The Queer Composition of America's Sound

The Queer Composition of America's Sound

Gay Modernists, American Music, and National Identity

NADINE HUBBS

University of California Press

BERKELEY   LOS ANGELES   LONDON

An earlier version of chapter 3 appeared in *GLQ: A Journal of Lesbian and Gay Studies* 6, no. 3 (2000): 389–412, published by Duke University Press, copyright © 2000 by Duke University Press. Reprinted by permission.

University of California Press
Berkeley and Los Angeles, California

University of California Press, Ltd.
London, England

Library of Congress Cataloging-in-Publication Data

Hubbs, Nadine.
   The queer composition of America's sound : gay modernists, American music, and national identity / Nadine Hubbs.
      p.   cm.
   Includes bibliographical references and index.
   Discography: p.
   ISBN 0-520-24184-3 (cloth : alk. paper).—ISBN 0-520-24185-1 (pbk. : alk. paper)
      1. Music—United States—20th century—History and criticism.
   2. National music—United States—History and criticism.   3. Gay composers—United States.   I. Title.

ML200.5.H83 2004
780'.86'640973—dc22   2004003478

Manufactured in the United States of America
13   12   11   10   09   08   07   06   05   04
10   9   8   7   6   5   4   3   2   1

The paper used in this publication is both acid-free and totally chlorine-free (TCF). It meets the minimum requirements of ANSI/NISO Z39.48–1992 (R 1997) *(Permanence of Paper)*.

Philip Brett
in memoriam

Contents

Acknowledgments

This book would not have been possible without the substantial kindness, generosity, and expertise bestowed by a number of individuals, organizations, and institutions. It is a pleasure to acknowledge them here.

As dean of the University of Michigan School of Music when I began this project, Paul C. Boylan lent pivotal support through a junior-faculty nurturing leave and through his vocal encouragement. A grant from Earl Lewis, dean of the Rackham School of Graduate Studies at Michigan, funded my travel to East Coast archives in the summer of 2001. The Institute for the Humanities at Michigan provided a faculty fellowship in 2001–2 that was indispensable to the realization of my project; Linnea Perlman, Mary Price, Tom Trautmann, and Eliza Woodford of the Institute staff all contributed importantly to this book during my happy and productive year with them. The University of Michigan Office of the Vice President for Research and College of Literature, Science, and the Arts generously provided a subvention grant for photograph and permission fees incurred in the publication of this book.

I am grateful for the kind and expert assistance I received from staff in the libraries and archives on which my research depended: in the Music Library and Harlan Hatcher Graduate Library at the University of Michigan, especially Amy Marino, Charles Reynolds, and Paul Barrow; in the Irving S. Gilmore Music Library at Yale University, particularly Suzanne Eggleston Lovejoy; in the Kinsey Institute for Research in Sex, Gender, and Reproduction, from Catherine A. Johnson, Shawn C. Wilson, and Liana Zhou; in the Rare Book and Manuscript Library at Columbia University; and in all the archival institutions that provided photographs for use here. As Special Collections Librarian in the Sibley Music Library of the Eastman School (and my erstwhile classmate at the University of Michigan), David

Peter Coppen went above and beyond the call of duty to help me secure necessary items under urgent circumstances.

Parts of this book and related work were presented under various auspices from the fall of 1999 through the spring of 2003. I am indebted to all those who facilitated forums in which I aired my ideas and findings, and to the audiences and participants whose input helped me to strengthen and refine my work. For their session-organizing and hosting efforts I thank Paul A. Anderson, George Chauncey, Mark Clague, Susan C. Cook, Nancy Guy, David Halperin, Marianne Kielian-Gilbert, Beth Levy, Fred Maus, David Patterson, Michael Sherry, Valerie Traub, and Eliza Woodford.

I received sources, ideas, and leads from a number of persons, including Byron Adams, Paul A. Anderson, Carol Bardenstein, the late Philip Brett, Peter Burkholder, Elizabeth E. Cole, Richard Crawford, David Halperin, Nancy Z. Hubbs, Lawrence D. Mass, Carol Oja, Howard Pollack, Annie Randall, Gayle Rubin, Michael Sherry, James B. Sinclair, George Steinmetz, Tim Stewart-Winter, Lloyd "Chip" Whitesell, and Eben Wood. Several colleagues generously shared their unpublished work: Philip Brett, Kara Gardner, Neil Lerner, Daniel Mathers, Howard Pollack, Martin Puchner, and Michael Sherry. Greg Laman, Andy Mead, and Margarete Thomsen kindly provided technical assistance. My editor, Mary Francis, has been attentive to every detail in the publication process; this book has reaped rich rewards from her expertise and guidance, and from that of its project editor, Lynn Meinhardt, and manuscript editor, David Anderson.

For astute comments on and criticism of earlier versions of this book and its various parts I am profoundly indebted to Ross Chambers, George Chauncey, Sophie Fuller, Neil Lerner, Fred Maus, Susan McClary, Howard Pollack, Martin Puchner, Robert Walser, and Chip Whitesell. Likewise Sidonie Smith, who, along with Domna Stanton, also gave me superb suggestions concerning the book's organization. I received help and support in various forms from Sara Blair, Dena Goodman, George Haggerty, Anne Herrmann, Valerie Kivelson, Maren Klawiter, Judith McCulloh, Kyle Morgan, Mitchell Morris, Guthrie Ramsey, Pamela Reid, Abby Stewart, Valerie Traub, Elizabeth Wingrove, my band mates in The Pittsfield Ramblers, and my family. I owe a special debt to two members of the gay tonalists' circle, David Diamond and Ned Rorem, for kindly sharing their time, thoughts, and memories of the people and events treated in these pages.

Certain friends and colleagues' sustained and prodigious contributions to this project can only be described as heroic. Andy Mead served as primary interlocutor and infinite source of imaginative ideas, critical insights, and encouragement throughout the time of this writing, and of every scholarly project I have undertaken. David Halperin shared liberally of his singular erudition and wisdom and provided crucial guidance, criticism, and support at every point. Michael Sherry was an invaluable and indefatigable critic, and his trenchant input has greatly strengthened this book's historical and readerly dimensions. Carla McKenzie sustained this work and its author in innumerable ways, from discussing hypotheses and reading drafts to helping me through illness that might have derailed the project were it not for her kindness and caring.

Philip Brett informed and inspired this work from its inception and even earlier. Before I could clearly "see" the book, Philip cast a glowing vision of it that served as a beacon for my efforts over the months and years to come. His confidence in me and in this project have been critically enabling, as has his courageous, path-breaking, and brilliant scholarship, which provides the basis for this and all other inquiry in queer music studies. Philip passed away in October 2002—a few days after I had completed the draft of this book. These pages attest to the ongoing effects of his words and insights, and of his extraordinary, beloved person.

Finally, I thank those who taught me the pleasures and disciplines of solitary work, of concentration and craft: my music and art teachers, and my mother.

INTRODUCTION

Composing Oneself

Aaron Copland stands as "America's most prominent composer." The fact is confirmed by no less an authority than the United States Army, which recently released a pair of recordings of Copland's music as performed by the organization's "premier touring musical representative," the United States Army Field Band, and its "vocal complement," the Soldiers' Chorus.[1] These recordings were accompanied by educational materials, scrupulously researched and handsomely produced, and timed to coincide with the year-2000 centenary of Copland's birth. Texts distributed in hard copy and on a special web site teach student-readers about a "quintessentially American" history in an essay whose title, "The Legacy of Aaron Copland," echoes that of the set. Presented here are a number of interesting facts about Copland and his legacy, and their national significance: We learn, for example, that the Library of Congress's Aaron Copland Collection comprises nearly 400,000 items, "[e]xhibited alongside the nation's most precious documents."[2]

As I encounter these sentences the year is 2001. I am intrigued to note that the text produced by "Today's Army" is unmistakably, even conspicuously, attuned to contemporary consciousness around minority identities. It highlights Copland's "Jewish heritage," for instance, and the values of hard work, self-reliance, and striving instilled by his Russian immigrant parents. Elsewhere the narrative sheds particular light on the composer's racial attitudes: We are told that Copland's "only effort as a lyricist" was registered in his alteration of a folk-tune lyric insensitive to African Americans, and that in premiering certain of his midcentury works he collaborated with the great African American baritone William Warfield.[3] I note too that the Army has taken pains to provide its target audience of school-age readers with documentation of its sources, giving meticulous endnotes and drawing on respected, up-to-the-minute research that would satisfy the demands of even scholarly audiences. One prominently cited work is Howard Pollack's 1999 Copland biography, a monumental and acclaimed study, and a landmark in its frank treatment of its subject's homosexual—as well as Jewish and leftist—identity.[4]

There can thus be no doubt that the Army's authors were aware of Copland's gay identity status. But the topic is never hinted at. Likewise unmentioned are the most remarkable events in Copland's life as an American citizen: the censoring of his patriotic *Lincoln Portrait* from the 1953 Eisenhower inaugural (though the work is included on the Army Field Band recording, with CBS *Sunday Morning* host Charles Osgood narrating), and his testimony under subpoena, the same year, before Joseph McCarthy and the Senate Permanent Subcommittee on Investigations.[5] Of course, the composer celebrated here as a national treasure and nationalist figure, were he alive today, would be subject to dishonorable discharge from the institution that now brandishes—selectively, to be sure—the facts of his work, career, and life in its production of American patriotism and nationalism for the new millennium. In fact, Copland, a peace-loving artist and intellectual who never belonged to the Army and, at any rate, has been dead for over a decade, is treated here to its latter-day "don't ask, don't tell" policy. As such he can be invoked as exemplar of all-American patriotism, Today's Army–style. It is a patriotism that embraces the immigrant, the "common man," racialized minorities, and Jews no less assiduously than it excludes queers—and so delineates a twenty-first-century recruitment ideal in whose sights millennial youngsters might position their own identities.

Meanwhile and elsewhere on the cultural horizon circa 2001, Copland would surface more visibly. On Sunday, September 16, for example, several memorial events were nationally broadcast in the wake of terrorist attacks on the World Trade Center and the Pentagon. As in many other times of national observance and celebration over the previous six decades, Aaron Copland's music featured prominently. On this day his setting of "At the River" was chosen by programmers and cited by commentators as one of the most eloquent expressions of the nation's mourning. A work of stark beauty, it evokes a simple dignity and noble melancholy that are perceived as characteristically American.[6]

Comparably, another work heard in the days, weeks, and months following this national tragedy was the *Adagio for Strings*, written by another gay composer, Samuel Barber. Long distinguished as the American opus most frequently performed by U.S. orchestras, the *Adagio* too is an American classic, but its meaning seems less specifically American.[7] The movement conveys an extraordinary emotional intensity, partly by its

timbral lushness, partly by its gestural restraint, and even more by the juxtaposition of the two. But the rhetoric of fatefulness and grief here in the
Adagio is understood—no doubt in connection with the qualities of its
idiom and, as well, its purely instrumental (nontextual and nonballetic)
medium—as more universal than particular, more cosmic than national. It
is one of the best-known and best-loved works of American art in America,
but it is not primarily received as a statement about or representation of
America. Or, to put it another way: Barber's piece, like Copland's, is decidedly American music, but, unlike Copland's, it is not "America" music.[8]

Indeed, the sound of Coplandian Americana is heard by many listeners
as ubiquitous and belonging to the public domain—and as *the* American
style in music for purposes of movies, television, and all events of national
significance, whether stately, celebratory, or mournful. For in addition to
the recent uses of it already mentioned, Americans know this idiom from a
half-century of western and other movie scores rife with genuine and imitation Coplandiana; from television and radio commercials touting such
brands as Oldsmobile and Continental Airlines, the U.S. Navy and American beef ("It's what's for dinner"); and from media products including the
basketball-themed film *He Got Game* (1998), whose creator Spike Lee
readily explains his use of an all-Copland soundtrack: "When I listen to his
music, I hear America, and basketball is America."[9]

And so one was scarcely surprised to hear televised from Salt Lake City,
in the multimedia extravaganza that opened the 2002 Winter Olympics,
strains of Copland's 1942 ballet *Rodeo*. For representation of the spirit of
the wide-open American West, and of America writ large, has long been
entrusted to this Brooklyn-bred Jew, communist sympathizer, and homosexual composer. More surprising, perhaps, is how little questioning
attaches to such facts. We have already glimpsed some reasons for this, in
the Army's *Legacy of Aaron Copland:* Copland so brilliantly succeeded in
composing a musical portrait of the American landscape and people, one
that the nation wholeheartedly embraced, that his life and music have been
appropriated with uncommon eagerness to the whitewashed, heterosexualized mainstream. And here they have been voided of any difference not
sanctioned within current conceptions of the "melting pot." Questions
have scarcely arisen about Copland's queer identity vis-à-vis his (apparently incongruous) identity as national cultural spokesperson—so long as
facts of the former have been denied. And such denial persisted over-
whelmingly until the recent appearance of Pollack's biography.[10]

It is not Copland alone, however, whose life and art raise questions about
the interrelations of national, social and sexual, cultural and musical iden-

tity in twentieth-century America, or about their meanings within U.S. musical modernism. Such questions also readily arise, for instance, from the 1983 scene of Virgil Thomson's acceptance of Kennedy Center Honors for lifetime achievement in the arts, which made him not only the third classical composer-musician thus honored since the awards' 1978 inception, but the third queer classical composer-musician thus honored: Copland and Leonard Bernstein had preceded him in 1979 and 1980, respectively.[11] Accordingly, this book focuses not on one composer but on a circle of gay composers who were central to the twentieth-century creation of an emblematic "American sound" in concert music—Copland and Thomson, and their more or less junior colleagues Marc Blitzstein, David Diamond, Bernstein, Paul Bowles, and Ned Rorem.

Copland was indeed the most visible and illustrious senior figure here, though Thomson was a prime source of the musical innovations on which the "Coplandian" Americana idiom was founded—as this book argues. One thrust of our inquiries will be to discover the identifications and affiliations by which members of this circle composed themselves as artists and subjects, individually and collectively, in the context of twentieth-century culture and of artistic modernism. How, for example, did these gay men forge public lives, careers, and successes as artists amid the newly refined mechanisms of modern sexual classification and pervasive homosexual panic?[12] A larger question to be revisited throughout these pages concerns the nature of the relationship between music and homosexuality in this historical and cultural context; it is addressed not singularly or linearly but multiply and cumulatively, via ongoing rumination.

And we will further ask, How did these artists compose a nation? What might it mean that the long-awaited creation of a distinct "American style" in serious music was realized at last by (most prominently) the Jewish, homosexual, leftist Brooklynite Copland, who rendered musically vivid an America of prairie cowboys and pioneer newlyweds?[13] What can we conclude from the fact that the quintessential boy-girl romance in modern American musical theater, *West Side Story,* was the fruit of collaboration among the gay artists Leonard Bernstein, Arthur Laurents, Jerome Robbins, and Stephen Sondheim?[14] By what social, cultural, and artistic mechanisms did Copland and Thomson's circle of queer composers serve, during America's most homophobic era, as architects of its national identity?[15] Do their remarkable successes flag music's function as a redeemer—or regulator—of twentieth-century homosexuals? And what is at stake in acknowledging the facts of queer lives, achievements, and presence so long and so fiercely silenced? These interrogations are directed toward a richer, more balanced and accurate accounting of American culture and its sources, by means of a perspective that places queerness centrally—in contrast to previous accounts that have positioned it peripherally or, more often, banished it altogether.

IDENTITY PERSPECTIVES

The denial and erasure of queer lives and contributions in historical accounts of twentieth-century U.S. culture reflect that culture's suffusion in homophobia. Homophobic culture provides ample incentive for non-queer-identified commentators to uphold queer-effacing views, including the dominant myths that assert heterosexuals' exclusive place in cultural and social production and reproduction. Most fundamentally, these myths sustain the profound "privilege [that] lies in heterosexual culture's exclusive ability to interpret itself as society"—to invoke Michael Warner's trenchant summation—and its view of itself "as the elemental form of human association, as the very model of intergender relations, as the indivisible basis of all community, and as the means of reproduction without which society wouldn't exist."[16] In the shadow of these self-affirming heterocentric myths, the extraordinarily culturally productive role of alliances and networking activity among gay modernist composers, and equally, the fertile queer interart, intergender partnership carved out by Virgil Thomson and Gertrude Stein, have gone unacknowledged. Such relationships, no matter how prolific, do not figure in the stories we tell about the production of American art and national culture.[17]

These reverberant omissions follow from the fact that such alliances and networking flourished in relation to these artists' shared queer identity, an identity generally presumed to be specially sexual (in a way that "normal" heterosexual identity, for instance, is not)—and one of stigmatized sexuality, at that. Regarding this presumption, we might note that in certain instances queer sexuality and desire can indeed be seen to have directly imprinted twentieth-century American musical culture—as in the case of Copland's pederastically modeled mentoring of American composers, to be discussed anon. The most consequential and neglected aspect of queer identity, however, was more social than sexual. The social aspect on this site bore an intensity owing not only to shared minority status, but to the unspeakability of this status among the outsider majority. A freighted sociality attached, in other words, to bonds forged by the secrecy that is (according to Philip Brett and Elizabeth Wood) "arguably the most important attribute of 20th-century homosexuality, more defining and universal in Western culture than sex acts themselves," and that has in recent decades come to be symbolized by the closet.[18] These historical circumstances provide a context for understanding gay men's alliances and networking in U.S. musical modernism, where gay identity was both sexual and social and was, simultaneously and inextricably, professional and artistic as well.

A case in point is Copland's crucial contact with and absorption of Thomson's musical innovations in the later 1930s, which followed the two men's drawing close earlier in that decade, as co-mentors to a captivating youth with whom Copland was in love: Paul Bowles. Further illustration can be found in Blitzstein's lifelong engagements with musical composition, proletariat activism, and working-class "rough trade" men—and the inextricable mutual influence of these artistic, political, social, and sexual preoccupations within his work, career, and life. Or take the fact that Blitzstein at nineteen (having not yet discovered his preference for rough trade and for the "active" sexual role) lost his virginity to the same man, Alexander Smallens, who would ten years later conduct the first run (1934) of the Stein-Thomson opera *Four Saints in Three Acts* and would also (in 1940) connect the newly repatriated Thomson with his all-important critic's post at the *New York Herald Tribune*. Through this position Thomson, in turn, would hire Bowles into a critic's post that proved crucial to his composing and writing careers. All these instances can suggest the small-world character of the big-city concert music scene within its significant gay sector, and the integration here of social, sexual, artistic, and professional dimensions.[19]

This decisive interdimensionality connects with the fact that classical music was, for queer musicians, a rare sphere in which one's "in-tribe" gay social contacts were often the same as one's professional contacts, and vice versa. And it connects, too, with certain defining qualities of twentieth-century queer life and subculture that mark them to this day, as Warner illustrates:

> Try standing at a party of queer friends and charting all the histories, sexual and nonsexual, among the people in the room. . . . You will realize that only a fine and rapidly shifting line separates sexual culture from many other relations of durability and care. The impoverished vocabulary of straight culture tells us that people should be either husbands and wives or (nonsexual) friends. . . . It is not the way many queers live. If there is such a thing as a gay way of life, it consists in these relations, a welter of intimacies outside the framework of professions and institutions and ordinary social obligations.[20]

The foregoing discussion suggests the dominant culture's part in neglecting and suppressing the history of queer lives and contributions in American musical modernism. But we cannot ignore the evidence that many queer subjects, including composers, musicologists, biographers, and critics, have themselves served as stalwart guardians of the silence around queer alliances in musical modernism. Undoubtedly they found compelling reasons, even beyond "internalized homophobia" (or what Erving Goffman more precisely termed the "ambivalence" of "stigmatized identity"), to act in this way.[21] First, there was a shared queer ethics (discussed below) of protecting oneself and one's fellow homosexuals by maintaining secrecy. Moreover, to acknowledge queer networking activities and alliances at all was to invoke conspiracy archetypes that would automatically dismiss queer composers and their work as meretricious; and it was, further, to arouse an insinuatively sexualized taint of corruption casting any associated successes as ill-gotten. The historian Robert D. Dean notes with regard to Cold War "lavender baiting" that "conspiracy theories of sexual subversion often recur in the history of Western politics," including fears of "a conspiratorial 'state within a state.'"[22] In various eruptions the same rumor-forms recurred in twentieth-century musical politics, especially in the notion of a homosexual cabal secretly running the music world—a hidden, sexually subversive "state within a state" of music.

But on a more fundamental level, homosexual men and women in this era before Stonewall and gay liberation just generally guarded the facts of each others' queer identities and associations from mainstream circulation, as a point of principle and of a specifically queer ethics. In *Gay New York* George Chauncey acknowledges a diversity of positions, in the pre–World War II gay male sphere, on the question of whether to acknowledge one's gay identity to other gay men. But he reports that there was little question about coming out to the straight world:

> Most middle-class men believed for good reason that their survival depended on hiding their homosexuality from hostile straight outsiders, and they respected the decision of other men to do so as well. Indeed, a central requirement of the moral code that governed gay life and bound gay men to one another was that they honor other men's decisions to keep their homosexuality a secret and do all they could to help protect that secret from outsiders.[23]

Motives for secrecy included the threats of familial and social ostracism and professional and economic loss, as well as a variety of legal sanctions that attached to being, looking, and acting queer in 1920s–1950s (not to mention earlier, and later) America. In this light it is not difficult to understand why homosexuals of this era might have joined with their own kind in forming social, professional, and artistic alliances—as indeed they did in classical music. Still, persistent taboo has attached to the facts of such alliances in American music, despite their extraordinary cultural fecundity, such that even positive or neutral acknowledgment of these is readily rendered as shameful accusation or confession. State prohibitions on public assembly of homosexuals (as effected through the regulation of New York bars ca. 1933–69, chronicled by Chauncey) may be defunct, but the force of such prohibitions' internalization within "free liberal subjects" clearly persists. And being internalized this force extends, as Foucault would have us recognize, far more broadly and deeply than that of any externally imposed regulation.[24]

Within the music profession, hiding one's homosexuality also linked to more specific motives. As Sherrie Tucker discusses in a recent essay, many queer professional musicians of the 1940s believed then, and long continued to believe, that exposing their sexuality would undermine their chances for garnering artistic and professional legitimacy.[25] But the subjects of Tucker's ethnography had multiple reasons to fear not being taken seriously as musicians: They were female instrumentalists and performers of popular swing music—many of them African American—who plied their craft in a radically male-dominated realm while the men were away during World War II. The queer sexuality of some of these performers was the one damning element of their identities they could choose not to disclose. And so they chose, claiming the identity of "real musician" over "queer" or "lesbian" while operating in an arena where the two were perceived as mutually exclusive—and even decades later, when Tucker interviewed them.[26]

That the gay white male classical composers discussed in this study do not present the same accretions of identity stigmata as do Tucker's subjects surely accounts, in some part, for their having been able to attain the levels of national and international fame and recognition they achieved. Being visibly male and, at least sometimes, *in*visibly homosexual was an identity combination that, although stigmatized and thus limiting, afforded certain possibilities unavailable to persons plainly marked as, for example, female or black. The Jewishness of four of the seven members of this gay composers' circle—Bernstein, Blitzstein, Copland, and Diamond—was another stigma that might be regarded as partially or sometimes visible, even granting that many theorists locate Jewishness in a nonwhite or "off-white" realm of racial identity in pre-1945 America.[27] As we shall have opportunity to observe, however, both homosexual and Jewish identity had special status in the classical music world, where they were "tolerated" more often and to a greater extent than in most other sociocultural quarters, including certainly—in the case of homosexuality—that of jazz and popular music. Indeed, the relative amenability of twentieth-century concert music toward these identities attests certain parallels and overlappings in the pathways along which such outsider identities as "Jew," "homosexual," and "artistic genius" have historically evolved.

Whatever the effects of their various other identity factors, there can be no doubt but that the composers named here, when they were identified as homosexual, occupied a marked identity position. As such, they would automatically be relegated to membership in a qualifying class, much like their (rare) colleagues "the female composer" and "the Negro composer," or "the girl saxophonist" in a swing band. In other words, whenever a gay white male composer was identified *as* gay, he was subject to a (here, marginalized) *collective* identity that threatened to displace the radically individualized identity to which he was otherwise entitled as a white male, and that was essential to his creative relevance and authority.[28] For this and other reasons (surely including the fact that by the late forties Red baiters imputed subversive connotations to the very notion of collectivity), in dealings with the dominant culture these composers' queerness was long guarded, if not actively denied, by the composers themselves and by their allies. And the requisite identity dodges and doubles were readily afforded by the established economy of compulsory heterosexuality, especially via the archetype of the artist "married to his art" and its bachelor-based variants like "priest of music."[29] Hence Copland in a 1974 interview could say at once cagily and altogether truthfully, "I'm a bachelor, in the tradition of Beethoven and Brahms."[30]

In the light of music's important ties here both to illicit sexuality and to its containment, we might recall Adorno's contention that "music represents at once the immediate manifestation of impulse and the locus of its taming."[31] And as the previous examples suggest, such taming is not only visited upon classical music from the outside. Indeed, on Philip Brett's analysis, "[t]he attempts to appropriate music for the enforcement of patriarchal order, to anesthetize listeners from its effects, and to defeminize it, lie most notably . . . within its own domain." Brett indicts a "collusion of musicality and the closet" via a "social contract" whereby queer musicians have willingly sacrificed self-determination in exchange for a degree of respectability and elite status. He further theorizes bohemia as the marginal realm to which (musical and sexual) deviance has been consigned, and handily self-policed, under the terms of the closet's double-bind, its simultaneous stimulation and suppression of desire. In this view, then, "our [bohemians'] public demonstration of feeling serves the function of keeping the rest of society in a state of decorum and restraint," and hints of forbidden sexuality issuing from bohemia's margins have served to reinforce the dominant culture's dichotomy of public/private in relation to hetero/homo.[32]

Decades of silence, from both within and without gay circles, on the operations and significance of gay composers' alliances reflect our culture's privatization of the facts of gay persons', gay networks', and gay politics' profound influence on the constituency and movements of (revered) classical music. Even now, any acknowledgment of the predominance of gay men among American modernist composers risks being co-opted under discourses of wholesale discreditation or delegitimation—of the composers in question, their music, and of U.S. tonal modernism generally. Relatedly, according to prevailing views, those men of the past, presumed heterosexual, who achieved compositional renown were singular *individuals*—men of genius—and this fact above all accounted for their achievements and status. Like the celebrated Great Composers of the European canon, Thomson, Copland, and company were white men of deep acculturation in Western musical and other traditions, and as such they could be construed as more or less fitting the traditional, post-Beethovenian mold of the composer-*artiste*. But in truth these American composers' successes in creating a national music had more to do with collective effort and mutual influence than with radical individualism.[33] And further, the cohesion of the collective and the richness of knowledge transmission within it were essentially grounded in intense bonds of shared sociosexual minority status.

QUEER GENEALOGIES

A central project of this book is to illumine the specifically queer lineaments of a musical idiom that serves as one of the most potent and recognizable cultural emblems of Americanness—a sonic representation of American vastness and rugged, simple beauty primarily associated with Aaron Copland (1900–1990). In its appropriation into the national-symbolic imaginary, and even in some of the scenarios in which it was originally presented, Copland's Americana idiom is outfitted with a sentimentalized national heterosexuality. So, too, the legend of Copland himself, cast as "Dean of American Music," as paterfamilias to American composition during a period, circa 1933–53, encompassing its most legendary fertility.

We can see a characteristic celebration of both of these nationalist tropes, of the man and his music as "quintessentially American," in the recent Copland recordings and educational materials by the Army Field Band and Soldiers' Chorus.

Copland was ideally suited to his position, within the exclusively male realm of twentieth-century composition, of generous and patient mentoring—but not by virtue of any identity or experience in the paterfamilias role, for indeed he had none. Copland's qualification, rather, was that he was a gay daddy par excellence. His embrace of the classic pederastic model and his belief in the societal benefits afforded by pederastic love and mentoring were cast early in Copland's life as a gay man. Around or after 1924 he read *Corydon* by André Gide (of whom Copland was already, by his own 1923 description, an "ardent 'disciple'"), a defense not so much of adult homosexuality as of *pédérastie* in the narrower sense of intergenerational erotic and mentoring relationships between men and youths.[34] Throughout his career as "Dean of American Music" many of Copland's relationships with younger composers were nonsexual, others included erotic dimensions, but all were fundamentally influenced by his self-identification as a homosexual with a penchant for young men, and by his Gide-informed embrace of a pederastic ideal. Thus we perceive a lineage crucial to the history of twentieth-century American music, albeit never before discussed by its chroniclers: a lineage that extended from classical Greek pederasty to Copland by way of Gide, and thence importantly shaped twentieth-century American musical modernism and national culture.

Copland's music, meanwhile, his idiom of the American, is deeply enmeshed in another queer lineage. Copland had been composing for some eighteen years—in the Stravinskian high-modernist idiom he had refined during his early Paris apprenticeship under Nadia Boulanger—before breaking through in the popular style with which his name would become synonymous.[35] This breakthrough, achieved in his 1938 ballet *Billy the Kid* and soon followed by several now-classic works including *Rodeo* (1942), *Fanfare for the Common Man* (1942), and *Appalachian Spring* (1944), was a result of Copland's adoption of a simpler, leaner, more accessible, and, especially, tonal and (relatively) consonant idiom that was modeled on the compositions of his gay American colleague Virgil Thomson.

Thomson's music in turn was fundamentally influenced by the avant-garde work of the lesbian American writer Gertrude Stein. While a Harvard undergraduate, around 1919, Thomson discovered Stein's *Tender Buttons* (1914) in the college library. After moving to Paris in 1925 he befriended Stein and eventually collaborated with her on two operas, *Four*

Saints in Three Acts (1928) and *The Mother of Us All* (1947).[36] Thomson followed Stein in her practice of composing "portraits" (his were always done from live sittings) and of automatic writing, which he applied throughout the process of composing *Four Saints*. But most formatively Thomson was inspired by Stein, and by the French composer Erik Satie (himself a queerish figure, as Sophie Fuller and Lloyd Whitesell have recently noted), to flout the Romantic-modern tradition of the *Meister* and *Meisterstück* by adopting everyday American vernacular as the basis for an avant-garde idiom.[37] Thus, following an epiphany around 1926, Thomson took up "the discipline of spontaneity" he had learned by reading Stein, which translated into a consonant, triadic, diatonic (i.e., "white-key"), and tonal musical language featuring indigenous folkish and popular elements—this at a time when an internationalist "post-tonal" dissonance was the sine qua non of musical modernism.[38] (Some commentators therefore treat such music binaristically as if it were outside or even opposite to modernism, though this is erroneous in the case of both Thomson's avant-garde brand of neoclassic tonality and Copland's popular one.)

We might note at this juncture that Stein's surfacing introduces the only woman who features prominently in the present account of twentieth-century musical modernism. This book's depiction of the scene of U.S. modernist composition circa 1927–54 reflects the historical realities of women's near-total exclusion from this arena—and surely, to represent things otherwise would be to revise the past and thus to do injustice to the women involved. From outside the gentlemen's club of U.S. modernist composition, however, the noncomposer Gertrude Stein is figured here as "Mother of Us All" in relation to America's long-awaited establishment of a national musical identity: Her work provided the crucial inspiration for Thomson's musical language, which in turn became the model for Copland's Americana idiom.

Another important woman among the present composers' group was the Parisian pedagogue and performer Nadia Boulanger, "the greatest teacher since Socrates," by Ned Rorem's (rather spectacular) appraisal. Though she is not foregrounded within the present story, Boulanger was unquestionably a pivotal figure in the lives and careers of the Thomson-Copland circle, and one whose own sexual identity status—presumed lesbian by at least David Diamond and seemingly more than one present-day Boulanger scholar—may have borne implications for American musical modernism yet to be revealed.[39] Likewise crucial to the creation of the music at issue here was the work of women in patronage roles, including that of Claire Reis in the League of American Composers and of Minna

Lederman as editor of its quarterly *Modern Music*. Although informed by recent work in this area, the present study does not focus on the history of women's patronage in American musical modernism.[40]

One thing this study does attempt, however, is to inscribe a history of influence and patronage among certain twentieth-century queer American artists, and of these artists' own efforts to locate a past and inscribe a history, and even a family tree, in a place where none was supposed to exist: That is, on the site of their own lives, in that narrative void surrounding the newly labeled tribe of the homosexuals—"discovered" and named circa 1870, by Foucault's well-known account.[41] This self-composing and -historicizing project is readable in various moments witnessed in these pages, including not only Copland's embrace of a Greek-Gidean pederastic lineage; but also Stein and Thomson's engagement with early-modern monastics Teresa, Ignatius, and others in *Four Saints* and with Susan B. Anthony and (her partner in life and work) Elizabeth Cady Stanton in *The Mother of Us All;* and Lou Harrison's self-avowed self-constitution in relation to those he regarded as his gay mentors and forebears—Henry Cowell and Virgil Thomson, Tchaikovsky and Handel.

CAREER MATTERS

As various instances in this book can suggest, the course of Copland's—rather than Thomson's—success, and thus of history, may well have been affected by his more advantageous positioning in relation to the homophobic conditions of their shared cultural moment. Whereas Thomson's ambivalence about his queer identity occasionally registered in involuted expressions (verbal and musical) that undercut their own ingenuousness and credibility, Copland's apparent self-acceptance gave solid footing to his high-profile career in the public spotlight, and bolstered the aura of forthright sincerity that is essential to his music's acclaimed American character.[42]

It seems likely, moreover, that Copland and Thomson's differences here had something to do with differences in gender identity: Copland's avuncularly masculine, thus gender-normative, homosexual persona occupied a privileged position relative to Thomson's, which was typically perceived as effete. This observation aligns with a metaphor casting Copland and Thomson as "father and mother of American music" and registered by a junior colleague, Ned Rorem, who clearly deems himself among their progeny.[43] Certain further implications of Rorem's camp metaphor seem worth exploring in connection with these composers' gender positioning under patriarchy. For it would appear that what were, in large part, the fruits of Thomson's creative labors have been known in the world by the name of "the father," Copland—or so Thomson and his once-pupil Rorem have claimed, and so this book maintains.

Thomson, a campy homosexual whose personal identity fell under the rubrics of "pansy" and "fairy," conceived the musical emblematics of Americanness, that sonic vocabulary by which America came to be represented as a nation.[44] Certain of the works in which this tonal rhetoric was forged were governmentally commissioned, deployed for political and patriotic purposes, circulated and reproduced at home and exported (especially via Hollywood) abroad. Also significantly shaped therein by this "fairy" composer were the emblematics of rugged American virility as these would be disseminated in the Hollywood western: The now-standard musical tropes of cowboys and western plains were pioneered in Thomson's film scores for *The Plow That Broke the Plains* (1936) and *The River* (1937), both produced by the Resettlement Administration, a Depression-era farm relief agency funded by the Works Progress Administration (WPA).[45]

The queer composition of "America's sound" owes not only to Thomson or to the better-known Copland, however, but to the productive intercourse between these two gay composers whose social, professional, and artistic relationship began in Paris, in 1921–22, when both were among Boulanger's first American students. Pivotal to Copland's eventual triumph was the elevation of his musical language to "universal" status, a shift enabled, according to one recent argument, by a late-twenties turn to abstraction through which Copland expunged telltale traces of homoeroticism—a decidedly nonuniversalized valence.[46] In this book's reading, however, such an "abstract turn" in Copland would figure as prerequisite to an equally crucial turn toward even greater concretization: For if indeed a late-twenties move toward abstraction wiped clean the signifying surface of Copland's musical idiom, it served ultimately not to leave a blank slate, but to clear space for the projection of vivid images of a mainstream (albeit relatively pluralistic) heterosexualized America. Bearing such concrete Americanist meanings, Copland's populist idiom was propelled to the iconic status that it attained in the ballets and other works of the thirties and forties, and holds today.

By contrast with Copland, we might regard Thomson as a gay modernist who never succeeded convincingly in "straightening up" his musical act. As "father of American music," Copland, a "queer" (i.e., conventionally masculine homosexual) type according to the terms of his time, was advocate of and mentor to innumerable American composers, the great conciliator who brought a modernist Americanism to the masses. The "pansy" Thomson, Rorem's "mother of American music," created a singular idiom with his self-described "darn fool ditties" and "plain as Dick's hatband" harmonies, and his transparently simple forms. Thomson's idiom shares with that of Stein an engagement with commonplace American vernacular and (less obviously) with African American language and style, and both revel in repetition, rhythm, and run-on, all in ways that were received as incomprehensibly abstract.[47] In their respective fields, both Copland and Stein's once-protégé Ernest Hemingway redeployed some of these inventions, rendered them more familiar and palatable, and so formulated popular Americanist idioms and works that entirely eclipsed Thomson's and Stein's queerer, ostensibly blacker, ultimately unmainstreamable models.[48] Indeed, the characterizations most often accruing to Thomson's music—of "witty urbanity," "deceptive simplicity," and "feigned naïveté"—telegraph his trouble within what Eve Kosofsky Sedgwick calls the "epistemology of the closet," that modern cultural-discursive economy in which "the homosexual topic" is now the primary object of knowledge itself.[49] For it seems Thomson—invariably glossed in terms of a feigned, false, or mock naiveté—just could not conceal his knowingness. In France he found praise for music that "achieves the utmost of sophistication; perfidious and perverse in its naïveté, it ends up as naïve through perversity."[50] Back home in America, similar perceptions were sometimes registered less appreciatively.

The considerable depth and span of networking among queer artists in American modernism, including Stein, Thomson, Copland, and many others, and the central role of queer collaboration in twentieth-century American concert music are attested in narrations throughout this book—which necessarily broach only a small fraction of such activity. Relatedly, the book examines the conditions that underlay networking activity among queer artists and its abundant productivity in this period of U.S. cultural life. An initial and basic observation we might register in this regard is that the twentieth-century American music world showed high concentrations of, and relative amenability to, queer ways and persons. One consequence of this for queer musicians was that they expended less energy, as compared with their counterparts in other careers and milieus, in cultivating a double life. Chauncey notes that

> [t]he degree to which men participated in the gay world depended in part on their jobs. Some occupations allowed men to work with other gay men in a supportive atmosphere, even if they had to maintain a straight façade in dealing with customers and other outsiders. Men who

worked in the city's restaurants, department stores, hotels, and theater
industry, among other occupations, often found themselves in such a
position. . . .

Some men were even able to use their gay contacts to find jobs,
particularly in those occupations in which many gay men worked or
that tolerated a relative degree of openness on the part of their gay
workers.[51]

That Chauncey does not mention composition here (although the first-
generation modernist Charles Tomlinson Griffes figures importantly among
his book's gay informants) may reflect the small number of composers relative to that of waiters, store clerks, or even actors in early-twentieth-
century New York. But classical music was undoubtedly one of those occupational realms that attracted comparatively high numbers of gay men and
"tolerated a relative degree of openness." And these conditions were crucial
to the remarkable success of many significant U.S. composers of the era—
so many that gay artists can be, and indeed at times have been, said to have
predominated in the field. We might further note that just as the relative
freedom from presenting an alternate sociosexual persona in the music
world surely benefited gay American composers generally, so would the
freedom from cultivating an alternate gender persona in the public sphere
have benefited Copland—contrastingly with Thomson, who assiduously
put forth a heteronormative masculine mien in public appearances.[52]

COMING TOGETHER

The story presented here traces the origins of a ubiquitous, ostensibly pub-
lic-domain Americanist musical idiom to Aaron Copland, its most prominent exponent, and to his 1940s Manhattan circle of gay colleagues. Copland's populist idiom is traced in turn to Virgil Thomson, inventor of the
tonal and folkish simplicities on which it was founded. And Thomson's innovations are traced to Gertrude Stein, whose writing and theoretical insights fundamentally inspired and grounded them. These points of lineage
connect with one of the central aims of this study: to illuminate some of the
dense and productive interpenetrations between, on the one hand, queer
lives and subculture, and on the other, modern U.S. national culture and self-
representation, in all their profound and effortful heterosexualization.

To take a long-overdue nonheterocentric perspective on the markedly
queer scene of American musical modernism is to vex the conventional
wisdom positing queerness and national identity as mutually antithetical.

For such a perspective reveals an intriguing scenario behind the long-standing curtain of queer denial and effacement—a scenario of thriving symbiosis between twentieth-century homosexual subculture and U.S. national culture. This book seeks to enrich and complicate our understanding of the role of queer artists in conceiving and producing American cultural identity, and doing so in a time of intense homophobia. It also reveals how movements in the little-known realm of concert music have shaped, and continue to shape, American queer life and world-making.[53] More broadly, this book explores the sites of U.S. gay modernist composers' individual and collective achievements to account for the ways in which queer lives and culture have shaped American musical, and larger, life and culture. In the process, it underscores the extent to which the Manhattan-centered milieu in which these artists moved and worked, and likewise its Paris "annex," was occupied not only with musical and artistic modernism, but with queer sexuality, identity, life, and culture.

1. Modernist Abstraction and the Abstract Art

Four Saints *and the Queer Composition of America's Sound*

Meaning! It is a piece of mu-sic, in which I have skillfully e-lu-ded ALL meaning!

CYRIL VANE, WILDEAN HOMOSEXUAL DANDY
IN JOHN TODHUNTER'S *The Black Cat*

It is not what is apprehended what is apprehended what is apprehended what is apprehended intended.

SAINT TERESA, IN GERTRUDE STEIN AND VIRGIL THOMSON'S
Four Saints in Three Acts

The premiere of Gertrude Stein and Virgil Thomson's *Four Saints in Three Acts* in Hartford, Connecticut, on February 7, 1934, was a major cultural and social event, a watershed spectacle that left its high-bohemian audience cheering wildly and weeping for beauty. The inspiration for such outpourings was an opera, performance, and occasion whose implications remain compelling and elusive even at some seventy years' remove.[1] In the moment, however, audience members scarcely lacked for explanations of their ardent catharsis. Kirk Askew and Julien Levy, important New York art dealers both and leaders in the crying that night, readily explained their tears of joy. Their account suggests they had witnessed a glorious and redemptive birth—of nothing less than the national culture: Askew and Levy wept because they "didn't know anything so beautiful could be done in America."[2]

"Everyone thought *something*" of the performance, in the words of one society reporter assigned to the event, "and was earnestly trying to express it."[3] And surely this was key in the work's success: Audience members were not only captivated by *Four Saints* but impelled to find meanings in it. Indeed, though it presented no linear narrative—nor even clearly interpretable sentences or mimetic sequences—the opera seemed to radiate meaningfulness. Set by Thomson's music and the dramatic scenario by his life partner, the painter Maurice Grosser, Stein's abstract avant-garde language appeared, in its way, more lucid than ever before. To much of the Hartford audience at *Four Saints'* premiere, as to many readers and critics since, Stein's writing presented itself not as mere nonsense but as "suspiciously *significant* nonsense."[4] But in February 1934 Stein's words, and the opera in which they were heard, conferred neither mere nonsense nor mere significance: Their effect was nothing short of numinous.[5]

That the opera inspired such fervent engagement while availing itself to multiple interpretations fostered its use under various identificatory aegises. Or, to put it another way, *Four Saints* beckoned audiences to make of it what they would, according to their own needs and desires. Thomson had been honing his skills at setting Steinese in ways that optimized this effect. That his prior, "tryout" project, a setting of *Capital Capitals* for four male singers and piano (1927), reminded the actress Fania Marinoff of a Jewish synagogue, the painter and folklorist Miguel Covarrubias of a Mexican church, and the writer Jean Cocteau of the Catholic liturgy evinces the extent to which Thomson's diatonic idiom could evoke a distinct religiosity even while maintaining an extraordinary blank-screen quality, subject to viewers' projections.[6] Audiences' similar response to *Four Saints'* open-endedness must have pleased its creators, for it is precisely the receptive stance endorsed by Grosser in his prefatory "Scenario" to the 1948 score edition. "One should not try to interpret too literally the words of the opera, nor should one fall into the opposite error of thinking that they mean nothing at all," he explained: "On the contrary, they mean many things at once."[7] But if interpretive pluralism was the order of the day at the opera's opening, there is nevertheless a reception standard that seems to have operated over the whole range of responses: that of whether or not one "got it," as judged by one's own perception in the matter.

Olin Downes was among the operagoers who got it—or so he unequivocally indicated in his music column for the *New York Times*. "The trail of foppishness and pose and pseudo-intellectuality is all over it," wrote Downes of *Four Saints'* opening (February 20, 1934) in what would prove to be an extended Broadway run. Criticizing the performance by way of its audience, Downes reported that "[e]very snob and poseur in town" showed up to simulate "from a distance and across a decade or two the poses of certain Parisians" at this opera "that was performed with such eclat for the precious." The *Times* critic was at pains to reveal Stein's text as constituting "far from an innocent or naïve creation," as audiences might have assumed from the work's religious theme and its stereotypic staging of African Americans as people of simple faith. On the contrary, readers were warned, the opera presented "a specimen of an affected and decadent phase of the literature of the whites." Downes appears intent to articulate something against *Four Saints'* creators and audience as a perceived in-group, particularly to expose the alleged falsity of their pretensions (aping 1920s Parisians, they are merely ersatz) and of the opera's ostensible naiveté—which masks its true, "affected and decadent" nature. Invoking and interlinking perversion, privilege, and Paris, Downes purported to illumine the nature of this " 'opera,' if such it is to be called," and its secretive meanings: I know something of such secrets, he assures his readers—and you need not bother.[8]

The critic and novelist Carl Van Vechten was another operagoer who clearly deemed that he got it, albeit along very different lines. A queer member of the avant-garde like his friends Stein and Thomson, Van Vechten inscribed some morning-after annotations on *Four Saints* while still basking in the afterglow of its premiere, at his Hartford hotel. He broached the topic of meaning: "It is unfortunate, perhaps, that I can have very little to say" to people "who seek a key to some more perfect understanding of Miss Stein's text," Van Vechten wrote. He continued, "It becomes more and more evident to me that if appreciation of the text of Miss Stein is not instinctive with a person he never acquires it."[9] Van Vechten thus all but says it outright: If you have to ask, you'll never know. Somewhat comparably, the press agent Nathan Zatkin "comforted the uncomprehending" on opening night in a manner Steven Watson recently characterized as "sly": "Either you get it or you don't—and, really, you shouldn't feel ashamed if you don't," Zatkin counseled.[10] Whether or not intended "slyly," Zatkin's response, like Downes's, evokes an intriguing question: Apropos *Four Saints,* who might have greater reason to feel ashamed—those who get it, or those who don't?

That notions of shame, or decadence, or contrived innocence should arise at all in proximity to *Four Saints* and its premiere already suggests a circulation of meanings beyond those attributable to "pleasurable nonsense"—to invoke the terms in which the opera is typically glossed. And we might wonder what could inspire such notions in relation to a staging of (not just four but) nearly thirty Spanish Catholic saints, real and imaginary, named and anonymous, in song and movement depicting daily devotions, a country picnic, fishnet mending, and the witnessing of visions (among other things), all to represent in three acts their earthly life. A further, apparent bonus act bestows an afterlife no less sanguine, a brief postlude in which the saints reminisce together in heaven. So, in addition to the innumerable pleasant acts performed by its personae, the opera itself

FIGURE 1.   Virgil Thomson and Gertrude Stein study the
score of their first opera, *Four Saints in Three Acts,* circa
1929. Yale Collection of American Literature, Beinecke Rare
Book and Manuscript Library. Reprinted by permission of
the Virgil Thomson Foundation, Ltd., copyright owner.

presents four acts—and thus (by either calculation) proffers an abundance
of saintly acts beyond the three announced by the title, and required by the
Vatican for saintly recognition. These acts' pageantry is set throughout by
strikingly lucid tonal music neoclassically evoking Anglican chant in the
same breath as Yankee hymns, and nineteenth-century American music-
hall ditties alongside operatic gestures redolent of Mozart, Bizet, and
Puccini.

Four Saints in Three Acts was a landmark collaborative creation of U.S.
modernist artists engaged in early-twentieth-century efforts to establish a
distinctly and genuinely American voice in transatlantic high culture. This

chapter examines the opera at close range and in historical perspective, as an artistic object and event that has stood continuously since 1934 as a pre-eminent example of illegible modernist abstraction, and one that issued from a heterosocial and intergenerational artistic marriage of lesbian and gay Americans living and working in that "capital of hedonism" that was interwar Paris.[11] It particularly interrogates the meanings that have attached to this putatively nonsensical work, in both production and reception, and the fertile scrutations that have attended *Four Saints* in all its legendary inscrutability. These interrogations highlight the queer expressive potential of artistic abstraction within the homophobic context of twentieth-century U.S. culture, and the crucial confluence, within that context, of queer lives and culture with artistic, particularly musical, activity and culture. The discussion here also raises questions that are explored throughout this book—concerning abstraction and identification; national, artistic, and sexual identity; and the predominance of queer artists in the twentieth-century creation of an American voice in concert music. More immediately this discussion illuminates the paths of influence and interaction, collaboration and rivalry, that were forged in Manhattan and Paris in the interwar years and led to the remarkably queer composition of America's sound.

STEIN'S QUEER ABSTRACTION

As a notoriously abstract production of the modernist avant-garde, Gertrude Stein's *Four Saints* libretto evades conventional meaning and likewise resists the reigning scientific and psychological apparatus of identity—that is, of social, sexual, racial, and other constructs of classification and normalization—that flourished in early-twentieth-century America and Europe.[12] Indeed, identity evasion is a frequent theme in recent Stein criticism, which often reads Stein's texts as resisting (in Sidonie Smith's words) "the evolutionary story, the self-conscious narrator, the identification between . . . narrator and . . . subject, the unitary voice"—in short, "all the rhetorical and narrative components of a patriarchally inscribed identity."[13] Stein's (negative) relation to identity is central in *Four Saints,* as it is in her modernist literary project generally: "Now identity remembers and so it has an audience and as it has an audience it is history and as it is history it has nothing to do with the human mind," she wrote in *The Geographical History of America; Or, The Relation of Human Nature to the Human Mind.*[14] Since identity, or human nature, according to Stein, "has nothing to do with the human mind," and masterpieces are rooted precisely "in the human mind," identity has no place in a master-piece.[15]

Speaking of masterpieces in the wake of Dada and anti-art, anti-master-piece developments, Stein (1874–1946) might appear as if clinging to nine-teenth-century aesthetic values. But in fact her stance is bracingly modern, for what she insists on by these statements is a reversal of the values attending drama and literature: Stein placed the inner experience of the spectator or reader—that of "the human mind," with its continuous sense of present moments—over and above the narrative representation of a past event, an outer reality that is a matter of "history." In contrast to the nine-teenth century's championing of an artwork conceived as absolute and autonomous, Stein conceived of the artistic object and its observer in terms of mutual interdependence. In her avant-garde work Stein therefore focused her creative efforts not on crafting narratives or histories, but on fully expressing "presentness," in congruity with that of the perceiving mind, locus of all masterpieces.[16]

Stein's definition of a masterpiece fixes on its ability to convey the essence of a subject by nonnarrative—that is, nonlinear and atemporal—means. Her corresponding and self-consciously cubist notion of landscape theater, of which *Four Saints in Three Acts* stands as the most distinguished example, is one of "eternity as an unrolled filmstrip, a simultaneous pres-entation of an image in all its possible projections into time" in which "everything that has been and will be is *there*, and merely needs to display various angles of itself." Thus is *Four Saints*, in Daniel Albright's reading, "an opera that tries to be a picture—an opera in which the text defies discursivity."[17]

We might further note that in creating an opera text that tries to be a masterpiece, the text's author defies cultural precepts concerning sex and gender identity. Stein's defiance here is evident from her presumptions to the (cross-) gendered role of "master." And it is likewise in a well-known passage from her notebooks: "Pablo [Picasso] & [Henri] Matisse have a maleness that belongs to genius. Moi aussi, perhaps."[18] In claiming "male-ness" (here a marker of gender qualities) for herself, Stein flouts her cul-ture's rules for sex-gender mapping, in language and in life. But by the same gesture she accepts and reinforces the fundamental terms of the cul-tural norm, that is, the gendered definition of genius by which she—failing her bid for special exception—would be excluded from the running.

About 1907, the year when she met her soon-to-be life partner Alice Toklas, Stein had come under the influence of Otto Weininger's just-pub-lished book *Sex and Character*. Theorizing that all humans are bisexual, the Viennese psychologist placed homosexuality within a relatively non-pathological schema: It is easy to imagine how this aspect of the work might have appealed to the queer-identified Stein. But Weininger also expounded on genius, writing that a female genius "is a contradiction in terms, for genius is simply intensified, perfectly developed, universally conscious maleness."[19] That Stein embraced such writings surely had to do with the enormous cultural currency of psychology at this time among Europeans and Americans of Stein's privileged (haut bourgeois) class and educational background—not to mention her specialized training in the field at Radcliffe College (under William James) and at Johns Hopkins Medical School. Inevitably there would also have been a *faute de mieux* factor: With male superiority and gynophobia inhering in the very foundations of the culture, what were the chances of eluding them? Stein's response was not to give up her principal aspiration—to be a genius. Rather, she constructed herself, personally and artistically, in the terms of sex-exceptionalism we see crystallized in her "Moi aussi" annotation, which dates from this early-Paris period. And here Weininger's theories would have provided further affirmation: For within his modern scientific scheme, lesbians were already "half male."[20]

Many critics have regarded the obscure language of Stein's writings as a means for her to evade detection as a sexual outlaw, queer in gender and sexuality. Catharine R. Stimpson offers a subtle but meaningful twist on this reading, by her proposal that Stein's linguistic coding serves as "a privileged, and a distinguished, 'anti-language.'" Borrowing the concept from the sociolinguist M. A. K. Halliday, Stimpson defines an anti-language as a speech system of an anti-society, one (in Halliday's phrase) "set up within another society as a conscious alternative to it."[21] Asserting that Stein and Toklas, "in their own home and in the social circles they inhabited, were citizens of a homosexual anti-society," Stimpson cogently argues that the speech Stein formulated in and for those private inner realms, "as part of her vast experiments," has become increasingly public "as the dominant society has become less hostile to her subjects."[22]

Of course, society's hostility on this front has not diminished in a constant or steady fashion, and in fact the United States saw an acute escalation of homophobia in the twenty years following Stein's death in 1946. Notably, the Stein-Toklas "homosexual anti-society" conjures precisely the "state within a state" that queer baiters most feared, and sought to flush out, in the stateside lavender scare of those Cold War years.[23] But following the peak of the Cold War, particularly in the post-Stonewall era, Stein's encoding of lesbian sexuality has been progressively deciphered, thus rendering her anti-language indeed more public and her work effectively less abstract.[24]

In the close of his introductory notes to *Four Saints,* Stein's longtime intimate Van Vechten seems to foretell the (eventual) evolution in reception that Stimpson identifies: Citing Stein's description of her work as (not a blurring of anything, but) "an exact reproduction of . . . an outer or inner reality," Van Vechten notes that Thomson's music too possesses " 'an inner and outer reality' of its own," which, "perversely, but none the less with intention, has led to a rich and strange collaborative creation which very probably a future generation may be pleased to regard as a work of art."[25] Veering, himself, toward hermeticism in this sentence, Van Vechten underscores simultaneously the "pervers[ity]" and "intention[ality]" of Thomson's contribution to *Four Saints,* as well as the distinction between "inner and outer" dimensions in both Stein's and Thomson's art. In lieu of any explanation of the scene he has just sketched, Van Vechten then offers his conjecture on future audiences' probable embrace of this "rich and strange" work—thus leaping over the present triumph of the opera's dazzling premiere the night before.

The abrupt turn toward some "future generation" and its receptive inclinations presents as a non sequitur, at least if we insist on the euphemistic distancing conventionally imposed in such instances—here, in the clustered company of unelaborated references to "perversity" ("with intention"), "strange[ness]," and realities distinguished as "outer" and "inner." But Van Vechten's gaze toward future *Four Saints* appreciators seems less curious if we allow these latter references simply to signify at apparent face value. Then his closing statement may emerge as a fond prediction of a more highly evolved future, one wherein *Four Saints,* with its perverse, rich, strange—its *queer*—vision, might be readily received in both its "inner" and "outer" dimensions, and with the same pleasure as Van Vechten finds there in 1934. That is, a future in which the authors' private anti-language is rendered public by a society (in Stimpson's words) "less hostile to," and thus more inclined to apprehend, the subjects of their work.[26]

The present discussion of Stein and her multifariously queer abstraction attempts to establish our own time as that ideal moment for *Four Saints* reception. It reads *Four Saints* from the standpoint of a twenty-first-century sensibility more accepting of and accustomed to articulations of queer meaning than would have been possible in any previous cultural moment. This perspective, however contemporary, is directed toward cultivating knowledge of the past, by examining *Four Saints* historically in the light of its contemporaneous receptions and of Stein's own artistic theories and preoccupations. These are repositioned in relation to pertinent historic models and kindreds, particularly from the queer world—as when we consider the opera's religious topic in relation to the rich history of religious thematics in Western queer art.

Stein and Thomson's *Four Saints in Three Acts* thus emerges as an influential instance of composing oneself in twentieth-century American modernism, a portrait of Americanism rendered by native queer artists living abroad. It was in Paris (a city then relatively lacking in musical cachet) that these artists found a congenial locus for sexual and artistic bohemianism, as well as an otherness that reflected back to them images of America more vivid than they had ever glimpsed at home.[27] The renderings of Americanism they in turn reflected back to America were informed by their lived experiences and perspectives as Americans, but also—albeit unspeakably— by their lived experiences and perspectives as twentieth-century queer subjects. At issue here, and throughout this book, are both the queerness and the normality of such artists' predominance in the creation of American national identity via concert music.

Surely Van Vechten would have been gratified to know that *Four Saints* would reverberate so richly decades after its premiere. But if he imagined the opera and its subjects enjoying ready transfer among later generations, he was no doubt aware that at its opening *Four Saints'* idiom and its subjects did not present themselves as fully commutable. Indeed, the identity ascriptions telegraphed by Olin Downes's "foppishness" and "Parisian poses" were evidently so difficult to pin on either the opera or its creators that Downes resorted to criticizing the audience. In so doing he may well have "violated a long-standing principle of criticism," as the current *Times* critic and Thomson biographer Anthony Tommasini attests.[28] But we might nevertheless view Downes's critical indiscretion as fortuitous, inasmuch as it affords a glimpse of homophobic anxieties and antipathies that were occasioned by the opera's performance, and that might not have been documented but for his agitated lapse.

Having noted Downes's remarks, however, and their evident homophobic thrust, perhaps we should not lend them credence as anything more than a displaced attack on *Four Saints'* queer *auteurs*. Stein's and (less famously) Thomson's sexuality was no secret, after all, to cognoscenti in the transatlantic arts and critical community circa 1934—especially given the previous year's publication of *The Autobiography of Alice B. Toklas*. But I do read in Downes an ascription of queerness—qua perversion, foppishness, and quasi-Parisian decadence—to that work which he placed at phobic arm's length (literally, in *scare* quotes) by his disdainful reference to the " 'opera,' if such it is to be called."[29] Downes thus evidently read *Four Saints* auto-biographically in relation to its queer authors (and to a perhaps similar opening night audience). Though without Downes's homophobic impetus, I will likewise read Stein and Thomson's opera in autobiographical terms.

I take my cue for such a reading from the facts of *Four Saints'* reception and its production. In the reception sphere we have already seen some hints of autobiographical interpretation both in Downes's negative take on the opera's opening and in Van Vechten's euphorically positive one. Admittedly, this is more clearly legible from Downes's accusatory (homo-exposing) review than from Van Vechten's circumspect (homo-protecting) commentary—which becomes vaguest just at the point when it gestures to draw together queer artists, art, and audience across boundaries of inner and outer reality, and across generations from the (then) present to the (unspecified) future. Elsewhere, the opera's initial coproducers—including the scenarist Maurice Grosser, set and costume designer Florine Stettheimer, and choreographer Frederick Ashton—display their own indications of interpreting Stein's libretto in autobiographical terms.

Grosser's scenario, for example, presents the saints in sex-segregated groupings: "Saint Teresa and her women," "Saint Ignatius and his men."[30] Of course, this is congruous with the opera's characterization of Catholic religious in the sixteenth century, and it is compatible with (not to say inevitable to) Stein's highly indeterminate text. Though the drama stages considerably more than the "Four Saints" of the title, this designation points nonetheless to a significant element in the work. For the titular four comprise the principal saints, in two pairs—a schema incanted punningly in *Four Saints'* prologue: "Four Saints two at a time have to have to have to have to."[31] Following Stein's own casting conception along these lines, Grosser opted to highlight specifically homosocial pairings: of Saint Teresa of Ávila and Saint Ignatius Loyola with "their respective confidants," Saint Settlement and Saint Chavez.[32] However apt, the monastic term "particular friend" is absent from Grosser's introduction of these last two saints in his "Scenario."[33] Even so, their function, here and in the opera, as inseparable companions to the principals is clear. Grosser did remark of Saints Settlement and Chavez that they are "without historical prototypes": Thus we see the authors taking up where history had left off, providing suitable companions for Saints Teresa and Ignatius.

And suitability here is in the eye of the opera's queer creators. The female pair particularly seems to reflect the librettist's own tastes in the companionship realm. Saints Teresa and Settlement, as announced by the latter's name, mirror a "settlement" in the Stein-Toklas coupling that has

FIGURE 2.   *Four Saints* scenarist and painter and Virgil
Thomson's life partner, Maurice Grosser, with Alois de
Gaul's wife, de Gaul, and Thomson circa the early 1930s. The
Virgil Thomson Papers in the Irving S. Gilmore Music
Library of Yale University. Reprinted by permission of the
Virgil Thomson Foundation, Ltd., copyright owner.

been remarked in many contexts, including this 1966 recollection from
Thomson: "Gertrude lived by the heart, indeed; and domesticity was her
theme. . . . [A]fter 1907 her love life was serene, and it was Alice Toklas
who made it so. Indeed, it was this tranquil life that offered to Gertrude a
fertile soil of sentiment-security."[34] Whether or not the principal male pair
is especially suggestive of Thomson and Grosser, the connection of Stein
and Toklas with the female pair—especially of Stein with Saint Teresa—

emerges strikingly from numerous facts within and without the text.[35] Certainly Stettheimer would seem to have understood Saint Teresa in this way: How else to explain the designer's inspired travesty—Teresa's costuming in the full regalia of a cardinal's vestments, fashioned in velvet and (like the opera's sets) the very latest modern material, cellophane?

Several critics have read the character of Saint Teresa in other terms: as a tribute to Alice Toklas. The character does bear one of Gertrude's pet names for Alice: Thérèse (the French spelling is used in Stein's libretto). And Saint Teresa made her home in Toklas's favorite Spanish city, Ávila, where Alice passionately proposed staying on forever when she first visited Spain with Gertrude in 1912.[36] Saints Teresa and Settlement notably bear the initials of Toklas and Stein.[37] Moreover, Stein writes about Saint Teresa in ways she characteristically uses to write about Toklas—as, for example, one who is always right: "Saint Therese could never be mistaken";[38] and as the happily married, sexually desirous, and sexually fulfilled wife. This latter theme arises in connection with the following passage, in which Thomson (circa 1971) finds Saint Teresa/Therese, in line 4, enjoying "high sexual delight":

> Saint Therese. To be belied.
> Saint Therese. Having happily married.
> Saint Therese. Having happily beside.
> Saint Therese. Having happily had it with a spoon.
> Saint Therese. Having happily relied upon noon.

Thomson's commentary indicates (by discreet verbiage) that the particular sexual meaning he ascribed here was one of cunnilingus, and identifies the "it" being spooned as "the sexual effluvia" (notably slipping into the ecclesiastical tongue).[39] I will say more about this passage in my discussion of Thomson's music in *Four Saints*.

Thus far this consideration of abstraction has focused on Stein's *Four Saints* text and its staging, and on certain issues attending her famously abstract writings—issues of meaning and nonsense, legibility and opacity; of production and stated intention; of reception, positioning, and effect; of queerness, autobiography, "inner" and "outer" realities. And in the interest of illumining the particular local context in which Stein and Thomson's avowedly autobiographical opera arose, this discussion frequently explores these various issues in connection with statements (on Steinian abstractness and related matters) from Thomson and other members of the authors' inner circles.

A further type of abstractness that will concern us is invoked by the present chapter's title: "Modernist Abstraction and the Abstract Art" refers to music's status in nineteenth-century art and philosophy discourses as the most abstract of all the arts. In its nonrepresentational abstractness music was deemed by nineteenth-century thinkers—including, most influentially, Schopenhauer—the purest, most absolute, and hence most exemplary of art forms.[40] Toward the end of the century the queer aesthete Walter Pater wrote in *The Renaissance* (1873) that "all art constantly aspires towards the condition of music. For while in all other arts it is possible to distinguish the matter from the form . . . yet it is the constant effort of art to obliterate it."[41] Of course, twentieth-century modernist literature and arts were characteristically directed *against* the prior ideals of the nineteenth century, and they generally cited no special debt or reference to music. Even so, the art known as modernist—emergent following the birth of psychology and of the homosexual, and following the Wilde trials' cautionary spectacle—undoubtedly displays a far greater fascination with abstraction than any previous art.

Although critical consensus long held high-modernist abstraction "above" concrete signification, latter-day Stein scholarship has found in her allegedly inscrutable avant-garde texts privately coded narratives, and landscapes, of queer life and sexuality.[42] Still other recent scholarship reads literary abstraction as a means of racial masquerade for Stein, T. S. Eliot, Ezra Pound, and other modernists who sometimes figured their American identity in significant, albeit undeclared, relation to African American voice and identity.[43] These sexual and racial analytical projects highlight a preoccupation with "nonestablishment" identities, and with arcane means for self-representing through them, that aligns with Robert M. Crunden's definition of modernists as "intellectuals in a philistine society, Catholics in a Protestant society, Jews in a Christian society, women in a male society, blacks in a white society, southerners in a northern society, [and] homosexuals in a heterosexual society," all of whom "often identified with oppressed colleagues in comparable marginal circumstances."[44]

The linkages with African American identity in Stein, Eliot, and Pound, and surely in Thomson's casting of *Four Saints,* are also symptomatic of modernist primitivism, with its racialized "emphasis on the innately creative, the unformed and untamed realm of the prerational and the unconscious, indeed that vitality of the naive which was so especially a leading edge of the avant-garde," in Raymond Williams's description.[45] Thus, in its original moment, Thomson's unprecedented casting decision—using African American performers in a sixteenth-century Spanish locale to represent the lives of twentieth-century white artists—served to stage, at a somewhat abstracted remove, the characteristically modernist sentiment

FIGURE 3.   *Four Saints'* British dance master Frederick Ashton with
Maxwell Baird, Floyd Miller, and Billie Smith, dancers in the original
1934 cast. Photo by George Platt Lynes. The Kinsey Institute for
Research in Sex, Gender, and Reproduction, Inc.

(expressed here, with all customary white-cultural ambivalence, by Eliot)
that the artist "is more *primitive*, as well as more civilized, than his contemporaries."[46] As several writers have by now remarked, *Four Saints'*
African American performers also served, at least for those worldly among
its 1934 audiences, to emblematize a queer sexual freedom associated with
Harlem and projected onto black bodies—a freedom of whose pleasures
Thomson, Grosser, Van Vechten, and other queer men in their circle were
known to partake.[47] More generally, blackness visibly represented identity
difference, and as such stood in for other, unspoken and typically less visi-

ble minoritized identities—as in Stein's "Melanctha" it had, at some level of abstraction, stood in for the author's Jewishness and queerness.[48]

Virgil Thomson's abstraction in the (reputedly) already-abstract medium of music, though regarded as on a par with that of his literary colleagues, has been subject to far less exegetic speculation than theirs. One could cite certain obvious reasons for this, especially involving music's undeniably nondenotative nature, which indeed makes it difficult to read meanings or even associations here, as compared with verbal or visual media. And Thomson's idiom presents special challenges by its notorious "blankness," its obscurity in—not abstruse complexity, as with Schoenberg, Sessions, and other modernist composers of the day—but vernacular simplicity. His musical language has long been recognized for its remarkable commensurability with Stein's literary one but, in its queer eccentricity, has yet to be recognized for the full extent of its influence on America's sound.

THE MUSIC OF *SAINTS*

Thomson's music in *Four Saints* has been described as humorous, eclectic, nostalgic for his Missouri Southern Baptist boyhood, the perfect counterpart to Stein's textual style, and a "primer on American musical declamation and drama."[49] What goes curiously unremarked in this music is its frequent gorgeousness—and it is frequently gorgeous in any number of styles. In its neoclassic troping of musical idioms and style markers it stands with Satie (e.g., *Embryons desséchés* of 1913) and with the Stravinsky of *Pulcinella* (1920) and *The Rake's Progress* (1951). In its effect, the music of *Four Saints* can often resemble that of Prokofiev: Both idioms skillfully manipulate music-rhetorical conventions that push listeners' emotional buttons, and then each (in its own way) abruptly leaves them hanging, without continuation of the narrative framework that is normally illustrated by, and the justification for, such catharsis. Among the vast range of musics heard in *Four Saints* are styles and idioms that would be at home in Anglican chant; in baroque opera or cantata (this includes but is not limited to Thomson's recitatives); in Mozart's Italian operas; in the Puccini of *Suor Angelica* and elsewhere (most obviously in surging lyric passages: e.g., at rehearsal no. 104); in nineteenth-century American music-hall entertainments and Protestant Sunday school classrooms; and in Bizet's *Carmen* (though exclusively that of Micaëla's pure white-key pastoral, and never of Carmen's chromaticized, rhythmically Latinized worldly and sexual knowing).[50]

Close examination of a few specific passages will serve to highlight some features of Thomson's score that are useful to our purposes. We noted above one textual passage in which Thomson professed to find Saint Teresa in "high sexual delight." His 1971 testimony on this point gives us a rare item of knowledge—of a particular, concrete, and specifically sexual interpretation of a certain passage in this oblique opera, from one of its authors. We must not underestimate the significance of such concrete representations as Thomson began, in his later years, to ascribe to *Four Saints.* The ramifications of his revelation here are substantial: It clearly suggests that Thomson understood Stein's words as not merely abstract but denotative, as bearing specific meanings, including sexual ones—even in this explicitly religious-themed work, and in relation to Teresa's sainted personage. If only we heed him, Thomson is advising us (as Stein would similarly do by her own example: see below) to perceive in this "abstract" modern art those things which it seems to present—to see the naked woman on the canvas as a naked woman, and thus to defy the reigning modernist bourgeois and aesthetic prescriptions that would label such perception unschooled, vulgar, or philistine (by contrast with a purely symbolic, sensory, or otherwise abstracting reception).

Thomson is, moreover, providing a queer byline for Saint Teresa: Her erotic pleasure taken (in Thomson's reckoning) by the spoonful must exempt her from what Gayle S. Rubin maps as the "charmed circle" of "Good, Normal, Natural, Blessed Sexuality," and relegate her to the "outer limits" of "Bad, Abnormal, Unnatural, Damned Sexuality" including homosexual, autoerotic, manufactured-object, and other nonconjugal and nonprocreative sex. Rubin traces this hierarchic conception of inner- versus outer-circle sexual practices to Western ideological structures rooted in Christian (particularly Pauline) teachings, but she adds that such notions "have by now acquired a life of their own" and thus persevere even apart from religion.[51] *Four Saints,* as seen in the light of Thomson's own reading, not only stages conventionally banished sexual personas and practices centrally in a charmed circle, but explicitly reunites them with the Mother Church, among her saintly elect—or, inversely: It links blessed personages with pleasures supposedly damned. As we shall soon discuss, *Four Saints* is neither the first nor the last instance in which Thomson treats religious topics, and treats them with subtle, particularly sexual, unorthodoxy.

Armed with such knowledge, one might well inquire as to how Thomson set the text in question. We find the answer in the opera's second act (score rehearsal no. 94 + 8 bars, Example 1): Saint Teresa's sexual ecstasy-apparent is set statically and repetitively, presenting a musical poker face throughout. The passage is marked by a slight increase in tempo, but the score direction *un poco animato,* which might serve as a clue to sexual excitement, bears

EXAMPLE 1. Saint Teresa's private ecstasy, *Four Saints in Three Acts,* act 2, Virgil Thomson on a text by Gertrude Stein (Elektra Nonesuch 9 79035, CD 2, track 1, 3:39–3:50).

more impact on the page than by its scarcely perceptible effect in perform-ance. The particular moment of purported sexual delight, "Having happily had it with a spoon," falls in line indistinguishably with those surrounding it, and the passage overall is distinct from its surroundings in only one way: by its consummate blank neutrality and stasis. Throughout most of *Four Saints* Thomson's music juxtaposes the feeling that (in John Cage's words) "something is about to happen" against the feeling, evoked by Stein's text, that "nothing is ever going to happen."[52] But this textual passage seems to inspire a reversal of roles on Thomson's part, its ostensibly hot implications calling forth a cool, vacant setting. And while such a musical-textual role reversal might appear as a radical move, its effect is decidedly conservative:

It serves to maintain the established (hot/cold) complementary dynamic and its steady, semantic-circuit-jamming ratio of "suspiciously significant" elements to "nonsense" elements.

Now we might similarly inquire about the opera's only "tender scene," an act 2 duet between the characters Commère and Compère (rehearsal no. 109 + 3, Example 2).[53] A pass here reveals this designated "Love Scene" as anything but ardent. It comprises eighteen bars in which the lovers regularly alternate in the singing of their fragmentary lines. In classic operatic instances, tragic lovers' intertwined voices soar to the heights; here, the couple's notes never so much as overlap. The "lines" themselves comprise prosaic particles of authorial self-mutterings ("Scene eight."—"To wait." / "Scene one."—"And begun."), all of which, in the singing, remain at a constant pitch level and on unchanging rhythm. The accompaniment is a sustained, arrhythmic F♯-major triad, its voicing immobile throughout this scene. Of course, passages of stasis in music can be used to create serenity and, contrastingly, to create tension. This static episode does neither: It creates little beyond a blank, banal white noise.[54] As we have remarked, Thomson offers up ardency and gorgeousness in this score. But he is always careful to do so *dissociatively*—that is, apart from any comparable implications in the staged scenario, and never in moments wherein the latter would conventionally call for such effects. It is in this regard that his music surely can be called abstract and a perfect complement to Stein's text: Where "something is about to happen" for one, the other always adopts the counterbalancing pose that "nothing is ever going to happen"—and what is "about to happen" in any case never does.

Not long after Teresa's moment of (muted) ecstasy, Thomson scores a "Dance of the Angels" (rehearsal no. 97 + 10, excerpted in Example 3). The passage's opening line constitutes a recurring question within Stein's authorial-musings-spoken-aloud in *Four Saints:* "How many saints are there in it." Answering her own query, Saint Teresa I sings, "There are as many saints as there are in it."

The ballet music here is immediately reminiscent of that of Thomson's colleague Aaron Copland, in his *Rodeo* and *Billy the Kid,* and even *Appalachian Spring.* It presents a textbook example of that "sound of the American prairie" by now recognizable—via Copland's scores and countless echoes in Hollywood westerns, TV, and film music—as a beloved national cliché. Here the distinctive elements of this sound inhere in a number of features: first, in the straightforward bugle-call triadicism and gentle syncopation of the ten-note tune, and in its trot-step accompaniment of pizzicato strings, conjuring a pioneer folk ensemble of washtub

EXAMPLE 2. Commère and Compère's "Love Scene," *Four Saints in Three Acts,*
act 2, Virgil Thomson on a text by Gertrude Stein (Elektra Nonesuch 9 79035, CD
2, track 3, 0:00–1:08).

(continued)

EXAMPLE 2. *(continued)*

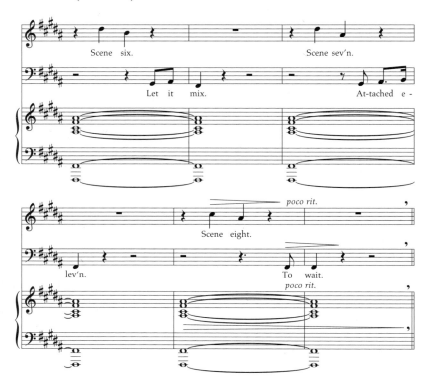

bass and backbeat banjo chords.[55] The tune and its accompaniment are stated, echoed by solo clarinet, and then slightly varied, all in E major.

And Commère breaks in with one of Stein's saintly laundry lists—"Saint Teresa Saint Settlement Saint Ignatius Saint Lawrence Saint Pilar Saint Plan and Saint Cecilia." Her litany is set by a reciting-tone formula that is effectively a four-bar fermata: It sustains the E-major tonic and confirms the established accompaniment style—while the now-monotone voice shifts to the less danceable, speechlike rhythms of through-composed baroque recitative. Here in the stasis of recitative, we may notice more plainly a certain modernist twist present in the harmonic dimension: the quartal aspect of its emphasis on the IV harmony. By showing equal regard to the fourth above and the fourth below tonic (IV and V, respectively), Thomson's harmony in this "Dance of the Angels" evokes the pitch symmetries of modernist harmonic palettes like Debussy's, Stravinsky's, Satie's—and later,

EXAMPLE 3. Saint Teresa I states the theme in "Dance of the Angels," *Four Saints in Three Acts,* act 2, Virgil Thomson on a text by Gertrude Stein (Elektra None-such 9 79035, CD 2, track 2, 0:06–0:13).

Copland's.[56] By a sort of music-rhetorical pun the usage also manages, in this setting, to evoke African American blues harmony, with its character-istic enjoyment of "nonprogressing" I–IV–I successions no less than I–V–I (the obliged teleology in conventional Germanic tonal grammar).[57]

The theme tune reenters following Commère's interjection and resumes its scheme of vocal and instrumental call and response. As before, echoes and answers are given by solo woodwinds, in the reedy innocence of their midregister timbres—another Americana hallmark familiar from *Appalachian Spring* and other Copland classics. Now, however, such thematic statement imparts an air of expectancy, having broken away from E to move up into G major's brighter realm, and having broken free of foursquare regularity into a more breathless pace of irregularly shifting meters. This setup will in turn break away, to another through-composed episode that forsakes the theme to climb ever more breathlessly through a succession of momentary tonics. At its peak a muted trumpet recaps the ascent, and the dance reaches its terminus. Saint Teresa II, resummoning baroque *stile recitativo,* delivers a dignified closing remark: "Thank you very much." Then, suspended on the recitative's characteristic half (i.e., open) cadence, we are jolted back into G major by a sudden, glorious, and poignantly lyrical outburst from Saint Teresa I, entering *forte* on a high G cradled in the barest, most exquisite of settings. Her descending phrase serves as coda to the entire passage, conceding the last lovely gasp of what was, while it lasted, an exhilarating whirl.

Teresa's gesture, here a closing and recapping, is simultaneously in another realm a beginning and foreshadowing. It is indeed, as suggested by the opening-night response of Kirk Askew and Julien Levy, a birthing moment for American music. For although this little-known passage is likely to recall for contemporary listeners Coplandian Americana, Thomson's music for *Four Saints*, written in 1927–28, considerably predates works like *Billy the Kid* (1938) and *Rodeo* (1942). Relevant, later-to-be-classic ingredients in Thomson's "Dance" surface in the musical idiom and orchestral soundscape of its tuneful country trot, in the melancholy beauty of its starkly lyric coda, and, not least, in the abrupt and heart-searing shift between the two.

To home in on some of the specific resemblances between the tonal neo-classicism Thomson introduced in *Four Saints* and Copland's Americana idiom, we might compare the brief passage from "Dance of the Angels" (see Example 3) with another sixteen-beat excerpt, taken from the famous "Hoe-Down" music in Copland's *Rodeo* (Example 4). We can readily identify several essential structural and stylistic similarities. First, each consists of a simple, triadic melody above a standard "boom-chuck" bass and chord accompaniment. And each melody emphasizes the notes of the tonic triad (i.e., main chord) of its major key, with particular emphasis on the descent from scale tone 3 to scale tone 1. Further, both melodies highlight pentatonicism and use the same folkish-sounding pentaton (i.e., five-note scale), consisting of 1-2-3-5-6 in the major scale, omitting 4 and 7; each melody presents a strong syncopation immediately in its opening bar; and each accompaniment is syncopated via a dropped downbeat at beat 13, creating a moment's musical wit by a trip-step in the approach to the cadence. Both examples also present a transparent style of orchestration with prominent pizzicato strings and trumpet, among other voices and instruments. All these features are shared between Thomson's and Copland's compositions, and moreover, all constitute key elements of the catchiness and distinct Americanness we hear in each "tune."

Of course, these two settings for the dance, while markedly similar in structure and effect, were composed some fifteen years apart. Copland's 1929 *Dance Symphony*, on the other hand, adapted from his early ballet *Grohg* (1922–25), exemplifies the balletic style in which he was writing around the time of Thomson's 1927–28 "Dance of the Angels." Here, how-

EXAMPLE 4. "Hoe-Down," from *Rodeo,* Aaron Copland (London Records 448–261, CD 2, track 14, 1:41–1:49). Compare the strongly syncopated opening bar and the dropped downbeat at beat 13 to those in Example 3.

ever, we find music strikingly different both from Thomson's "Dance" and from Copland's own later Americana ballets like *Rodeo, Billy the Kid,* and *Appalachian Spring.* For whereas Copland's Americana idiom is neoclassically tonal, his writing in *Grohg* and *Dance Symphony* is more harshly dissonant and unmistakably Stravinskian. Specifically, it evokes the primitivist Stravinsky of *The Rite of Spring* (1911–13) and *Les noces* (1914–17), as contrasted with the neoclassic Stravinsky of *Pulcinella* (1919–20) or *The Rake's Progress* (1948–51).[58]

One could similarly examine other passages in *Four Saints,* such as the closing comment of Thomson's lone muted trumpet, which presages his more expansive exposition of this instrumental "persona" (unmuted) in the hymnodic prelude to act 3 (again engaging the "Dance of the Angels" theme). Between the prelude's quietly prayerful beginning and its soaring climax the trumpet goes from street-corner salvation band to courtly heraldic duties. This music gives a foretaste of the musical trope that would come to represent American majesty and simple integrity, when, some years later, it became widely known via the compositions of Thomson's gay coeval and colleague Copland. In Copland's work and that of his followers, such writing would be presented not amid abstraction but with concrete thematic cues through which listeners could interpret the music. Take, for example, Copland's ballet score for Martha Graham's *Appalachian Spring* (1944): This presents the Shaker hymn "Simple Gifts" in a lucid, widely spaced orchestration comparable to that of Thomson's "Dance" and prelude, but now in explicit relation to Graham's themes of pioneer strength and austerity, prairie vastness and beauty, and—despite the ballet's theme of Shaker life (which, notably, is celibate)—joyous love and marriage between a man and a woman.

Growing evidence suggests it was in large part from such Thomsonian models as are given here and in the ballet and documentary film scores of 1936–37 that Copland learned, as it were, how to be Copland. The composer was characteristically candid in expressing to Thomson his admiration for *Four Saints,* its innovativeness and particularly its orchestration, and he was equally generous a few years later in his praise for Thomson's film music.[59] Thomson's scores for two New Deal government documentaries, *The Plow That Broke the Plains* and *The River,* have only recently received serious critical attention. In close analyses of this music and that of Copland's film and other scores from the period, the musicologist Neil Lerner details the extraordinary dramatic and musical innovations of Thomson's long-forgotten documentary work and concludes, "Copland's U.S. pastoral sound is in no small part indebted to Thomson's landmark film scores."[60]

The notion of Copland having derived essentials of his populist language from Thomson has arisen in other quarters as well. Ned Rorem has registered the point on many occasions, most recently with this summary: "[I]t was [Thomson] who first legitimized the use of home-grown fodder for urbane palates. He confected his own folksong by filtering the hymns of his youth through a chic Gallic prism. This was the 'American Sound' of wide-open prairies and Appalachian springs, soon borrowed and popularized by others."[61] A similar genealogy surfaces strikingly in a memorial penned for the *New York Times,* upon Thomson's 1989 death, by Copland's most illustrious disciple Leonard Bernstein, who wrote that Thomson would "always remain rightly alive in the history of music, if only for the extraordinary influence his witty and simplistic music had on his colleagues, especially on Aaron Copland, and through them on most of American music in our century." Bernstein closes: "I know that I am one twig on that tree and I will always cherish and revere Virgil, the source."[62]

All these assessments affirm Thomson's own frank statements, apparently intended for the record, in his 1970 book *American Music since 1910*—to the effect both that Copland was the author of "the most distinguished populist music style yet created in America," and that he had modeled this style directly on Thomson's music. According to Thomson, his own *Four Saints* was the inspiration for Copland's first opera *The Second*

Hurricane (1936); his *Plow* soundtrack (1936), replete with folkish tunes, cowboy songs, and war ditties, and his Americana ballet *Filling Station* (1937) were the models for Copland's breakthrough ballet *Billy the Kid,* its western-genre successor *Rodeo,* and Copland's first Hollywood score, *Of Mice and Men* (1939); and his *River* score (1937), with its use of Southern hymn tunes, was the "direct source" for Copland's use of nineteenth-century hymns in *Appalachian Spring.*

Thomson claimed it had not occurred to Copland, "a self-conscious modernist," that an American composer at this time could write an American opera or ballet, nor had he imagined *how* one might write for a large, popular audience without sacrificing "intellectual" (i.e., high-cultural) status. By Thomson's report, his own musical simplicities showed Copland that one need not preserve the limiting "correct façade of dissonance" their Paris training had instilled. And these simplicities gave Copland, in his own words, "a lesson in how to treat Americana."[63] If all this sounds like sour grapes, that fruit was almost surely present *chez* Thomson in 1970, and with the fermentation of some three decades. But it must be said that Thomson's book, a survey and assessment of sixty years of American music and composers, is throughout an exemplar of generosity, even-handedness, and peerless musical and professional discernment. And his account therein of Copland's influences, whatever its etiquette implications, appears verifiably on the mark.

While both Thomson and Copland lived, there was never any question— not after about 1938, anyway—as to whose idiom was the more recognized "American music." In *Four Saints* and other works, Virgil Thomson, in the estimable view of the former *Times* critic John Rockwell, "has given us as profound a vision of American culture as anyone has yet achieved."[64] But Copland's willingness and ability to link his own lean, tonal music with seemingly apposite, broadly embraced mainstream images of America's land and people positioned him more optimally in that period, following the Great War, when the U.S. hungrily scanned its horizon for a native musical bard and national language.

CREATIVE IDENTIFICATIONS:
COMPOSING ONESELF IN *FOUR SAINTS*

To invoke the sixteenth-century mystic and seer Saint Teresa of Ávila is to invoke one of the defining icons of vital passion and ecstatic rapture in the Christian world. It is equally to invoke one of the beloved heroines and patron saints of Western queerdom, a woman who in her life knew intense intimacy with other women and endured on account of her rapturous s/m-tinged "visitations" both scandalous rumor and incarcerative scrutiny in the Spanish Inquisition—and a woman who has since her death inspired the devotions of queer writers from the English baroque poet Richard Crashaw to the earlier-twentieth-century English writers Ronald Firbank and Vita Sackville-West and the contemporary American poet Gloria Anzaldúa. In their literary paeans and in Stein and Thomson's *Four Saints* the critic Corinne E. Blackmer examines Saint Teresa's role as a "queer diva" whose "bravura negotiation of the speakable and the unspeakable" in her *Life* (written under order from her inquisitors) manages to reveal, "in a double movement of concealment and disclosure, the sources of her *jouissance*."[65] By this description Teresa may seem a most fitting heroine for Gertrude Stein, who indeed read her writings with admiration.[66]

Stein also avidly read and admired the contemporary high-camp novels of Firbank, a prodigiously eccentric, sapphically identified queer friend of Van Vechten and others in Stein's circle.[67] His novels include treatments of Teresa and the religious life in *Valmouth* (1919) and *The Eccentricities of Cardinal Pirelli* (1926), which, like *Four Saints* after them, present historical and invented saints in fantastic scenarios that bear selective resemblances both to historical fact and to their author's contemporaneous queer realm. Such writing takes part in a long tradition, traced variously upon Anglo-American literature, of identification with Catholic monastic life on the part of queer subjects who (as Blackmer notes) have regarded its enforced homosociality as "an appealing refuge" and have felt attracted to a religion that was "for half of its existence" (in John Boswell's words) "most notable for its insistence on the preferability of lifestyles other than [heterosexual] family units."[68] Among early-twentieth-century lesbians in the arts worlds of Paris and London, queer Catholicism's tradition was carried on in the devotions and conversions of Vita Sackville-West, Violet Shiletto, Christopher St. John, Una Troubridge, Renée Vivien, and others yet to be discussed.[69]

Though she bears certain important resemblances to Toklas, Stein and Thomson's Saint Teresa, as we have noted, also seems to represent Stein, who was, like the historical Teresa, a "devoted artistic woman who achieved prominence later in life."[70] She seems Steinish already by virtue of being the central character in *Four Saints,* where her name is the mantra continually invoked and repeated—like that of Gertrude Stein in *The Autobiography of Alice B. Toklas.* The latter book, of course, leaves no room for doubt about Stein's ability to write a "tribute" to Toklas without disturbing her own place as central subject. In the light of Saint Teresa's evident duality we might borrow (from one of Stein's manuscripts) the formulation "Gertrice/Altrude" to designate the biographical-referential space staked out by this protagonist. Ultimately, such space may even be limitless: Meg Albrinck argues that Saint Teresa "gains plurality and multiplicity through the repetition of her name" and thus resists categorization and interpretation.[71]

"Can two saints be one," the libretto asks—as if to render these questions unignorable.[72] And *Four Saints'* operatic realization offers an answer, in the affirmative. Thomson staged two performers to make one Teresa, splitting her character into dual roles—Saint Teresa I (soprano) and Saint Teresa II (mezzo-soprano)—for reasons both dramatic and musical: He wanted her to be able to converse, and sing duets, with herself.[73] But however present Stein might be in the ever-expansive character of Saint Teresa, she is more nearly ubiquitous via the authorial commentary that crowds the prologue and resurfaces throughout the rest of the text—comprising nearly two-thirds of the whole, by Richard Bridgman's estimate.[74] Indeed, Albrinck observes that Stein's libretto "is a curious mixture of dialogue, stage direction, and authorial comment, making the author's voice as present as those of the saintly characters." Jane Palatini Bowers further develops this notion, marking the presence of "Stein, the writer, [as] a character in her own play" and reading *Four Saints'* text as a representation of the process of its own composition.[75] Surely much of the charm audiences perceive in the opera owes to Thomson's decision to set all of this "curious mixture" equally: "I put everything to music, even the stage directions, because they made such lovely lines for singing," he declared in 1982.[76]

Unlike the now-revealed queerness of some of Stein's other writings from this period, that of *Four Saints* is not manifested in lyric style or erotic subject matter.[77] Rather, queerness presents here in the engagement with a queer life cycle, located in a collective dimension embracing daily "tribal" or social life, vocation, and spirituality. Of course, my reading of *Four Saints in Three Acts* focuses on the opera, and not primarily on Stein's libretto. Within the latter, Thomson himself attested to finding a "quite impressive obscurity," upon receiving the manuscript from Stein in 1927.[78] Once rendered a singable, stageable work by Thomson and Grosser (thus realizing the imperative of Stein's subtitle, "An Opera to Be Sung"), *Four Saints* remained an exemplar of avant-garde abstraction, but it was now inarguably and inevitably more concrete, in some significant ways. This difference has been noted from the time of its premiere. Van Vechten, for instance, writes that "Thomson's music has perforce introduced an associational element into this prose"—just after quoting Stein on her desire to *destroy* "associational emotion in poetry and prose."[79] The latter-day critic Albrinck is at pains to emphasize the alteration of Stein's text, and the dilution of its resistance to dramatic and social conventions, that were wrought, in her view, by the operatic realization. But surely "[t]he transformations that were necessary for staging *Four Saints*" must be viewed in the first place "as a measure for the distance Stein's text maintains from the theater." This indeed is how Martin Puchner views them in his analysis of Stein's *Four Saints* libretto as an instance of modernist "anti-theatricalism" and thus of "closet drama"—a genre he defines in terms precisely of social resistance, via "the refusal of or withdrawal from social normativity."[80]

One can scarcely argue with Albrinck's claim that Thomson's addition of *commère* and *compère* characters constitutes a prime element in his (and Grosser's) alteration of the libretto. Indigenous to French theatrical revues, these stock characters are put to narrational use. In this capacity the pair have been likened to the Greek chorus and, often in connection with Thomson's all-black casting of the original production, to the end men of blackface minstrelsy.[81] In *Four Saints*, Commère and Compère "speak to the audience and to each other about the progress of the opera" (as Grosser explains) and frequently observe the action from their special place in a "box" offstage.[82] Significantly, only these two characters, among all those presented in the opera, are intended to represent the laity.[83] In the 1934 premiere they alone wore modern dress, twentieth-century street clothes, while the saints—excepting the resplendent Teresas—wore saintly robes of various sorts. And they are distinguished as the only characters that stage a "tender scene" and sing a love duet.[84] They introduce heterosexuality into the opera, and thus Albrinck regards Thomson's Commère and Compère as straightening up Stein's act, as normalizing the prior queerness of her text and "radically rewrit[ing]" it in a manner fundamentally at odds with its vision, which Albrinck reads as antipatriarchal and socially resistant.[85]

Albrinck fails to notice, however, an aspect of Thomson's "nonsaintly commentators" (as he calls them) that some other viewers have found most striking.[86] To wit: Commère and Compère fulfill the highly specialized function assigned them—that is, of nonsaintly commentary—"and are therefore kept apart from the 'saintly' primary cast." Puchner remarks that Commère and Compère are "segregated" from the saints both spatially and functionally: by their relegation to the outer stage, and as bearers of only "the diegetic parts—narrative, stage directions, commentary"—of Stein's libretto, at a remove from the saints' onstage mimetic action.[87] Thomson's

Commère and Compère are pleasant, they are helpful, they are demon-strably capable of affection with each other and of interaction with the saints. But they remain perennially outside the frame of *Four Saints'* spec-tacle. In their embodiment of the culturally ubiquitous and domineering topos of heterosexuality they invite the sort of reading that Albrinck gives them—as main attraction. They provide a focal point for (some) spectators' desire for the staging of heterosexual desire. But those spectators who seek other objects may readily see past them. And such queerish viewers are likely to notice that Commère and Compère, uniquely among *Four Saints'* dramatis personae, are presented as mainstream mortal folk, always out-side the realm of saints and of consecration.[88]

Of course, queer-attuned subjects in the pre-Stonewall era were accus-tomed to looking past standard surfaces, and adept at seeking out more rar-efied clues to meanings that might reflect their own lives and experiences. To the queer listener John Cage circa 1957, it appeared "significant"—albeit in an unspecified way—that his friend and colleague Virgil Thomson chose a seemingly self-emblematic musical figure (a Protestant hymn tune, for a former Kansas City Baptist church organist) to set the Steinian phrase "as they say in the way they say they can express in this way tenderness."[89] For other spectators similarly versed in the requisite encodings of pre-Stonewall queer life, a significant tenderness—at least in the way "they" can express it in *Four Saints*—is readable in the saintly spectacle presented on center stage, and with recourse to the creators' own queer lives. And it is readable despite the diversions of artistic abstraction and of heterosexual spectacle, with its exclusive claim on "tender scenes."

With reference to various past and present instances of reception, I have been arguing that *Four Saints*, its renowned abstractness notwithstanding, is in fact pivotally concerned with certain tender subjects: those of the authors' own lives, loves, and work as modern queer artists. Questions of "the way they say they can express" such subjects loom large and central here, given the proscriptions on queer representation and expression that obtained in American life throughout much of the twentieth century. By the century's final quarter, however, such conditions were beginning to change, and Virgil Thomson, born in 1896, was still around to bear witness. Even more remarkably, he remained until his death in 1989 capable of shrewdly assessing and continually adapting to shifting sociosexual and political terrains—contrary to conventional wisdom concerning old dogs and new tricks. Thus, although Thomson had been fiercely guarded and secretive about his personal life from the time of his 1940 U.S. return through at least 1966 when he published his memoir, in 1982 he saw fit to speak of his magnum opus in somewhat more personalizing terms than he or Stein had previously used (notably, in the 1980s Thomson also actively sought a biographer who would confront head-on the queer themes in his life and work).[90] He spoke now of *Four Saints* as concretely thematic in its collaborative conception—specifically, as an autobiography of the artists, Stein and himself (and not merely an account of Stein's creative process, as Bowers would have it), presented via an eccentric species of religious allegory:

> It was early in 1927 that Gertrude Stein and I first thought of writ-ing an opera. Naturally the theme had to be one that moved us both. "Something from the lives of the saints" was my proposal; that it should take place in Spain was hers. She then chose (and I agreed) two Spanish saints, Teresa of Avila and Ignatius Loyola. The fact that these two, historically, never knew each other did not seem to either of us an inconvenience. . . .
>
> Why did it occur to Gertrude Stein and myself to write an opera about saints? Simply because we saw among the religious a parallel to the life we were leading, in which consecrated artists were practicing their art surrounded by younger artists who were no less consecrated, and who were trying to learn and needing to learn the terrible disci-plines of truth and spontaneity, of channeling their skills without loss of inspiration. That was our theme; certainly that was our theme. That the daily life of saints could be, as regards their work and their prepara-tion for it, a model to ours.[91]

One senses here a very close identification between the authors and their brainchildren in *Four Saints*. And a fusion of the saints' personas and daily lives with those of their creators, within the imaginations of the lat-ter, had also emerged in dialogues from the collaboration years. In Septem-ber 1927, for example, Thomson wrote campily to Stein, "The saints are singing. . . . Gaily praising their maker and trying not to be too catty to one another" (in Thomson and Stein's own gay world, camp cattiness was a virtue and a defining performative element of the "anti-language" of their shared "anti-society").[92] Until Thomson's 1982 statements, however, neither he nor Stein had spoken in explicit terms of an autobiographical program in *Four Saints*. Of course, it was not the fashion among avant-garde or other modernists to make too much of artistic content. Rather, being modern meant glorifying form, as Stein did in connection with her notion of "landscape theater"—which not only granted writing a degree of abstraction commensurate with that of modern painting, but abstracted the very notion of writing by rendering it conceptually commensurable with painting (both here being apprehended piece by piece, and outside any temporal frame).

ABSTRACTION, *ACCROCHABILITÉ*, AND THE NAKED WOMAN

Undoubtedly Stein's *Four Saints* libretto is concerned with problems of form and intended to "oppose, subvert, and disrupt the dominant, conventional forms of drama."[93] Similarly, Thomson's setting is determined to instantiate an American music of directness and simplicity in line with his anti–German Romantic, antimasterpiece vision. Much of what is "abstract" in *Four Saints* surely arises in connection with its authors' avant-garde attempts to resist prior artistic forms and their effects—for example, with Stein's struggle against the disconnect between (on the one hand) a play's narrative and (on the other) the sensate response of its audience members. She described having felt herself caught, as a playgoer, between a rock and a hard place: forced to choose between keeping pace with the onstage narrative, or attending to her own emotional response to it, always unfolding at a different pace. Stein's linguistic and formal experiments in *Four Saints* were directed to this and to other perceived problems of conventional narrative and drama, and they were tied to her artistic theories, particularly her notion that "the business of Art . . . is to live in . . . and to completely express [the] complete actual present."[94] Her quasi-cubist approach to expressing the "complete actual present" in this "landscape play" eschews narrative, with its focus on the past, even while deploying the (conventionally narrativic) medium of language. The abstraction that ensues might seem all but inevitable, quite apart from any queer content in the work or in the authors' lives.

But the work was not created apart from the authors' queer lives, any more than the authors' métiers and methods—not to mention collaborative partners—were chosen apart from their queer identities. By virtue of its abstract formal characteristics, *Four Saints* already evinces a "refusal of [and] withdrawal from social normativity" that may be said to mirror queerness and other kinds of social marginality and resistance.[95] Moreover, the opera was received and produced in autobiographical relation to its queer creators. It presents a mise en scène so simply and fundamentally queer as to be unremarkable, in the manner of forgone conclusion and quotidian normality. As Blackmer observes of *Four Saints'* Teresian protagonist, her "sexuality is not treated as an 'incitement' to narrative or as a prurient secret to be unveiled for the delectation of her spectators."[96] Indeed, the signs of her and the other saints' queerness are simply present amid the toils and pleasures of devoted daily lives, an unquestioned element of "things as they are" (to invoke a line from elsewhere in Stein's oeuvre).[97]

Thus rendered mundanely, unspectacularly central, these signs ironically became illegible, "abstracted," from the perspective of the dominant culture. Through such "abstraction" the authors were able to compose and stage their artistic statement of collective and individual, national, sexual, and artistic identity. And surely Stein and Thomson had reason, beyond modernist fashion, to welcome abstraction and, in 1927 as for many years after, to avoid speaking of any autobiographical program in their hagiographic and American opera, or consecration vis-à-vis the lives they were leading: For such notions would have made their work unpresentable (or, as Stein would put it, *inaccrochable*) in America, where the dominant culture deemed queer persons dispossessed of such sacred themes and expressions.[98]

Not surprisingly, the receptive ideal that evolved in relation to high modernism applies to audiences the same expectations as are wielded by artistic producers—of placing form over content and of actively cultivating abstraction. Given the thorough training in not-seeing that modernist aesthetic culture thus engenders, perhaps we should not wonder that the fundamental queerness of *Four Saints'* spectacle is little registered in the still-growing discourse surrounding the opera and its libretto.[99] Given, too, the particular instance of *Four Saints* as well as the general facts of queerness among so many of American modernism's principal figures, we might consider the possible connections between, on the one hand, the historical exigencies of concealing queer meanings from the homophobic mainstream, and, on the other hand, the contours assumed by abstract modernist style—and herein lies one of this chapter's key propositions. A related proposition, which will be pursued substantially throughout this book, links the exigencies of concealing queer meanings in twentieth-century America and, in the same cultural-historical context, queer subjects' extraordinary engagements with the putatively abstract art of music.

Twentieth-century Anglo-American queer subjects knew a great deal about abstracting meanings and speaking in code, especially in the decades following the (1895) Wilde trials. "You didn't mention it" in the teens and twenties, as Thomson recalled in 1988, "but you understood everything." Silence among queer persons and their allies was assured by the fact that "everybody knew about the Oscar Wilde case."[100] And if this was not equally assured with outsiders and enemies, these at least could often be trusted to bring abundant ignorance to queer meanings.

Ernest Hemingway can serve as a case in point. For all his preoccupation in his Paris memoir, *A Moveable Feast*, with identifying queer markers and subtexts and ostentatiously distancing himself from them, Hemingway seems deaf here to the resonant queer implications of a certain piece of advice he received (by his account) from Stein. After reading (circa 1922) a short story of Hemingway's that contained vulgar language, Stein instructed the young writer, "You mustn't write anything that is *inaccrochable*" (unhangable, hence: unpresentable for public display). "There is no point in it," Stein emphasized. "It's wrong and it's silly." Hemingway appears to have been, even some thirty-five years later, so intent on portraying (by contrived understatement) the purity and instinctual integrity of his own literary vision that he misses completely the possible significance of Stein's statement in relation to *her* writing.[101]

Given Stein's emphatic stand on this principle (as well as her keen attention, as discussed above, to matters of reception) we might well suppose that she observed it in her own work: Never write anything that is *inaccrochable*. Do not offend the standards of bourgeois modesty and respectability, for there is no use in painting a picture that can be neither hung in a show nor displayed in a genteel home, and thus cannot be sold. Hemingway gave no indication that Stein encouraged him to alter his themes, but only the means of their conveyance, and then to specific, professionally strategic ends. Impressed by the naughty transgressiveness of his own slangy, tough-guy language in "Up in Michigan," however, Hemingway was apparently absorbed in a (retrospective) fantasy of himself as youthful challenger to the prior generation's orthodoxy, represented by Stein. He betrayed no awareness of the far more radical potential of Stein's conservative tactic, of its ramifications in relation to her own writing, or to the truly unorthodox meanings her assiduous avoidance of *inaccrochabilité* might have allowed her to pass under the public's nose. However useless as advice to Hemingway circa 1922, Stein's statement is valuable to us as an indicator of her priorities and strategies vis-à-vis obtaining exposure and getting her work, and its messages, before the public.

In light of such indications, perhaps the abstraction in *Four Saints* is best read as deferring rather than obviating meaning—and deferring it until such time as its audiences might be capable of receiving it. This notion is consistent with Stein's focus on the audience and their role of (in her view) completing the circuit of artistic process. It is also consistent with Stein's statement in 1939 to her young friend and admirer Samuel Steward that, while she deemed what she and Toklas did in bed their own business, "perhaps considering Saint Paul it would be better not to talk about it, say for twenty years after I die, unless it's found out sooner or times change." To Steward—who was approaching homosexual themes in his own work as a writer—she expressed regret at having written on same-sex affairs in *Q.E.D.*, at a time (1903) when "it was too early to write about such things in our civilization."

Perhaps it was, more precisely, too early for Stein to write about such things, for this early work—in contrast to her writing from *The Making of Americans* (1911) on—employs a legible, linear style resembling that of Henry James. In her conversation years later with Steward, Stein confessed that she had found the writing therapeutic, but that having done it caused her to feel ashamed, for "it was too outspoken for the times even though it was restrained." Stein told Steward that she would not permit *Q.E.D.* to be published during her lifetime, but that she had in this instance "changed it around and made a man out of one of the [romantically embroiled] women" to create "Melanctha" (1905)—which presents a style already vastly less Jamesian, more nearly Steinian. Something had had to be done, in Stein's view, to make the work responsive to the cultural requirements of its own time: "[I]t would not have been a graceful thing to publish it then."[102]

Stein's work—the meanings of which are increasingly deciphered and demystified by critics—and her comments on it suggest there is more to *Four Saints*, its creators' vision, and (at least some) modernist abstraction than pleasurable nonsense or even pure form. But "considering Saint Paul," that most influential critic of sexuality and expression, and considering her audiences, Stein respected the crucial difference between the coded and the constative. She had reckoned with "the tradition that we call Pauline"—in which, as Ellis Hanson remarks in his study of fin-de-siècle decadent Catholicism, "we are asked to appreciate saintly *jouissance* without ever analyzing it."[103] Interestingly, amid her acute awareness of abstraction and its crucial function, the writer best known as the prime exponent of nonsensical abstraction apparently neither trusted abstraction nor granted it mystique in other artists' work, and she further deemed the sense, or meaning, of her own work its very raison d'être.

Indeed, according to Thomson's recollection, Stein in the late twenties "did not trust abstraction in art" and believed it "constricted between flat color schemes and pornography."[104] Thomson's account finds fleshing out in an anecdote from *The Autobiography of Alice B. Toklas* that concerns Matisse's painting of "a big figure of a woman lying among some cactuses" and illuminates Stein's stance toward artistic abstraction:

> [O]ne day the five year old little boy of the janitor who often used to visit Gertrude Stein who was fond of him, jumped into her arms as she

was standing at the open door of the atelier and looking over her shoul-, der and seeing the picture cried out in rapture, oh là là what a beautiful body of a woman. Miss Stein used always to tell this story when the casual stranger in the aggressive way of the casual stranger said, look-ing at this picture, and what is that supposed to represent.[105]

Matisse's "cactus woman" was not relegated to the obscurity of *inac-crochabilité:* The picture hung in Stein's own studio. And yet, as Stein surely understood, it would have been sequestered, along with any number of other works, had many of her "casual strangers" or readers of *The Autobi-ography* followed Stein's (and her little visitor's) lead, allowing themselves to register its content as well as its form. Her friend Matisse knew and used methods for rendering his pictures *accrochable* without giving up cen-sorable content. Hemingway's story attests that Stein strongly approved of such methods, but it never suggests she was herself, as a receptor, "taken in" by them: In Matisse's work as in her own Stein expected, and found, con-crete meanings. This point is amplified by the description, given in 1931 by the young composer and writer Paul Bowles, of Stein's exhortations on the absolute primacy of "sense" in writing:

> She has set me right, by much labor on her part, and now the fact emerges that there is nothing in her works save the sense. The sound, the sight, the soporific repetitions to which I had attached such great importance, are accidental, she insists, and the one aim of her writing is the superlative *sense*. "What is the use of writing," she will shout, "unless every word makes the utmost sense?"[106]

And yet in her own time many, if not most, of Stein's audiences and crit-ics could be counted on to regard her avant-garde work as nonsense, and even to bring a willful, conditioned blindness to it and its meanings. The cultural frame into which her words were placed encouraged such not-see-ing—not only by its construction of high art in transcendent, disembodied, and (within modernism) abstracted terms, but also by its insistence on the nonexistence of female sexuality in general and (female and male) homo-sexuality in particular.[107] Of course, there have been both appreciative and hostile receptors who have trusted that they "got it" upon encountering *Four Saints* and other works of abstract reputation. But even as late as 1971 Thomson, in an otherwise appreciative review of a budding crop of code-breaking Stein scholarship, was at pains to point out (albeit subtly, surely not wishing to appear *too* knowledgeable about queer codes) the plain-obvious meanings in Stein's language that continued to pass under schol-ars' radar—which, as he also pointed out, was often hopelessly over-cali-brated toward the arcane.

Having cited one scholar's explanations for the word choices in *Tender Buttons* via Indo-European philology ("a subject of which Gertrude knew little"), and for those of another work via Jungian psychology, Thomson took the opportunity to drop a quiet little bomb concerning Stein hermeneutics. In "a stroke that demonstrated how simple it is to short-circuit the wiring of the open secret" (to borrow the description given in another context by Philip Brett), Thomson wrote, "I wonder why no one has ever reached out in public, at least to my knowledge, for the meaning of the title *Tender Buttons*, of which the literal translation into French will easily get anyone a laugh." Even Bridgman, whose book Thomson praised highly, "does not essay that one," despite devoting twelve pages to the piece. Here as in *Four Saints*, the exoticizing abnormalization of queer identity and life—their sequestering as tender subjects in receptions even of *Tender Buttons*—allowed them, in overt and mundane representations particularly, to pass undetected in the dominant culture: Queer abstraction indeed. And in case anyone might have missed the point—or perhaps because they can be expected to—Thomson closed this section of his discussion with an arch multipart pun, expressing his hope for further progress "toward opening up . . . the approaches to *Tender Buttons* presented in *A Long Gay Book*."[108]

QUEER CATHOLICISM GOES TO (RELIGIOUS) CAMP

Thomson's choice of Florine Stettheimer as *Four Saints'* set and costume designer was a bold move. The composer had previously considered Pablo Picasso and, separately, Christian Bérard in this capacity. But he fixed upon the cloistered and unknown Stettheimer as soon as he saw her flashy, tinselly paintings. When asked by Steven Watson a half-century later to explain the affinity between Stettheimer's paintings and the opera, Thomson got directly to the point: "Florine's paintings are very high camp, and *high camp is the only thing you can do with a religious subject.* Anything else gets sentimental and unbelievable, whereas high camp touches religion sincerely. . . . People who have been cured of an eye disease put little toy eyes in front of a statue of a saint. And then the world of tinsel can only be sincere."[109] Evidently Thomson, a camp virtuoso for whom Manhattan's great cathedral was "St. John the *Too, Too* Divine," could recognize a kindred spirit when he saw one.[110]

We should note in this connection that "camp" has only recently acquired the broad popular sense it now possesses—denoting a general sensibility, not necessarily in association with a particular sexuality or subculture—since the mass media appropriated camp, the word and sensibility, around the late eighties (capping a process begun in the sixties). Throughout the earlier decades of the twentieth century, camp was understood exclusively in its original relation to homosexuals and homosexual culture. This homo-specific usage surfaced as late as 1960 in Hemingway's memoir *A Moveable Feast:* His phobic ejaculation, "Take your dirty camping mouth out of here," was the means by which Hemingway outed a certain interlocutor to readers (or rather, to cognoscenti), the more insultingly because nonnominatively and insinuatively.[111]

Susan Sontag's landmark 1964 "Notes on 'Camp'" let readers of *Partisan Review* in on what had been an exclusively subcultural phenomenon. But Esther Newton attests that *camp* was still a homosexual "in-group word" in the midsixties when she conducted ethnographic research for her ground-breaking *Mother Camp: Female Impersonators in America.*[112] Newton's book defined camp in terms of incongruous subject matter, theatrical style, and humorous strategy, identifying all these elements in intimate relation to "the homosexual situation."[113] In a more contemporary context, Moe Meyer, responding to the recent mass appropriation and heterosexualization of camp, conceptualizes camp as a specifically queer social critique and emphasizes its "cultural and ideological analytic potential."[114]

When in early 1927 Virgil Thomson suggested a religious subject to Gertrude Stein for their operatic collaboration, he had already been engaged with Christian themes, both narrative and musical, for many years. Brought up in a devout Baptist family, he also earned his principal income in church, working as a professional organist from his Kansas City adolescence through his undergraduate years at Harvard. Thomson's intimacy with religious topics thus began in his youth, but by means of more recent explorations he had, by 1927, confirmed the singular qualities of such topics as vehicles for queer meaning. The close association of religion, music, queerness, and abstracting dissociation that characterizes Thomson's work in *Four Saints in Three Acts* would surface time and again in his creative projects, in such a way as to constitute a central and persistent theme of his artistic voice and oeuvre. But the theme predates *Four Saints,* and it appeared significant in Thomson's life some years before it emerged in his art.

Attendant with Thomson's entire adolescence was a friendship and mentoring relationship with the Kansas City church tenor Robert Leigh Murray. The relationship was formative for Thomson both as a musician and as a homosexual. Murray provided contacts with the crème de la crème of local music teachers and took Virgil to hear the most illustrious concert artists of the day, in their own city and on weekend trips to Chicago. Whether or not the young Thomson was involved sexually with the decades-older Murray—and there is strong suggestion that, in some fashion, he was—the association with Murray and his cohort provided Thomson's earliest initiation into the homosexual world, and particularly into the realm of homosexual arts devotees and professionals.[115] Here we might further note that in his youthful relationship with Murray Thomson experienced a fused, simultaneous initiation into musical and homosexual life and culture, which was itself, in this instance and elsewhere throughout his life, a fused entity: a life and culture that coalesced equally around homosexuality and musicality, mutually informed and mutually inextricable. The association with adult homosexuals would surely also have initiated the nascently queer Thomson into the ways and habits—including coding, silence, and double consciousness—that characterized the identity, discourse, and life of the reigning persona among early-twentieth-century middle-class queers: That is, of the "discreet homosexual."[116]

On his seventeenth birthday, in 1913, Thomson received from Murray a gift that he would keep until his death nearly seventy-six years later. It was a handsomely bound copy of Oscar Wilde's *De Profundis* (1897), inscribed, "To a lad whose friendship is a very pleasant thing to me," and initialed by the giver.[117] We might glean the significance of this gesture by comparison with a very similar instance in the queer youth of a Thomson coeval, the English writer Beverley Nichols. Alan Sinfield reports that Nichols was "taken up" during his World War I adolescence by a bachelor named Edwards who lived nearby. Though the two were sexually involved, Nichols's businessman father persisted in thinking the dandy Edwards a ladies' man until one day he came upon his son reading a book that Edwards had given him: Wilde's *Picture of Dorian Gray*. Mr. Nichols became violently frantic, calling his son a "pretty little boy" while hitting him in the face. He spat on the book and tore its pages with his teeth, exclaiming Wilde's name in disbelief.

Sinfield points out that Edwards, an effeminate, aesthete bachelor, was perceived by the elder Nichols as a "leisure-class philanderer" until Wilde's name arose, at which point he was instantly transformed into a homosexual. The meanings and effects of Edwards's gift to young Nichols, and Murray's to Thomson, owed to the facts of the contemporary symbolic economy, specifically the fact that after 1895 the effeminate, aesthetic, dandyish Wildean type was infamously the paradigmatic homosexual persona in Anglo-American culture, and "an Oscar Wilde" a male homosexual. Indeed, "the queer man as we know him is a consequence of the Wilde trials," which christened in scandal and shame an emblematics previously unknown.[118] And we need only look at *The Well of Loneliness*'s Stephen Gordon, or her creator Radclyffe Hall, to confirm queer women's contemporaneous involvements in Wildeanism and its effects.

The particular Wildean opus Thomson received from Robert Leigh Murray carried further and deeper resonances, however, at least for queer readers, than those merely of homosexuality or aestheticism. Wilde's *De Profundis,* his long letter (literally) "out of the depths" of his imprisonment in Reading Gaol, inflected the (now eponymously Wildean) figure of the homosexual in terms of persecution and suffering, and of longing for Christian consolation and deliverance. And in its delineation of "an intimate and immediate connection between the true life of Christ and the true life of the artist," *De Profundis* proffered a redemptive, indeed, Christ-like role for the abjected homosexual: that of the artist.[119] Throughout Wilde's oeuvre art is religion, and religion—Catholicism in particular, in all its theater and ritual—is art. This queer theology resembles that to which *Four Saints* pays homage, albeit with Teresa's (effectively) antipatriarchal cardinality displacing Jesus' status as supreme sacerdotal figure. The extent to which Thomson adopted such an aestheticized affiliation to the Church may be suggested by his 1943 reply to a *Herald Tribune* reader who had found his Easter Sunday review "both Christian and Catholic": Thomson was delighted, he claimed, for although he was "technically neither," indeed "Christian" and "Catholic" described his "religious sentiments" exactly.[120]

If *Four Saints'* religious theme was Thomson's suggestion, the queer theology instantiated there could readily have been formulated with reference to Stein's life. One time, in their early travels together, when Stein and Toklas went walking in the hot sun of Spain, the peasants assumed Stein's customary brown corduroys to be the habit of a religious order.[121] Such a notion was not far from the truth, for Stein's "strange steerage clothes" (in Hemingway's description) were a visible marker of her life's passionate devotion and vocation. As she would advise Hemingway, "You can either buy clothes or buy pictures."[122] Stein's chosen habit was to sacrifice the worldly pleasures of sartorial splendor for the divine riches of art, and to practice a kind of ascetic discipline in the material realm so as to dwell in art's consecration. Her perception of a similar devotion in Thomson preceded her decision to collaborate with him: Driving home after one of their first evenings together—during which Thomson had given his one-man rendition of Satie's *Socrate,* his lifelong musical touchstone—Stein remarked to Toklas that Thomson was "singularly pure *vis-à-vis* his art," which he appeared to regard (as she did her own) in terms of "discipline, humility, and loyalties rather than egocentric experience."[123]

Composing oneself in relation to the high church, in art or in life, appealed to queer modernist artists including not only Stein, Thomson, and their *Four Saints* collaborators, but also their contemporaries Firbank, Hall, W. H. Auden, Montague Summers, and others.[124] These moderns' conviction that "a cult of homoerotic community" could be found "[u]nder the cowl of monasticism" was an inheritance from their late-nineteenth-century queer predecessors. Wilde and Pater were leaders among the "late-nineteenth-century aesthetes, many of them homosexual, who found in the church a peculiar language for artistic and sexual expression."[125] A similar artistic sensibility merged with cultural and political vectors in the French literary movement dubbed Neo-Catholicism, which embraced the "decadent" symbolist poets Charles Baudelaire and Paul Verlaine, and took as its principal text J.-K. Huysmans's 1884 novel *À Rebours (Against the Grain)*.[126]

A subsequent generation of American twentieth-century moderns would adapt Catholicism to their own particular symbolic purposes: It functioned as antonym to a despised Protestantism and, in its exoticized mysticism and sensuality, signaled a resistance to further scorned elements of a contemporary scientific, moralist, Progressivist national culture deemed vacuous and provincial.[127] The further resonance of Catholic/Protestant within (what Sedgwick has called) "the new calculus of homo/hetero" is legible with many queer modernists, though none more clearly than Firbank. His *Valmouth* widows Mrs. Elizabeth Thoroughfare and Mrs. Eulalia Hurstpierpoint share both a homoerotic friendship and ornate Catholic pieties, the latter "aimed, in part, at converting their friend Lady Parvula de Panzoust from her 'fallen' conditions as heterosexual and Protestant."[128]

Virgil Thomson's fascination with a sacred Christian erotics was undoubtedly fueled by his experiences as a college student in the late teens and early twenties when, according to Humphrey Carpenter, "Harvard was largely occupied with trying to copy the 'aesthetic' style of Oxford in the 1890s. Undergraduates read the *Yellow Book*, discussed Walter Pater and [Aubrey] Beardsley, displayed crucifixes in their bedroom [sic] and declared that they found the Church 'voluptuous.' They posed as Decadent poets and wrote sonnets."[129] But *Four Saints*' particular genuflection to aesthetic religiosity was also importantly molded by Thomson's experiences with Protestant religion and music, and by Stein's style and input.

Stein's preoccupation with pleasure was central throughout her writing from about 1911, following completion of her grand chef d'oeuvre, the 925-

page novel *The Making of Americans*. But the flavor of pleasure fixation in Stein's writing is wholly distinct from that of the decadent poets. It bears, for instance, no hint of shame, and betrays no taste for what the Church has called "morose delectation."[130] Whereas Stein celebrated quotidian pleasures in occult language, the decadents celebrated occult pleasures in relatively quotidian language. Virgil Thomson partook of the latter sensibility in other sacred settings, but in *Four Saints* he aligned himself with Stein's singular approach to queer religiosity and, in certain ways, with camp style. And if Stein's queer anti-language is a thing apart from both decadent Catholicism and camp, it nevertheless functions much as camp does (in William Lane Clark's description) to cloak "the sexual projections of transgressive personality, allowing a sympathetic reader to read one side of ambiguous characterization and yet forestalling censure by providing the antagonistic reader equally plausible meaning(s)."[131] Such language functions, in other words, to exploit multivalence: It elevates ambiguity to an art form and thereby creates space for queer meanings, pleasures, and realities.[132]

Thomson's first formal attempt at composition was in July 1920, following his freshman year at Harvard (his matriculation at twenty-two having been delayed by Army service during World War I). The result was a choral setting of the Penitential Psalm *De Profundis*. Though Thomson's text here is conspicuously Old Testament, his title alludes obliquely to Wilde and his (by this time queer-emblematic) letter from the depths.[133] Thomson's first effort as a composer is notable not only for producing a "striking" choral work (in Tommasini's description) that he would later publish, but also for presenting certain general traits that would mark his subsequent composition, and sometimes his prose, including (1) an articulation of covert queer meanings in relation to musical works of overtly sacred theme, and (2) a commingling of Christianity and homoeroticism in which the latter topos appears always concomitant with (if not immanent in) the former.

More particularly Thomson's opus one shows an impulse to take up the banner borne by Wilde in that most poignant, emblematic statement of queer suffering, spirituality, and selfhood, *De Profundis*. It was an homage that would reach fuller—that is to say, both more substantive and more concealed—realization in *Four Saints in Three Acts*, Thomson's first large-scale work following his 1926 artistic epiphany and turn toward what would be his mature, tonal, vernacular style. Whereas Wilde's *De Profundis* "delineate[s] an intimate and immediate connection between the true life of Christ and the true life of the artist," *Four Saints* mediates this connection somewhat, inasmuch as its relations, likewise intimate and immediate, obtain between the artist and Christ's emissaries in the form of saints both male and female (this latter undoubtedly essential from Stein's standpoint).[134] But Thomson's 1982 statements on behalf of himself and his late collaborator convey a sense of artistic intentions no less sacred for this saintly mediation: If by the opera, he writes, "something is evoked of the inner gayety *[sic]* and the strength of lives consecrated to a non-material end, the authors will consider their labors rewarded."[135]

Another instance in Thomson's saintly repertory is "Commentaire sur Saint Jérome" (1928), a song inscribed *"pour Carl Van Vechten."* Thomson never attempted to publish this setting of a kinky, queer, and misogynist text by the Marquis de Sade, but Anthony Tommasini, as pianist, has brought it to performance and recorded it on a 1994 collection.[136] It yields a glimpse into Thomson's treatment of saintly themes outside, but roughly concurrent with, his composition of *Four Saints*. His nakedly simple, French-flavored and -inscribed setting soars to its pastoral apex on *"des fesses des jeunes bergers"* (the buttocks of young shepherds). The text in this song, evidently intended for exclusive inner-circle consumption, translates as follows:

> Saint Jerome reports that during a voyage he made among the Welsh he saw the Scots eat with delight the buttocks of young shepherds and the breasts of young maidens[.] I would have more confidence in the first of these dishes than in the second, and I believe, along with all the cannibalistic tribes, that the flesh of women, like that of all female creatures, must be far inferior to that of the male.[137]

Further interesting examples can be found in Thomson's published scores, including "Consider, Lord" (1955, on a text of John Donne); an arrangement of the Southern U.S. hymn tune "My Shepherd Will Supply My Need" (1959); and settings of multiple Crashaw texts, some of which notably revisit the shepherd motif. All of these exhibit the traits identified above in relation to Thomson's sacred settings. As for Thomson's "Commentaire sur Saint Jérome"—the word *covert* scarcely applies to the blatant homoerotics here, but it perfectly describes the status accorded this unpublished song within the composer's musical oeuvre.

The most extraordinary treatment of a religious theme in Thomson's prose catalog is found, again, in an unpublished manuscript, though in this case it appears that Thomson had sought publication. Thomson published a great deal of prose, mostly criticism, in numerous articles and books over many years. This writing began in his college days and peaked during his 1940–54 tenure with the *New York Herald Tribune*, a period that saw

Thomson become America's most important music critic and one of the most distinctive voices in music criticism of any era: trenchant, plainspoken, and lucid. But in 1924–25, about the time when Thomson penned an essay entitled "My Jesus, I Love Thee," he was still an unknown American composer in his late twenties, living in Paris. The essay was apparently submitted to H. L. Mencken for publication in his *American Mercury* (possibly in an earlier version and under its previous title, "Patented Praises"). Mencken's fame as a debunker of religion and irreverent critic of the American bourgeoisie likely raised Thomson's hopes of publishing an essay implicating Baptist hymnals and Christic erotics in a condemnation of (among other things) bourgeois materialism in American religion. But despite strategic efforts the argument in "My Jesus" falls considerably short of *accrochabilité,* and, fortunately for Thomson, Mencken responded with a firm (if vaguely bewildered) rejection.[138]

We can surmise from his life's work, and from his late-1980s revelation concerning camp and religiosity, that religion *chez* Thomson was a topic highly charged with queer erotics and camp, and as such was subject to techniques of encoding and abstraction. But in this early essay we see Thomson testing the limits of his ability to get sexy queer thematics past the censors, as it were, *without* abstracting them. In lieu of abstraction, his ingenious tactic for dissociation was one of displacement: First, "My Jesus" attempted, in a high-handed and at times puritanical tone, to indict "the popular religion of our time," defined here as a success rhetoric focused on love and on business, and characteristically Protestant. Then, along a (rather flimsy) thread of "individualism," Thomson endeavored to implicate this "cult of success" in the personalized, first-person eroticization of Jesus he purported to expose in contemporary Protestant hymns. Quoting from the selected, offending, hymnal, Thomson concocted long strings of suggestive lyrics: "I 'tell Him every longing that throbs within my breast,' and 'He gives relief'; 'He satisfies me.' "[139] This goes on for two full paragraphs, in the manner—or so we are to believe—of a prosecuting attorney relentlessly presenting his most damning evidence.

Ultimately, however, the target of Thomson's plaint is never fully clear, and it seems to shift throughout the course of his (uncharacteristically) blustery discourse. The righteous condemnation of Protestant hymnals that was Thomson's vehicle and opportunity for overt discussion of (homo-) erotics in Christic hymns (the question of their homo-ness is never named, but begged throughout) is therefore marked, from the reader's standpoint, as somehow fishy and perhaps disingenuous. Thomson managed cannily to confect a narrative frame through which his public dis-

cussion of sacred textual erotics might have been publishable. But crafting
the narrative and convincingly directing its accusations of prurience—
toward the hymnal and its users and away from himself—proved beyond
his rhetorical powers in this instance. Yet, however ill-calculated, "My
Jesus, I Love Thee" is an invaluable document of its author's queer apprenticeship as cultural spokesperson: We see Thomson experimenting with
techniques for balancing "inner and outer realities," exposure and silence,
that would later become practiced habits—if here they show need of further refinement. And the combination of religion, music, queerness, and
dissociation was fully realized in this essay, as it would be in *Four Saints*
and other Thomson compositions to come.

Although a posture of astonishment was essential to Thomson's indig-
nant mien in "My Jesus," his keen, seemingly exhaustive reportage on disavowed erotic markers in hymn texts leaked evidence of a knowing and
lack of innocence in this regard. Thus it was precisely in the deployment of
his ingenious rhetorical stratagem (i.e., of displacement) that the ever-bril-
liant Thomson proved to be—from a standpoint of *accrochabilité*—as too
clever by half. Thomson's over-eager cleverness exposed him within what
D. A. Miller has analyzed as the economy of the open secret, wherein the
"function of secrecy . . . is not to conceal knowledge, so much as to conceal knowledge of the knowledge."[140] Elsewhere, of course, Thomson's
knowledge in this realm is attested—albeit less flagrantly—by his sacred
text choices throughout his compositional career, which suggest a near-
connoisseurial ken of the homoerotic tradition in English-language sacred
verse.[141] These musical compositions managed somewhat better than his
earlier verbal one to maintain the simultaneous elusiveness and richness of
meaning that characterizes modern queer knowledge—which is, under the
regimes of homophobia, characteristically *connotative* and as such (in
Miller's words) "enjoys, or suffers from, an abiding deniability."[142] If
Thomson's "My Jesus" offered its young author any lesson, it might have
been about the oil-and-water polarity that his culture ascribed to church
texts and deviant sexuality, and hence about the (paradoxically) ample
maneuvering room that religious themes afforded queer meanings—provided, that is, such meanings were rendered sufficiently deniable.

For our own part, we might note that music's singular capacities vis-à-
vis "abiding deniability" render it commensurate with—and apparently
even equivalent to—modern queer knowledge as Miller defines it. As we
shall further explore in the next chapter, queer subjects in twentieth-century America would seem to have understood (however consciously) the
relation between music and queer knowledge in terms of some similar sig-

nificance—or so suggests the evidence of their extraordinarily frequent, devoted, and influential involvements with the "abstract" art of music.

A POSTLUDE

During her long years of solitude following Stein's 1946 death, Alice Toklas converted to Catholicism. Toklas had, like Stein, come from a Jewish family, but she had never been religious. In her later years, however, she was increasingly drawn to the Roman Church. At home in Paris, Toklas was deeply moved by an Easter mass she attended in 1956, and by the end of 1957 she had taken First Communion. Thus at the age of eighty did Alice B. Toklas become a Catholic, as she would remain until her death a decade later. She spent the fall and winter of 1960–61 in residence and devotions at the convent of the Sisters of the Precious Blood, in Rome. Friends visited and corresponded with her there, and to one she confided that, were she young again, she might have joined the "good sisters" in their simple life.

Among Toklas's visitors that winter was Virgil Thomson. What the two old friends might have made of the symmetries emergent between art and life at some thirty years' remove, we can only imagine. It is known that Thomson was among those who greeted Toklas's conversion with understanding and support. However skeptical elsewhere on matters religious (a Christian, Thomson notes in his memoir, "I surely was not"), he could well have apprehended his friend's "need for an all-consuming passion" and for "an ordered pattern of life."[143] Her embrace of Catholicism, its rituals and disciplines, fulfilled these needs for Toklas and lent her renewed energy in her waning years. Catholicism further provided Alice Toklas with the promise of a heaven where, after her long wait, she would be reunited with Gertrude Stein.[144] Thus, an abundant afterlife as postlude, as final bonus act: It was an ending worthy of *Four Saints*.

2. Being Musical

Gender, Sexuality, and Musical Identity in Twentieth-Century America

> Every profession is a secret society. The musical profession is more secret than most, on account of the nature of music itself. No other field of human activity is quite so hermetic, so isolated.
>
> VIRGIL THOMSON, *The State of Music*, Chapter 1: "Our Island Home"

> As a boy [I was] partially ashamed of [my love of music]—an entirely wrong attitude, but it was strong—most boys in American country towns, I think, felt the same. . . . And there may be something in it. Hasn't music always been too much an emasculated art?
>
> CHARLES IVES, *Memos*

> Music had stirred him like that. Music had troubled him many times. But music was not articulate. It was not a new world, but rather another chaos, that it created in us.
>
> OSCAR WILDE, *The Picture of Dorian Gray*

In April of 1940 Virgil Thomson dispatched from Paris that he had "discovered music all over again." "And it turns out to be just as it was when I was seventeen," he effused: "the daily joy of practicing a beloved instrument and of finding one's whole life filled with order and energy as a result." While Europe burned and France hovered on the brink of Nazi occupation, Thomson in his studio pressed on toward a solution to "the central esthetic problem in music today." This problem, by his report, occupied the pianists of Paris "[t]o a man, and at all ages," even as twenty years' tensions in Western Europe came to a head in Nazism and fascism—indeed, their engagement with it grew more urgent with the invasion's imminence. Writing to colleagues in America via the quarterly *Modern Music*, Thomson identified this pivotal contemporary concern: It was "the creation of an acceptable style-convention for performing Mozart."[1]

If this instance hints at certain incongruities between the music world and the outside world circa 1940, or between the concerns and values that characterize each realm, it can also point up some crucial parallels between music and religion in the functions and rewards each one offers its devotees. In the latter regard, we might notice that the musical rituals and disciplines Virgil Thomson first discovered in his youth, and rediscovered (perhaps more than once) in his adulthood, appear as the source of "daily joy" and of "order and energy" that fill his "whole life"—much as Alice Toklas, in her later years, found renewed energy, "all-consuming passion," and "an ordered pattern of life" in Catholicism's rituals and disciplines.[2]

As for Thomson's evident embrace of music to the exclusion of the momentous political events surrounding him: Whatever one might conclude vis-à-vis such practice-room sequestration, it should not be presumed unusual. For such diverting, all-consuming engagement appears as one of the salient features of musical devotion and one of the most characteristic uses to which music is put by its disciples, past and present.[3] The notion receives further expression, now tinged by noble heroic sentiment, in a credo attributed to Leonard Bernstein:

> This will be our response to violence:
> To make music more intensely,
> more beautifully,
> more devotedly than ever before.

The ideal so ardently articulated here continues to resonate with classical musicians to this day. By various formulations it was given voice and via many performances enacted in the American music world following the terrorist attacks of September 11, 2001. Indeed, I came by the above quotation in the weeks just following the tragedy, when a colleague posted it to the faculty e-mail list of the large university music school in which we both teach. He thought the passage would strike a chord with many in the school and larger music community, and he was right: Clearly it did.

As the foregoing instances and epigraphs suggest, music—certainly for musicians—is not something subject to simple definition. Rather, it is an object simultaneously of love and hate, of discipline and compulsion; both a "universal language" and a "secret society," all-consuming and all-rewarding, vocation and avocation, and more. And as we have seen, music appears to occupy in its devotees certain spaces more often associated with political allegiances; with lover, partner, or family relations; and with religious practice. Any attempt to explain such facts will necessarily come face to face not only with questions of what music is, but of what it means to engage with and even to dedicate oneself to music—that is, to be in a serious way *musical.*

Undoubtedly, in twentieth-century America to declare oneself musical was to claim membership in a special class or even a secret society. Initiates in this society shared arcane knowledge of forces that would appear forever mysterious to most "ordinary" citizens, including many who would have professed considerable susceptibility to such forces. For music, particularly high-art music, was the exclusive province of persons deemed to possess *talent*.[4] The elect were determined by birth, and others to a large extent remained outsiders.

But within certain circles, in at least the first half of the century, to declare oneself musical invoked a different meaning. The gay novelist Christopher Isherwood recalls, for instance, that his gay uncle Henry, circa 1930, "using the slang expressions of his generation . . . referred to himself as being 'musical' or 'so.'"[5] Thus in Anglo-American queer vernacular, "musical," as code for "homosexual," carried a denotation distinct from its conventional one. Yet its connotations were much the same in both instances: It implied membership in an exceptional class (exalted in one case, stigmatized in the other) of persons possessing knowledge and preoccupations alien to the majority.[6] And notably, such class membership was in both cases widely regarded as an inborn, fixed and immutable aspect of one's essential nature.

The semantic parallels just noted may have had something to do with the adoption of the designation *musical* for queer-identity coding purposes. But another factor that was certainly reflected in this usage is the historically tenacious association of music with femininity or effeminacy, of effeminacy in turn with homosexuality (conventionally figured in male terms), and of musical activity with queer persons.[7] Those who have dared to assert such associations have often done so in the context of homophobic incriminations. But it is not only hostile outsiders who have voiced these notions: As the gay vernacular instance illustrates, queer insiders have also done so. Similarly (or, obversely), some musicians have shown a willingness or eagerness to claim significant relations between their art and queerness—as chapter 3 will show.

As this discussion already suggests, the histories of musical and homosexual identity in twentieth-century American culture mirror and overlap one another significantly. As such, each has much to reveal about the other, and their intersections—as represented by queer musicians and queer musical subculture—are especially telling. This chapter examines these busy intersections and the identity constructs that trafficked there, particularly among prominent New York–based gay composers in the 1920s to 1950s. It thus interrogates the operative categories and constructs in their cultural and historical specificity, taking a social-constructionist view of what were often highly essentialized understandings of self and other.[8]

This inquiry addresses some questions that readily arise from recent years' popular and scholarly acknowledgment of the queer identifications of so many celebrated twentieth-century American composers, including Samuel Barber, Leonard Bernstein, Marc Blitzstein, Paul Bowles, John Cage, Aaron Copland, Henry Cowell, David Diamond, William Flanagan, Lou Harrison, Gian Carlo Menotti, Harry Partch, Daniel Pinkham, Ned Rorem, Virgil Thomson, Ben Weber, and others. For example, given the histories of these artists, and the growing evidence about Handel, Schubert, Tchaikovsky, and other canonic Western composers: What were the connections between composing and queerness? And taking into account such nineteenth- and twentieth-century phenomena as the cult of Wagnerism, lesbian diva worship, the opera queen, and the general prevalence of queer figures in concert music: Was there some special relationship between music and queer persons? If so, what was it?[9] And in light of the extraordinary preponderance of homosexual-identified men among America's best-known twentieth-century composers: What were the links between composition and modern homosexual identity? Were these peculiar to twentieth-century American culture, or artistic modernism? How has modern queer life and identity shaped—and been shaped by—American art music?

This chapter responds, in other words, to one of Wayne Koestenbaum's literary characters, an aging, semiretired lesbian accompanist who enjoins reverberantly, "[E]xplain the hole that's left in music when my kind is missing."[10] And it engages a related injunction: Explain the hole that's left in the story of my kind when music is missing.

IDENTITY JUNCTURES

In *Gay New York* the historian George Chauncey reveals an active early-twentieth-century male social and sexual landscape featuring three recognized roles: of markedly effeminate men, or "fairies"; of conventionally masculine denizens of the homosexual world, or "queers"; and of men (including uniformed soldiers, sailors, and policemen) who lived in the "normal" world but had sex with other men, or "rough trade." Such categories did not assume any fixed or exclusive *orientation*, as is assumed in the modern notion of sexuality or "sexual identity." Flagging this discrepancy, Chauncey emphasizes the cultural-historical locus of sociosexual practices on the streets of New York circa 1890–1940, and contrasts them with those "sexual practices and meanings . . . announced by the elite." He refers here to the elite institutions of science, medicine, and psychology that have been taken up in the theoretical work of Foucault and others, but that (as Chauncey shows) had little relation to the actual sociosexual lives of working folk in late-nineteenth- and early-twentieth-century America.[11]

It is true, as Foucault observed, that continental sexologists focused on individuals whom they invested with elaborate new schemata of sexual specification, and thus defined circa 1870 a new "species," the homosexual.[12] But Chauncey's point is that the preeminence of "the modern homosexual" was *not* thereby established throughout the Western urban industrial queer world. Especially in New York working-class culture, social practice among homosexually active men continued to be understood and organized in terms of sex and gender behavior (versus sexual identity) even into the 1950s.[13]

In middle-class culture, however, amid perceived threats to the position of Anglo-Saxon manhood from feminists and women generally, post-Reconstruction African Americans, waves of new immigrants, and allegedly overcivilizing industrialization, the gender-normative homosexual had displaced the maleness-abasing fairy several generations earlier.[14] And, of course, such object-fluidity as characterized the sexual behavior of rough trade, whose "manly" sexual acts were equally so whether they involved female or male partners, lay outside the homo/heterosexual paradigm (which is not to suggest that "trade" themselves were outside the realm of bourgeois queers' involvements). Thus, from around the end of the nineteenth century, homosexually active middle-class men generally conceived of their "sexual identities" within a homo/heterosexual dyad, and self-identified only with the queer node of the fairy-queer-trade triad. As Chauncey stresses, the class differences were never absolute, the role meanings were contested, and there were significant contacts between the middle- and working-class worlds. Still, fairies and trade in this period were predominantly located within the working class, where gender behavior (i.e., whether one took the "manly" or "womanly" role) notably "governed the interpretation of sexual practices," and "manliness was self-consciously performative" (i.e., produced by any "manly" sexual act, whatever the sex of the object). Among the middle classes after the turn of the century, however, gender was supposed to be rooted in anatomy, and one's sexual persona, or "sexuality"—either homo or hetero—was similarly understood as a given fact of one's nature and identity.[15]

Copland and Thomson typify the gay modernist composers on which the present study focuses, insofar as both came from middle- or upper-middle-class families—albeit geographically, ethnically, and religiously differing ones—and went on to personal and professional lives in which their social and cultural milieu was one of elite cosmopolitan culture, education, and wealth, while their finances were often on a par with members of the poor and working classes. That is to say, they occupied, in their adult lives, the liminal realms of bohemia. Only one member of the gay modernist circle defined herein had poor or working-class origins: David Diamond's Austrian-Jewish immigrant parents, a cabinetmaker and a dressmaker, were poor and working class both. But Diamond (b. 1915) early distinguished himself by virtue of his musical ability—first as violinist and later as composer—and thereby gained entry into elite musical and cultural environs from a young age, beginning with scholarship study at the prestigious Eastman School of Music during his high school years.[16]

Of the circle of gay American composers treated here—Bernstein, Blitzstein, Bowles, Copland, Diamond, Rorem, and Thomson—Marc Blitzstein (1905–64) had the most significant and long-term contact with working-class gay life. He had himself enjoyed a privileged upper-middle-class upbringing, but was throughout his adulthood a committed artist-activist on behalf of the proletariat, as well as a queer man sexually engaged with sailors, soldiers, and other "nonqueer" trade (by Rorem's assessment, "Marc . . . forever championed the working class but avoided rubbing elbows with them unless they were rough trade [which wasn't quite elbows]"). Blitzstein spent his last conscious moments with three such men on the island of Martinique, who robbed and beat him, then left him for dead.[17] The 1950s and 1960s diaries and memoirs of Ned Rorem (b. 1923) also chronicle brief, often anonymous encounters with rough trade in America and abroad, while indicating that his longer-lasting romantic and sexual liaisons more often involved middle- and upper-class men (his 1994 memoir places Rorem's total number of lovers at 3,000).[18] Rorem also ascribes to his friend Diamond, at least in the 1940s, a pattern, deemed troublesome, of "proffering deep love to those who by their very nature cannot reciprocate (rough trade)."[19]

Thomson had pursued illicit, race and class boundary-crossing encounters in Paris and in Harlem, but he curtailed such activity after being arrested in a 1942 police sting on a Brooklyn waterfront gay bordello frequented by sailors and soldiers. Thomson, then chief music critic of the *New York Herald Tribune,* was mortified: He had not only the Wilde case to remind him of the perils at hand, but much closer to home that of Henry Cowell, a pioneering modernist composer whose 1936–40 imprisonment in San Quentin on sodomy charges had ended less than two years earlier. Though Cowell made remarkable good out of a bad situation—teaching

FIGURE 4.   David Diamond circa 1947–48. Photo by Alexander Leventon. By permission of Mrs. Gladys Leventon, and courtesy of the Sibley Music Library, Eastman School of Music, University of Rochester.

music to over fifteen hundred inmates, composing fifty pieces, and writing a book and several journal articles during his imprisonment—and was granted a full pardon in 1942, neither he nor his career ever fully recovered.[20]

David Diamond, although notably strapped for funds at various points in his career (his nightly fiddling in pit orchestras for Bernstein musicals kept him afloat more than once), traveled in his adult life along the same routes of transatlantic cosmopolitanism, within socially and culturally elite strata, as his fellows in the gay composers' circle—indeed, Diamond's liaisons with American celebrity royalty are noteworthy even within this extraordinarily well-connected circle.[21] And Diamond's adult sexual identity appears to have formed in relation to the middle- and upper-class social and professional realms he inhabited as a youthful and adult musician. Of course, had Diamond forged his social-sexual persona within the working-class milieu into which he was born, it might well have been constructed according to the gender-performance scheme delineated by Chauncey. As Chauncey notes, "[e]very man had to position himself in relation to the ideology prevailing in the social worlds in which he was raised and lived."[22] But these were, for Diamond, two distinct worlds: His musical identity gave him access to a different class identity from the one in which he was raised, which difference in turn affected the sexual identity within which he lived—that of a (more or less) gender-normative man understood, by those to whom such sensitive information was known, to be queer as opposed to "normal," homo- as opposed to heterosexual.

Diamond's case, in which musical identity served as a determinant for class, gender, and sexual identity, illustrates the crucial interrelations that often obtained among all these identity positions within the twentieth-century American music world. And it suggests the important role musical identity could play in mediating the overall identity positions—entailing gender, race, class, national, sexual, and other vectors—of twentieth-century American musicians. For in music's rarefied realms, European Old World language, culture, and tradition exerted a constant (albeit variously resisted) "foreign" presence; the feminine—if not the female—occupied a central place; talent was a coveted commodity capable of trumping or trans-forming class status; and queerness was, at least, less queer than in the out-side realm, at most, more normal than "normalcy."[23] Thus, wielding musical identity—"being musical"—had substantial potential to change one's position in the world.

A MUSICAL MANDATE FOR THE AMERICAN CENTURY

Throughout the first third of the twentieth century the national and inter-national position of American music was closely watched, fiercely debated, and highly freighted on its home turf. The reasons for such anxious scrutiny toward American music lie in complex musical as well as cultural, political, and historical factors, some of which are illumined in certain recent writings. These include several studies of Charles Ives (1874–1954) that seek at last—following decades of musicological glossing over the composer's clamorous gyno- and homophobia—to confront those utter-ances comprising "the most extraordinary use of gendered aesthetics in the public testimony of an American composer" and to situate them in their cultural-historical context. Thus contextualized, Ives's diatribes present tellingly as expressions of musical, sexual, and cultural anxieties that prevailed in the United States within the early decades of the twentieth century. The composer appears less as an eccentric crank with personal issues concerning women, queers, and music than as a stentorian mouthpiece for interlinked cultural anxieties around gender, sexuality, musicality, and national identity that significantly shaped twentieth-century American music.[24]

Identifying a distinct American style in concert music and a great American composer became a fervent concern, beginning in the nineteenth century, for several generations of American audiences, artists, and critics seeking to counter the domination of European cultural products and values, and to prove America's high-cultural worth and maturation. Success on this front was not immediately forthcoming, however. Carol J. Oja's study of the 1920s New York music world chronicles numerous visits, tours, and premieres of European composers throughout the decade, concluding that these rendered New York increasingly less provincial and helped to make it an important venue for the emissaries of continental modernism. But by the end of the twenties America still lacked a compositional profile of its own, such that "visiting European luminaries," for example, while greatly impressed by American jazz, "seemed to pay little attention to American composers of concert music."[25]

And so, as Mary Herron DuPree has shown, the national concern with identifying an American style and a great American composer became in the 1920s an almost desperate preoccupation—with a majority of commentators concluding that American music had failed.[26] Amid a range of explanations for such failure, most critics seemed to agree that music was (in DuPree's words) "the most troubled and 'backward' of the American arts, immature and unrealized at a time when American poetry, prose, and the visual arts were blooming."[27] In view of American music's apparent inability to rise to the occasion, many critics blamed a feminization and emasculation in the field, charging—much as Ives had begun to do around 1911—that American music had grown too soft and lost its vital "manliness."[28] A more implicit sex-gender anxiety is also apparent in several of the commentaries DuPree examines, and in her just-quoted summary of these: Its characterization of contemporaneous American music in terms of "backward[ness]" and "immatur[ity]" notably resembles the language some sexologists were using to explain homosexuals as anomalous, primitive outcroppings on the path of human cultural and evolutionary progress.[29] Two decades later the same language had come to dominate psychological theories of homosexuality, as was illustrated in young Rorem's psychiatric evaluations as a candidate for U.S. military service in World

War II: On three separate occasions the openly gay composer was rejected, twice with 4-F status on grounds of having "not yet developed mature sexual impulses."[30]

One telling commentary in the teens and twenties' crisis around American music was the 1920 *Dial* essay "Introit," by the influential modernist critic Paul Rosenfeld—whose rhetoric of music criticism here might have been discharged directly from the antimasturbation tracts of his era's moral-purity literature. Citing a perceived lack of "interpenetration of the concert-hall and daily life" in America, he lamented the culture's attempts to "mechaniz[e] . . . the passions" and "to indulge them discreetly, patronizingly—in off hours . . . to toy with them, to prettify them, to parody them, to waste them in a myriad different fashions." In sum, Rosenfeld indicted a perversion in American cultural values that rendered the concert hall "that unnatural thing, a void," characterized by "the lugubrious, musty presence" that is a "sign of the misuse of music, the deposit of all the emotion wasted there."[31] His rhetoric of musical disdain shared vocabulary with the contemporaneous sexological, psychological, and, increasingly, popular language of sexual pathology, as it readily invoked the onanist (i.e., masturbator conceived as personality type), the invert, the homosexual, and, in the blurring-together of all these, another important figure: the polymorphous "sex pervert."[32] Lying within the shadowy space of modern sexual-definitional incoherence emergent in the late nineteenth century (and charted by Sedgwick a century later) is that terrain on which "homosexuality" and "onanism" overlap, are mutually implicated in undifferentiated perversion (as if perhaps their similarly specular prefixes erased any distinction between "*homo-*" and "*auto*eroticism"). Modern definitions of musicality, as Rosenfeld's "Introit" may suggest, reside in part on this tremulous turf.[33] Finally, amid the conceptual conflations undergirding Rosenfeld's rhetoric we can detect a further (and foundational) conflation, namely of femininity with emasculation, shallowness, and weakness, femininity figured as quintessential immature and unrealized condition: manliness *manqué*.

The previous examples evidence an identity crisis, peaking in the early 1920s, that was directed at the American music world and placed sex-gender issues at the rhetorical fore.[34] The crisis centered on the absence of an important national musical culture, particularly of a distinguished compositional profile, a condition frequently blamed on American music's enervation via feminization and emasculation. It may seem striking to us today, particularly given the low profile of concert music on the current U.S. cultural landscape, that musical composition some eighty years ago should have been the object of such anxieties implicating sex, gender, nation, and cultural empire building. To understand how and why such wide-ranging ambitions and polemics came to be focused on the music world, we will need to frame a cultural and historical context that exceeds the music world.

IVES, AMERICAN MUSIC, AND MUTATING MANLINESS

It is indeed a broadly informed context of musical and cultural history that Lawrence Kramer constructs in his keen analysis of Ives's musical rhetoric, which reveals in Ives's music an idealized mapping of American social space that is markedly exclusionist. Kramer's aim is to set forth an "exemplary test case for politically informed musicology," and his method—or a central element of it—is to take seriously the misogyny and gay bashing he finds symbolically enacted in Ives's Second String Quartet (1913).[35] The work is described in Ives's memoirs as an attempt to salvage the genre by making the musicians for once "get up and do something like men." In its second movement, subtitled "Arguments and Fight" and marked (in schoolboy pseudo-Italian) "Andante emasculata" and "Largo sweetota," the composer mocks a quartet tradition that he depicts as Europeanist and effeminate.[36] Ives uses, aptly enough, the second fiddle to embody the scorned character of his fictional nemesis Rollo, whose "nice," "pretty" music is, as Kramer notes, "violently hooted down" by the other three players.

In connection with his reading here and elsewhere in Ives's oeuvre, Kramer argues that, while the composer's "misogyny undoubtedly has personal roots, . . . its exclusionary logic is part of a broader field of cultural practices that bear closely on the problems of [social] heterogeneity and democratic social space." Examining Ives's cultural practices in relation to the nineteenth-century problematics of national-identity formation, Kramer concludes that Ives's music encodes "the same nativist ideal" as D. W. Griffith expresses in his notorious *Birth of a Nation* (1915).[37] In Griffith's film the birth of America, the great modern nation, is engendered in the domination of whites over blacks, of men over women, and of "true" Americans over foreigners.[38] Comparably, Ives's musical expression of a seemingly populist American ideal (e.g., through Protestant country-church hymn tropes) continually reverts to subordinating the feminine, the effeminate, and "the masses" themselves, and his vision of an invigorating American heterogeneity is revealed by Kramer as merely a retrograde affirmation of a "social order that is rural, white Protestant, patriarchal, and premodern."[39]

Ives's eruptions, deemed "extraordinary" within the immediate context of the American music world (as noted above), appear strikingly characteristic, hence ordinary, within the larger context of contemporaneous national culture delineated by Gail Bederman in *Manliness and Civilization*. Bederman's study illuminates the scene, circa 1890–1917, of America's Progressive Era, in which a notion of exclusively white "manliness" merging millennialism and imperialism defined the prevailing vision of American national identity and destiny.[40] In this period of rapid social change, middle-class white men, anxiously seeking to remake male power, interweaved race and gender in Darwinian accounts of the necessity and inevitability of male supremacy, distinctly racialized here in terms of Anglo-Saxon ethnicity.[41] "Manliness" was a frequent topic of discussion and debate and, along with "civilization," an oft-invoked cultural ideal. As Bederman shows, manliness possessed a very particular meaning in this moment, one that is not equivalent to latter-day "masculinity" but that signifies noble civility and superior humanity attributed exclusively to the Anglo-Saxon male. The qualities of manly civilization claimed by certain white men were defined against the primitivism and brutishness ascribed to the "lower races."

But the era's racialized ideal of male supremacy did not inhere merely in a simple duality like civilization/primitivism. Rather, the civilized and the primitive were figured dialectically, as complementary strengths within an American Anglo-Saxon man posited as the universal ideal, pinnacle of the species. By the 1890s middle-class white men were rejecting the genteel model of their Victorian forefathers in favor of a more physically strenuous standard of manliness, informed by—but not wholly given over to—the primitive. Primitivism in its unreconstructed forms was ascribed to the lesser races, including the non-Anglo-Saxon immigrants who were then arriving in great numbers and the African Americans whose changing status in U.S. society, like that of women in this era of suffragists and reformers, threatened the stability of white male hegemony. According to its own doctrine, American Anglo-Saxon manliness could, uniquely, both appropriate "brute" masculinity and transcend it.[42]

The dangers of "overcivilization" were much discussed among the middle and upper classes following the rapid, radical changes in society and labor brought about by nineteenth-century industrialization: Sedentary "brain work" amid increasing mechanization was thought to be depleting the nerve force of white American business and professional men, and Victorian ideals of manly self-restraint and -mastery appeared increasingly inadequate to the cultural, political, and economic challenges these modern men faced.[43] Around 1870 a new malady, "neurasthenia," was defined as a condition of nervous exhaustion, of enervation resulting from the pace and pressures of modern American civilization. By the early 1880s neurasthenia had reached almost epidemic proportions among American white-collar men (it was also diagnosed in women, but with different implications assumed).

As a disease that supposedly left many of these men incapable of drinking anything stronger than milk or even "of reproducing the species," neurasthenia was, in Bederman's analysis, an effort "to construct the *cultural* weakness of self-restrained manliness as a *bodily* weakness, and to 'cure' it."[44] Bederman locates significance in medicine's concurrent fascination with the male neurasthenic body and with that of the recently defined homosexual: "Attention to the homosexual man—newly dubbed the 'invert'—was one way to investigate, medicalize, and contain the wider social, cultural, and economic forces that threatened the potency of middle-class manhood."[45] Indeed, like other bodies now provoking anxiety on this front, including those labeled female, black, and non-Anglo-Saxon, the homosexual body was a frequent object of medicoscientific scrutiny in this period.

In her recent study *Queering the Color Line* Siobhan B. Somerville illuminates some particularities of the anthropometry, classification, and theorization to which such bodies were subject. Somerville's inquiries depart from the observation that "the emergence of a discourse on homosexuality in the United States occurred at roughly the same time that boundaries between 'black' and 'white' were being policed and enforced in unprecedented ways"—that is, following the 1896 *Plessy v. Ferguson* decision and its establishment of Jim Crow segregation.[46] Her cogent argument is that the cultural invention of racialized, black and white, subjects was not only concurrent but crucially interdependent with the cultural invention of sexually classified, homo and hetero, subjects. Scientific racism, as enacted via comparative anatomy and eugenics in the nineteenth and twentieth centuries, provided the paradigm for sexology, including its specific methods and assumptions. Indeed, some sexologists who developed influential models of homosexuality were themselves active participants in the miscegenation-opposed eugenics movement—including most notably (the Briton) Havelock Ellis.[47]

Even sexologists who were not eugenicists were apt, however, to construct their theories in ways that mirrored scientific racism structurally and substantively. For example, both comparative anatomy and sexology were intent on the image of the abnormally large clitoris as a key indicator of deviation from their racialized, heterosexualized somatic norm (female sexual anatomy having been, as Somerville observes, the object of both fields' most zealous scrutiny). Both projects served to authorize the reigning ideology of normalcy and social order, and so they provided concrete "scientific proof" of the lesser humanity of queer and African American persons, who were revealed by clitoral and other criteria to be throwbacks to an earlier stage in the evolution of the species, group instances of arrested human development.[48] We might note that the historical proximity, if not currency, of such notions in relation to *Four Saints* and its premiere suggests further lines along which audiences might have linked the opera's African American cast with queer thematics.

But even as the dominant white, male, bourgeois culture was at pains to define racialized primitivism in association with sexual abnormality and, particularly, excessive and uncontrolled sexuality, it began to claim primitivism among its own manly attributes. By the turn of the century modern manliness was an alloy of the civilized and the primitive—as exemplified by the Rough Riding, wild game–hunting, Harvard-educated blueblood Theodore Roosevelt. Temporally or historically speaking, an enervating "overcivilization" was now associated with the prior generation, while a manliness engendering primitive "masculinity" (a word coined in this era, as Bederman shows) was the current gender ideal for middle- and upper-class white men.[49] Frequently these constructs were also mapped geographically, with civilization corresponding to Europe, primitivism to Africa (especially), and a New World hybrid of the two ascribed to America. Popular, medical, and other discourses of this modern moment rehearse such a conception of American Anglo-Saxon manliness both in celebratory affirmations and in assessments anxious about its achievement. And musical discourse in the first third of the century reproduced the same formulation, in innumerable prescriptions for American composition as an ideal hybrid of classical and jazz idioms.

Charles Ives presented a particularly clear demonstration of gender affirmation and anxiety both, expressed simultaneously—or at least of betraying anxiety in his putative masculine celebratory. In Ives we encounter a forceful application of the era's white-masculinist ideology of gender-race-nation to the contemporary problems of musical identity. Concerning his individual musical identity Ives was wont to express ambivalence ("As a boy [I was] partially ashamed of [my love of music]"), and concerning America's national musical identity—and the European one to which it cleaved unmanfully—skepticism, criticism, and scorn. Thus Ives displays anxiety around American art music's adequacy to the manly ideals of his nation ("Is [America] gradually losing her manhood?"), his race ("Is the Anglo-Saxon going 'Pussy'?"), and his era, and around the personal identity he constructed in fundamental relation to all of these.[50] Ives, a church organist and composer, had reason to be anxious about his musical identity, given the contemporaneous stereotype of artists and intellectuals as physical weaklings, their suspect status in relation to masculinity and within the alleged general deterioration of the American male population.[51] And Ives's personal identity anxieties might have been further, more particularly exacerbated if he was, as Gayle Sherwood has recently argued, himself diagnosed as neurasthenic.[52]

Is American music manly enough? Can it strike out and make its own way? Will it ever launch a cultural empire to rival that of Western Europe? In such questions, voiced repeatedly in the teens and twenties, an anthropomorphized "American music" is anxiously held up to the contemporaneous standards and fears defining American manliness. Critics either detailed didactically or hinted darkly at the ways in which American music was insufficiently virile, hence insufficient *tout court:* American music, it would seem, was a woman, or a masturbator; it was neurasthenic, or a pansy. American music, inevitably a reflection of the national character, showed a failure of maturity, was arrested in its development. Within the anxious atmosphere of the time, not surprisingly, music's cultural history as a feminized construct reared its head.

For, as Brett has pointed out, the Western world has long constructed music in terms of femininity and hence danger.[53] In America particularly, music has been beset by gender anxiety probably since the first Protestant settlers arrived. John Adams's diaries invoke music as a prime marker of temptation: As a young man in 1759 Adams counted flutes and violins—and, of course, women—among the vices that could lead him into "a Life of Effeminacy, Indolence and obscurity," and in 1780 he prayed that his children should "make the choice of Hercules," confessing, "I sometimes tremble when I hear the syren songs of sloth, least they should be captivated with her bewitching Charms and her soft, insinuating Musick."[54] From Adams's time to Ives's, styles of American manhood shifted countless times in various ways, and yet the place of music and the feminine—as objects at once of allure and danger—appears remarkably consistent within this span.

"It's going to be a boy—some time!" quipped Ives with reference to music's birth moment.[55] Here as elsewhere Ives's sarcastic swagger marks the breadth of both fearfulness and entitlement in his position toward musical identity, national and individual. But such commentaries, from

Ives and others in the first third of the century, also usefully mark the depths to which twentieth-century aspirations to beget an American music and cultural identity were enmeshed, from the outset, in negotiations and contestations of gender, sexual, and racial identity.

THE WOMAN QUESTION AND OTHERS

Revisiting the scene of American music's gender and ontological crisis in the teens and twenties, Catherine Parsons Smith has investigated its effects on women musicians and composers. Smith cites census data to show that 1910 was the peak of a forty-year growth trend for women in the music professions. By 1920, however, and "in droves," women had left the music professions—including that of composition, where white middle-class women had, in the pre–World War I period of romantic Americanism, made the first significant inroads achieved here by women.[56] Smith attributes this decline of women's participation in American musical life to the first emergence of modernism, between 1910 and 1920. Surveying the professional and popular musical literature concurrent with World War I–era modernism she finds, much as DuPree does, a preoccupation and panic about the perceived emasculation and feminization of American music.

Amid the white middle class's contemporaneous celebration of manly and strenuous lives and its widespread fear of enervation, arts-inclined males found reason to worry over the legitimacy of their place in American culture. Women and "feminization" in music thus became targets for artistic males' anxieties born of self-doubt.[57] Smith argues that "the seemingly endless chorus of voices requiring that music be 'virile' and 'masculine'" in the 1910s effectively suppressed the advancing female tide in music and served, under modernism, "literally to transform the meaning of the phrase 'American music' to exclude biological females entirely, . . . along with the 'feminine.'" She suggests that both the advances made by middle-class white women in American music circa 1870–1910 and the broader social changes wrought by first-wave feminism sparked a backlash in the music world. That backlash, in her reading, *was* musical modernism.[58]

In *No Man's Land: The Place of the Woman Writer in the Twentieth Century,* the literary scholars Sandra M. Gilbert and Susan Gubar theorize Anglo-American literary modernism as a reaction against first-wave feminism, women's suffrage, and the changing sex roles of the late nineteenth and early twentieth centuries.[59] Smith applies this argument to music as well, and thus suggests the woman composer's place in the twentieth century was likewise in "no man's land." And Smith further suggests a corre-

lation between the twentieth-century inception of wide-scale debate over a
national music, and the disappearance of women from the field of composition: "In addition to the racial issues raised in this debate, part of it was
really about whether a national music might include, and perhaps even be
partially defined by, the work of women."[60] The latter claim is surely useful in its acknowledgment of racial and sex-gender stakes in America's
debates over national music and identity, but it forecloses on a further vec-
tor therein: sexuality. For, given the frequent coupling and conflation in
these debates of women with "effeminate" men, of feminization with
emasculation, and of all of these with homosexuality, we need to listen
carefully to the multiple resonances of the feminine topos, and to acknowledge its encoding of both women and homosexual men.

In this vein Smith is right to insist that Ives's attacks on male effeminacy—which are, more often than not, articulated through derogatory figurations of women—also bespeak misogyny.[61] Judith Tick also recognizes
the entangling of effeminacy and femininity here, but she locates Ives's
primary concern with male composers and the alleged emasculation of
male musicians. Tick's argument is that Ives's misogynist and homophobic
rhetoric appears in the service of what is in the first place an assault (i.e.,
specifically Oedipal and Americanist, I might note) on the male-dominated
institutions of European classical music. Real women, by this account, are
peripheral, and male emasculation is the prime object of fear and hostility
in Ives's antifeminine rants.[62]

The Ivesian tactic inspiring interpretive dispute here surfaces in countless other commentaries similarly presenting commingled misogyny and
homophobia and articulated by music critics and commentators in the
teens and twenties—and beyond.[63] A 1942 American *Vogue* article by the
British conductor Sir Thomas Beecham conjures several of the old, familiar bugaboos, now in the heyday of Coplandian Americana. Beecham's
monologue illustrates the enduring modernist equation of artistic vitality
and originality with the masculine, and of stagnation and decadence with
the feminine—and makes explicit what is frequently only implicit: the
clustering of both women and homosexual men with these latter topoi.
"When art is vital and creative, it is the almost exclusive property of man,
who is essentially the creative element in human kind. When it becomes
barren and stereotyped, then come the women; the conservative and the
reactionary, as well as that neutral type of creature, neither man nor
woman, which is rampantly prevalent in our stricken latter-day world."[64]

This instance from the genre of (what we might call) twentieth-century
American discourses of music-cultural hygiene leaves no doubt about its

targeting of both women and effeminate or emasculated queer men, and hence about its simultaneous misogyny and homophobia. Other instances encode and intermix the two in ways that may occasion multiple interpretations—as is evidenced by Smith's and Tick's differing interpretations of Ives.[65] To elucidate the frequent parallelism and merging, in twentieth-century discourses, of tropes of the homosexual and the feminine, we might refer to Sedgwick's "Axiom 5" in *Epistemology of the Closet*. Here she astutely points up the definitional incoherence of "homosexuality" and its condensation of prior, often contradictory, categories of sexual deviance, including (most relevantly for our purposes) that of gender inversion— according to which the male-deviant body serves as the vessel for a woman's soul.[66]

We have already noted how Chauncey's analysis of the roles engendered among actively gay men circa 1890–1940 points to a divergence of historically concurrent sociosexual conceptions and practices. The divergence here—of fairy and trade from queer—is structured by differences in class and, hence, in subjects' relations to official discourses and knowledge. Sedgwick too remarks the concurrence of differing and conflicting conceptions of queer identity and acts, though with reference to ongoing and contemporary discursive practices, and without recourse to any class-based analysis. Sedgwick's insight concerning the persistence of earlier, often contradictory, concepts under the modern aegis of homosexuality emphasizes the definitional disunity that is embedded in the concept even up to the present.

In other words, no matter how neat and tidy the notion of "homosexuality" as conceived by late-nineteenth-century sexologists, no matter how discrete—or even contrary—its conception in relation to other categories such as inversion, in actual usage the term, and idea, has persisted for over a century in dragging around lots of old, mismatched conceptual baggage originating in various folk and official locales.[67] Accordingly, we should recognize that "homosexuality" in actual twentieth-century discursive practice marks notions of gender inversion—of the manlike woman or womanlike man—perhaps as often as it represents its official meaning of same-sex object choice.[68]

Such recognition is suggestive for contemplating the Copland-Thomson circle, and imperative for interpreting these gay American composers' success in creating a long-awaited national music. It can suggest the irony of their accomplishment, as members of an identity group (i.e., a *feminized* identity group) repeatedly blamed for the failure of American music, in leading the way to a distinct national music and musical identity. This strain of irony was not lost on certain homophile activists writing for a 1965 issue of *One* (a magazine published by members of the Mattachine Society) in response to a concert manager's assault on the prevalence of male homosexuals in American concert music: "She says 10 of the 12 leading U.S. composers of serious music are homosexual—but doesn't add that U.S. music has never before been rated so high by the world. And what would it be rated WITHOUT the 10? And who in the hell are the 2 odd ones?"[69] Given the mid-century homophile movement's emphasis on cultivating dignity and respectability for homosexuals, it should come as no surprise that the old tainted and derogatory labels were shunned in *One* magazine. Nevertheless it is clear what "odd" stands in for here: The last sentence rhetorically questions who is really *queer*, and who normal, among elite American composers, suggesting thereby a reversal of the standard assumptions.

Notably, the passage from *One* takes up national music with reference to an international standard, focusing on how U.S. music is rated "by the world." This was, in Oja's reading, likewise a hallmark of Copland's own efforts to create an American music, starting in 1924 when he returned to New York from three years of study in Paris. Oja places Copland among leading 1920s "visionaries of a postwar American cultural renaissance" for whom cultural nationalism was a necessary means to cultural internationalism. Forging a national identity was not merely a chauvinistic exercise but a way toward cosmopolitan engagement, and hence within this vision the two goals were fused, interdependent. Copland's pursuit of this fusion, his cultivation of a "transatlantic gaze," made him a prototype for U.S. culture building in the twenties and defined his subsequent career. That is, at least, until he reached the Cold War era, as we shall discuss in chapter 4.[70]

Returning to *One* magazine's Cold War–era commentary, we might ask: If American composition circa 1964 is—by the agreement of both friends and enemies—rife to the highest levels with homosexual men and their gay ways, then what do we make of Catherine Smith's contention that American musical modernism is an artistic movement founded on and essentially defined by hypermasculinity? So pervasive does this exclusionary masculine ethos seem that Smith exhorts that we "investigate whether there was a different, more broadly defined, perhaps less hostile or more gender-inclusive form of modernism that until now has been wholly hidden from view."[71] Does this imply that the tonal, variously Americanist music of Thomson, Copland, and company is not modernist music? Or perhaps that these composers and their work were driven by the same hypermasculine, antifeminine impulses Smith indicts in her essay? Smith makes no gesture toward the latter claim, and indeed no writer, to my knowledge, has characterized the work of these gay tonalists in hypermas-

culine, antifeminine terms (such a reading certainly would find little support in critical or popular reception history). Nor does Smith here explicitly classify the music of the Copland-Thomson circle as nonmodernist. If
implicitly and effectively she does so, it is not by virtue of any express relegation of these composers' twentieth-century tonal music to some other,
nonmodernist category. Rather, it owes to her use of a certain exclusive, and
distortive, notion of modernism that has circulated in musical discourse
since the end of World War II.

WHOSE MODERNISM?

The characterization of musical modernism in terms of antifemininity and
hypermasculinity is more apt to certain modernist strains—including
those of Italian futurism, Schoenbergian atonality, Ivesian dissonant experimentalism, and the midcentury serialism of Boulez, Babbitt, and others—
than to the modernist practices exemplified by Thomson and Copland.
Smith emphasizes modernism's opposition to Romanticism, particularly
romantic Americanism, and these gay tonalists indeed directed their efforts
against Romanticism—specifically German late Romanticism, which they
regarded as ponderous and overblown.[72] Still, their music does not figure
within Smith's depiction of musical modernism, which designates Ives as
"father figure and role model for modernist composers in the 1920s and
1930s" and clearly assumes subscription to the "prevailing aesthetic discourse that equated masculine or virile with vital and original."[73] Members
of the Thomson-Copland circle active in the twenties and thirties had no
particular engagement with Ives or his music, and the Dada-influenced
Thomson and many of his associates rebuffed the virile-original compositional ideal—as exemplified in Thomson's mocking references to what he
called *le style chef-d'oeuvre* (the big-statement, or masterpiece, style).[74]
Still, they unequivocally considered their work modernist, as I do here. And
I do so with regard to both of the compositional styles typically associated
with Copland, commonly, if problematically, known as his "severe" and
"simple" styles. Whatever distinction is to be drawn between the two
idioms, it is not one of modernism versus nonmodernism. Indeed, with
regard to Copland's simplicities we must keep in mind that mixing highbrow and lowbrow, popular and learned styles and genres is, as the cultural
theorist Robert Crunden has noted, a defining characteristic of (not just
postmodern but) modernist art.[75]

Smith's exhortation that musicologists investigate the possible existence of a kinder, gentler musical modernism appears to invoke the fre-

quent musical usage of "modernist" as a *stylistic* marker designating atonal, dissonant, and/or experimental music as distinct from tonal, consonant, and/or neoclassical music. In perpetuating this narrowed use of the term Smith may inadvertently collude with Schoenberg's and his successors' exclusive appropriation of the banner of modernism for their own music, thereby attempting to define for it a central and even exclusive place in the twentieth-century history of Western art music.[76] The critic Terry Teachout writes, "To revisit the postwar literature of serialism is to be struck by the smugness with which it proclaimed that the lineage of classical music descended not through the tonal modernists [including Stravinsky, Hindemith, and Copland] but through Schoenberg and his successors." As illustration he quotes the serialist Charles Wuorinen, in a confident and categorical 1979 statement that the tonal system "is no longer employed by serious composers of the mainstream." Teachout summarizes: "[I]n classical music, as in the other arts, there were really two modernisms—one conservative, the other profoundly radical—and the chief architect of the second modernism [Schoenberg] made it his life's work to subvert the first."[77]

The restrictedness and effective co-optiveness of Schoenberg's—and, hence, Wuorinen's and Smith's—conception of musical modernism is confirmed by Leon Botstein's entry on musical modernism in the *New Grove Dictionary of Music and Musicians*.[78] Modernism in music, as Botstein notes, embraces many styles, all of which are linked by a "common debt to the historical context from which [they] emerged." His delineation of "five distinct strands" of modernism that had come into being by 1933—the Second Viennese School, the French-Russian axis, German Expressionism, "indigenous Modernisms," and experimentalism—expressly includes tonal and neoclassical composition. Botstein's observation that "[a]fter 1945 the implications of Webern's music . . . defined not only the legacy of Viennese Modernism but became emblematic of Modernism *per se*" is revealing for our purposes: It can help to historicize and trace that conception of musical modernism invoked by Smith. Notably this conception also aligns with images of both "modern art" and "modern music" that proliferated popularly, as in magazine cartoons of (especially) the Cold War decades, in which "modern" as it applied to music was synonymous with the alien, the noisy, and the bewilderingly complex.

A useful practice employed by Oja and other writers is to distinguish the dissonant, experimental, and masculinist circle of Ives, Ruggles, Cowell, and their cohort as "ultramodernist," hence as a particular subset of the larger and more diverse modernist movement.[79] The subset thus invoked included at least one woman, Ruth Crawford (later Seeger). Now as then,

Crawford (1901–53) stands as the most renowned woman of this period of American composition from which a scant handful of women's names arises—Marion Bauer (1887–1955), Crawford, Miriam Gideon (1906–96), and Vivian Fine (1913–2000).[80] And it seems telling that Crawford's diaries document an awareness and troubledness about her own acquisition of "withering" masculine attitudes and behaviors while active in the ultra-modernist circle circa 1927.[81]

DEAN AND DADDY

Richard Franko Goldman's 1961 paean to Copland typifies a well-represented and, by this date, well-established genre: "If any one musician today can be singled out as the 'dean of American music,' it is Aaron Copland. . . . He has created, encouraged, and enriched the repertory, leading the way to a musical climate genuinely 'made in America.'"[82] Celebrated here and in numerous other contexts since the 1930s, Copland's "appointment" to the deanship of American music surely must be considered ironic in the light of both his homosexual and his Jewish identities.[83] As a Jew Copland was deemed an outsider to Anglo-Saxon culture, and thus incapable of composing American music, by colleagues and critics who assumed a racialized and Protestant standard of true Americanness. This position was made explicit in commentaries by Daniel Gregory Mason (1920) and Henry Cowell (1930). The composer and critic Mason "claimed that Copland's Jewish background precluded him from writing genuine American music, . . . that 'the speciousness, superficial charm and persuasiveness of Hebrew art, its brilliance, its violently juxtaposed extremes of passion, its poignant eroticism and pessimism' were diametrically opposed to the American character, . . . the 'poignant beauty of Anglo-Saxon sobriety and restraint.'" Cowell plied a different argument: He grouped Copland with other Jewish American composers who used jazz, which he (like many others at the time) regarded as "Negro music seen through the eyes of Jews." And Cowell judged these composers inimical to the creation of any genuinely American music—represented here by the work of Ives and Ruggles, "the two genuine Americans." Thus did Mason and Cowell arrive at identical conclusions concerning the impossibility of Copland composing American music—despite their being at this time, as Pollack notes, "principal spokespersons for the old guard and the avant-garde, respectively."[84]

I would point out that a slight majority of members of the gay American composers' circle identified herein—Bernstein, Blitzstein, Copland, and Diamond—had Jewish backgrounds, the other members—Bowles, Rorem, and Thomson—being of WASP origins. Any detailed account of the former fact or its apparent ironies is beyond the scope of the present study, which focuses on these composers' important impact on American music in the light of their queer sexuality. Within my chosen focus, however, I am conscious of the dangers of constructing a false or overdrawn collective unity by ignoring or suppressing differences within the group.[85] And so I am at pains to remark religious, ethnic, and class identity differences within this gay composers' circle—though I leave the investigation of Jewish identity in American musical modernism to future writers. I am also aware of a further danger, in a project such as this, of inferring an overdrawn unity among these gay composers at the expense of, not ethnic or religious identity differences, but differences in sexual identity itself. With this in mind I present, following this chapter, an intermezzo exploring the case of Paul Bowles. Bowles's remarkable evasion of the standard categories of sexual, as well as national and artistic, identity can afford a useful corrective to tendencies toward false unitarity and reification around such identity categories.

But now, returning to the subject of Copland's "deanship," I wish to recognize a further important dimension of irony therein. A certain 1947 reader of the *New York Herald Tribune,* having written to comment on Virgil Thomson's column, received from its author this rather curt private reply:

> Aaron Copland is certainly the most famous living American composer, but he is not the dean of anything. That word means, I believe, the oldest member of the profession or the longest in business.
>
> Most sincerely yours,[86]

Thomson left it for the reader to deduce that there were American composers on the scene older, and perhaps with more seniority, than Copland. Thomson would have known this only too well, for he had himself been "in business" longer, had preceded Copland in coining the tonal idiom through which the latter had long since become the most famous representative of American music. The point with which Thomson chooses to take issue, however, is one of semantics: What does it mean to call someone the "dean" of some profession or group—and does the word really apply to Copland?

Copland's legendary mentoring of so many composers, gay and straight, from the thirties through the fifties (and beyond) was indeed crucial to the attainment of an American profile in art music, as the title "Dean of American Music" serves to acknowledge (while also acknowledging the crucial role of Copland's own compositions). One thing that was certainly not acknowledged—by any faction, homo or hetero—in connection with this honorific and its invocations is the fact that Copland found the model and impetus for his momentous mentoring activity in Classical Greek pederasty. The evidence for this is readily available, however, in Copland's most recent biography. Howard Pollack quotes Erik Johns, one of Copland's "more significant partners," in describing Copland's adult sexual-romantic relationships in terms of " 'the classic Greek thing with an older man adoring and mentoring a younger guy.' " Pollack then notes,

> Copland believed that, in love relationships, every man was either a father or a son. "He had been the baby," observed Johns, "and he'd had all of that. He wanted to dote." A number of the young men he became involved with had problems—including sexual identity confusion, alcoholism, and clinical depression—beyond those typically found among adolescents; even in his professional relations with composers, he often guided and supported troubled young men. A similar impulse animated his love life; indeed the line was often a thin one.[87]

Copland was profoundly influenced, from perhaps as early as 1924, by *Corydon*, Gide's Platonic defense of pederasty.[88] And Copland's adult relationships unswervingly align with the second, the pederastic, category of David M. Halperin's four "pre-homosexual categories of male sex and gender deviance"—indeed, they illustrate the historical persistence of this "pre-homosexual" category long past the birth of the modern homosexual.[89] Halperin's category of "paederasty or 'active' sodomy" is constructed in terms of hierarchic difference between two partners, based on age, role, and/or gender performance.[90] The nature of pederastic coupling thus contrasts with the sameness that defines the notion of *homo*sexuality. As Halperin explains:

> Here [in paederasty] sex implies difference, not identity, and it turns on a systematic division of labor. It is the younger partner who is considered sexually attractive, while it is the older one who experiences erotic desire for the younger. Although love, emotional intimacy, and tenderness are not necessarily absent from the relationship, the distribution of erotic passion and sexual pleasure is assumed to be more or less lopsided, with the older, "active" partner being the *subject* of desire and the recipient of the greater share of pleasure from a younger partner who figures as a sexual *object*, feels no comparable desire, and derives no comparable pleasure from the contact. . . . The junior partner's reward must therefore be measured out in currencies other than pleasure, such as praise, assistance, gifts, or money.[91]

FIGURE 5.   Aaron Copland and Leonard Bernstein publicize a 1946 performance of Copland's *Concerto for Piano and Orchestra* with the New York City Symphony, Bernstein conducting. Photo by Fred Fehl. Leonard Bernstein Collection, Library of Congress. Reprinted by permission of the Aaron Copland Fund, copyright owner.

Copland's "senior" role in numerous pederastic pairings, from at least his thirties onward, is consistent with what we know about his self-conceptions as masculine ("queer," as opposed to "pansy," in the early-twentieth-century vernacular) and physically unattractive.[92]

Surely America's cultural growth and achievements have been shaped in various instances by forces and structures of gay and lesbian desire—though such instances have mostly been appropriated to heteronormative culture, their queer origins disavowed and erased. The case of Copland and his national musical leadership provides uncommonly clear demonstration of such shaping forces and provides an opportunity to correct the heteronormalizations of the historical record. Copland's role as "father of American music" (as Rorem puts it) was enacted in his loving, patient, and remarkably generous paternal mentoring of young American composers of several generations—who were, within modernism, virtually all male.[93] But, of course, the cultural image of paternity is a fundamentally heterosexual icon, constructed in terms inextricable from the nuclear family of the father's (presumed) dominion. Thus, in the light of this fact, and of the facts of the homosocial male milieu of modernist composition, and certainly of the gay (sub-) cultural context in which he learned and practiced his extraordinary mentoring skills, Aaron Copland appears less as the father of American music, and more precisely as its gay daddy.

ABSTRACTION REVISITED

> DIANA TRILLING: Did Gertrude Stein formulate a theory of the obscure? Consciously, I mean? Or did she just work that way?
>
> VIRGIL THOMSON: No, no, she had theories. Don't forget that she was very elaborately educated in psychology and medicine, and when she had really mastered the obscure thing with *Tender Buttons*, she described it by saying, "This is an effort to describe something without naming it," which is what the cubist painters were doing with still life.
>
> DIANA TRILLING: But it's also what musicians are always doing.
>
> VIRGIL THOMSON: Well, I got myself into a lovely little—shall we say controversy—with André Breton, by pointing out that the discipline of spontaneity, which he was asking his surrealist neophytes to adopt, was new for language but something that composers had been practicing for centuries.[94]

In chapter 1 we examined *Four Saints in Three Acts* as an illustrative instance of the queer expressive potential of artistic abstraction within the context of modernism and of earlier-twentieth-century U.S. culture. As was evident from Stein's example, it takes considerable effort to effect abstraction—or "the obscure thing"—in literature, "to describe something without naming it" using the medium of language. But, as the foregoing interview passage suggests, the matter was quite otherwise in music. Here abstraction is generally harder to escape than to enact: It has been thus at least since the nineteenth century when, as Brett observes, the Romantics elevated "abstraction, formalism, and organicism" over naturalism, imitation, and realism, as "the best way to rescue music from its own irrationality."[95] Within the purely instrumental genres that comprised the bulk of nineteenth- and twentieth-century concert music, abstraction was virtually inevitable. Hence the suspicion, doubt, and avowed hatred with which Henrik, the aged military general and protagonist in Sándor Márai's 1942 novel *Embers*, regards "this incomprehensible, melodious language which select people can use to say uninhibited, irregular things that are also probably indecent and immoral."[96] But if, in this uneasy reading, music is nonsense, "incomprehensible," it appears nonetheless—like Stein's writing—as "suspiciously significant nonsense."

Whatever suspicions may be projected onto music or its devotees—and as we have seen, these have often been considerable—significance (in the semantic sense) in music is generally impossible to pin down. The ready "abstractness" of music as an artistic medium can render it unusually resistant to the mechanisms of identity labeling and regulation by which society and culture classify and control subjects. Of course, music as an activity, as a social-professional realm, and as an identity aegis is still subject to and indeed saddled with such classification and regulation. And within twentieth-century American culture, "music" in all these latter senses was classified as sexually suspect—even as it was, as a cultural form, idealized, revered, and consecrated (a paradox rendered more familiar if we recall Brett's linkage of music and femininity, the latter of which is likewise both idealized and sexually suspect).

But music qua cultural form—"the music itself," music as sonic artistic medium—is largely held separate from concrete interpretation, whether in terms of sanctioned or illicit, sexual or other meanings. As Koestenbaum observes, writing of twentieth-century queer musical devotions, "Historically, music has been defined as mystery and miasma, as implicitness rather than explicitness, and so we have hid inside music; in music we can come out without coming out, we can reveal without saying a word. Queers identify with shadow because no one can prosecute a shadow."[97]

It is notable that in an era of tremendous industry in the classification and often brutal enforcement of racial, gender, and sexual identity norms, certain groups thereby relegated to the margins of American society—homosexuals, African Americans, and Jews, at the least—made in music a place for themselves and their expressions, and indeed distinguished themselves here in radical disproportion to their numbers in society. I see more than coincidence at work in this confluence of cultural-historical facts. Admittedly, the present study does not analyze African American or Jewish involvements in twentieth-century music but focuses on homosexual male involvements, particularly those of the Thomson-Copland circle from the mid-1930s to mid-1950s. I am convinced that music's extraordinary qualities of, at once, semantic obscurity and (what feels to the music lover like) affective-expressive specificity had much to do with twentieth-century gay men's frequent, fervent, and highly successful endeavors in U.S. classical composition and performance.[98] And it seems likely that these qualities played a part, too, in Jews' and African Americans' important engagements with classical and popular music in the period.

But what does music really offer its devotees inhabiting society's margins? Does music serve to liberate voices oppressed by the chains of silence? As a medium for expression and catharsis, is music a lifeline for subjects who cannot find outlet in other, more specified mediums? Or is music an anodyne, a harmless release that keeps marginalized subjects from channeling frustrated energies in ways more lucid and immediate, and perhaps more threatening to the status quo? In *The Queen's Throat* Wayne Koestenbaum provides passionate testimony on both sides of the argument just sketched. For woven throughout his rhapsodic musings on queer opera-loving are confessions that bespeak opera's sustaining role in the queer devotee's perennially smoldering abjection. Indeed, Koestenbaum attests that he learned from opera how to inhabit the shame and oblivion of queer subjectivity: "The voice of Marni Nixon, ghosting for Audrey Hepburn in *My Fair Lady* and for Deborah Kerr in *The King and I*, told me everything about singing in the dark, singing without a body, singing from an erased, invisible place in the universe. . . . I opened my mouth, in a wide, vapid O of awe and shame, while women's voices streamed from my green Magnavox."

Elsewhere he writes that "[t]he grandiosity of operatic utterance is a wild compensation for the listener's silence."[99] But the adequacy of such compensation is always already in question, for Koestenbaum's register in this ode to queer opera fandom is, knowingly, one of pre-Stonewall homosexual delectation-in-abjection.[100] Having come of age into the pre-Stonewall life now figured in terms of the closet—in which a covert, coded deviance from mainstream social norms was all the resistance one usually dared, and the code itself (i.e., camp), along with the homophobic oppression that inspired it, provided a basis for intense bonds within the subcultural "family"— Koestenbaum waxes elegiac for a past, richly tragic condition known as homosexuality. Deploying his opulent poetic gifts and a fetishization of abandoned cultural objects (principally, and synecdochically, opera) to conjure this homosexual condition, Koestenbaum manages at the late date of 1993 to evoke the ardor of its protracted ambivalence, and the bittersweet flavor of its fervent abnegation.[101]

But what Koestenbaum (like any of us) cannot readily conjure is a credible sense of realness around, or necessity for, tragic homosexual abnegation and abjection. Such a sense is by now nearly impossible to reconstruct for post-Stonewall, postmodern subjects, unless they have lived long enough to have experienced firsthand the twentieth-century phenomenon of (so-called) closeted homosexual identity. Within the cultural logic of postmodernism, grounded as it is in assumptions of identity's social constructedness, the bitter and sweet sensibilities of homosexual abjection and camp may inspire nostalgia, envy, admiration, or horror. But neither old-school homosexual worldviews and feeling-tones nor their myriad collective and individual "symptoms" can be understood outside that frame—now regarded mostly as an artifact of past false consciousness—in which homosexuality constituted an inborn, immutable stigma; a tragic accident of fate and nature; a damning originary wound that might, however, hold redemptive and beatific potential à la Wilde in *De Profundis*.

It is perhaps relevant that Brett spent considerably more time than Koestenbaum in abject homosexuality's "golden age" (or alternately, its dark ages), and thus in that realm wherein—to borrow Koestenbaum's words (scented, to be sure, with camp irony)—"the states to be savored are absence, sacrifice, and search."[102] Like Koestenbaum, Brett recognizes classical music's role in teaching queer devotees how to sing "from an erased, invisible place in the universe." But unlike Koestenbaum, he betrays little ambivalence in his response on this point. In Brett's reading the music profession has, in its role as twentieth-century homosexual refuge, served an anodyne function, and as such has been a prime regulator of the patriarchal social order:[103]

> For the musician in general, and particularly for the gay or lesbian
> musician, there is an involvement in a social contract that allows com-
> forting deviance only at the sometimes bitter price of sacrificing self-
> determination . . . [and] elite status in exchange for something more
> like a commodity: bohemia, "a respectable place for marginality . . .
> [that] had to justify its unorthodox practices by its intellectual and
> artistic achievement."[104]

Notably, the artistic-intellectual achievement required by the terms of this "social contract" was understood to depend on the double-binding conditions of the closet, particularly on that "homoerotic/homophobic process in which desire is stimulated and simultaneously suppressed."[105] It is a familiar formula: no art without pain—here, the pain of homophobic oppression, both from without and, as ensured by the artist's complicity in such a "contract," from within. Having probed twentieth-century queer musicianship as a constructed identity position bearing the contours just outlined, Brett ultimately regards the role as more suppressing than liberating, its compensations unequal to its exactions.

"What good," Brett asks, "is the 'discretion model' [British gay modernist composer Benjamin] Britten maintained, and musicians still maintain today, if it merely reinforces dominant culture by confining homosexuality to the private sphere while making it obscurely present in public discourse as an unthinkable alternative?"[106] Brett's 1994 question was, and remains, crucial, and his associated analysis comprises a quantum leap in the (previously nonexistent) realm of formal understandings of the functions and interrelations of homosexuality and musicality in twentieth-century Anglo-American culture. Now, a decade after Brett first sounded his trenchant critique, American culture has moved into a new century and millennium and into the fourth decade of the "post-Stonewall" era, that pride-filled promised land of postcloset liberation. And, of course, our current assessment of queer and musical identities and their social functions, past and present, must be situated in relation to current, rapidly shifting cultural realities—including gay-themed network sit-coms and cable series, the call for lesbian and gay marriage, and various other signs of increasing normalization and commodification of gay and lesbian identities.

We can trust, in other words, that our twenty-first-century present and future will surely ask new questions of our twentieth-century queer past. Having acknowledged music's anodyne function among twentieth-century queer music devotees, for example, how do we reconcile the problematics of that past situation with the present crisis of queer identity and politics—in which the "liberation" of formerly closeted devotions (such as that of music) opens the way to a stifling mainstreamed lesbian-gay identity that may offer even less social resistance than did the old, "discreet" type? For indeed, as *Four Saints* shows and the following pages will attest, twentieth-century homosexuals often took part in subcultural, including artistic, practices that fostered alternative social and cultural values, and that offered some degree of resistance—however marginalized or hidden—to those of the mainstream. And even as the outlaw zone of bohemia shielded straight culture from the reality of queer lives, it also (to varying degrees) protected pre-Stonewall queers from the normalization of conventional, institutionally sanctioned sociosexual life.

Suzanne G. Cusick's first-person account of her cultivation, as a lesbian in the latter half of the twentieth century, of an intimate relation with classical music illustrates the potential potency of queer musical engagements as ongoing exercises in social resistance. As Cusick observes, music can afford alternative modes of psychic, erotic, and affectional interaction and thus can help music-lovers in modeling culturally unsanctioned, variously queer—including same-sex and antipatriarchal—forms of intimacy and relationship.[107] But music must already be counted as a force of resistance, at an even more basic level, insofar as it helped many twentieth-century homosexual men and women to survive. For such theorists as Leo Bersani and Michael Warner have suggested that same-sex desire by its very nature is capable of disrupting coercive social orders.[108] However, I would argue that for pre-Stonewall homosexual subjects to defy the dominant culture's paramount message to them—that they should not exist—was the most crucial form of queer social resistance. To survive, then, and go on to live a queer life, however "discreet," was to contest and thus (in some measure) to erode the foundations of the twentieth-century homophobic cultural order. Indeed, as Warner notes, queerness in its stigmatization

> is connected with gender, the family, notions of individual freedom, the state, public speech, consumption and desire, nature and culture, maturation, reproductive politics, racial and national fantasy, class identity, truth and trust, censorship, intimate life and social display, terror and violence, health care, and deep cultural norms about the bearing of the body. Being queer means fighting about these issues all the time, locally and piecemeal but always with consequences.[109]

Music in the twentieth century afforded homosexuals, among other things, a means for abstracting and encoding its queer devotees' battles on all these fronts, and for blurring—to outside eyes—potentially incriminating differences that the mechanisms of homo/hetero definition had brought into sharp focus. As such it served as a magnet for queer life and culture, and a hotbed of individual and collective queer identity, expression, creativity, and survival.

MUSIC, HOMOSEXUALITY, AND A "SUBLIME LACK OF RESPECT FOR THE TRUTH"

This chapter opened to a scene of Paris in the terrible spring of 1940, in which Virgil Thomson, showing remarkable disregard for political—and some would say, more fundamental—reality, obsessed over Mozart interpretation even as Europe burned and bled around him, and Nazi forces moved in toward the very spot where he (and his beloved piano bench) stood. The instance, as we noted, is suggestive vis-à-vis the variety of functions music can serve for its devotees, and the intensities these may bear.

But it also witnesses Thomson's detachment from conventional wisdom and values, and a serious dismissal of the discursive truths circulating around him. Heeding the forecasts and warnings of Nazi invasion, most Americans and other foreign nationals had left France well before the 1940 New Year (by mid-June Thomson, having resolved the Mozart dilemma, also left Paris).[110]

Thomson's deviant actions in this context connect with another attraction music held for twentieth-century queer subjects: It has no standpoint, or is at least understood as such; makes no truth claims or assertions; and can seemingly obviate words altogether. The lines along which these attributes might render music appealing and even uniquely trustworthy to homosexuals are inferable from a remark of Ned Rorem's: "Having first-hand knowledge of homosexuality, and seeing that the world is mostly blind to, or wrong about, homosexuality, wised me up early. Jews are similarly wised up about their status."[111] Rorem suggests that both Jews and homosexuals develop a generalized skepticism toward majority knowledge and its truth claims as a result of their personal experience as minoritized subjects, and of their firsthand knowledge of alternative, contradictory truths. In his subculturally influential 1951 book *The Homosexual in America* the pseudonymous Donald Webster Cory registered the same observation, albeit in terms more apt to his sociological orientation:

> [T]he homosexual, . . . as a result of his anomalous position in society, is likely to become a skeptic and an iconoclast. Why? Because in that area of his life with which he is so vitally concerned, he is forced to reject an attitude [i.e., condemnation of homosexuals] which he finds so universally taken for granted by others. . . . He sees that there is room neither for inquiry nor argument, and that even men who are otherwise of rational and scientific mind wish to dispose of homosexuality with rash invective or with scornful pity.
>
> But he, the homosexual, is firmly convinced that the great mass of humanity is wrong in its judgment. Though his opinion grows out of necessity, its implications for his intellectual activity are widespread, for having come to reject a viewpoint held by so many to be beyond dispute, he must question whether many other tenets, similarly held to be beyond discussion, are not based on unthinking faith, blind passion, illogical reasoning, or lingering prejudices that at one time or another were part of the ruling mores of society.[112]

Chief among the "tenets" toward which twentieth-century homosexuals had reason to be skeptical—though few would have managed not to absorb them to some degree—were the pronouncements on homosexuality issued by the era's most elite, irrefutable sources of official knowledge: the discourses of science, including psychology and medicine. For twentieth-century America, scientific authority was the ultimate authority, and scientific fact that which was ultimately denoted *by* "fact." And in this light we might consider another of Rorem's remarks: "Facts don't exist. The sole truth lies in a tone of voice."[113] This *petite phrase* can suggest certain paths by which mid-twentieth-century queer discursive skepticism might connect with musical devotion: We need only note that its author is also America's most illustrious creator of art song, a composer who, in over sixty years and more than five hundred works, has cultivated an extraordinary devotion to the "truth" indwelling in "a tone of voice."[114]

At this point I would also flag the possibility of a connection between the "skeptical" homosexual's evident estrangement from the discourses of science, and gay American composers' radical noninvolvement in the science-affiliated "complexity music" that ascended after World War II.[115] Elsewhere, we might note that Rorem's position statement on "facts" and "truth" may hint, in its rather dramatic absolutism, at possible connections between what I am calling "queer discursive skepticism" and gay camp sensibility. Such connections emerge clearly in Koestenbaum's ruminations on "Divaspeak": "Divas talk like Oscar Wilde. Or Oscar Wilde talked like a diva. The diva *turns* a phrase and reverses it—substitutes praise for blame, pride for chagrin, authority for vacillation, salesmanship for silence. I long to imitate this language, if only to inhabit, for a sentence or two, its sublime lack of respect for the truth."[116] This passage's camp performativity is capped by the *sublimity* of the "lack of respect for the truth" it celebrates. But its counterpart in Rorem's or even Cory's more sober testimony is no less insistent on "truth"'s meretriciousness: Indeed, "Facts don't exist," in Rorem's estimation; and the culture's unquestioned tenets are fatuous, according to Cory's midcentury homosexual perspective.

Bernstein's musicianly response to violence (cited at the beginning of this chapter) also speaks at some remove from certain mainstream discourses of authority and power, and locates faith and redemption in music and musical acts. Though Bernstein, like Copland and Blitzstein, was actively engaged in political causes, his statement in this instance seems to posit musical deep engagement as a means of political disengagement (i.e., as a "response to violence"). Bernstein's elder colleague Virgil Thomson possessed a superb mind and sophisticated understanding of affairs and exchanges from intraprofessional through international levels. But while Thomson, especially in his years as chief critic for the *Herald Tribune*, exercised his skills and influence to affect musical matters, he steered remarkably clear of matters legal and political. Even when he might have readily used his position as the nation's most powerful music critic to respond, and to generate response, to Copland's McCarthy troubles, Thomson was silent. Other leading critics had weighed in on the removal, just two days before the event, of Copland's *Lincoln Portrait* from the 1953 Eisenhower inaugural program, and "[e]veryone in the cultural community was waiting for Virgil Thomson's strong voice."[117] But he wrote nothing about the incident, explaining in private that he "fear[ed] that public protests and similar manifestations might result in merely publicizing the incident to Mr. Copland's disadvantage."[118]

Thomson's biographer Tommasini writes, "What the events of 1953 had made clear . . . was that Virgil Thomson, the scrappy critic, picked his battles judiciously."[119] But surely they showed more than this—at least if we understand such instances to signify in social and cultural dimensions, beyond the purely individual and psychological. It is not difficult to see in these events and Thomson's (non-) responses the operation of reflexes culturally conditioned by twentieth-century queer identity and experience, and by the "discretionary model" of homosexuality that was, for him and his contemporaries, "absolutely necessary for survival"—to quote Brett.[120] By Thomson's own admission he feared publicity, feared public exposure and expected it to bring "disadvantage." At the first sign of trouble with officialdom Thomson's impulse, here on his colleague's behalf as elsewhere on his own, was to freeze and hold silent. That is, to behave as any discreet homosexual would in a bar raid, in a bordello sting, or in an anxious attempt to "straighten up" his public persona.

Thomson showed a comparable closeting impulse at many other points: As Rorem notes, he was "oddly mum about anything that might compromise him publicly."[121] At many pivotal moments, however, Thomson was not merely silent; he was silencing. On the day after his 1942 morals arrest in Brooklyn he called a woman colleague, Minna Lederman, and inexplicably insisted that she don elegant evening attire and accompany him to the symphony where he, also elegantly attired, made a point of lingering and being seen with her.[122] In 1966, when Rorem published his *Paris Diary* with its frank accounts of gay lives and loves, Thomson hastened to remove from his own memoir, then in press, all references to this longtime friend and once-student.[123] When in his eighties Maurice Grosser (1903–86), Thomson's life partner (the two were lovers for twenty-six years and mutually devoted "most important persons" to each other for sixty), was dying of AIDS, Thomson's urgent imperative was to convince Grosser to tell no one the truth of his illness (not even his friends, who might have offered support and sympathy), after which Thomson kept his distance.[124]

No friend or relationship was above being sacrificed, or foisted as decoy, in the public denial of queerness.

Thomson's actions in these instances can resemble a sort of desperate and unfunny version of Ma Rainey's classic "Prove It on Me Blues," whose final couplet shades various queer pleasures and behaviors boasted in the preceding verses: "'Cause they say I do it, ain't nobody caught me, / Sure got to prove it on me." But Thomson in his public denials practiced more than silence or silencing; he also engaged in projective displacement. In instances concerning minority identity Thomson tended not only to reticence, but even to thrusting a surrogate in front of himself, as shield and camouflage: Recall, for example, the prurient Baptist hymnal adherents he posited in "My Jesus, I Love Thee." Such a move evokes the so-called "Albertine strategy," inasmuch as it involves displacing one's queer identity onto others. The term arises out of Marcel Proust's putative practice, in *À la recherche du temps perdu*, of effectively representing his own homosexual affairs as heterosexual by transposing the sex of his lovers to create female characters—thus rendering an "Albert" an "Albertine." At least one critic further applies "Albertine strategy" to Proust's having "transposed the male homosexuality he did not dare treat openly onto the lesbian character Albertine."[125]

In like fashion, referring to his first meeting with Stein in 1926, Thomson in subsequent years would often repeat the insinuatively loaded phrase "Gertrude and I got on like Harvard men." More explicitly, in his 1966 memoir Thomson did not hesitate to underscore Stein's, Toklas's, and other Paris women's "amazon" status, even while confecting elaborate heterosexual fictions about himself and his gay male friends, lovers, and associates.[126] But the prime instance of transposed identity otherness, stigmatization, and sexualization in Thomson's oeuvre is that of *Four Saints*, whose public staging of improbable crossings in 1934 (Negroes singing opera? embodying Catholic saints?) taunted the forbidden display of other, real-life crossings. Surely Thomson, who harbored shame and resentment about his queer identity and its social status, had personal—and, as a composer outside the mainstream, professional—investments in using the cast's color "to sully . . . the rarefied white world of opera."[127] In *Four Saints'* African American casting we see surrogate Others pushed to the fore by a queer author who observes, from a safe perch, the public's response to these performers' stigmatized identity—and to the possible scandal of its presentation here in the context of grand opera and a historical Spanish Catholic setting.[128]

These latter examples instantiate the Albertine strategy even as they serve, with the preceding examples, to illustrate a crucial distinction between types of "truth." It is a distinction that Thomson and other homosexuals of his era were compelled to observe. To wit: Mainstream, heterosexual, public truth—"their" truth—is not at all equivalent to "our" marginal, queer, private truth; and we had better, for our own sake, seek diligently to control any encounters between the two. The perception of a gulf between these two "truths" is at the heart of camp sensibility as an expression of acute queer awareness toward the absurdity of *shame*—one of the attributes that naturally cleaves to queer identities, if we are to believe the dominant "truth."[129]

CAMPING OUT AT "OUR ISLAND HOME"

Brett identifies a pivotal truth about music and its function among twentieth-century queer devotees: It served here as an anodyne, and as a locus of nonverbal, depoliticized, even "meaning-free"—or at least untranslatable—expression. At the same time, music served other, sometimes contradictory functions vis-à-vis queer subjects. Chief among these was that of ministering to the wounds of twentieth-century homosexual identity: Even as music helped to keep its queer devotees more or less sedated in the sociocultural margins, it also served at various points to keep many of them alive. For music, as Brett also notes, particularly in the form of singing or playing an instrument, can appear "as a veritable lifeline" to "gay children, who often experience a shutdown of all feeling as the result of sensing their parents' and society's disapproval of a basic part of their sentient life."[130] But it was not only for children that music served this function in the twentieth century: Adults too, including queer adults, found refuge from social rejection and alienation in nonverbal, embodied, intimate engagements with music.

Moreover, it is worth noting that in an era when medical-psychological authorities offered sublimation as the best thing homosexuals could hope to do with their erotic and affectional impulses, music was often figured as a lover, spouse, or surrogate. "Music is my mistress," for example; "He is married to his music"; So-and-so (e.g., the unmarried gay midcentury conductor-composer Dimitri Mitropoulos) is a "priest" of music.[131] Salient among music's devotees in this era, of course, were persons for whom "real"—that is, conjugal—love was deemed and legislated unattainable: homosexuals. And yet, by Cory's midcentury reckoning, homosexuals coveted marriage: "The homosexual is . . . simultaneously frightened by fly-by-night, unstable relationships and attracted by the seeming permanence of marriage as a family institution. Despite the high rate of divorce among the general populace, the homosexual notes that the majority of marriages endure, and many seem to be happy, especially when they are viewed from without."[132] Surely Cory did not speak for all postwar homosexuals in his characterization of this exiled desire, on the part of "the homosexual," for marital heteronormativity. But Cory's emphasis on homosexuals' idealization of an object, conjugal love, that the culture constructed as perennially outside their grasp finds support in contemporaneous sources, including literature and art about homosexuals, and literature and art created by homosexuals about heterosexual life and love (e.g., Laurents, Sondheim, Bernstein, and Robbins's *West Side Story*).

And if, as Warner remarks, idealized conjugal love possesses "world-canceling force" and seems "beyond . . . the law," music's similar powers in the lives of its twentieth-century betrothed are evident in the Thomson and Bernstein examples that opened this chapter.[133] We might well suspect the operation of something like sublimation in such queer musical deep engagements. But we might also note, in connection with Warner's statements, that the world effectively—or at least ideally—"canceled" by queer musical devotion is that of the heteronormative mainstream: the "outside" world, *the* world. It is the world of identity labels and heavily policed subjecthood, of those "bewilderingly fixed categories" from which music—like lesbian sex, in Cusick's 1994 analysis—offers an escape, allowing one "to wallow in the circulation of pleasures that are beyond danger and culturally defined desires."[134] It is also the world whose social margins contain and define sexual and artistic bohemia and thus render queer musicality (as Brett reveals) a relatively harmless, even status quo–enhancing, outlet for potentially disruptive persons and energies.

We have been examining some of the kinds of appeal music held for twentieth-century homosexuals, who flocked to it in great numbers and served therein as prime movers and shakers. First, we noted that music, being nonverbal and understood (in this site and era) as an abstract medium, makes no truth claims, and that such a nonconstative, "value-free" medium appears to have been attractive to persons—including queer persons—whose lives and identities were particularly subject to the regulatory claims and values of prevailing identity discourses.[135] Second, we have begun to consider the ways in which music, being nonverbal and experienced as deeply embodied and unmediated by social structures, affords alternative modes of emotional and erotic intimacy that may have (a) provided critical succor for persons, including queer subjects, who felt excluded by and alienated from social structures, and (b) (not only evaded but) weakened the tyranny of the gender and sexual classifications in which twentieth-century queer persons found themselves invidiously caught (a point developed further in chapter 3 and its discussion of "desubjectivation"). And now, third, we will explore how the subcultural world of twentieth-century American classical music sustained alternative kinship networks to those defined by heterosexuality and blood ties, and as such offered a relatively hospitable realm for queer lives and expressions.

Chauncey writes of the double life maintained by most gay men in early- to mid-twentieth-century New York:

> Managing a double life was relatively easy for many men because they did not consider their homosexual identity to be their only important identity. Identities are always relational, produced by the ways people affiliate themselves with or differentiate themselves from others—and are marked as different *by* others. All men managed multiple identities or multiple ways of being known in the many social worlds in which they moved, because they had to present themselves in different ways in different contexts.[136]

As we noted above, Chauncey's discussion of gay men's occupations and identity management in this period does not explicitly treat classical music, but it is informed by the diaries of Charles Tomlinson Griffes (1884–1920), a brilliant gay American composer of modernism's first generation.[137] And though it was less so during Griffes's lifetime, by the 1930s and 1940s American classical music, and particularly composition, was an exceptionally gay and gay-supportive occupational realm. The music world constituted a sympathetic sphere for gay men and lesbians in this period and, insofar as it required relatively little expenditure of energy for cultivating doubleness, a productive locus for work.

Moreover, for gay male composers particularly, gay contacts and professional contacts often overlapped considerably, were one and the same. In fact, typically one's gay (or largely gay) musical-artistic "family" circle could be the fabric, ground, and sustenance of one's professional life, providing acculturation, mentoring, introductions, jobs, loans, and various other forms of connection, specialized knowledge, and moral and material support. Such networking among U.S. gay modernist composers was crucial to their activities and successes—and, as such, crucial within American twentieth-century music overall—and is the subject of chapter 3. Of course, gay composers did not invent networking or kinship structures, both of which have perennially formed the bases of personal and professional life in mainstream heteronormative culture. But the culture's classification of homosexual ties as illicit and of patriarchally heteronormative ties as exclusively sanctioned has meant that gay composers' kinship and networking has long been denied by queer-identified artists and scholars, while ignored or acknowledged only in accusations by many nonqueer-identified commentators: What is "family" in a heterosexual context is rendered "cabal" when marked by the sinister taint of putative sexual perversion; "connecting" becomes "conspiring"; "support" translates to "pulling strings."

Nevertheless, in comparison with other arenas of the time, the zone inhabited by many twentieth-century gay modernist artists, and certainly composers, was a relatively utopic one lying somewhere between the realms of the "overts" and "coverts"—to invoke Newton's classifications for pre-Stonewall U.S. gay social-occupational organization. In her theoretical scheme "[t]he overts live their *entire* lives within the context of the [homosexual] community," while "the coverts live their entire *nonworking* lives within it." These groups generally correlate to disrespected (especially sex work and sexualized entertainment) and respected forms of work, respectively, and hence to lower- and middle-class positions.[138] But if, as Gayle Rubin remarks, "the vast majority of [pre-Stonewall] homosexuals had to choose between honest poverty and the strain of maintaining a false identity," then the homosexual composers discussed here represent a rather privileged minority.[139] For gay American modernist composers and other artists—in New York and certainly in Paris—enjoyed both a relatively "overt" working sphere and a respectable, if not terribly lucrative, professional identity. Such conditions accrue, of course, to the liminal realms of bohemia. And in no quarter of bohemia did such conditions bear more cultural-artistic fruit than in the "island home" of gay American modernist composers.

This chapter has explored multiple meanings of "being musical" in twentieth-century America, and particularly how gendered, sexual, and musical identities interacted and intersected, inflected and informed one another. Such exploration establishes a context in which to understand the work of the Copland-Thomson circle and the significance of gay white male composers' leadership in the establishment of an American national music. Before focusing on these composers' profile and activities as a group, however, we will take time to examine some individual differences within the group, through a brief consideration of Paul Bowles's youth among queer American modernist artists abroad, and of his later life and career as a sexually obscure American writer-composer permanently resident in Tangier. The spotlight here is on Bowles's identity status as a sort of queer among queers who defied definition on multiple fronts, including sexuality, nationality, and artistic specialization. Bowles's case forces us to confront the complex nature of the identifications at hand and the always-contested nature of identity, and thus discourages any reification of overly simple, tidy, or reductive notions in connection with the identity-based arguments to follow.

My Dear Freddy

Identity Excesses and Evasions
chez *Paul Bowles*

Ned Rorem first met Paul Frederic Bowles (1910–99) in the summer of 1941. Bowles at thirty was living in Taxco, Mexico, and the seventeen-year-old Rorem was traveling there with his father. Two years later, when Rorem and Bowles were both living in New York, they struck up a friendship. Rorem recounts vividly his first visit to Bowles's apartment of 1944, a small penthouse with a "spectacular view of downtown Manhattan": "The larger of the two rooms was all in white," Rorem writes, "white sofas, a white piano, with long white curtains moving slightly in April's first warm breezes, and a white fur rug wall to wall. A white telephone with the number removed." The account continues:

> Like his room at the Chelsea a year ago, this one reeked of perfume, as indeed did Paul himself, wherever he went. He had spent the better part of his Guggenheim fellowship on raw ambergris which he combined with other basic essences to confect heavy oils that imbued the furniture, never to disappear. A luscious cage of scent for him to hide behind.

Rorem reports further details attesting Bowles's creation of an esoteric and, at points, dark, worldly mystique, and then writes, "All of this would be chitchat were it not relevant to another aspect of the man which grew clear in the next half hour, and which changed my life as [Satie's] *Socrate* and [Stravinsky's] *Sacre* had."[1] Bowles played a recording of an arietta from his *zarzuela* (operetta) *The Wind Remains* (1942). "I was bewitched and remain bewitched after five decades," Rorem wrote in 1994. He confesses to having appropriated then, and retained thereafter, what he perceives to be Bowles's signature (albeit unconscious) musical mannerism: an expressive "dying fall" by minor third. The same gesture was favored by Mahler in his late-Romantic *Weltschmerz*, but it is used to opposite effect in Bowles's music, which Rorem describes, by contrast to fin-de-siècle decadence, as "the picture of health."[2]

Lamenting that "the bulk of [Bowles's] fans today are unaware that he ever composed," Rorem (displaying a characteristic fixation on national types) sees this as a symptom of Americans' exclusive engagement with specialists. "So," Rorem proclaims,

> for the record let it be said that Paul Bowles is, like Europeans of yore (Leonardo, Cocteau, Noël Coward), a general practitioner of high order. Unlike them, his two professions don't overlap—neither esthetically nor technically. . . . Bowles is the sole fiction writer among [composers who prosify: Schumann, Debussy, Thomson], and his fiction is as remote from their prose as from his own music. His stories are icy, cruel, objective, moralistic in their amorality, and occur mostly in exotic climes; they are also often cast in large forms. His music is warm, wistful, witty, redolent of nostalgia for his Yankee youth, wearing its heart on its sleeve; and it is all cast in small forms.[3]

A QUEER YOUTH AMONG THE MODERNISTS

We know of Bowles's self-introduction at eighteen (in late 1929) to Copland, and to many other artists and literati.[4] At this time the young Bowles was, according to his biographer, "less interested in getting to know new people than he was obsessed with adding names to his list."[5] Copland and Bowles, however, would indeed get to know each other. Soon after their first meeting they began daily composition and harmony lessons together. And when Bowles's parents insisted he return to the University of Virginia for the 1930 spring term to finish his freshman year, Copland made a visit to Charlottesville that Easter. In the fall Bowles joined Copland in Saratoga Springs, at the artists' colony later to be known as Yaddo, where Copland worked on his *Piano Variations* and took his young friend on long rides, one time meeting the composer Carl Ruggles, another time Roger Sessions.[6] But it was Bowles who introduced Copland to Gertrude Stein and Alice Toklas—in spring 1931, a few weeks after he himself had first knocked on the door at 27 rue de Fleurus. Stein and Toklas had immediately dubbed their young visitor "Freddy," deciding that this diminutive of his middle name better suited him than his first name. Still in Paris, Bowles connected with Virgil Thomson in the summer of that year[7]—the same summer when, accompanied by Copland, he visited and thus began his lifelong love affair with Tangier. It is a city where, in Ned Rorem's words, "virtually all males practice what we call homosexuality, [and] virtually no males are homosexual"—which is to say, male-male sexual behavior flour-ishes apart from any assumptions of homosexual identity.[8]

Bowles at twenty was by every account striking and elegant in appear-ance and extraordinary in intelligence, wit, and social manner. But for all his travels and time spent with Copland—whose penchant was for pretty young men like Bowles, within just the sort of mentoring association they were cultivating—the raciest note in Bowles's life at this time might have been in his relationship with Stein. Staying with Stein and Toklas at their vacation home in the French countryside, Bowles daily donned the *Leder-hosen* Gertrude prescribed, and ran circles around the garden each morn-ing while she watched from a second-story window—shouting "Faster, Freddy, faster!"—and her standard poodle Basket chased him and scratched his legs. According to Bowles's biographer Gena Dagel Caponi, Stein "enjoyed [Bowles's] discomfort, while he interpreted her attention [per-versely] as 'a sign of the most personal kind of relationship.'" Caponi sees the scene as a reenactment of Bowles's relationship with his despised and abusive father, though with Stein "Paul was happy to be allowed" to play this role of "naïf, to be taken care of, to be 'naughty,' even though it meant undergoing humiliation and personal discomfort."[9] His delight in this dynamic shows in his choosing one of Stein's letters to him, written when he was ill, abject, and thus most deeply in the naïf role, and she at her most grandmotherly, to set as a song he called "Letter to Freddy" (1932, Example 5).[10]

Bowles's setting readily evokes several of the characterizations that typ-ically attach to his music: charming, gracious, French. He begins with a slow introduction that might have served well to open a 1930s radio melo-drama: Moving through shimmering chords (featuring added ninths and other coloristic elements), it briefly presents two descending gestures in search of a key and meter. Then, before either issue is clearly settled, the piano launches into an elegant Parisian café waltz. A supple vocal melody enters, shifting nimbly between waltz time and declamatory stretches that draw out the speech rhythms of Stein's unrhymed, unmetered epistolary address. Lasting less than ninety seconds, the song glides easily through several distinct atmospheres including that of the cabaret, at the point where Stein urges "Freddy," the "poor boy," to come to Paris where he can be "looked after." Equally vivid is the extraordinary peace and security in which Bowles swathes the final phrase, "Always, Gertrude Stein."

By comparison to his Freddy act with Gertrude, the young Bowles's relations with Copland can seem vanilla-wholesome. Eva Goldbeck, friend of Copland and spouse of Marc Blitzstein, reported from Paris in summer

EXAMPLE 5. Opening, "Letter to Freddy" (1932), Paul Bowles on a text by Gertrude Stein (Albany Records TROY043, track 14, 0:00–0:22).

1931 that Copland had fallen "madly in love with this youngster of his"— and to her sorrow, for she distrusted Bowles's character. But he and Copland had separate rooms when they traveled on to Berlin together. And though Bowles reportedly played coy around others, doing "nothing to prevent suspicions of a homosexual affair," Copland's love evidently went unrequited. One of Copland's letters even found him dispensing patient counsel on Bowles's apparent sexual noninvolvement: "When you really want to [make love]," he wrote, "you will."[11]

Undoubtedly Virgil Thomson was fond of Bowles too, though he regarded him more shrewdly: "Paul made like being queer," Thomson reportedly asserted, "and he got money out of that and friendships. But he was really not interested in the physical side."[12] It is not that Thomson presumed Bowles straight: Concerning what he called the "strange and elaborate marriage" between Paul Bowles and the writer Jane Auer Bowles, he remarked, "They probably never slept together. Oh, they may have tried it once or twice. But they were terribly devoted."[13] And where Thomson's biographer Tommasini identifies Jane Bowles as "thoroughly lesbian," Paul Bowles is described as *essentially* homosexual."[14] From these accounts Bowles does not seem straight, but neither does he seem gay, exactly. Nor, particularly, is there any indication of bisexuality. Rather, Bowles appears, as the title of a 1993 documentary put it, *The Complete Outsider*—or better, as the most thorough and extreme embodiment of "queer," broadly construed, within a modernist context already markedly queer.[15]

IDENTITY STAKES

My engagement with these questions of classification in relation to Bowles and the modernist arts world connects to my considerations in this context of sexual, musical, and national identity and their interrelations. In particular I intend for these perspectives on Bowles to situate the consideration of identity and identifications among the Thomson-Copland circle to be pursued in chapter 3. My work in this area began with observing certain shared musical-biographical motifs among this intergenerational circle of important gay composers working in New York in the 1940s. These shared motifs include, in addition to their homosexual identification: foreign apprenticeship, especially in Paris; studies with Boulanger; self-alignment with things French, often in express opposition to things German; and cultivation of a tonal compositional idiom, usually pursuing clarity and economy.

It is a narrative in which I had, initially, included Paul Bowles. He had seemed a likely candidate for inclusion—at least up to the point when he moved to Tangier in 1947.[16] But later I wrote him out, unsure whether his positioning quite matched the story I was telling. Later still, having delved back into Bowles materials, I was tempted to write him back in. And if at one time I was annoyed with all this waffling on my part, by now I have come to see some usefulness in it: It underscores the difficulty of discussing

Bowles in relation to categories generally—his multidimensional status as enigma, a veritable queer among queers. But it also reveals the difficulties and limitations inherent in the identity categories that frame this study. I hope here to exploit this revelation, as an opportunity to clarify what is and is not assumed in my invocations of identity categories, and how my assumptions might differ from those that would have applied in the original historical instance. In the case of Bowles, for example, his being sexually involved with men while also being married to a woman, Jane Auer Bowles (notwithstanding her lesbian identification), allowed him to be labeled "normal" from one perspective, but tainted him as queer from another. Other perceptions of Bowles's sexual identity would tag him as a "P.H.," or phony homosexual, in a phrase of the day; or as unknown and mysterious.[17]

My own inclusion of Bowles in the circle of queer composers around Thomson and Copland is rooted in a definition of queerness that emphasizes issues beyond the rote clinical facts of subject-object sex configuration, and beyond the legal and official facts of marital status—issues including one's self-identifications and social and cultural affiliations. The African American writer James Baldwin (1924–86) was another artist and expatriate of this era whose life and work exceeded the sexual—and in Baldwin's case, racial—identity binarisms reigning then and in many present-day accounts as well. Both Bowles and Baldwin had personal liaisons with members of both sexes, while explicitly offering neither homosexual nor heterosexual self-labelings. I regard them as *queer* figures whose frequent contemporary appearance under the banner of "gay artists" can usefully trouble the category of homosexual identity—and its apparent continuing presumption of a miscegenation model.[18] Baldwin's and Bowles's respective expatriations are further indicative here: We might note Baldwin's views on America as the "house of bondage" (racial and sexual), on race and sexuality as mutually constitutive, and on American culture's infantilization of sexuality (see his "Here Be Dragons"); and Bowles's permanent expatriation to Tangier, where (as Rorem put it) "virtually all males practice what we call homosexuality, [and] virtually no males are homosexual."

One might argue for Bernstein and Blitzstein to be viewed in similar terms. Surely their respective marriages account for the "bisexual" label that sometimes accrues nowadays to each (though rarely to Bowles, which may owe to his being the only one of the three whose spouse was herself famously queer—a fact that helps to confound labelings). But in self-identification both Blitzstein and Bernstein aligned more with homo- than hetero- or bisexuality. In fact, by standards of self-definition Blitzstein, although married, was unequivocally queer. The also-married Bernstein appears queer by virtue of his own self-identification, which he seemed to conceive (not only in the years before and after his marriage) in relation to homosexuality; his collaborator and longtime friend Arthur Laurents described Bernstein as "a gay man who got married," adding that he "wasn't conflicted about it at all. He was just gay."[19] Bowles, as I have suggested, exceeded categories and refused definition, and in this way might be regarded (again invoking a broader sense of "queer") as queer-plus, or queerer than queer.

Having written him back into my story, I will discuss Bowles's place and influence within American musical modernism. First, he emerges in Pollack's Copland biography as the tie that binds Copland and Thomson in the period of their closest, most familial relations. According to Pollack this relationship "was probably warmest in the early 1930s, when together, like older brothers, they fretted over the musical education of Paul Bowles," and during this time the elsewhere-brusque Thomson signed his letters to Copland "Love, Virgil."[20] Their biggest point of disagreement concerned study with Boulanger, which Copland strongly urged and Thomson was against. Ultimately, it is hard to say who won: Bowles attended two of her counterpoint classes in the fall of 1931 and then quit.[21] Though Copland and Thomson both made their musical knowledge available to Bowles, he was not at his best in the role of pupil. He managed, as Thomson notes, to become accomplished as a self-taught composer.[22] But Bowles (like Rorem) did learn from Thomson a finely honed art of orchestration. And Bowles credited to Copland the formation of his "whole musical and intellectual background."[23]

Rorem, recalling their Mexico encounter of 1941, reports that Bowles played a record for him, Copland's *Music for the Theater* (1925). This music, Rorem writes, "bowled me over. . . . The lean but telling language of a land I knew well but had never heard spoken! American music!" Bowles then performed one of his own pieces, and Rorem remarked, "It sounds like *Music for the Theater*." At this Bowles presented an issue of *Modern Music* and quoted an essay remarking of himself and Copland, "The master has been more influenced by the student than vice versa," thus quashing Rorem's implication about the direction of influence.[24] Three years later Bowles would play for Rorem another of his compositions, the little five-minute arietta from *The Wind Remains* that imprinted Rorem and his own music forever after.[25]

Rorem reports that "Lenny" Bernstein at twenty-four (1943) "apotheosized" Bowles, was "beguiled" by him as man and musician, and that he would throughout his life laud "his idol" Bowles as "one of America's least-sung heroes." But Rorem also reports that "Bernstein, who had absorbed Bowles's jazzily perfumed modes by osmosis, eventually allowed himself to believe that he was their originator." (In Paris in 1954, Rorem at the piano noodled briefly over a theme from *The Wind Remains,* and Bernstein asked, "O God, Ned, when did I write that gorgeous thing?")[26] Another admirer was Gian Carlo Menotti, operatic composer of *The Medium* and *The Consul,* and life partner of Samuel Barber. When in his teaching at the Curtis Institute Menotti used Bowles's "wonderful" music to illustrate a perfect match between orchestration and dramatic characterization, it was an instance of high praise, coming from the most successful American opera composer of the era.[27]

Rorem even places Bowles centrally in a shift toward things queer and gentile that he attributes to postwar American music and art:

> After the [1945] opening night of [Tennessee Williams's] *The Glass Menagerie*—heightened, or rather, delineated, by Paul Bowles's background score, which came later to be known among musicians as "the Tennessee sound"—it was clear that *something* had happened. . . . A queer goyische flavor was sprouting out of the war and would burst in a few years.[28]

The postwar scenario of queerness, sprouting, and bursting sketched here is explored at length in chapter 4.

All these examples attest Bowles's musical impact on fellow modernists and modernism, including Copland, Bernstein, Menotti, Rorem, and those postwar musicians who came to know the by-now-unheard-of "Tennessee sound." These examples suggest that Bowles's influence as a composer was more profound than current historical accounts, not to mention concert and publishing practices, would begin to indicate. As for other modernists' influence on Bowles, that of Gertrude Stein was probably most decisive. She announced to young "Freddy," after scanning his poetry in 1931, "As a writer you're a good composer."[29] This should not have been so harsh a blow as one might assume, for a couple of years earlier Bowles had written of longing to be told what to do: "If a composer said to me: 'You are a composer,' that would be all right. Or if a poet said: 'You are a poet,' that would be acceptable, too. But somebody had to say something."[30] Stein did, but the criticism reportedly stung, and bothered him for a long time.[31] In any event, for the next sixteen years Bowles would pursue composition, and some journalistic music criticism, to the exclusion of poetry and fiction. Upon Stein's death in 1946, however, Bowles claimed to have undergone a purge. He then returned to writing fiction, and his compositional output dwindled, though it did not cease entirely. Rorem cites two mediums in which Bowles continued to compose, both of which are now, by Rorem's account, extinct: The first was incidental music for plays; and the second, piano duos, commissioned—like 1949's sparkling and sultry *Night Waltz*—by Arthur Gold and Robert Fizdale. Fizdale and Gold were a gay couple and perhaps the most important two-piano team of all time, both for their performances and for their numerous and varied commissions.[32]

By 1948 Bowles was still the most in-demand composer for the theater in midtown Manhattan (later "Off Broadway"). By Rorem's account he had "inherited the mantle from Virgil [Thomson] in the WPA days, and achieved fame with *The Glass Menagerie*."[33] Actually, it was a role that had been embraced by all of Bowles's seniors in the Thomson-Copland circle: Besides Thomson, Copland and Blitzstein too had taken up composing a sort of accessible, entertaining, classically informed yet commercially viable music for theater, ballet, movie, and sometimes radio audiences. And likewise Bowles's junior colleague and compositional admirer Bernstein. In fact, it was when Bowles passed on the chance to score Jerome Robbins's 1944 ballet *Fancy Free* that Bernstein got the project and created, with Robbins, the work that catapulted composer and choreographer both to fame.[34]

His successes as a theater composer notwithstanding, with the appearance of his novel *The Sheltering Sky* in 1949 Bowles's public image quickly shifted, in Rorem's words, "from the role of composer-who-also-writes to that of author-who-used-to-compose." By August 1950 Bowles owned a house in the Casbah, endlessly under construction and having no furniture "except for a box of sapphires," and showed little interest in ever composing again, remarking, "But nobody remembers that I ever wrote music."

Rorem writes of first meeting Bowles that his

> direct Americanness, . . . blond thirty-year-old good looks, and informality . . . made him seem accessible in the extreme. . . . With passing years I would discover that Paul was accessible to no one; whether involuntary or by design his oxymoronic stance was one of aloof friendliness, beckoning unapproachability. . . . His affably smart conversation was identical with everyone, from concierge to countess, serving as a neutral screen between him and you—not to mention the active screen of exotic perfume which always enveloped him.

It struck Rorem as "against nature that anyone could be in the driver's seat with Paul; [he] was just not accessible."[35]

To Rorem, Bowles was "the artist as voyeur, more concerned with the hopeless sensuality of all men than with the eager sexuality of one man."[36]

FIGURE 6.   Tennessee Williams and Paul Bowles in
Morocco circa early 1949, some three years after their collaboration in *The Glass Menagerie* gave rise to the "Tennessee sound." Harry Ransom Humanities Research Center, the University of Texas at Austin.

Though his friends report meeting various of Bowles's boyfriends over the
years, they seem perennially mystified vis-à-vis his erotic life. On one
"liquory evening" in Paris in 1949, Truman Capote asked Rorem what he
thought Paul did for sex "with all those Arabs": "My silent reaction,"
Rorem reports, "was that he should know better than I."[37] Both had known
Bowles for years, but neither, evidently, could fathom a guess about him as
an erotic being.[38]

I never met Paul Bowles. All I know of him I have gleaned from books,
music, and films. Still, I suspect that I may have glimpsed his erotic persona:
in Gide's Michel, title character in *The Immoralist* (1902).[39] My recognition dawns specifically from the queer-theoretical reading of *The Immoral-*

ist given by Leo Bersani in *Homos*. Michel is a cultured Frenchman who renounces his privileged social-national position to live among Arab natives in North Africa. Suffering from tuberculosis on his arrival, he is "beguiled back to health" by the health and beauty of the Arab boys there. Like the often sickly Bowles, Michel takes deep pleasure in sunbathing, in baring his body to the harsh desert sun and wind: For Michel this becomes the means of recovering an authentic self—by peeling away "layers of acquired knowledge" and culture to expose a true self, not beneath the skin, but finally *in* it.[40] With skin newly sensate Michel feels himself a part of the landscape, expanded into the grass and soil, and extended without bounds into beautiful Arab-boy bodies. His satisfaction lies not in coupling with these bodies, but more impersonally, in basking in their proximity. Michel's homosexuality is thus "a matter of positioning rather than intimacy," and Gidean pederasty here comprises "the narcissistic expansion of a desiring skin": Like nude sunbathing, "it too works against the narcissism of a securely mapped ego."[41]

Hence such an eroticism, in Bersani's view, comprises a more radically *homo-* form of homosexuality, and one to which he ascribes significant psychological and political liberatory potential. For it "eliminates from 'sex' *the necessity of any relation whatsoever*" and so is unaccompanied by that (more Proustian) condition of "an essentially doomed and generally anguished interrogation of the other's desires."[42] Here I am suggesting a parallelism between this radically *homo-* homosexuality, by which Michel qualifies in Bersani's reading as a "gay outlaw," and the sexual persona of Paul Bowles. In the next chapter I draw parallels between such homo-homosexuality and (what I will call) *musico*sexuality—that is, eroticism defined in terms of neither same-sex nor opposite-sex relations, but musical relations. For now I would note that while Bowles appears atypical of queer modernist composers in his radical evasion of identity categories, he also appears exemplary in his engagement with techniques of subjectivity shattering via subject-object merging—techniques that were central to modern homosexual and musicosexual practices and penchants, as the next chapter demonstrates.

"BECKONING UNAPPROACHABILITY," MUSICAL MASKS

The nineteenth-century proliferation of medicoscientific discourses classifying and regulating gendered, sexual, and racial subjects created hothouse conditions of identity definition and discipline, conditions that haunted the twentieth century and its modernist movement. With regard to these conditions and their effects, Paul Bowles's life and music both offer intriguing perspectives. He stands in ambiguous relation to central categories of modern subjecthood—of nationality and sexuality, and even to kingdom identifications, to the extent that he often seems more vividly relational to land sites, in their botanical and mineral particularities, than to human (or any other) animals.

The detachment and aloofness remarked in Bowles's life and person also turn up in discussions of his fiction. Ned Rorem's assessment of Bowles's novels has been severe, on grounds of severity. He regards Bowles's fiction in general as "willfully cold, but readable and satisfying to the cruel streak in us all." He deems *The Sheltering Sky*, however, "unsettling . . . in the wrong way; a touch vulgar, . . . and also a touch facile," professing, "I neither believed it, nor in it." Rorem, like some other readers, finds the best characterizations in Bowles's writing ("as in his life") in depictions of scenery and landscapes. "But when discussing real people," Rorem wrote in 1972, "the effect is desperate, touching, even sad, sometimes humorous, though only secondarily the effect he intended, that is, a pose of noninvolvement. That effect, which fills the novels, no longer seems viable for our troubled world—perhaps precisely because the world has turned into a Paul Bowles novel."[43] This last phrase echoes Norman Mailer's much-quoted assessment of Bowles's influence on modern American literature: "Paul Bowles opened the world of Hip. He let in the murder, the drugs, the incest, the death of the Square . . . the call of the orgy, the end of civilization."[44]

Bowles's music is usually read in quite other terms: as gracious, witty, and charming.[45] But in connection with the topic (again) of modernist abstraction, I might be tempted to take a different angle on Bowles's charming, attractive musical idiom. Abstraction is often discussed in standard accounts of musical modernism, which locate the modernist movement's very roots in obfuscating abstraction and in "secret languages," all the while begging the question, What is the secret?[46] Abstraction in these accounts is most often associated with dissonance, chromaticism, atonality, and minimized perceptible patterning—as in the language of Schoenberg and his followers.

But we find quite different musical means of abstraction in the work of certain gay American modernists, and some indications, finally, of the nature of one secret in those "secret languages." This secret is laid bare in a recent essay by the musicologist David Metzer, who finds Copland encoding gay desire in his early songs via musical orientalism and African-Americanisms, and later straightening up his act, as it were, by abstracting these corporeally and sexually marked signs of the racial Other. Metzer describes Copland's "turn to abstraction" beginning in the late twenties as a "compositional scorched-earth campaign" to void the corporeal and homoerotic language he had developed in notably exoticist works earlier in the decade: Invoking characteristic gestures from these works, Copland's later "abstract" idiom desensualized and whitewashed them by various means, including a literal silencing of the human voice, and afforded his music the perceived "universality" that helped propel it to the iconic status it attained in the ballets of the thirties and forties and has maintained since then.[47]

By contrast to the standard image of modernist musical abstraction, which is rendered in terms of Schoenbergian complexity and atonality, the abstraction that we can trace in Copland plays out within an idiom that is relatively nonchromatic, mild in its dissonance, quasi-tonal, and clearly patterned. And Thomson's famously abstract idiom—in all its remarkable congruity with the literary idiom of his collaborator Stein—is thoroughly white-key diatonic, consonant, plainly tonal, and (not just patterned but) conspicuously repetitious: Thus is Stein and Thomson's *Four Saints in Three Acts* a notorious instance of modernist abstraction even as it exhibits, both verbally and musically, the plainest everyday vernacular and simple formal clarity. Bringing Paul Bowles's musical idiom into this considera- tion of syntax and semantics in modernist abstraction can raise some intriguing and complicating questions. Perhaps this lean, tonal, audibly French-affiliated music marks an even further point of encoded queerness on the abstraction continuum we have begun to map using the musical lan- guages of Schoenberg, Copland, and Thomson as coordinates. Bowles's lan- guage, however, is not conspicuously abstract; perhaps most conspicuously, it is *charming*—which certainly seems a less freighted, more innocuous quality. Thus, it may be that I was right earlier, in judging that Bowles did not fit into my story here.

On the other hand, addressing Bowles's music now, I cannot help but recall Rorem's description of the composer's "beckoning unapproachabil- ity" and "aloof friendliness," and to hear in this famously charming music something of the "affably smart" discourse that Rorem perceived "serving as a neutral screen" (none of which is to imply a diminishment in my appreciation of the music, for indeed, I grow ever more intrigued by it). And if such a character inheres in Bowles's music, it may help to account for the utter Americanness so often heard there. Or so one might infer from Baldwin's short story "This Morning, This Evening, So Soon," whose pro- tagonist, making passage back to America after long expatriation in Paris, registers this observation: "The Americans on the boat did not seem to be so bad, but I was fascinated, after such long absence from it, by the nature of their friendliness. It was a friendliness which did not suggest, and was not intended to suggest, any possibility of friendship."[48] If an ability to charm without engaging or revealing oneself appeared around the mid–twentieth century, to no less keen an observer than Baldwin, as a distinguishing feature of American character, the notion might also provide useful perspective onto both the style of art music that came in the thirties and forties to signify the "American" and the extraordinary involvement of homosexual composers in its creation. After all, much of what we know of homosexual (including camp) culture from this era is in the form of humor, wit, or charm that serves to conceal and distance a speaker from (at least some) interlocutors or onlookers. Even today the trait may persist as a gay-male discursive modality: As the critic and theorist Ross Chambers notes, "being affable-but-guarded is still something you can see in (certain) gay men."[49]

For a final word on Bowles's music we might turn to his longtime friend Rorem, whose assessments of the Bowlesian oeuvre have differed dramatically between the musical and literary realms. The always-outspoken Rorem has emphasized the important influence of Bowles's music on his and others' work and even placed Bowles at the forefront of his own field, of twentieth-century American art song. "No American in our century has composed songs lovelier than his," Rorem proclaimed in 1994. "None of these songs is currently in print," he continued. "That fact echoes the indifferent world that he elsewhere so successfully portrays."[50]

3. A French Connection

Modernist Codes in the Musical Closet

> Male homosexuality has certainly been prevalent in this country since the time of the Norman conquest.
>
> ENGLISH BARRISTER WRITING ON THE WILDE TRIALS

> The word is *gay*. . . . I have been told by experts that it came from the French, and that in France as early as the sixteenth century the homosexual was called *gaie;* significantly enough, the feminine form was used to describe the male.
>
> DONALD WEBSTER CORY, *The Homosexual in America*

> I never found (as the anguished Foucault did) that the French were intolerant of homosexuality, or Americans either for that matter. Admittedly, the only people I've ever known have not been the stone-throwing bourgeoisie, but artists, the idle rich, and similar misfits.
>
> NED ROREM, *Knowing When to Stop*

In 1919, in a Pennsylvania town, a nine-year-old boy summoned his courage, composed a letter, and set it out for his mother to find. The boy, then known as Sam, would grow up to be Samuel Barber, a celebrated American composer and a gay man. His letter begins:

> NOTICE to *Mother* and *nobody else*

> Dear Mother: I have written this to tell you my worrying secret. Now don't cry when you read it because it is neither yours nor my fault. I suppose I will have to tell it now without any nonsense.

Having prepared the difficult ground, he continues:

> To begin with, I was not meant to be an athlet *[sic]*. I was meant to be a composer, and will be I'm sure. I'll ask you one more thing.— Don't ask me to try to forget this unpleasant thing and go play football.—*Please*—Sometimes I've been worrying about this so much that it makes me mad (not very),
>
> > *Love,*
> > *Sam Barber II*

The tone and language leave little doubt but that this letter constitutes what we would call, in contemporary parlance, a coming-out statement.[1] Sam Barber had already, precociously and secretly, come to terms with his irrefutable desire and resolved to follow it in spite of his society's expectations. The pursuit of this desire attached to a particular identity, and it was a dangerous one: As its (repeated) binary juxtaposition with athletics makes clear, this identity was figured in opposition to conventional masculine and heterosexual positions.

But just what was this desire, this identity, so contrary and threatening to prescribed norms of gender and sexuality, and so fraught with anxiety and heartache for this gifted son and, ostensibly, his mother? Was it the named object—music, and the identity of composer—that challenged the social order around this prominent upper-middle-class family? Or was it, following the semantics of the closet, the absent term—queerness—that resonated menacingly here, undenoted and thus everywhere connoted? Indeed, was it—*is* it—possible to disentangle one meaning fully from the other, musical desire from queer desire, musical identity from queer identity?

MUSIC AS SEX AS IDENTITY— AND AS IDENTITY SOLVENT

The answer to my last question, according to some recent discourse in queer music studies, is no. A seminal essay by Philip Brett, for example, constructs an extended and revealing correlation between musicality and homosexuality. In "Musicality, Essentialism, and the Closet" Brett notes the deviant status of both roles (one privileged, the other punished), their close association in the popular imagination and queer vernacular (in the use of "musical" as code for "homosexual"), and their shared status as a putative moral threat—music's place here being traceable back to Plato and Aristotle and their cautions about music's effects on the citizenry and its youth. "Lurking beneath [these, Augustine's, and Calvinist] objections against music," Brett writes, "is the long tradition of feeling that it is different, irrational, unaccountable. . . . Nonverbal even when linked to words, physically arousing in its function as initiator of dance, and resisting attempts to endow it with, or discern in it, precise meaning, it represents that part of our culture which is constructed as feminine and therefore dangerous." This gendered and highly charged construction of music tints every musician's identity, queer or straight: As Brett notes, "*All* musicians . . . are faggots in the parlance of the male locker room," and hence the musical profession displays anxious, compensatory preoccupations with mastery, rigor, and competitiveness.[2]

Brett's analysis illumines perilously freighted congruities between musicality and homosexuality as perceived from without, and anxious reactions to these from within the music world. In "On a Lesbian Relationship with Music" Cusick reveals similar congruities, now pleasurably freighted, through an intimate examination from within her own relationship with music as a lesbian, musician, and music-lover. She observes, "For some of us, it might be that the most intense way we express or enact identity through the circulation of physical pleasure is in musical activity, and that our 'sexual identity' might be 'musician' more than it is 'lesbian,' 'gay,' or 'straight.' . . . If music isn't sexuality, for most of us it is psychically right next door."[3] Developing this line of speculation leads Cusick to posit an identity relation: "What if music IS sex?" That is, "If sex [freed of reproductive associations] . . . is then *only* . . . a means of negotiating power and intimacy through the circulation of pleasure, what's to prevent music from *being* sex, and thus an ancient, half-sanctioned form of escape from the constraints of the phallic economy?"[4]

Both music and lesbian sex, in Cusick's figuring, allow a more diffuse channeling of pleasure than does the prevailing phallic economy, and "more varied positions than we think we're allowed in regular life, . . . enabl[ing] us . . . to escape a system . . . of bewilderingly fixed categories, to wallow in the circulation of pleasures that are beyond danger and culturally defined desires." Both realms afford freedom to choose and to change positions within the "power/pleasure/intimacy triad" and consequently, in Cusick's musicianly view, "no one accumulates the consolidated power we call 'identity,' because the pleasure of the game is living in a world free of fixed categories."[5]

This last thought is one I would like to appropriate for my purposes below, of considering categories of meaning and affiliation attaching to certain gay modernist composers. (If I read Cusick fairly, it seems possible to do so in connection with these gay men's status as musicians—thus without ascribing to them any special lesbianism beyond that mirrored, in Cusick's account, by any true music-loving.) We might note the extent to which Cusick's first-person narrative of musical experience, while unmistakably informed by late-twentieth-century sensibilities and postmodern critical perspectives, coincides with earlier modernist testaments to the intimate, desirous, and pleasurable nature of musical experience. And we can find such testaments from ardent music-lovers including not only the young Sam Barber but T. S. Eliot in "The Dry Salvages," from *Four Quartets* (1943):

> music heard so deeply
> That it is not heard at all, but you are the music
> While the music lasts.[6]

Eliot's cathectic representation of a consummate self-music merging describes the particular musical experience that is epitomized by many music-lovers, hearers and players alike. Cusick circles near this idea in her reference to the nonaccumulation of identity in both musical and lesbian-sexual activity. She later homes in on it: "the moments wherein I have felt most fully alive, most fully myself, have been when I have *become* the music." We might invoke Cusick's and Eliot's descriptions of musical experience to address the question (paraphrasing Bersani), "Who are you when you listen to or perform a piece of music?" The answer they suggest is "I am the music—no longer myself and/or more fully myself." For in both of their accounts the supreme musical experience is a music-induced intensification, and dissolution, of subjective identity, an experience in connection with which the phrase *musical identity* resonates at once paradoxically and polysemously.[7]

Cusick's declaration that she has "felt most fully alive" at times when she has "*become* the music" suggests that she has found *jouissance* in moments when she has lost herself, or self-consciousness, in the sort of musicosexual intercourse she chronicles. Eliot's paean to musical penetration extols the same blurring of subjective boundaries and intensely pleasurable loss of self. And these examples elucidate an oppositional pair of thematics arising from modernist musical activity: of identity production and enforcement, and identity resistance and dissolution—both of which are salient in the intensively queer realm of American musical modernism. In such musical examples we may also see—as in Foucault's explorations in s/m, drug use, and gay bathhouse sex—a pursuit of pleasures that exceed interiority, that blur this with exteriority and push against the constraints of modern subjective identity.[8] Here we might further compare Warner's remarks on men who seek in gay public sex "the negation of identity through anonymous contact": He notes that "much of sex lies at the limit of consciousness and will"—that sex "is a kind of experience in which we are supposed to be most ourselves, while at the same time least in control of ourselves."[9]

Relatedly, the musicoeroticism described by Cusick can be seen to afford the same radically *homo-* sexual experience that Bersani highlights in his reading of Gide's *Immoralist*. It, too, "eliminates from 'sex' *the necessity of any relation whatsoever*" and so offers an alternative to "intersubjectivity as we have come to prize it in Western culture." In "gliding into an impersonal sameness" with the object, thereby seeking "nothing more than to touch . . . extensions of himself," the musicosexualist—like Gide's nonpederastic pederast—invites "self-impoverishing self-expansions [that] block the cultural discipline of identification," that is, of *self*hood. But notably, whereas such a means of erotic self-subversion is ultimately judged immoral in its Gidean version, where according to Bersani it violates the real personhood of the other, it remains at least "half sanctioned" (to borrow Cusick's phrase) within musical experience, where the object's (potential) animate "otherness" is merely figurative, clearly *not* real.[10]

Here and elsewhere Bersani acknowledges the possibility and even inevitability of aloneness in sexual relations with others—that is, of "the irrelevance of the object" in sexuality, and even sex's "shattering of the psychic structures that are the precondition for the very establishment of a relation to others."[11] Sex in this view is both a potent source of an intersubjectively grounded sense of self, and a potent technique of self-dissolution, or desubjectivation. In his essay "Is the Rectum a Grave?" Bersani elaborates a definition of the sexual in terms of "a moving between a hyperbolic sense of self and a loss of all consciousness of self." He cites both Foucault and Freud in connection with this notion, particularly the latter's

> speculation, especially in the *Three Essays on the Theory of Sexuality,*
> that sexual pleasure occurs whenever a certain threshold of intensity is
> reached, when the organization of the self is momentarily disturbed by
> sensations or affective processes somehow "beyond" those connected
> with psychic organization. . . . [T]his definition removes the sexual
> from the intersubjective.

Surprisingly, Bersani points to important social benefits of sexuality that accrue to its very "remov[al] . . . from the intersubjective" and its subversion of the self. The self, "a practical convenience," becomes a "sanction for violence" when elevated to the status of an ethical ideal. Thus sexuality, albeit socially dysfunctional in that it "brings people together only to plunge them into a self-shattering and solipsistic *jouissance* that drives them apart," is also "our primary hygienic practice of nonviolence": Its shattering of the psychic structures that are "the precondition for [any] establishment of a relation to others" is a shattering, precisely, of the proud and serious subject, that phallic self willing "to kill in order to protect the seriousness of [his or her] statements."[12] Perhaps the same logic can illuminate certain mechanisms by which another self-shattering technology, music, functioned hygienically as (in Brett's reading) a social anodyne to twentieth-century queer indignation and rage. And further, if we assume that the stigmatization of queer identity would have enhanced the appeal, for queer subjects, of *any* means of escaping subjectivity (as compared with the presumable lesser urgency of such escape for unstigmatized subjects), then we might surmise that music's capacities for desubjectivation contributed to its position as an extraordinary magnet for queer persons—listeners, fans, and professionals—during the markedly homophobic decades, of the 1930s to 1950s, that comprise the focus of this book.

Both Cusick and Eliot describe an experience and a perception of music as a potent, pleasure-giving solvent, capable of dispersing and thus subverting identity. It is useful to acknowledge this perception, which very likely played a central role throughout the twentieth century in many musicians' self-identification *as* musicians. But such acknowledgment must not be taken to imply that an involvement with music allows a musician, any more than anyone else, to escape the sociopolitical operations and impositions of identity categories (on the contrary, a musician's identification may only bring on more, and more arcane, categories, as in Ned Rorem's formulations, below). Indeed, Cusick's rhapsody on the pleasures of "living in a world free of fixed categories" underscores the extraordinariness, the anomaly, of the escape experience that music and/as lesbian sex offers, from the perspective of one who lives within the "fixed categories," musician and lesbian, that accrue to this very experience. We might similarly note that young Sam Barber circa 1919 articulates his "worrying secret" as a problem of identity, of being a composer versus being an athlete—and not one of, say, compositional versus athletic *acts*. Certainly "musician" served as a decisive identity category when Bowles was labeled 4-F, deemed psychiatrically unfit for World War II military service on the basis of his being someone who "[wrote] symphonies" (in yet another demonstration of the U.S. Army's canniness as herald of sociosexual actuality).[13]

Brett's and Cusick's notions of musical and/as (homo-) sexual identity appeared in the 1990s, but their aptness to earlier discourses of musical modernism is readable through various historical texts. Brett's analysis of the sexual anxieties attending Anglo-American musicality is, in fact, formulated specifically in relation to the midcentury modernist composer Benjamin Britten. And we have already examined the musical, sexual, and cultural anxieties expressed by the experimental modernist Ives and in the 1910s–20s sex-gender panic around American music. All these instances attest the forceful operations of identity in the earlier twentieth century and the sex-gender anxiety attending musical identity in particular, and thus provide crucial contextualization for any consideration of modernist composers, male or female, straight or queer.

ROREM'S TAXONOMY

The foregoing discussion and its quotations of Barber, Brett, Cusick, and Eliot suggest some qualities—intimate, pleasurable, homosexualized—associated with musical identity and identification in twentieth-century America. The following passage lends these constructs a further dimension: Reflecting insider positioning and acutely self-conscious musical, sexual, ethnic, and other identifications, it presents not so much a picture of modern musical identity as a dazzling plurality of highly particularized modern musical *identities:*

> Harpists (of whom, like hairdressers and cooks, most are women though the best are men) are all homosexual—the males, that is. Male string players are all Jewish and all heterosexual. Male brass players, wind players, and percussionists, though not necessarily Jewish, are also all heterosexual, at least those in orchestras; among soloists the percentage wavers. Of male pianists, also mostly Jewish, half are gay. ("Gay" was not standard usage then, at least among straights.) Male organists, all gay. Of classical singers no tenors are gay, most baritones are, but few females. In jazz the reverse obtains: the women are lesbian, the men are macho—but alcoholic. Choir directors, all gay. Among composers, who until the war had been mainly Gentile and defiantly effete (Thomson, Griffes) or defiantly virile (Ives, Sessions) the ratio was fifty-fifty. The ratio remained fifty-fifty. Stravinsky's flock of Americans, which overlapped with Aaron Copland's, was straight and Jewish. Virgil [Thomson]'s was mixed. (Rumors still abound that Aaron championed mainly his gay entourage. What entourage? Leo Smit, Irving Fine, Arthur Berger, Harold Shapero? For a gay goy like me he never lifted a finger.)

This taxonomy—indeed, cosmology—was first articulated in 1948 by Ned Rorem, then twenty-five, in an informal conversation with Dr. Alfred Kinsey. The conversation followed a formal interview that the young composer granted for Kinsey's famed sex research. Some forty-six years later, in his 1994 memoir *Knowing When to Stop*, Rorem reproduced the passage, adding some postscript annotations and an explanatory introduction: "Since I knew more than Kinsey about who 'was' and who 'wasn't' among musicians, I generalized as follows."[14]

Surely there are any number of points in this excerpt on which one might comment. One could start with the breezy, smug misogyny with which Rorem launches his list. Or with Rorem's bold brandishing of sensitive labels like *gay, alcoholic, Jew,* and *goy;* its inflection by his self-identification elsewhere with three of these, *gay, alcoholic,* and *goy;* and his self-avowed erotic penchant for persons under the remaining one, *Jew.*[15] One might also remark Rorem's tone, particularly his terse pronouncements in absolute terms of "all," "none," or "fifty-fifty," which underlines the need for any attuned reading here to be conversant with classic gay camp, and hence to locate itself at camp's rhetorically potent juncture of grave seriousness and transparent artifice.

Another telling aspect of Rorem's ascriptive litany is its construction as a taxonomy, and one with a specifically sexual dimension. Sexual taxonomy making enjoyed a heyday around the mid–nineteenth century when various categories of human sexual type were posited, such as the masturbator, the pedophile, and the zoophile, and sexual definition became a central locus of modern meaning and power.[16] But the taxonomic impetus (as Sedgwick has pointed out) later radically condensed, leaving only one classificatory lens—that focusing on the sexual configuration between an individual and his or her chosen object (i.e., same or different)—to determine *tout court* what would come to be known as "sexual orientation."[17] Rorem's taxonomy of musicosexual types is thus an undertaking thoroughly modern in spirit and puts a special, musical twist on the constructions of sexologists like Ulrichs, Krafft-Ebing, Hirschfeld, and Freud.

Taxonomic in form, in substance Rorem's litany invokes nearly all of the most pervasive and powerful categories of social differentiation and hence of identity construction operative in America circa 1948—namely, gender, race-ethnicity, and sexuality, arising here in terms of male versus female, Jew versus Gentile, homo versus hetero. Rorem's particular taxonomy emerges from the linkage of these differentiations, central and hegemonic, with a second set, arcane and largely opaque for the majority of his contemporaries: harpists versus string players, section players versus soloists, tenors versus baritones, Stravinskians versus Thomsonites. As such, it speaks from the doubly rarefied intersection of the already rarefied realms Rorem occupied, as a member of both the contemporary gay subculture and the American classical music world—this latter referred to by Thomson as "Our Island Home." Hence Rorem's deliciously droll excerpt also deserves our serious attention: His armchair taxonomizing bespeaks a vantage point that was significantly and rather singularly shared by the members of his important artistic circle and was, I contend, vitally implicated in their constructions of identity, style, and musical idiom.

RECASTING THE CIRCLE

We have already variously invoked a particular artistic circle comprising Virgil Thomson, Aaron Copland, Marc Blitzstein, Paul Bowles, Leonard Bernstein, David Diamond, and Ned Rorem. We shall now define this circle more specifically *as* a circle, by demonstrating the links and commonalities among its members as well as its historical identity as a circle, its having been perceived as such. But first we might qualify the very notion of an artistic circle by noting that all such circles are dynamic and infinitely overlapping: Circles of various sizes and constituencies coexist in a given pool of contemporaries, and any such circle may be selected out for the particular narrative purposes at hand. Among the dramatis personae constituting the present circle, we can see several significant shared identity attributes: All were white, male, American modernist composers active on the New York music scene in the 1940s; all associated closely with a plurality of the others; all worked within a tonal idiom of relative clarity and simplicity; and all were, or are, queer-identified.[18]

Accordingly, one might argue for the further inclusion of composers like Samuel Barber, John Cage, and Lou Harrison in the present group, but I view them as occupying skirting circles, as I do (for example) William Flanagan, Donald Fuller, Robert Helps, Lee Hoiby, Daniel Pinkham, and Charles Turner. Barber and his life partner Gian Carlo Menotti were tonalists, but their tonality was distinctly different from the lean Americana variety: It was Brahmsian via Rosario Scalero (their teacher at Curtis) and was thus affiliated with the German Romanticism against which Copland and Thomson self-consciously constructed their art. John Cage, Lou Harrison, and Harry Partch formed around Henry Cowell what must be counted as a queer modernist circle in its own right.[19] Both Harrison and Cage had close ties with Thomson, too, but musically the former four composers were experimentalists, with no interest or involvements in tonal nationalism.[20]

Alternatively, one might argue against any presumption of cohesiveness within the gay tonalists' circle identified here by pointing out, for example, that the tonal idiom of a Copland is a thing apart from that of, say, Rorem. And indeed it is, in numerous identifiable ways. Still, by Rorem's own account his music was grouped under the Coplandiana label in the 1940s, insofar as it was "diatonic, even nonmodulatory in the extreme" and

clearly not subsumable under the opposing rubric of "twelve-tonish" composition.[21] Finally, one might object to the present grouping on grounds
that Copland and Thomson themselves should occupy separate circles, as
indeed Rorem indicates at points in his writing, thus reproducing the dipo-
lar archetype accruing to Schoenberg and Stravinsky, Brahms and Wagner.
But ample evidence points to multiple overlappings of Copland's and
Thomson's circles—via Rorem and Bowles, for instance—and moreover to
their own long-standing and mutually important collegial and friendly
association. Rorem himself, amid his talk of "rival factions," dubs Copland
and Thomson the "father and mother of American music," which suggests
a closer conjunction even as it drops camp-coded clues to their respective
sexual and gender styles.[22]

In defining a gay modernists' circle encompassing Copland, Thomson,
and the others, I emphatically make no claims for the inevitability of this
particular grouping, nor for any naturalized, numinous, or essential gay
musical brotherhood, aesthetics, or idiom. This gay composers' circle is a
construction—and for present purposes, a heuristic as well. It is not my construction, however, but one that operates tacitly and explicitly in discourses
from Copland and Thomson's time up to our own. Within the history
(extending as far back as Ives, though still mostly buried) surrounding a
binary opposition of "gay composer" and "straight composer" and its workings in American musical modernism, the circle of New York gay Americana
composers has been regarded as a more or less cohesive body since the 1940s
(certain composers being added or subtracted in various accounts). This
point is illustrated most dramatically by the conspiracy theories that centered on the group in their 1940s prime and charged them with operating as
a secret cabal to control the music world from their gay Manhattan head-
quarters, denying access and power to straight male colleagues in America
while Britten, Pears, and Tippett ran the London branch.[23]

Another invocation of the gay modernists' circle attests the grouping's
enduring epistemic vitality in latter-day musical thinking and discourse:
That is, Susan McClary's 1994 statements in the *New York Times* on American modernist composers, which are poised so as to cluster the "gay" modernists together and in connection with the attributes "tonal" and "popular," in contradistinction to modernists figured as "straight," "atonal," and
"elitist."[24] These formulations, like those of the 1940s conspiracy theorists,
are not merely descriptive but overtly valuative. But whereas the conspiracy theorists reproduce both the straight-gay dichotomy and the status quo
homophobic valuation it serves to enforce, McClary's statements reproduce the dichotomy and reverse its valuations.

McClary further seems to say not simply that straight modernists happened to be difficult (read: complex, atonal), elitist, and unpopular, and their gay contemporaries accessible (read: simple, tonal) and popular, but rather that she infers some more significant connection, beyond random coincidence, between modernist composers' sexual identities and their musical and ideological styles. That McClary's public articulation of such a notion is rare, perhaps unprecedented, does not mean that she invented it ex nihilo. On the contrary, her statement frankly references a cluster of attributions long circulated in more furtive and disavowed, hence quite potent, forms. Its history is traceable to the first third of the twentieth century and connects with the still-older history of a more general practice of sexual classification of musicians (especially) by musicians. We can trace this history in Ives's fulminations against "sissy" composers and their putatively ruinous influence, and in the 1930s and 1940s purges of homosexual faculty and students from the Eastman School under Howard Hanson's directorship. Both instances exhibit a concern—or more precisely, an obsession—with classifying musicians in hetero/homosexual terms. And, notably, both attach to the "homo" term the same fiercely negative valuation.[25]

RHETORIC AND ENCODINGS:
SEXUAL POLITICS IN MUSICAL MODERNISM

But there is another, nearly opposite, historical phenomenon evinced here, particularly in Ives's rhetoric—that of a musical discursive practice remarkable for its preoccupation with "homosexual" precisely as this does *not* attach to actual persons. When Ives remarks of Chopin, for example, "one just naturally thinks of him with a skirt on, but one which he made himself," the simultaneous effeminizing and queering implications of the statement are unmistakable.[26] Yet Chopin was, as Ives surely knew, a conspicuously heterosexualized figure, famously associated with a female lover, George Sand (among other female love objects).[27] Thus a literal reading, one that called into question Chopin's normative sexuality, would render Ives's remark meaningless. But in fact the remark would have been abundantly meaningful within the music world, understood here in its proper function of music criticism—as calling into question, on multiple fronts, the value of Chopin's music by invoking terms of gender and sexuality. Ives placed his remark into an established music-critical tradition in which qualities of gender and sexuality were made to figure qualities of musicality. Indeed, Chopin's "skirt" here is a complex and heavy garment: It weaves together scorned images of the old European cultural order,

French aristocracy, and their perceived music-stylistic emblems, and presents these in the form of ultimate fear, loathing, and ridicule, as a feminized, emasculating object.[28] Within the present argument Ives's modernist rhetoric may ramify in yet another direction: For whereas in Ives we see queer sexuality encoding certain musical meanings, in Sam Barber we saw the converse, musical designations encoding sexual meanings.

We can find further illustration of the modernist musicosexual order, and of the reciprocity of musical-homosexual coding just noted, in the story of Virgil Thomson's first meeting with Ben Weber. Thomson characteristically began his questioning of the younger composer with a non-question: "I hear that you are homosexual." Weber affirmed that he was. Thomson continued, "I hear that you're a twelve-tone composer." Weber affirmed this too. "Well," Thomson rejoined, "you can't be both. Now which is it?"[29] Among the American dodecaphonists of his generation, which included Perle, Babbitt, and Carter, Weber was indeed the only homosexual.[30] With his tongue-in-cheek mandate Thomson invoked (at least half seriously) a "nonce taxonomy" of his own that was, like Rorem's, essentially "musicosexual"; and he showed thereby a self-conscious awareness of the centrality of homo-hetero definition in the music world.[31] He thus also described some contours of the landscape he inhabited: It contained serialist and nonserialist composers, who were, to whatever extent, heterosexuals and homosexuals, respectively.[32] And we should not be misled by the absolute terms in which Thomson stated the correlation: When he had finished, neither category, serialist/nonserialist or heterosexual/homosexual, was indicated as progenitor or prime determinant of meaning; indeed, they appear as mutually constitutive, each figuring the other. What *is* indicated in Thomson's characteristic tone is his legendary and epigrammatic camp ("It was like living with Oscar Wilde," the architect Philip Johnson once remarked of Thomson as houseguest). And this is a significant point, as mainstream ignorance of camp codes has at times given rise to consequential misreadings of Thomson's words and his music.[33]

Ned Rorem, in a 1994 passage recounting his own first meeting with Ben Weber in 1943, inscribed a related recollection: "Once I quipped that some of my best friends were twelve-tone composers." Rorem described the landscape of "two generations" earlier as offering a fashionable, diatonic, Coplandian camp and an unfashionable, twelve-tone, Schoenbergian camp. "One didn't have friends in both camps," he averred. Hence his erstwhile parody of the classic liberal phrase "Some of my best friends are ———," wherein the blank designates some identity group that is alien to and estranged from one's own and (crucially for Rorem's joke) the purported beneficiary of the speaker's largesse. Whether or not Rorem circa midcentury meant his quip to imply any sexual group identity, it clearly implies a vastness in the gulf separating the worlds of diatonic and twelve-tone composers. In either case, the Rorem of 1994 expressly linked questions of sexuality and compositional voice here, musing that Weber's "heart was tonal," and that if he had been heterosexual, "all other things being equal, his music would have been different."[34]

Now, it is not my point to claim that the stereotypic associations highlighted here were either accurate or justifiable, but rather to remark their historical existence and influence. There were, of course, many prominent straight-identified composers of tonal Americana music, including Roy Harris, Douglas Moore, William Schuman, and Harold Shapero, to name a few. And there were, even beyond Ben Weber, homosexual-identified composers of non-Americana as well as nontonal bents. These included the experimentalists Cage, Cowell, Harrison, and Partch as well as the "conservative" Samuel Barber (whose tonal idiom, being Brahmsian, would have been perceived by Copland and some others almost as antithetical to Thomson's or Copland's lucid "French" tonality). But, these facts notwithstanding, the ideology of the time linked tonality—particularly of the neoclassical and (beginning in the late thirties) Coplandian strains—with homosexuality, and defined it by contrast to nontonality or atonality—especially of dissonant and serial leanings—and masculine heterosexuality. The latter association readily connects with earlier Ivesian rhetoric—particularly of the "a good dissonance [is] like a man" variety—and with Ives's (and comparably, Ruggles's) compositional practice, in which, as Lawrence Kramer aptly observes, "the innovative energy of his music is fringed by defensive [sex-gender] panic . . . made audible in the arbitrary harshness and discontinuity on which Ives so candidly prided himself."[35] If express articulation of these sexuality-to-style associations was—like discussion of sexuality generally—taboo and thus rare, their past and recent hegemony in the music world is nevertheless evident in various surfacings.

The composer Robert Parris (1924–1999), for example, in his 1994 letter to the *New York Times* recounting the Thomson-Weber anecdote, concluded, "Perhaps Weber was one of those exceptions that prove the rule. But," he added, *"the mystery behind the 'rule' remains."* It is conceivable that the "unimpeachable (though secondhand) authority" on which Parris stakes his anecdote in the *Times* might have been that of Copland. For indeed Copland, decades earlier, had been Parris's teacher. In Parris's *Times* correspondence, however, that relationship goes unmentioned, and the source of his campy and irreverent queer anecdote is discreetly left anonymous. One thing the heterosexual-identified Parris did make clear in 1994 was his own subscription, undoubtedly conditioned by the music-world order of his time, to Thomson's apparent notion of a "rule" whose governings ("myster[ious]," according to Parris) linked gay modernist composers, perhaps exclusively, to tonal music.[36]

In an ostentatiously homophobic 1951 article published in the *American Mercury* under the title "The New Taste in Humor," Alfred Towne gives an analysis of homosexual humor that seems apt to the Thomson-Weber anecdote: Such humor functions to bring "out in the open . . . something that is forbidden," according to Towne—who exhorts that it should remain hidden. Here that forbidden something—an acknowledgment of the preponderance of homosexuals in American musical modernism, and a perception of their special relationship to tonality—appears to have kept gay and straight composers alike alternately biting and wagging their tongues for decades.[37]

The potency and persistence of the notion of a gay-tonal linkage is illustrated in another anecdote, conveyed to me by a colleague in 1999. The story concerns a well-known American composer who was teaching in the early 1970s at an Ivy League school. The composer was at pains to assure an undergraduate pupil (my colleague) that the tonal writing he had recently taken up, having abandoned his previous twenty years' cultivation of atonality, had "no relation to the tonality of a Britten or a Rorem." Perhaps this straight-identified composer would claim not to have had any thought in this instance of sexuality or gender, but only of schools of "purely" musical affiliation and style. The names he invoked signify tellingly nevertheless: Britten and Rorem were not the only well-known tonalists of the period, nor were they kindred in compositional style or outlook. The most conspicuous distinction shared between the Briton and the American was their status as the most famously homosexual figures in the modern music world. In fact, high-profile tonalists of the time included numerous nonqueer composers, such as Leslie Bassett, Walter Piston, and Karel Husa—all 1960s Pulitzer Prize winners in composition—but this tonal convert had expressed no anxiety about comparison with these artists. His invoking here instead Britten and Rorem might point to a lag between the musicosexual reputation of tonal writing and its actuality in this period. If so, the instance illustrates a remarkable persistence within the music world of queer-tonal associations, perhaps reflecting the logic of taint or miscegenation, by which something once marked with a stigmatized meaning cannot readily regain a neutral, unmarked status.

Undoubtedly, too, it illustrates the persistence of dualistic conceptions of music-stylistic affiliation, whose history in European art music is traceable through the *stile antico/stile moderno* and Brahms/Wagner controversies of the seventeenth and nineteenth centuries, among others. In the 1920s, Schoenberg, the inventor of twelve-tone "atonality," was at pains to discourage what appeared to many observers as the dualism most apt to the contemporary musical landscape: tonal/atonal. Schoenberg particularly resisted certain attributions that clustered here casting the atonal pole—hence his project—as a radical break from musical tradition, construed in terms of a Viennese succession including Haydn, Mozart, Beethoven, Schubert, and Mahler. Given that Schoenberg defined himself above all in relation to this lineage, it is hardly surprising that he rejected "tonal/atonal" as the pivotal dichotomy for genealogical, historical, and stylistic identity in modernist composition. As we shall soon discuss, Schoenberg's *Three Satires*, op. 28, shows him mocking the question *"tonal oder atonal?"* (tonal or atonal?) in movement 1, and in movement 3 proposing an alternative binarism: Schoenberg/Stravinsky.

STAKING A CLAIM ABOUT QUEER NETWORKING: A REVERSE DISCOURSE

Much of the foregoing discussion makes a bid to reconstitute the group of gay modernists around Copland and Thomson. We will seek thereby to engage the still-resounding question of what an artist's homosexuality might have to do with his or her work, and more specifically with the question of how these particular artists managed to achieve preeminence in the high-culture mainstream while residing in certain stigmatized sociocultural margins. Our approach to both questions involves examining the construction on this site of personal and professional identities and of compositional idioms, from within and against prevailing cultural contexts. Here we will consider the role of the usual identity binarisms—including those of gender, race, and sexuality—plus a few far less usual that emerge as potently meaningful within this group.

Among the further questions raised by this inquiry is one broached in the introduction: What is at stake in acknowledging such facts of gay lives, achievements, and presence so long and fiercely silenced? Any attempt to answer this question must reckon with the constant shifting of the cultural and political stakes involved. What is at stake as you read these words in the early twenty-first century is different from what was at stake in the

1930s, the 1940s, or the Cold War 1950s for the composers in question, their rivals, American music, or American national identity. The stakes importantly shifted from the twenties to the late thirties, when the crisis over the perceived lack of an American music was brought to an end by the musical solutions Copland and others put forward. In the thirties and forties higher stakes attached to concealing queer identities, as their representation in American culture was increasingly regulated and proscribed. With the dawn of the fifties and the Cold War, the social and political stakes in identity and identification were critical and frequently quite visible in American composition, as the next chapter will show.

From the 1930s to the present, however, at least one issue has always been at stake in any acknowledgment of queer involvements in American music: That is, disclosure of the pivotal role of homosexual persons and sensibilities in a modernist musical idiom that came to define the very essence of twentieth-century American national identity—of *mainstream* America, even, in all its radical disidentification with queerness. We might note a striking paradox here, in the fact that queer artists should have served, during this deeply homophobic era in America, as architects of American national identity. Our inquiries into this circumstance will complicate its apparent paradoxicalism. For, it turns out, the modern figure of the homosexual—as outsider—shows a marked congruity with, and a historical relation to, modern conceptions of artistic identity and genius.[38]

But our immediate concern lies elsewhere, in tracing the particular identificatory paths along which homosexuality was inscribed in twentieth-century music of American national identity. We will begin by identifying several themes shared among members of the gay modernist circle named above—of Thomson, Copland, and company—and contemplating their possible significance. These themes emerge from certain shared musical-biographical motifs, in addition to the composers' homosexual identification—particularly those of foreign apprenticeship, especially in Paris; studies with Nadia Boulanger; self-conscious affiliation with things French, often in express opposition to things German; and cultivation of a tonal, perhaps neoclassical, compositional idiom, usually pursuing clarity and economy.[39] Our argument here will be that these motifs provide key elements of an influential definitional axis—heterosexual/homosexual, complex/simple, atonal/tonal, German/French—along which gay modernists created identities for themselves and for American music, and colleagues and commentators sometimes targeted them with homophobic censures and conspiracy theories.

The remainder of this chapter thus illuminates the centrality of homo/ hetero identity in the musical politics and styles of American modernism from the 1930s through World War II. Already by the 1920s, however, the axis just outlined had begun to take shape. Examining the scene of New York musical modernism in that decade, Oja notes that, "[i]ncreasingly, consonant music . . . was linked with women or effeminacy, while dissonance was quickly labeled 'manly' or 'virile.'" Elsewhere she flags contemporaneous associations of tonal neoclassicists with femininity, homosexuality, and "impotence," and with Boulanger as female teacher:

> Gendered language was used against the so-called neoclassicists of the day, . . . most of [whom] had studied or had extensive contact with Nadia Boulanger, a female teacher. And a few key figures, most notably Copland and Thomson, were gay. In aesthetic arguments of the period . . . "neoclassicism" often was posed as the antithesis of "experimentation." Thus in a gendered scheme, neoclassicism became feminine—or "impotent," as Edgard Varèse was on record as saying— and experimentation was masculine, as Ives registered it.[40]

In addition to the workings of clustered gender-sexual-national-stylistic associations (i.e., here: "closet codes") the present argument highlights the crucial role of gay social-sexual-professional networks not only in the lives and careers of the gay composers under examination but, more broadly, in the creation and operations of twentieth-century American modernist and Americana music. This analysis also illuminates the homophobic mechanisms that have served to enforce the virtually complete and universal silence that has, until now, attended the facts of these gay composers' networks. These mechanisms have granted exclusive space to rumorous incriminations about gay networks, in part by rendering any acknowledgment of them immediately rumorous and incriminatory (regardless of intent).

Under such a discursive-ideological regime, guard-keeping over long-held secrets of homosexual networks and their importance in American music has been nowhere more fervent than among gay composers, performers, and musicologists themselves. This should not be surprising if only for the fact, as noted by Chauncey of the pre-Stonewall New York gay male world, that "a central requirement of the moral code that governed gay life and bound gay men to one another was that they honor other men's decisions to keep their homosexuality a secret and do all they could to help protect that secret from outsiders."[41] And I would stress that this code is still in place "post-Stonewall," being honored to this day, by many

FIGURE 7. The choral conductor Robert Shaw, Leonard Bernstein, and Marc Blitzstein recording Blitzstein's *Airborne Symphony*, 1946. Wisconsin Center for Film and Theater Research.

men and women whose ethical habits were conditioned by the harsh homophobic realities of an earlier era (hence my scare quotes around "post-Stonewall," with its connotations of historical slate wiping and overnight transformation). The evidence can be seen in instances like Lawrence D. Mass's "Interview with Ned Rorem," with its glaring generational disjuncture between the gay sensibilities of composer and interviewer on questions of sexuality and its suitability to public discourses on art and artists.[42]

We have noted the persistence of the negative, condemnatory valences attaching to the facts of gay networking in the twentieth-century American composition world, the facts of gay white men's prevalence here with respect to their various and productive personal and professional interrelations—giving and receiving moral and material support and guidance, knowledge and contacts, in roles variously collegial, familial, and intimate. Within the context thus produced, which has persisted for many decades, it has been most advantageous—even and especially from an antihomophobic standpoint—to discuss the remarkable collective and individual successes of gay composers *without* reference to any queer collectivity. For to acknowledge networks or networking among homosexual modernists at all is to invoke the specter and indictment of the "homosexual syndicate," and insinuations about gay composers as cheaters whose cunning and clubbishness (founded on shared perversion) outweighed their genuine talent and achievement.

Thus in writing this book and directing it to antihomophobic ends, I must seek to effect something akin to Foucault's "reversal of the discourse." Halperin explains a "reverse discourse" as one that "recapitulate[s] in an affirmative vein" a prior oppressive discourse, "while strategically reversing the object- and subject-positions assigned by it."[43] Foucault cites the example of the early homosexual emancipation movement, whose members reiterated the terms of pathology and perversion wielded against them from about the 1870s by psychologists and physicians, but strategically turned these around. He characterizes their move: "All right, we are what you say we are—by nature, disease, or perversion, as you like. Well, if that's what we are, let's be it, and if you want to know what we are, we can tell you ourselves better than you can." The effect, Foucault observes, is that of "strategic turnabout of one and the 'same' will to truth."[44]

Foucault's notion of reverse discourse can elucidate some crucial aspects of the definitional axis sketched above. Its profile of homosexual (as tonal, simple, etc.) composers presents characterizations that were variously embraced from within and imposed from without, hence that functioned as both self-affiliations and objectifying stereotypes. Where, then, in this gay tonalist profile do we locate the line between the etic and the emic, between reductive reckonings of the Other and informed representations of the self's truths? The answer is that, in an important sense, there is no such line. Twentieth-century homosexual subjects and their nonhomosexual contemporaries both found their conceptions of (sexual and other) identity in the same cultural knowledge bases. Hence the point of queer histories generally is to show, not how queer subjects engaged any separate or unique set of cultural definitions, identities, and practices from that engaged by their nonqueer coevals, but rather how they operated either more or less productively within and against those definitions, identities, and practices that structured the historical and cultural moment in which they lived. Accordingly, the definitional axis presented above should be understood to begin at the modernist preoccupation with identity—with classifying subjects in terms of race, nationality, gender, sexuality, and other individual and collective, personal and professional identity constructs.

CREATIVE IDENTIFICATIONS

Another preoccupation, carried over into modernism from Romanticism, is that of defining the identity of the artist. This concern connects readily with the Romantic-modern artist's aura as producer, and with the ardent, sometimes covetous, desire thus attaching to the identity "artist." Such desire certainly attaches to the identity of the musician, as witness several instances already cited in this chapter (e.g., involving Barber, Cusick, Ives, Rorem). Inspired in music's devotees by its extraordinary penetrative powers, this desire is intensified by cultural constructions of talent (e.g., as inborn, ineffable, unlearnable) that regulate one's achievement, or failure, in acquiring the consecrated status of "musician."[45] Further illustration of this desire can be found in the considerable energy with which musicians routinely map their own lineages within the classical music world, as when, for example, a pianist declares herself a student of a student of Liszt.

Indeed, Liszt seems especially oft cited in this regard. For example, Marc Blitzstein in his student days "proudly claimed Siloti as his teacher, thereby making himself a 'grandson' of Liszt." In fact, Alexander Siloti not only studied piano with Liszt in Weimar (1883–86), but had earlier studied theory with Tchaikovsky in Moscow.[46] Thus Blitzstein could have readily claimed a lineage from Tchaikovsky—as Lou Harrison would later do even without any particular teacher-pupil link (see below). That Blitzstein as teenage virtuoso (ca. 1922–25) emphasized his Lisztian lineage might reflect an early stage in the development of his personal and musical identity—one, perhaps, in which "composer" (versus "performer") and "homosexual" did not yet occupy the place they would occupy in his adult self-identity. But it is also conceivable that the adult Blitzstein too, a mustached queer top with a penchant for rough trade, would have identified more with Liszt, avatar of potent virtuosity, than with Tchaikovsky, frequent symbol (e.g., in connection with the "Pathétique" Symphony) of a frail and fatal Romantic sensitivity.[47]

The play of markedly masculinized and feminized images here can usefully suggest the centrality of gender as well as sexuality (as defined by the sex relation, of sameness or difference, between subject and object) in modern "sexual identity" formations, and ways in which these can cut against—or concur with—conventional associations of male homosexuality with effeminacy, and lesbianism with mannishness. In these terms, even within the present, relatively homogeneous circle of gay tonal composers, homosexual identity is no monolith. For if homosexual identity in Rorem and Thomson appears to have correlated to effeminacy, that of Bernstein,

Blitzstein, and Copland did not; nor did Thomson himself betray such tendencies in his *public* persona. Moreover, as the foregoing proposes in relation to Blitzstein, even in connection with a particular subject, identity in this regard (and others) is mutable over time.

We might return now to the Romantic-modern identity of the artist. Notably, this is cast in terms of the outsider, a singular individual, characteristically male (as Gertrude Stein had occasion to remark) and specifically positioned outside society. And the modern homosexual, a figure born at the twilight of the nineteenth century, is likewise defined above all in terms of his or her positioning outside society and its norms—which outsider status here is further inflected as degenerate or pitiable, and so on. Thus we see a congruity between the coveted identity of musician—or, in its most artistically exalted form, composer—and the ostensibly abject identity of homosexual, and hence the potential for reassignment or at least slippage between their conventionally opposing valuations. In other words, the parallels between the identities of composer and homosexual open up possibilities for a depreciation of the former, an appreciation of the latter, and even for the existence of some special correlation between the two.

We know from the reactive vitriol of figures like Ives that the possibility of music's depreciation-by-homosexual-association did register on certain nongay-identified parties. A less ponderable question is whether the foregoing cluster of possibilities registered, presumably with different effect, on persons themselves simultaneously occupying both homosexual and composer categories. For to confront this question would entail acknowledgment that homosexual-identified modernist composers might have found space within which to regard their sexuality, in relation to their creative-artistic identity, as a nonliability—or even as a special, inborn, and exclusive *asset*.[48] Hence this question is "less ponderable" because it is fraught with taboo, colliding as it does not only with the prevailing heterosexism and homophobia of American culture but with its idealized images of a caste-free democratic social structure (which would reject any such notion of inborn privilege).

It is also possible, of course, that the same implications—of homosexuality as a creative asset—registered on nongay colleagues and observers, and contributed (as jealousy) to the homophobic anxiety and hostility that sometimes erupted around the gay modernists' circle. And indeed, fulfilling the identity requirements of the modern artist was perhaps easier for Copland, Thomson, and company than for such compatriots as Hemingway, Jackson Pollock, and other macho modernists whose attainment of outsider status exacted such a heavy, effortful toll in self destruction.[49]

Evidence that gay modernist composers actually conceived of their sexual and creative-artistic identities in positive relation to one another comes
from the intriguing testimony of Lou Harrison (1917–2003), who referred
to his having "early learned" that Tchaikovsky and "the divine Mr. Handel" were gay, like the two prominent American modernist composers,
Henry Cowell and Virgil Thomson, whom he identified as his principal
mentors.[50] "Early" in Harrison's career much of the official knowledge of
Tchaikovsky not only ignored homoerotic possibilities, but plied heterocentric insinuations and fictions focusing on his ephemeral marriage and
his relationship with his patron Madame von Meck. And apropos Handel,
the first musicological discussion of his possible homosexuality—Gary
Thomas's 1990 presentation to the American Musicological Society—
followed Harrison's "underground" revelation at a half-century's distance,
and even then aroused considerable controversy in the mainstream. More
important here than the veracity or verifiability of any claims about Handel's homosexuality, however, is the folkloric circulation of knowledge
among queer musicians.[51]

Chauncey documents some of the means and mechanisms by which
queer persons and their allies produced and circulated queer histories, creating a largely oral and underground queer tradition in an era when such
discourse scarcely existed in print or other official media. He traces these
queer folkloric and other historical practices back to about the same time in
the late nineteenth century when the homosexual was defined and made
the object of pathologizing attributions. The classics scholar John Adding-
ton Symonds's 1883 essay on male same-sex love in ancient Greece was
suppressed by the British government, but *Ioläus*, Edward Carpenter's
compilation of "writings on male 'friendship'" (including Byron, Shakespeare, Whitman, and ancient Greek and Roman sources), was published in
1917 and would influence queer readers for years to come. By the 1930s
such readers could find lists of their own purported ancestors among the
great in the popular gay novels *Strange Brother* (1931) and *Better Angel*
(1933).[52] And as I suggested in chapter 1, Stein and Thomson's 1934 opera
Four Saints is in part a construction of homosexual prehistory, mapping a
lineage from modern homosexual artists back to early modern Catholic
monastics and saints.

A 1935 letter places Sigmund Freud among the subscribers to certain
homosexual historical narratives then circulating: "Many highly respectable individuals of ancient and modern times have been homosexuals,
several of the greatest men among them," Freud wrote to an American

mother seeking his "help" for her homosexual son. He lists some examples, "Plato, Michelangelo, Leonardo da Vinci, etc.," before continuing: "It is a great injustice to persecute homosexuality as a crime and a cruelty too. If you do not believe me, read the books of Havelock Ellis." Freud thus recommends to his correspondent—and perhaps more deliberately, to her son—another prime source of queer historical narratives being passed among homosexual readers of the era.[53] In a related vein, we might note that the American sex researcher Alfred Kinsey gathered extensive data in the 1940s for a planned study of sexuality in the arts, possibly with expectations of finding some significant relation between homosexuality and creativity.[54]

Even up to the present, no light has been shed on the workings of the genealogical-historical oral tradition among gay composers that is evidenced by Harrison's statements, or on the mechanisms by which its knowledge was gleaned and conveyed. On the latter point I would posit two possible scenarios, in the form of questions: Did gay modernist composers reach a verdict on Handel's sexuality contemporarily and intuitively, via posthumous "gaydar" readings of his music, texts, and dramas? Or did word of Handel's social and sexual liaisons carry through generations of musicians, from his associates, lovers, and pupils, to theirs, and so on, over some 180 years down to Harrison and his circle of gay twentieth-century classical musicians?

As a longtime denizen of the classical music world and its queer subculture, I find both of these possibilities viable. But clearly, no matter how his notions about Tchaikovsky and Handel reached him, Harrison's mention of them was situated precisely in a sentence that served to define his own place in a musical lineage. And it is specifically a *gay* musical lineage. He began, "My two main mentors, Henry Cowell and Virgil Thomson, were gay," before leaping historically back (and geographically over) to retrieve Tchaikovsky and Handel.[55] Others, including Harrison's own students (one of whom is among *my* former students), could undoubtedly deepen and widen the genealogy thus sketched, as in: The gay Henry Cowell taught not only the gay Lou Harrison but likewise the gay John Cage (who also studied, like the gay Marc Blitzstein, with the straight Schoenberg).[56] Cage's friend Harrison worked as an assistant to the gay Virgil Thomson, as did the gay Ned Rorem, who studied with both Thomson and the gay Aaron Copland and would years later teach *(my* former classmate) the lesbian composer Jennifer Higdon—and so on. One could go very much further with this, and what is perhaps most remarkable is that so many musicians do. Indeed, classical musicians cultivate keen awareness of their place in an extensive musical family tree—and hence of their membership in certain musical communities, and of the attendant myth and lore—and they make such awareness a fundamental basis of their artistic and personal identities.

FRENCHNESS AS QUEER AMERICANNESS

Surely such awareness was cultivated among the gay modernist circle named here, who defined their place in relation to various identifications, several of which we have already touched on: aesthetic simplicity, tonality, homosexuality. I now propose that one further identification, Frenchness, functioned pivotally to ground and interlink these others—and thus constituted a French connection, so to speak. Frenchness was othered, effeminized, and sexualized from both the vantage point of Englishness, which infused American cultural views generally, and that of Germanness, which was the basis of American serious music culture particularly. The meaning of Frenchness in modernism was further inflected by Paris's status as the arts and culture capital of the world in the 1920s, when its cultural scene was specifically lesbian ruled.[57] The conventional attributions to Frenchness are inscribed in language, where it encodes the sensual, sexual, elegant, and exotic and is a particular preoccupation in gay vernacular. Indeed, within certain quarters of modern American gay subculture, signs of Frenchness have served as redolent signs of queerness. This is illustrated variously in the classic gay novel *Dancer from the Dance* (1978), as when one character—in camp parody of an epigrammatic style itself characteristically French—identifies the "two requirements for social success with those queens in the Hamptons: a perfect knowledge of French and a big dick."[58] Members of the Copland-Thomson circle were exceptionally well endowed in their knowledge of French language and culture. Beyond this, they manifested French musical affiliations and Francophile mannerisms to differing degrees and in different registers. Copland placed Frenchness—against Germanness—at the heart of his musical identity and his accountings of his compositional approach. A famously unpretentious, unflamboyant personality, he nevertheless drew repeatedly on certain favored French idioms, particularly in his teaching and discussions of music—Boulanger's *dépouillement* and *grande ligne* being among these.[59]

Thomson had set forth a French-versus-German cosmology as early as 1925, in his essay "How Modern Music Gets That Way," but had cultivated his views in this regard since his adolescence in the 1910s, in early discoveries of and devotions to Debussy and Ravel (a dandy of enigmatic sexual persona), and to the soprano Mary Garden (a champion of French repertory, and Debussy's original Mélisande).[60] He explicated his French musical affiliations even more elaborately than did Copland, across multiple dimensions, including his approach to orchestration—which he ascribed to a tradition that he anatomized and identified as French and essentially transparent, as distinguished from one identified as German and essentially dense. Thomson's primary musical allegiance was to (the ultra-French) Satie, and his trademark verbal style owed, in Rorem's account, to his speaking "French in English."[61] He spent many years in Paris and affiliated himself with what he saw as its unrivaled musical discernment and cutting-edge role as "the accepted world capital of first performances." In this city where "concert halls are invaded by Corybantic troupes of classics-worshippers and seekers after soul-states," Thomson predicted to *Modern Music* in early 1939, "the exiled German composer" (of which there were many after 1933) would have little effect: "France has all she can take on . . . with sixty thousand unrestrained music lovers." Consequently, "[t]echnical complexity unjustified by expression, emotional vagueness, most particularly that air of owning all Musical Truth that German composers so naïvely and so impregnably assume, all get short shrift here," Thomson reported from Paris, with evident satisfaction.[62]

Diamond identifies two French composers, Ravel and Satie, as his earliest and most significant influences.[63] Rorem affiliates primarily with (the ultra-French and ultracampy) Poulenc and exhibits musical and personal French identification to an obsessive, all-encompassing, and often (knowingly) absurd degree. "I went to France because I was already French, not the other way around," he writes characteristically: Rorem's discourse is rife with such quips, "these glib—these *French*—truisms," in which both form (concise and self-contradictory) and content show a concern with distilling essential Frenchness.[64]

Concerning the (mainly French) expatriations of the gay modernist composers at issue here, I would point out that these are first of all readable as literalization of the outsider status they had already occupied—variously as secret, open secret, nonsecret—at home in the States. Second, their creating self-consciously American music while living abroad might be read as emblem, precursor, or synecdoche in relation to their careers overall, as native artists defining a voice for America while, to an important extent, residing outside its sociocultural limits. In expatriating and self-affiliating with Frenchness specifically, these gay modernists became affiliated with its general valences—of culture, elegance, sensuality, queerness—and its art-musical valences—of blurry, effeminized other, outside and against the Austro-German masterwork mainstream.

FIGURE 8.   Virgil Thomson received this photo in 1958 "with love from *Ned.*" Rorem's youthful beauty was famed on two continents. The Virgil Thomson Papers in the Irving S. Gilmore Music Library of Yale University.

Besides turning away from the masters, members of this circle revered a mistress, Nadia Boulanger.[65] Copland and Thomson in the early twenties were among her first American pupils, followed in the later twenties by Blitzstein. Diamond, with Copland's urging, became a Boulanger pupil in 1937 and recalls having urged Bernstein in 1939 (on Diamond's return from two years abroad) to study with Boulanger, but Bernstein's conducting studies at the Curtis Institute of Music and the outbreak of war prevented it. Though Bernstein was never resident in France nor a Boulanger student, the two hit it off upon first meeting (with Copland's help) in 1946 and maintained a warm association up through Boulanger's final illness.[66] Rorem received compositional guidance and personal mentoring from

Boulanger around 1950 and was affiliated with her throughout his mid-century years of expatriation in Paris.[67] Boulanger's Gallic orientation to the individual and his or her singular, presumedly inborn nature *(la nature bête)* seems to have resonated deeply with these gay composers: Copland underscored Boulanger's ability to "inspire a pupil with confidence in his own creative processes."[68] Within the contemporaneous musical and political context, their affiliation with Boulanger linked them with the Stravinskian pole of the reigning binarism: Schoenberg versus Stravinsky. To the varying extents to which these composers embraced Boulanger's approach, they further linked with an aesthetic orientation to directness and *dépouillement*, or stripping away, and to a tonally based musical idiom.

These gay composers linked, moreover, with each other, professionally and personally, and hence collectively constructed and circulated "tribal" lore and meanings, in connection with which they forged musical selves, idioms, and oeuvres. In an age obsessed with identity categories, they lived under the headings of composer, American, and homosexual, and they infused their lives, personas, and work with signs and experiences of Frenchness. This further aligned them with multiple coded resonances understood, if rarely acknowledged, from within and without their circle: resonances linking sexual, national, and stylistic positions and thus defining signifying codes importantly operative in musical modernism.

As we have seen, Frenchness carried homosexual associations within queer discursive realms. This was also the case in nonqueer American (likewise British) discourse of the twentieth century. In homophobic discourse particularly, Frenchness—often in association with notions of aristocracy, cosmopolitanism, and/or foreignness—was at times presumed proximate, if not equivalent, to homosexuality. These connotative pathways are illustrated in Robert Dean's recent examination of the U.S. government's sexual inquisition of federal employees during the Cold War. Here the composer Nicolas (cousin of Vladimir) Nabokov, an aristocratic Russian émigré who was working for the Department of State's Voice of America radio division, came under suspicion in part for his association with "the *Parisians*" Jean Cocteau and Sergei Diaghilev, and with a "refugee group" of "French artist[s] and musicians, among whom it was the practice," according to government documents, "for the men to sleep together." Between his divorce and subsequent remarriage Nabokov shared an apartment with Charles Thayer, a high-level officer in U.S. foreign service. Both men came under suspicion for briefly hosting a certain French refugee artist who, by the report of their building superintendent, "drew a lot of nude pictures and read a lot of French books." This artist was adjudged to belong to "the obvious type that one calls a 'queer.' "[69] From the assiduous and repeated inclusion here of the relevant markers, it would seem that the queer "type" emerges as particularly "obvious" in the presence of things French (or Parisian) and aristocratic, artistic, literary, and/or musical.

Now, in arguing that Frenchness, tonality, and *dépouillement* carried coded meanings of homosexual identity in U.S. musical modernism I emphatically have not asserted, nor would I assert, that these particular mappings of sexual, national, and music-stylistic meaning were inevitable, universal, or transhistorical. Further, I make no claims that Copland's music, or Thomson's, Rorem's, or that of any of the other composers of this circle, was devoid of influence from Germanic music. Nor am I engaging any questions about whether their work was verifiably more French-influenced than that of particular other composers, gay or straight. I am noting, however, that these composers often identified their work, and that their work was often identified by others, in terms of salient Frenchness. And I am arguing that the connotative freight of "Frenchness," "tonality," and *"dépouillement"* in this cultural-historical context could exceed their denotative freight, and could include sex-gender ascriptions that were less readily conveyable by direct utterance—at least until the Cold War advent of overt and unbridled finger pointing.

Henry Cowell's brief note of introduction to Copland, written in 1929 upon hearing some music by the eighteen-year-old Paul Bowles, described the aspiring composer's work as "very French," adding, "but it might interest you."[70] Cowell's wording suggests both that he placed compositional "Frenchness" outside the realm of his own interests, and that he assumed Copland more likely to engage with the perceived Frenchness in young Bowles's oeuvre (perhaps, too, with his striking person—with which Copland was indeed taken). Particular musical meanings attaching to "French" or "German" in such labelings are rarely specified. Occasionally the intended meaning is clear, as when Thomson delineates the orchestrational characteristics of the traditions he labels as French and German, respectively, listing composers exemplary of each type; or in a work such as Bowles's *Night Waltz* (1949), which presents a stylistic kinship to Poulenc, Ravel, and Parisian café idioms that is saturative and immediately obvious.

Both Thomson and Copland at points expressed admiration for certain German and Austrian composers and works, including Hindemith, Mozart (whose "Best Friend" status in relation to Thomson is proclaimed by a chapter title in the latter's memoir), and Mahler (who, not only German but German Romantic, was nevertheless admired by Copland). But both were quite vocal in claiming primary and even exclusive French stylistic affiliations for their own music.[71] Comparably, Blitzstein in 1928 publicly praised the music of Paul Hindemith, whose every work was "usually a model for succeeding compositions of like form," in Blitzstein's assessment.[72] But generally Blitzstein, like Copland and Thomson in this period (and Rorem later), used "German" to characterize artistic effects and works he deemed least worthy of modeling. Elsewhere in 1928, for example, he summarized a film that he disparaged for being "a burdensome, long, unwieldy opus" as "monotonous, unarticulated, *German*."[73]

READING CLOSET CODES: A METHOD

Within the twentieth-century American music world, including its offshore activities, the binarisms discussed above served to define the operative battle lines, drawn through a whole cluster of meanings that could thus encode one another. Hence at points we can see "French versus German" clearly functioning as code for "Stravinsky versus Schoenberg"—that is, invoking the latter, more polemically charged meaning without expressly naming it. The reductiveness surely engendered in such usage in no way undermines the argument presented here. For the reductive move, the diminishment of semantic specificity, occurs in the historical instances of encoding—as when these render "French" (or "Franco-Russian") as synecdoche for Stravinsky, as composer and person; or in Thomson's sweeping indictments of what he called the "German-Austrian musical complex."[74] The present argument aims to trace the historical meanings and cultural work of such usages, whose codings provide surrogate (sometimes euphemistic) and shorthand—hence frequently reductive—terms for pivotal stylistic, political, and sexual designations.

My approach in this regard is informed by what Halperin calls "the basic method of Foucauldian discourse analysis," that is, "to refuse to engage with the content of particular authoritative discourses . . . and to analyze [these] discourses in terms of their overall strategies." Halperin's lucid explication of this method, with particular reference to Sedgwick's deployment of it in *Epistemology of the Closet*, is worth quoting at length:

> The reason it is pointless to refute the lies of homophobia is not that they are difficult or impossible to refute—on the contrary, taken one at a time they are easily falsifiable . . . —but that refuting them does nothing to impair the strategic functioning of discourses that operate precisely by deploying a series of mutually contradictory premises in such a way that any one of them can be substituted for any other, as different circumstances may require, *without changing the final out-*

come of the argument. Sedgwick's account recalls us, specifically, from our natural impulse to try and win . . . the game . . . [and] encourages us, instead, to stop playing long enough to stand back from the game, to look at all its rules in their totality, and to examine our entire strategic situation: how the game has been set up, on what terms most favorable to whom, with what consequences for which of its players.[75]

In focusing on who wields labels like "French" and "German," "tonal" and "serial," toward whom, in what circumstances, and to what ends, I am analyzing modernist musical discourses "not [just] substantively but strategically."[76] In this analysis I do not look to particular musical texts either to prove or to refute specific music-stylistic claims that might attach to these heavily freighted labelings. Admittedly, such a method puts my argument at odds with the musicological (including music-theoretic) orthodoxy that locates ultimate—and often eternal and universal—truth in "the music itself." I hope my neglect of music-textual "proofs" in this chapter will not serve to distract readers, whether or not grounded in musicological orthodoxy, from my main points. One of these, perhaps at greatest risk of being missed, is that, whether or not (say) Copland's *Rodeo* sounds "French" or even especially "tonal" to a particular listener, we would do well to pay attention to the composer's and others' persistent claims for his music's French and tonal character. Granted, the work's (relative) tonality is uncontroversial and readily verifiable, whereas its "Frenchness" poses a more complex and contestable problem for textual demonstration—even in the light of Rorem's observation that Frenchness is Stravinskian in Copland's case, while Satiean in Thomson's.[77] Still, both attributions, of tonality and of Frenchness, are significant in my reading, which highlights their strategic deployment in a modernist music realm structured by dynamics of identity and affiliation—sexual, national, and stylistic, among others—and by struggles for power and influence.

An illustrative instance of the coded usage mentioned above—of "French/German" denoting "Stravinsky/Schoenberg"—can be found in a 1927 remark from Schoenberg to Blitzstein, then his pupil in Berlin: "Very well. Go ahead, you write your *Franco-Russische Hübschmusik*" (Franco-Russian pretty music).[78] Examining Schoenberg's remark in relation to its relevant local and wider contexts can highlight the signifying heft of his term *Franco-Russische Hübschmusik*. With reference to Blitzstein's positioning vis-à-vis Schoenberg, the phrase readily evokes the young American's just-prior studies with Boulanger, in whose Fontainebleau studio "Franco-Russian"—which is to say "Stravinskian" (for in music, unlike painting and dance, "Franco-Russian" indicated one artist unmistakably)—

music flourished: It was no secret that Boulanger deemed Stravinsky the master of the age. Generally, Schoenberg brandished "Franco-Russian" as an indictment of Blitzstein's music, much as Blitzstein brandished "German" in relation to a film he found burdensome and unwieldy.

More particularly, Schoenberg's sarcastic, feminizing "pretty" points toward the relatively consonant, tonal, and *depouillé* idiom cultivated by Blitzstein and other Fontainebleau composers (and contrasting with Schoenberg's dissonant, atonal, and complex idiom). It is difficult to know whether the term might have further connected—in Schoenberg's intention or Blitzstein's reception—with what was perceived (by the refractive light of exclusive male hegemony) as the quasi-matriarchal structure of the "Boulangerie," or to the prevalence of homosexuals therein. But surely the sardonic and belittling tone begs for comparison with another instance: Schoenberg's *Three Satires*, op. 28 (1925), whose text mocks "kleine Modernsky" in his (putative) periwig, looking "just like Papa Bach." The connotations here and in "Franco-Russische Hübschmusik" are markedly trivializing and feminizing, hence homosexualizing. Whatever else these utterances do, both clearly stake a rhetorical claim for Schoenberg's masculine superiority over his perceived rival (the straight-identified) Stravinsky.[79]

We might further compare these examples with another remark of Schoenberg to Blitzstein circa 1927: "It is only since the war that you American composers have been cut off from your source of supply, which is Germany, and have been writing Franco-Russian music. Ten years before the war you were all writing German music; and ten years from now you will all be writing German music again."[80] This passage, with its reductive gloss on the stylistic terrain of U.S. composition circa 1904–27 (and, by prognostication, to about 1937), affords a vision of imperial expansion in which America figures as the contested object of cultural annexation. Conspicuous here is Schoenberg's express confidence about the eventual triumph of the German musical empire in the New World. More important for the present argument, however, is his tacitly presumed mapping of the known compositional universe in dualistic terms of French ("Franco-Russian") versus German.

All these utterances function to define particular terms and, more fundamentally, the general binary structure by which modernist composers often constructed self and other, for themselves and others, and by which critics and audiences also conceived of them, their musical idioms, and the relevant political, personal, and stylistic movements. The terms in which Schoenberg conceived this binarism circa 1925 appear inscribed in his foreword and vocal texts for *Three Satires*. The musicologist Glenn Watkins reads something of a manifesto here: "Henceforth, one would be obliged to make a choice: Paris or Vienna: Stravinsky or Schoenberg; an ongoing tradition (now spelled Serialism, despite Schoenberg's railing against fashionable movements) or a retrograde Neoclassicism."[81] Indeed, these three Schoenbergian examples of 1925–27 resonate on multiple nodes of the definitional axis posited above: on feminine/masculine and hence homosexual/heterosexual (in this cultural context, imputing femininity to a man is generally tantamount to imputing homosexuality), and on French/German, with implicit links to Stravinskian/Schoenbergian and tonal/atonal. Schoenberg's statements vividly illustrate the discursive mechanism I ascribe to the musicosexual definitional axis posited here—a mechanism by which attributes conventionally deemed cognates (i.e., those clustered together) are capable of implying one another and, by binary logic, of implying those conventionally deemed their counterpoles. In the above context, for example, Schoenberg's reference to "Franco-Russian pretty music" reinforces the conventional clustering of French music *with* feminine, queer, tonal (and perhaps simple) characteristics, and implicitly ascribes the "opposite" gender, sexual, and stylistic attributes to that national music figured *against* it: German music.

IMPLICATIONS FOR MUSICAL AND QUEER HISTORY

Recognizing musicosexual "closet codes" and their workings may clarify and complicate any number of issues in musical modernism concerning the activities and work of artists both gay and straight. One such issue concerns the anti-Romantic, antifeminine, and hypermasculine impulses in musical modernism, in connection with which Catherine Parsons Smith exhorts us to "investigate whether there was a different, more broadly defined, perhaps less hostile or more gender-inclusive form of modernism that until now has been wholly hidden from view."[82] Might this description apply to the modernism of the gay tonalists considered here? Certainly not by standards of gender inclusivity: To my knowledge, no serious claim for this circle's special advocacy of or involvement with women composers has been put forward. Indeed, theirs was a markedly homosocial male sphere—albeit no more so than the mainstream modernist compositional establishment, whose exclusion of women was already virtually complete.[83] And notwithstanding their important associations with women artists and *auteurs*—including those with Boulanger, Thomson's with Gertrude Stein, Copland's with Martha Graham, Blitzstein's with Lillian Hellman—such expressions of misogyny as typify the period can be found in the annals of this circle.[84]

As we have seen, Smith is among those musicologists who identify an antiwoman impetus in the reaction against romantic Americanism in the teens and twenties.[85] Along similar lines one might assume that the gay tonal modernists' anti-Romantic aesthetic position perpetuated the misogynist status quo. But in fact, this is where we can indeed detect a kinder, gentler musical modernism, one marked by sexual difference. For the musical Romanticism against which Copland, Thomson, Bowles, and Rorem (in particular) positioned themselves was specifically German Romanticism (whose continuation they—like Schoenberg himself—heard in the modernism of Schoenberg and his followers).[86] In locating their musical affiliations and idioms outside and against the Germanic mainstream, these gay composers were also repudiating the tradition that had been most assiduously and successfully directed toward containment and quashing of music's effeminizing threat. This latter was effected through the great-man and masterwork ideologies of the Germanic musical tradition and, as Brett argues, through its "Teutonic abstraction" and hierarchical ordering, by which music could be appropriated for patriarchal purposes and its sensuous, irrational, feminized qualities disowned, kept at bay.[87] In this connection we might further note that the gay Americana composers' use of tonality circa 1927–54 was *not* accompanied by theoretical claims for the natural or historical inevitability or the timeless transcendence of their chosen method; it is thus significantly distinct from the contemporaneous Germanic practices of Schoenberg vis-à-vis twelve-tone music, and Hindemith and (the music theorist) Heinrich Schenker in the tonal realm.

As for the sensuous, irrational, and feminized: These were alive and well in the French tradition—at least according to its critics, and, at times, even its proponents. The gay tonal modernists, in staking their music to French ideals, reclaimed qualities of music elsewhere rejected as feminine and opposed the patriarchal authority of canonic musical Germanness. Such opposition could include self-conscious resistance to the long-reigning musical ideology of the absolute, as it did when Thomson, displaying a critical acumen no less sharp than his tongue, upbraided Copland for perpetuating the conventional wisdom of analytic listening in his just-published book *What to Listen for in Music* (1939):

> Your book I read through twice and I still find it a bore. . . . Not that [it] doesn't contain a hundred wise remarks about music. But it also contains a lot of stuff that I don't believe and that I am not at all convinced

you believe. Supposing you do believe that analytic listening is advantageous for the musical layman, it is still quite possible and not at all rare
to believe the contrary. It even remains to be proved that analytic listening is possible. . . . I suspect that persons . . . do just as well to let
themselves follow the emotional line of a piece, . . . which they certainly can't do very well while trying to analyze a piece tonally. . . .

I'm not trying to write your book for you. I'm just complaining that
you didn't write it for yourself.[88]

Thomson's critique of analytic listening deftly targets authoritative establishment discourses that abstract and objectify art music by denying its subjective bodily and emotional engagements, and that uphold its elite cultural
status by merging this denial with exclusive and perhaps even impossible
terms for "correct" listening. Thomson and Copland long shared common
cause in actively opposing the canonical "museum music" establishment—
which may explain why, even in its severity, Thomson's commentary conveys an implicit sense of concordance and solidarity of purpose.[89]

In their code-accreted identification with Frenchness and hence its cognates—tonality, simplicity, homosexuality—and against the Germanic
musical mainstream, the gay tonalists' circle begot an alternative form of
musical modernism. It was a form of musical modernism more inclusive of
feminized values, if not of actual women. And it was founded upon and
shaped by both collective networking activities and particular identifications and identity cross-associations. These associations were constitutive
in the stylistic and professional categories that governed U.S. composition
during the Copland-Thomson circle's prime, and sometimes beyond: associations of dissonance and atonality, stylistic complexity, and Germanness
with heterosexuality and masculinity; and of consonance and tonality, clarity and cultivated simplicity, and Frenchness with (male, and hence feminized) homosexuality.

Though thoroughly ignored even up to now in any official discourses,
such clustered codings featured prominently within the potent discourses
of gossip and rumor in the period and functioned as vital indices of meaning and identity in American modernist music. The "closet codes" structured boundaries along which composers constructed themselves, each
other, and their work in this era; lent their resonances to veiled political and
identity meanings within professional and critical musical discourse; and
exerted important influence on the musical, personal, and professional
affiliations and activities of American composers in the twentieth century.
The historical reasons for silence around these stylistic, sociosexual, and
national signifiers and their effects are much the same as for the more gen-

eral (queer and nonqueer) hush surrounding homosexual presence and networking in this context. Such silence, however, would not appear to have diminished the impact of (what I am calling) the closet codes of musical modernism; if anything, they gained impetus from the force of insinuation and eluded close, potentially damaging scrutiny by virtue of their effective unspeakability.

Recognizing and interrogating these codes can shed new light on various aspects of musical modernism, by sharpening our historical vision of the defining boundaries among relevant factions—here, for example, separating significantly different anti-Romantic positions. Cracking the closet codes, and acknowledging the important collectivity of the gay composers in relation to whom they primarily operated, can also elaborate musically on Chauncey's historical work demonstrating an extensive gay New York subculture circa 1890–1940 and thus exploding the "myth of [gay] isolation."[90] Undoubtedly, engaging these codes is essential to any genuine understanding or appreciation of the lives and work of this gay modernist composers' circle and their contemporaries. But it is also essential to any understanding of the mutual cross-coding of homosexuality and musicality that continues to shape our own cultural universe.

4. Queerness, Eruption, Bursting

U.S. Musical Modernism at Midcentury

[H]ere, today, now, in the middle years of the twentieth century in America . . . the dominant factor in my life, towering in importance above all others, is a consciousness that I am different. In one all-important respect, I am unlike the great mass of people always around me, and the knowledge of this fact is with me at all times, influencing profoundly my every thought, each minute activity, and all my aspirations. It is inescapable, not only this being different, but more than that, this constant awareness of a dissimilarity.

DONALD WEBSTER CORY [PSEUDONYM],
The Homosexual in America (1951)

Once the young protégé of his intergenerational circle of gay tonalists, Ned Rorem today is an elder statesman in the American arts world, a Pulitzer Prize–winning composer of hundreds of songs and other works, and a prolific author of diaries, memoirs, and criticism. And among the many vivid observations and recollections inscribed in Rorem's prose is this 1994 account of the American midcentury music scene, which presents an arresting intrigue for any student of artistic modernism, or of queer history:

> Nor can you imagine the talent that seemed to mushroom from the fertile ooze of war. After the [1945] opening night of *The Glass Menagerie*—heightened, or rather, delineated, by Paul Bowles's background score, . . . it was clear that *something* had happened, a hypodermic for American theater which could already be called postwar art. A queer goyische flavor was sprouting out of the war and would burst in a few years.[1]

Surely J. D. McClatchy is justified in his recent claim that Rorem's writings constitute "the most extensive and intimate account we have of any composer's mind and heart."[2] But Rorem's longtime friend and colleague David Diamond may be equally justified in declaring, as he did in a recent interview, that he hopes never to be the subject of, and thus subject to the vagaries of, Ned's pen.[3]

The products of that pen by now comprise a voluminous catalog and remain remarkably as Janet Flanner found them at the 1966 publication of Rorem's (1951–55) *Paris Diary:* "worldly, intelligent, licentious, highly indiscreet."[4] Flanner's ironic juxtapositions echo Rorem's own characteristic style, perennially cast in the French tradition of urbane wit issuing from paradoxical epigram—a stylistic tradition to which Oscar Wilde and Rorem's mentor-cum-colleague Virgil Thomson also hewed. And if Rorem's abundant name-, date-, and datum-dropping annals of his half-dozen decades among the international cultural elite represent an acknowledged contribution to belles lettres, they also constitute an invaluable cache for the historian—not least for their extraordinarily frank treatment of queer subjects. Here they must also raise caveats, however, as texts in which one can never fully separate the learned from the gossipy, the banally concrete from the grandly conjectural, or the artful from the archival.

Caveats and contradictions notwithstanding, this chapter explores the mid-twentieth-century American music world, and the role of sexual identity therein, by embarking from Rorem's provocative remarks. For although, admittedly, I have not been able to substantiate Rorem's claims for the late-wartime eruption of a peculiarly "queer goyische flavor" in American arts (nor to elicit any elaboration even from Rorem himself), I find his commentary heuristically useful. It is certainly intriguing vis-à-vis accounts, by John D'Emilio and other historians, of the general postwar, post-Kinsey "eruption" of greater queer visibility.[5] And it resonates with many other contemporaneous indications (or, often, indictments) of a shift toward homosexuality in American arts and media after World War II; indeed, Kinsey's plans for a book on the sexuality of art and artists suggests the topic's currency in the immediate postwar years.[6] Ultimately the argument presented here corroborates at least some aspects of Rorem's narrative: to wit, that a certain queer "flavor" in American art music, whether or not "sprouting out of the war," did establish an important presence, and then "burst" a few years after war's end.[7]

These explorations thus trace a new history of U.S. midcentury musical modernism, emphasizing political and cultural factors—in addition to the usual musical and genealogical ones—as determinants in compositional style and regime shifts. Central in this history is the decline of Copland's career as "Dean of American Music," and of tonal Americana as well, under conditions of Cold War anxiety and postwar scientism that helped to launch twelve-tone serialism and other complexity music into prominence. This chapter thus completes, circa 1954, a rise-and-fall narrative that began on the stage of the Wadsworth Atheneum in February 1934, with the premiere of *Four Saints in Three Acts.* It is a rise-and-fall narrative with a twist, however. For as we shall see, the Coplandian idiom enjoyed a renaissance following the height of the Cold War, one that continues to this day.

WHOSE QUEERNESS? WHAT BURSTING?

We might begin our inquiry by addressing a pair of questions begged by Rorem's proposition, namely, What is this "queer flavor"? and, How and why did it "burst"? A part-response to the second question appears in certain other passages from Rorem. At one point he writes (invoking more lurid imagery of sprouting and bursting): "Nontonal or serial composition was scarcely in fashion, though when the war ended, and for decades beyond, it would seep over and damage the globe like a liquid tumor."[8] Elsewhere, when Rorem defines American music as that composed after 1925 by Americans, like Copland, who eschewed German traditions in favor of a Boulangerian leanness, he tellingly locates its end at "around 1955 when the serial killers took hold with a fearless canvas that could in no way be identified as national."[9]

Virgil Thomson described a similar scenario. In his 1966 memoir Thomson recalled his 1954 retirement from his fourteen-year post as chief music critic for the *New York Herald Tribune,* noting that he thus reported little of what he calls "the modern-music war that went on throughout the Eisenhower decade." Thomson continued: "That war, which was fought between Europe and America for world control over music's advanced positions, was won by Europe. Pierre Boulez, Karlheinz Stockhausen, and their aides now occupy lots of space in the world's press, ride high, make money, and instruct the young."[10] Thomson's account posits "world control" by the serialist avant-garde as the outcome of a dualistic struggle between vying musical powers circa 1953–60. His reading thus concurs with Rorem's image of serial composition "seep[ing] over . . . the globe." And notably, in both cases it is American nonserial (read: tonal) music that is perceived as overtaken thereby.[11]

Implicit in both Rorem's and Thomson's remarks is a conception of twelve-tone serialism and tonality as principal, and mutually antithetical, compositional languages. This conception was prevalent in American music even before World War II, though lines appear more clearly drawn following the war and its concomitant influx of Germanic musicians and scholars.[12] We saw in the last chapter that tonality and dodecaphony (twelve-tone music) in the thirties and forties carried further valences attaching to another prevailing binary, that of sexual identity. The story of Virgil Thomson and Ben Weber's first meeting illustrates the operations and particular alignment of these valences, with Thomson's witty camp highlighting the virtual absence of homosexuals from the ranks of well-known American twelve-tone composers of the era.

Among American tonalists, however, many, of course, were queer-identified—including Barber, Bernstein, Blitzstein, Bowles, Copland, Diamond, Menotti, Rorem, and Thomson. Collectively these tonal composers enjoyed considerable prominence in the thirties and forties. Most famously, Copland succeeded in forging a distinct "American style" in serious music. Thus, after much clamor and hand-wringing from nationalistic culture-watchers in the teens and twenties, the thirties at last saw the creation of an "American sound," thanks to Copland and his studied adaptation of Thomson's tonal simplicities.

Hence, in connection with the composers just named and others, one might say that there was indeed a "queer flavor" in American music as a domain. But can such a flavor also be ascribed to the work produced therein? Well, in a medium as nondenotative as music the meaning or even presence of some particular "flavor" is by no means self-evident (accordingly, we may never know what Rorem had in mind with his reference to postwar music of a "queer goyische flavor"). But we have seen that a certain musical idiom was associated with queer composers and queerness, a tonal idiom self-consciously oriented to transparence, simplicity, and other perceived "Frenchisms."

This queer "flavor," however, had its "eruption" long before the end of World War II, in works like Thomson's *Four Saints in Three Acts* (1928), premiered in 1934, and Copland's populist works of about 1938–44, including *Billy the Kid* (1938), *Fanfare for the Common Man* (1942), and *Appalachian Spring* (1944). Subsequently, "Coplandiana" was taken up by many American composers, and not only gay ones: It was "the sound of America," sonic embodiment of U.S. national identity. Still, even in its heyday, being associated with this idiom or with the reputedly Coplandian League of American Composers could, in certain inside circles, make a composer the object of sex-gender suspicions and innuendo from rivals and critics.

RUMORS, PURGINGS, AND CONSPIRACY THEORIES— FIFTIES STYLE

Both Thomson and Copland were involved with the League of American Composers beginning in the 1920s. Oja cites numerous examples of gendered rhetoric in criticism of the League from this decade, when Edgard

Varèse's International Composers' Guild was its rival (the League formed in 1923 as a splinter group from the Guild, which disbanded in 1927). As Oja shows, such gendered rhetoric assailed its targets on the basis of women's involvements with the organization—women figured importantly as patrons and leaders—and on the basis of associations with men whose heteronormative masculinity was deemed suspect.[13] Rorem gives an account of the League in the 1940s that suggests the persistence of such associations. His description of the League and of the group that was by this time its rival, the International Society for Contemporary Music (ISCM), invokes the sex- and gender-coded French/German binarism: "In the forties the ISCM represented the Germanic side of a spectrum on which the League was French. . . . To the ISCM the writ was twelve-tonish and the junk was Coplandiana."[14] Also tellingly, Bernstein's biographer Humphrey Burton reports that the League "was once dubbed the Homintern" owing to the (perceived) concentration of homosexuals among the "leading musical figures in the New York left-leaning intelligentsia."[15]

Indeed, during the years when tonal Americana reigned supreme, homophobic rumors flourished among some nongay-identified, often nontonal, composers. Varèse, for example, in a 1944 letter to a colleague, railed against Copland and his "competing boy friends" with the charge, "use your arse as a prick garage—or your mouth as a night lodging and . . . N[ew] Y[ork] is yours." A recent book chapter on Varèse and his place in 1920s modernism is titled "Creating a God."[16] Thus, perhaps it should come as no surprise that the nontonal and electronic pioneer perceived himself as persecuted: "Christ," he writes (in the same letter), "it seems impossible to get help and support for something healthy and white."[17]

Elsewhere, another recent biographer of Bernstein cites a nongay composer who claimed that a heterosexual-male identity placed one at such disadvantage that "many a well-known composer . . . had deliberately changed his sexual orientation . . . to improve his career prospects"— though the author neglects to identify even one such composer.[18] Diamond and Rorem, on the other hand, have chronicled dismissals of gay faculty and students from the Eastman School of Music in the thirties and forties. And Diamond identifies himself and several other gay musicians who were made to leave the prestigious school or chose to escape its conservative environment and administrative "spying" on homosexuals.

So the prominence of a "queer flavor" was confirmed, by friends and foes alike, in both the constituency and compositional products of the American music world from at least the midthirties onward, with Copland its most eminent representative. And as we have seen, networking activity among gay composers in Manhattan (and Paris) was significant for creating and transmitting professional and artistic knowledge, opportunities, and even shared stylistic tendencies. It further afforded gay composers a self-conscious awareness of the presence of homosexuals in the highest— as well as middling, and lower—ranks of their field, in a period when the very existence of gay persons was increasingly denied and erased from American cultural discourses and representations. In fact, the situation in art music—composition and beyond—was such that it functioned as a significant site of queer world making in the U.S. throughout much of the twentieth century.

Following unprecedented success and renown in the thirties and throughout the forties, Copland's career reached new heights in 1949 when he received an Academy Award for Best Score with *The Heiress:* He thus became the first composer to garner both an Oscar and a Pulitzer.[19] But it was also in 1949 that Copland's career began a decisive downturn. In March of that year Copland served as sponsor and speaker for the U.S.-Soviet Waldorf Peace Conference and hence suffered considerable negative press and scrutiny. Events of that summer—the communist takeover in China, the Russians' testing of an atomic bomb—would only intensify suspicions about "subversives" and "infiltrators." Elsewhere in 1949, the composer and critic Lazare Saminsky published a five-page diatribe on Copland as composer: "drenched in anti-Semitic and homophobic innuendos," it remains "perhaps the most scathing attack on Copland ever penned," according to his biographer Pollack.[20]

Of course, Varèse's 1944 letter shows gay-conspiracy theories bubbling up from the rivalry and envy around Copland even a few years before this. Indeed, rumors of homosexuals controlling the modern music world had simmered, flaring up periodically, since at least the 1930s.[21] But by the dawn of the fifties this established rumor form would converge with other factors that arose after the war and granted it new legitimacy. One such factor was the increased awareness of homosexuality, following (as D'Emilio has shown), first, the war's radical homosocialization of both battle and home fronts and, then, publication of Kinsey's reports, which set off a national sensation with their picture of extensive homosexuality in America. Concurrently there was a preoccupation, as evinced in the Red Scare, with the "infiltrator" as insidious other, indistinguishable from you or me: Here "communist" and "homosexual" became interchangeable as terms that could fill in the menacing blank.

All these factors would converge to yield the image of a more potent and sinister homosexual presence in American art music, vividly represented in the Cold War notion of the "Homintern." The word is a neologism troping on *Comintern*, the name of the Moscow-based organization that served till 1943 as the parent group for the worldwide communist movement, including the American Communist Party. In 1966 *Time* magazine helped to disseminate the term and provided this phobic explication: "The notion that the arts are dominated by a kind of homosexual mafia—or 'Homintern,' as it has been called," relates to conditions "in the theater, dance and music world, [where] deviates are so widespread that they sometimes seem to be running a closed shop."[22]

Whispered rumors and theories of a homosexual syndicate had swirled around Copland and other gay artists for decades. But postwar conditions lent gay-conspiracy theories apter ideological vehicles, greater sanction and credibility—and thus lent fuel to the popular notion that a "homosexual cultural takeover" was on the rise.[23] This might explain why in the fifties and sixties, even as his power as a composer dwindled, "the long familiar notion that Copland was prejudiced in favor of Jewish or homosexual composers gained ground."[24]

John D'Emilio has written that a chance revelation during 1950 congressional loyalty hearings "led to the entanglement of homosexuality in the politics of domestic anticommunism" already in motion.[25] By similar conception, the antihomosexuality of the postwar period is often regarded as a symptom, subsidiary, or annex of its anticommunism. But in fact, the paranoid and punitive force of antihomosexuality sometimes overtook that of anticommunism, in government and elsewhere. In investigations of federal employees at the Library of Congress, for example, more people lost jobs during the six-month purge of "perverts" in 1950 than at any time within the nine years of loyalty investigations, 1947–56.[26] Cold War ideology traded on the image of emotionally unstable, morally weak "perverts" yielding national secrets under pressure from the enemy and being ever susceptible to blackmail, and traded simultaneously on the opposing image of invisible-but-potent homosexual predators infiltrating and (somehow) subverting America from within. Hence the U.S. Senate, in 1950 hearings and a related report, emphasized the national security risk posed by "susceptible" individuals in government employ.[27] Such concerns were unabated by the 1960s: In 1964 the Florida Legislative Investigative Committee published a report on its concerted efforts to root out homosexuality and thus to prevent it from destroying the United States in the manner of a Trojan horse or a fifth column.[28]

In the early fifties, homosexual-conspiracy theories were already the stuff of blaring tabloid headlines: "HOMOSEXUALITY IS STALIN'S ATOM BOMB

TO DESTROY AMERICA."[29] But the notion that sexual perversion was a communist plot, engineered to undermine the government and destroy America's strength, also flourished in right-wing quarters of government from state legislatures to the U.S. Senate. And in journalism, "respectable" sources were no less instrumental than tabloids and scandal rags in advancing homophobic paranoia and conspiracy allegations, particularly in the 1960s. Those focusing specifically on homosexuality in the arts included *Partisan Review* (1950), *American Mercury* (1951), *The New York Review of Books* (1965), *Commentary* (1965), *Time* (1966), the redoubtable *New York Times* (1961, 1963, 1966), and a *CBS Reports* documentary (1967) featuring Mike Wallace.[30]

Such instances support the historian Michael Sherry's observation that "[t]o submerge postwar homophobia under Cold War anti-communism won't come to grips with its substantial autonomy."[31] Indeed, examining the construction and circulation of antihomosexual ideology "at every level of government" in the 1950s, D'Emilio concludes that "the Cold War's preoccupation with the homosexual menace appears less like a bizarre, irrational expression of McCarthyism and emerges, instead, as an integral component of postwar American society and politics." As he argues, it was a social and political project directed at eliminating political dissent, social nonconformity, and sexual deviance.[32] And as we shall see, its entanglements and effects in music would have a profound impact on the fate of the American art.

POLITICS AND SILENCE, INSIDE AND OUT

Among the creators of a musical "queer flavor" in the Copland-Thomson circle, it was undoubtedly Copland who took the hardest hit from government-led anticommunism—with all its homophobic and anti-Semitic entailments—and from its popular reverberations. Copland was never a member of the Communist Party. But he was in the thirties and forties a "fellow traveler" and member of what would later come to be called "front groups," including the Composers Collective of the communist-controlled Workers' Music League.[33] In 1950 his name was published in *Red Channels*, a widely known source used in blacklisting practices. And in 1953 Copland was among those artists and intellectuals who were called to testify before Joseph McCarthy and Red Scare congressional investigative committees.

Other queer composers suffered inquisitions and listings of their own in the postwar years, particularly Blitzstein and Bernstein.[34] Rorem spent 1949–57 in Paris, with no such troubles: "The anti-Communist turmoil in

America was not a fact of life to expatriates," he has written.[35] In 1947 Bowles had moved to Tangier for good, and thus would be similarly untroubled by McCarthyism.[36] Diamond, expatriated in Italy nearly throughout the fifties, has said that his leaving America in 1951 was motivated by a desire "to escape the repression of the McCarthy period."[37] Financial and family matters forced him to return home briefly, however, and while in New York in 1956 he was subpoenaed out of an orchestra pit (for Bernstein's *Candide*) and questioned by members of the House Committee on Un-American Activities (a.k.a. HUAC). Diamond reports that his interrogation was directed to politics and sexuality—his own and that of other composers and writers.[38]

Thomson, though in New York, had no McCarthy troubles. Diamond attributes this to his respectable position as chief music critic of the *New York Herald Tribune,* a Republican paper.[39] But it must also be noted that Thomson, unlike Copland, Blitzstein, Bernstein, and sometimes Diamond, cultivated no political engagements and kept an extremely low profile in this regard—the extremity of which may well have been enhanced by his own brush with J. Edgar Hoover's FBI, and with public scandal, in the 1942 gay bordello raid. Thomson's most notable ties to the left came from his having worked for New Deal agencies in scoring two Pare Lorentz films for the Resettlement Administration, *The Plow That Broke the Plains* (1936) and *The River* (1937), and one for the Office of War Information (OWI), *Tuesday in November* (1945). Such involvements might seem peripheral, though Copland and his biographer Vivian Perlis speculated that it was his own association with the OWI (later renamed the United States Information Service), as film composer for *The Cummington Story* (1945), that brought Copland under Red baiters' suspicion in later years: McCarthy believed the agency to have been taken over by communists.[40]

As we know, Thomson's avoidance of public politics extended to maintaining complete silence in his influential *Herald Tribune* column when Copland's *Lincoln Portrait* was pulled from the Eisenhower Inaugural concert program in early 1953. In the event, other critics—even without the personal ties to, or common cause with, Copland that Thomson had—were speaking up in Copland's behalf. Thomson, however, privately explained to a colleague his position that "publicizing the incident might be more disadvantageous to [Copland] than protesting about it," and he declared his more general views on overt protest: "I do not think individual action is ever very effective and I know that agitational or editorial protest can be a two-edged weapon."[41] Thomson's response to the events of 1953 was consistent with his responses to many others over the years, including his public self-heterosexualizing "campaign" (deploying Minna Lederman) following the 1942 morals arrest in Brooklyn, his distancing of Rorem upon the 1966 release of the latter's homosexually frank *Paris Diary,* and his arm's-length response when Maurice Grosser was dying of AIDS in the 1980s.[42]

Proximately, Thomson at various points showed an aversion to taking any position on matters of minority identity—the potential surfacing of which he surely would have perceived in Copland's McCarthy troubles. We have examined certain instances of not only silence but also active (and to whatever degree, voyeuristic) smoke screening on Thomson's part, in his failed early essay "My Jesus, I Love Thee" and through projection of conspicuous Otherness onto lesbian associates in interviews and memoirs, and similarly onto the African American performers staged in *Four Saints.* Unquestionably *Four Saints'* spectacle partook of a "mixed erotic economy of celebration and exploitation" betraying "what Homi Bhabha would call its 'ambivalence'" and what Eric Lott terms "love and theft."[43] Both Bhabha and Lott are speaking of racialized identity ambivalence, which is abundantly present in this instance. But we might also flag here the strong commingled presence of sexual identity ambivalence, particularly around the sexuality that Thomson, a queer subject in a deeply homophobic society, simultaneously claimed and denied, relished and loathed—in ways that significantly imprinted American music and culture. Thomson's ambivalent silence, disavowals, and disengagement illustrate in microcosm those conditions—including homophobia and self-defensive and other protective impulses—that have led commentators on all sides to leave unremarked the eminently remarkable histories arising from the conjunction of gay identity and classical music in twentieth-century America.

In any case, Thomson too, his political detachment notwithstanding, experienced rough going in his compositional career at midcentury. In 1949 he had captured the Pulitzer Prize for his score to Robert Flaherty's film *Louisiana Story,* but by the midfifties he found it difficult to get performances of his music. Surely Thomson's circumstances were affected in part by his loss of status and power upon stepping down from his critic's post at the *Herald Tribune* in 1954.[44] But other Americana tonalists also found the U.S. musical and cultural climate increasingly less hospitable in the Cold War fifties and sixties. According to Glenn Watkins "the end of World War II" had "signaled the end of America as a musical backwater." The time had come to abandon the ideal of a self-consciously American music in favor of a reckoning with all the "aesthetic forces," national and international, operative in this moment—and Thomson, in his role as critic, was among the first to recognize the new postwar musical realities.[45] Such facts may suggest the implausibility of any simple equation between McCarthyism and the "bursting" of tonal Americana. To what, then, might we finally attribute this bursting, and how might it relate to the social, political, and other contours of the postwar American landscape?

COMPLEXITY MUSIC AND THE AMERICAN WAY

The factors discussed up to this point have been social and political, but we shall consider another factor now on the cultural front. The brand of music that gained prominence for those Thomson would call the "complexity boys" was ideally in step with American culture's postwar preoccupation with modern science: Electronic, serial, and other musics of complex compositional *systems* were perceived as characteristically mathematical and scientific.[46] Such music was thus attuned to the supreme contemporary cachet of science and technology, following extraordinary wartime gains and innovations in this realm. During this atomic age in which science became a central preoccupation in official and popular discourse, and "scientific" the highest possible recommendation for everything from shoe polish to sex surveys, the nerve center for American art music shifted from the concert hall, ballet, and opera house to the university.[47]

New musical "laboratories" were erected by such institutions as Columbia and Princeton, arcane studios where learned men used the latest scientific equipment to create and manipulate electronic sounds. Ivy League scholars Milton Babbitt, Allen Forte, and their graduate students began publishing quasi-scientific papers on the formal characteristics of certain compositions, especially those of the Second Viennese School (comprising Schoenberg and his pupils Berg and Webern). The writings and compositions produced by these men deployed new technical vocabularies and methods intelligible only to themselves and each other. Babbitt would defend this state of affairs by comparing it to that of contemporary physics, in which the most advanced knowledge had indeed become *so* advanced that it was incomprehensible to all but a handful of the world's scientific elite. His manifesto appeared in 1958, in an essay he called "The Composer as Specialist"—better, if sometimes infamously, known by the title under which it was published, "Who Cares if You Listen?"[48]

Such a position was not entirely new. From its beginnings atonal and dissonant music had been associated with exclusivity and elitism, as well as heteronormative masculinity, not only by audiences, but also by its creators. Carl Ruggles, a New England composer whose harsh dissonance fostered ideals of manly American "ruggedness," regarded large audiences disdainfully, as a sign of pandering artistic mediocrity. Arnold Schoenberg, inventor of the twelve-tone system and principal figure in musical high modernism throughout the first half of the century, inscribed this view epigrammatically: "If it is art, it is not for all, and if it is for all, it is not art."[49] Comparing these examples with Babbitt's position in "Who Cares if You Listen?" we may perceive a consistency between earlier twelve-tone and later serialist composers' embrace of exclusivity. But we should also note Babbitt's adroit adaptation in the terms of his rationale, which now invokes not art but science.[50] Such an appeal was perfectly pitched in relation to the postwar cultural authority of science and technology, but its strategic effectiveness may have accrued to other factors as well.

For in the decades between high modernism's first notoriety and the postwar serialists' bid for power, America had witnessed the birth and growth of its own national music and musical identity in the concert realm. And this music, from the public's perspective, differed crucially from much of the "modern music" they had heard before: It did not "sacrifice beauty on the altar of Scheme" (as Blitzstein wrote in 1927 of his then-teacher Schoenberg) or insist on "divorcing art from life."[51] When Thomson, by his own account, "then Copland, Piston, Blitzstein," and others began composing for the theater and for documentary films in a straightforward, simple style, they proved in "the 1930s, especially their highly productive last half," that "music could be contemporary without being hermetic."[52] American audiences engaged with the tonal Americana thus launched, and it was woven into the fabric of American life, in the concert hall, ballet, and opera house, but also, increasingly, in the mass cultural forms of movies, radio, and television. Following this musical breakthrough—and breaking down, of high/low boundaries—in the left-leaning, populist thirties and forties, elitist appeals to Art, however they might have played for Schoenberg in pre–World War II Germany and Austria, were not likely to get serial composers very far in postwar America.[53] Midcentury U.S. concert, radio, and other musical audiences were no more enamored of dissonant complexity music now than they had been earlier in the century. If anything, the normalizing tenor of the postwar times provided a less hospitable environment than had the wild and experimental decades of the teens and roaring twenties.

Invoking high science (i.e., physics in the atomic age) as the standard by which his project should be judged, Babbitt staked his claim upon a greater authority in that Cold War era than mere high art, and thus managed to garner considerable support from the academy and the foundation, "those twentieth-century American equivalents to the outmoded courts of Europe."[54] But in this way he also, wisely, sidestepped the criteria by which his project would never prove persuasive, critically or popularly: those of artistry and artistic merit. Constructing his exclusivity-rationale on scientific, rather than artistic, foundations further allowed Babbitt's project some protection from the erosion, much accelerated within the Cold War period, of high art's position on the American cultural landscape—an erosion itself exacerbated by the midcentury ascendance of masculinized complexity music (a point to be discussed shortly).

Such exclusivity, if not a means of attracting listeners, was productive in other ways. Serial and other "formalist" music, even beyond its particular scientific associations, was aligned with the postwar American Zeitgeist more generally by means of its conspicuous "difficulty."[55] Indeed, in the late-forties Red Scare the "common man" and any art purporting to address him became suspect, this being the prescribed focus of artists working under Stalinism. Hence, in its 1942 debut Copland's tonally accessible *Fanfare for the Common Man* was heard in terms of American nationalism, but the ensuing decade brought a diametrical shift in meaning. Anticommunists like Ayn Rand and Illinois Congressman Fred Busbey flagged the phrase "common man" as a mark of political subversion and drummed up suspicion around demotic art.[56]

In this political-ideological context serial music was at times invoked as an emblem of intellectual and artistic liberty. Such an association appears counterintuitive in the light of popular conceptualizations of serialism as a method engendering "lockstep discipline," or an instance of musical totalitarianism—of "comprehensive, world-ordering systems" embraced by "cultural ideologues" who found ripe opportunity in "[t]he chaos into which the West had been plunged by World War II."[57] But in America in late 1949 and early 1950, public discourses directly linked serial composition—contrastingly—to Soviet and Iron Curtain prohibitions.[58] And in this regard at least, serialism would seem to have enjoyed a certain moral-political privilege on the U.S. compositional scene of the Cold War era: When presented as an art form off limits to Soviet artists, serial music acquired emblematic status as *the* music of democracy and Americanism.[59]

Serge Guilbaut has advanced an argument very similar to the one just sketched with regard to music, but concerning America's Cold War visual art scene, in *How New York Stole the Idea of Modern Art: Abstract Expressionism, Freedom, and the Cold War.*[60] The situation in modern art has also been vividly glossed by Dave Hickey:

Mussolini's coup [of preemptively appropriating Italian Futurist rhetoric for fascism] would not meet its match until the early nineteen sixties when Ivy League Cold Warriors in Washington coöpted the cultural chauvinism of Abstract Expressionism, mounting touring exhibitions that effectively converted [Jackson] Pollock's canvases into muscular, metaphorical billboards for a virile, imperial, "all-over" America.[61]

In music, notions linking severe formalism with virile American imperialism had entered the culture stream by the time Copland's *Lincoln Portrait* (1942) was censored from the 1953 Eisenhower Inaugural program, at the behest of Representative Busbey.[62] The congressman led an ad hominem campaign, citing Copland's "long record of questionable affiliations," but it is conceivable that Busbey was aided by the shifts in musical emblematics, or the politics of musical style, that his own rhetoric elsewhere had helped to produce.[63]

THE BURSTING: COPLAND IN THE FIFTIES

In 1950, amid the dawning of his Red Scare troubles, Copland had turned in a new and unexpected compositional direction. The composer whose populist music was widely viewed as the antithesis of twelve-tone serialism, and whose 1941 book *Our New Music* had regarded twelve-tone music as elitist and ineluctably Germanic (and hence passé), by 1950 had adjusted his position such that he made use of serialism in his own *Quartet for Piano and Strings*—as he would do again in *Piano Fantasy* (1957), *Connotations* (1962), and *Inscape* (1967). Copland later attributed this turn to a realization, inspired by Boulez and certain coevals, that he could use serial technique in the service of his own self-avowedly French aesthetic.[64]

In her study of Copland in the 1950s Jennifer L. DeLapp presents a cogent exegesis of the *Quartet* that weds musical analysis to a semiotic reading of the composition as Copland "staging his own fight against the Cold War."[65] DeLapp draws on Copland's 1949 speech to the Waldorf Peace Conference, in which he criticized the media for a Red Scare rhetoric of false dichotomies including "blacks and whites, East and West, communism and the Profit System," and "mass-appeal music . . . and [Schoenbergian] musical radicalism."[66] Copland was certainly not alone in feeling the hegemony of crude dichotomies in this moment: Though he cites only "the media" in this regard, a primary source of such ideology—particularly the radical division of the world into capitalist and communist camps—and one much discussed as such in its day, was the so-called Truman doctrine, announced by the U.S. president in a nationally broadcast speech of March 12, 1947.[67] DeLapp argues that Copland's 1950 *Quartet* engages several reigning dichotomies—serialism/tonality, elitism/populism, and capitalism/communism—and that in literally reconciling the first of these, it symbolically resists and reconciles the others. Of course, Copland, as a "discreet homosexual" of his time, would never have expressly enumerated the heterosexual/homosexual dyad in the context of a public speech. Nevertheless, both the Thomson-Weber anecdote and the definitional axis discussed in the previous chapter suggest that homo/hetero must figure among the dichotomies resisted in Copland's *Quartet*—as do, further, the facts of sexuality's ubiquitous and overweening significance in the lives of midcentury homosexuals, as attested in 1951 by the pseudonymous Cory ("the dominant factor in my life, towering in importance above all others, is a consciousness that I am different").

Copland's forays into twelve-tone composition, however, were embraced neither by his established listeners nor by the adherents of serial music. The entire decade of the fifties, moreover, would prove difficult for the composer. Following his McCarthy troubles and cancellation of *A Lincoln Portrait* he lost commissions, speaking engagements, and support in some quarters; his only "grown-up" opera, *The Tender Land* (1954), an object of enormous effort and high hopes, was a dismal flop; he suffered a serious writer's block and composed very little—which DeLapp directly links to the morale-destroying effects of the Cold War and McCarthyism.[68] The musicologist Richard Taruskin has written that "Copland ended his career embittered" for being held to his "regionalisms" at the point when he sought a serious hearing for his twelve-tone works. But clearly Copland, whether or not he was embittered (DeLapp, for one, cites evidence to the contrary), had more than this reason to be so.[69] At a time when he should have been enjoying accolades, Copland was targeted in a witch hunt—one that called into question the very national loyalty to which he felt he had devoted much of his life's work—and subsequently blacklisted in certain quarters. By the time the accolades arrived, Copland's composing career was long over, and as Rorem notes, while Copland's "fame swelled during the sixties and seventies, his influence waned."[70] And in a further irony, highbrow perceptions of Copland's musical nationalism in regional and parochial terms around this time contrasted diametrically with the goal he had pursued throughout his career: of deploying nationalism as a vehicle for internationalism.

Writing on film music, Lerner describes Copland's "sound (or more correctly, sounds)" as having "permeated Hollywood in the 1940s and . . .

FIGURE 9.   Composing oneself *chez* Thomson, 1950: The American tonalists
Samuel Barber, Virgil Thomson, Aaron Copland, Barber's life partner Gian Carlo
Menotti, and the straight-identified William Schuman. Photo by John Stewart.
Aaron Copland Collection, Library of Congress. Reprinted by permission of the
Virgil Thomson Foundation, Ltd., and the Aaron Copland Fund, copyright owners.

become even stronger since the U.S. Bicentennial."[71] This periodization
frames the present-day popularity of Copland's music more as a continuation of a late-seventies revival than as any continuous fact since the composer's 1940s prime. Lerner bases his perspective in part on a 1990 ethnographic study by Claudia Gorbman, in which she "described her interviews
with composers working within the [film and TV] industry who said that
after the bicentennial, television music 'went' Copland. By the mid-1970s,
then, the Copland sound was a recognized idiom within the industry,
although . . . it had surfaced earlier in such scores as [that of Hugo Friedhofer in 1946 for] *The Best Years of Our Lives*."[72] Thus, Copland's music
recovered from the battles and witch hunts of the Cold War, even if his
career did not.

CONCLUSION

By 1954 the United States had long since acquired the musical-cultural profile it coveted in the teens and twenties, and America at midcentury was no longer a cultural backwater or mere wannabe. There is nevertheless a notable symmetry in our story here, to the extent that American classical music shows a masculinizing, imperialist impulse on either end of it: first in the 1910s' and 1920s' drive toward establishing an important national musical-artistic culture, and again in the 1950s' move toward music of scientistic, international, and complex character. Throughout the Cold War years complexity music would possess considerable cachet within the academy and the foundation, but would never (even as yet) succeed in finding a listening public. Still, some would argue that its consequences for listeners have been decisive, for it was during the years of serialism's prominence, concurrent with homophobic government and media attacks on the arts (indicting thus that music which *was* known and embraced among the public), that concert music radically diminished in cultural relevance and prestige, and thus became far less visible on the American cultural horizon—a process fairly well completed by the mid-1980s.[73]

American art music was a significantly queer locus in the 1930s and 1940s when the nation found its signature sound in the lean, tonal, French-affiliated idiom of Copland and company. The marked queerness of the tonal Americana realm constituted an open secret in the U.S. music world, provoking some direct responses in private (e.g., Varèse on Copland ca. 1944) and oblique responses in public (e.g., Downes on *Four Saints* ca. 1934).[74] But circumstances had shifted by the end of World War II, with the advent of a significant "queer eruption" in America. That is, with the eruption of greater visibility of queer activity, persons, and communities—all of which had been driven ever more underground since the end of the Prohibition-era "pansy craze," by Hollywood's Hays Code, sex-crime panics, and other cultural and legal repressions.[75]

Wartime homosociality and liberality were answered by vigorous postwar renormalization (which is to say, imposition of constructed norms—as distinct from some return to prior conditions). In music, cultural, social, and political changes brought about or intensified by the war shifted the meaning and status of tonal Americana, often in relation to its homosexual associations.[76] And whereas in the thirties and forties homophobic purgings and conspiracy theories had a hushed presence in and around the music world, increasingly in the fifties antihomosexual accusations were voiced publicly and attached to more elaborate, sinister imputations and harsher sanctions. In the Cold War fifties Coplandian music was among the objects, activities, and persons coming under public fire from those who subscribed to theories of interlaced communist, foreign, and homosexual conspiracy and coercion.

The notion of an eruption and then bursting of a queer "flavor" in the American arts thus appears apt in the case of midcentury music. After the war, homosexuals who had established a place in various domestic arenas were forced, like Rosie the Riveter, to step aside and let the "real men" resume control.[77] The Cold War co-construction of homosexuals and communists as infiltrators and subversives lent further force and sanction to the purgings of lesbians and gays from government, culture, and other domains. In American art music, postwar renormalization manifested itself in composition's elitist and masculinist turn toward serialist and quasi-scientific methods (often inimical to homosexuals, along the lines of discursive and ideological estrangement previously argued),[78] heightened and more hostile scrutiny toward gay composers' sexual identities, and stigmatization of homosexual artists and their work. All these factors must be implicated in the contemporary "bursting" of Coplandian tonality and ascent of university-based complexity music.

Concurrently, post-Webernian serialism and other music of cultivated complexity benefited by certain conditions emergent on the Cold War cultural-political landscape, including (1) America's orientation, following the Second World War, toward global perspectives and away from any seemingly parochial nationalism; (2) the perceived relations of serial, electronic, and other complexity musics to a masculinized high science in the context of a postwar, post-atomic emphasis on American scientific and technological power (concurrent with the U.S.-Soviet arms race); and (3) a new positioning of serial composition as emblematic of artistic freedom and U.S. creative-expressive prerogatives in the (contrasting) light of Stalinist prohibitions against serialism and other "formalist" art.

Further, the musical style and power shift emergent in this moment may itself be implicated, along with Cold War arts-directed antihomosexuality, in concert music's loss of status and authority in postwar American culture. Some commentators have blamed the midcentury rise of serialism for the American public's abandonment of contemporary music, in particular. This view is articulated by Terry Teachout: "By the 1960's . . . the general perception was that serialism had triumphed; even Stravinsky and Copland finally converted in old age. As more and more composers submitted . . . the public, too, came to agree with this judgment—and it responded by, in effect, giving up on new music altogether."[79] Examining the proliferation of homophobic attacks on American arts and artists in U.S. Cold War media, Michael Sherry speculates more broadly, positing that these attacks may well have contributed to the overall decline of concert music in the United States.[80] Don't be fooled by the homosexuals and their so-called art, critics warned America: Like their characters and their lives, it is merely ersatz—gleaming on the surface, but hollow inside.

None of this is to suggest, however, that the midcentury scenario Thomson dubbed a "modern-music war" was simply a showdown between the forces of a gay tonality and a straight serialism. Several factors preclude such a reading. First, it was never the case that "gay and "tonal," or "straight" and "atonal," mapped onto one another either perfectly or exclusively in American musical modernism. As we have seen, there were always straight-identified composers among tonal modernists, even in the 1930s and 1940s when the best-known tonalists were disproportionately gay-identified. Conversely, the ranks of nontonal experimentalism—a project constructed in distinctly masculinized terms—also included a prominent queer circle in the 1940s: of Cowell, Cage, Partch, and Harrison. And the careers of Cage, Harrison, and even the eccentric Partch (a longtime member of gay hobo subculture) flourished in the viciously homophobic Cold War era. We might surmise that this was because (1) their (mostly nonserial) music—perceived as internationalist, advanced, and cerebral—aligned well with prevailing masculinist and imperialist values; and (2) their homosexuality, whether or not rumored, remained *deniable*. It was deniable in part by virtue of these men's association with a markedly masculinized project: Nontonal experimentalism was figured as masculine and heteronormative, and so, by a kind of circular logic of the closet, were these gay experimentalists presumed masculine and heteronormative.

The choreographer John Taras, who created a 1965 ballet on a Copland score, recalled that "[t]here was a great deal of opposition to Copland at the time—it was fashionable not to like him." By 1979 the serialist Charles Wuorinen would pronounce tonality, the compositional system with which Copland and the other gay Americana composers were associated, unserious and outside the mainstream.[81] The frequent disdain and belligerence with which serialism was proclaimed superior and tonal and Americana music dismissed in the fifties through the seventies flag the presence of stakes beyond the musical and intellectual—particularly of the gendered and sexual attributions popularly attaching to each musical category. We should not look to such attributions—elsewhere known as stereotypes—for precise and accurate depictions of the actual circumstances of composers and composition, tonal or serial, gay, straight, or other. Of course, American tonalists were not all gay, though many were. And neither were post-war serialists (born after the twelve-tone composers of Ben Weber's generation) all straight; indeed, insiders have long known the gay reputations of certain leading figures in national and international postwar serialism.

And so our assessment of the midcentury modern music war, as of the closet codes that preceded it, must pay close attention to movements and struggles in the discursive realm, historical perceptions and representations that may, or may not, correspond to verifiable historical realities. With regard to the relevant discursive movements we would do well to remember that homophobia has never been wielded or upheld only by heterosexuals; this is true in the music world as in the larger culture.[82] In sum, both tonality and serialism had prominent queer adherents in the postwar era; but tonality had been tainted as queer and feminine, and serialism decidedly had not. We are looking at a midcentury struggle, then, not between a queer tonality and a heterosexual serialism, but between a queered and feminized tonality and a heterosexualized and masculinized serialism—both of which had, to differing degrees (and with differing degrees of secrecy), gay- and straight-identified practitioners and defenders.

It was not only Americana music's homosexual associations that weakened its position on the macho imperialist landscape of the Cold War, however, but also its tonal accessibility (versus scientistic complexity, or Stalin-defying formalism), its nationalism (now read: parochialism), and the gendered associations accruing to these—their feminized status. All these elements contributed to the decline of tonal modernism in America, which in turn likely contributed to the late-twentieth-century decline of classical music generally. Homophobia—vocal, virulent, and misogyny-entangled in the Cold War period—thus notably appears as a factor in the descent of Coplandiana, the ascent of complexity music, and the considerable abandonment of concert music by American audiences.

But certainly there were further factors at work in classical music's shift of cultural position. Mass media developments contributed enormously to the lessening importance of the concert hall and opera house. Also significant was the dissolution of the high/low divide. This was accelerated and greatly advanced by the gay modernists themselves, including Bernstein, Blitzstein, and Copland with their vital, accessible theatrical and balletic settings. And few figures in any field were more influential in this regard than Thomson, with his relentless two-pronged assault—compositional and critical—on revered wisdom and unquestioned hierarchies of value. As chief music critic for the *Herald Tribune* Thomson quickly became the most powerful arbiter of musical taste in America, a position he used to erode the

reigning cultural hierarchy of high and low: Thomson's singularly penetrative, eminently readable commentary was as liable to praise Eugene
Ormandy and the Philadelphia Orchestra as to "skewe[r] the pretensions
of the Metropolitan Opera" or to review, on Easter Sunday, a "Negro
preacher in New Jersey who wore frilled white paper wings over his blue
serge suit and played swing music on an electric guitar."[83] Such discourse
did not denigrate classical music, but it certainly redefined it in relation to
vernacular expression, accessibility, and everyday life. And it undoubtedly
sought to debunk, not the music known as classical, but the classical—that
is, elite, transcendent, unquestionable—status conferred on certain music.

In the antipopulist, internationalist push of the 1950s, however, the classical music America had embraced, tonal Americana, would be trivialized
and pronounced tainted, even insidious, by the self-styled defenders of
high culture. Such paragons of musical Americanism as Copland's *Lincoln
Portrait* and *Fanfare for the Common Man* were subject to 180-degree
turns of interpretation in the new ideological climate of the Cold War.
Meanwhile, the music that was presented as having *real* merit was largely
unpalatable to U.S. audiences. But if the American public never developed
a taste for serial and complexity music, nor, in the long run, did they lose
their taste for Coplandian Americana—as has been amply demonstrated
since September 11, 2001.

Appearing under the rubric of classical music, the Americana idiom
derived much of its meaning from those meanings—of class privilege,
wealth, Old World European tradition, and elite cultural capital—that
attached to this category, a category itself inflected and altered (in its U.S.
version) by the advent of tonal Americana and its merging of high and low
elements. By now in America, however, there is scarcely any meaningful
sense in which classical music can be called "classical." Such music no
longer occupies a status analogous to that of Barthes's "classical writing"
(*écriture classique*), a mode once understood "not as a style at all, but as
inevitable, right, and suitable for all times and places."[84]

Of course, the position of those who create classical music has also
shifted. In Rorem's retrospective view, composers circa 1944 "were an
accepted, if rarefied, fragment of general society," and artistic matters were
granted importance such that composers and other artists "could afford to
bicker about which language was holy writ and which was negligible junk."
Writing a half-century later, Rorem laments the contemporary situation in
which "art is not even a peripheral concern. Composers of classical music
are not despised pariahs, for to be a pariah one must exist." Nor do music
wars figure on a landscape where former rivals and enemies the "aleatorics,

the dodecaphonics, the minimalists, the neoromantics" all occupy the same status of invisibility and irrelevancy, and so are all "mutually tolerant bedfellows."[85]

Whether or not we find cause for lament in the changes that have taken place throughout postwar American culture, we cannot deny their effects. Composers, classical music, and tonal Americana unquestionably occupy different positions now from those they occupied in the Thomson-Copland circle's prime. Intriguingly, of these three former major players on the cultural stage, tonal Americana arguably manages best to sustain a vital cultural profile in the present day. Perhaps this owes to the fact that this music's contemporary profile and prestige are little dependent on any elite status that might accrue to the classical art. For Coplandian Americana now exists as part of the U.S.-dominated global media stream and possesses cultural presence as such, largely apart from high-cultural associations. And so the sound of America composed by the Thomson-Copland circle lives on—beyond many of the cultural forms, institutions, and strictures within which, and against which, it was created.

Composing Oneself (Reprise)

The meanings of classical music, of homosexual identity, and of American-ness have changed substantially since the zenith of U.S. tonal modernism. Nevertheless, the history of the gay Americana composers and their work has much to tell us about ourselves today. For in highlighting the queer dimensions of central objects and figures in America's cultural life and national identity, this history elucidates the ways in which all of us—queers and nonqueers, musicians and consumers, Americans and global cit-izens—compose ourselves in concert with modern homosexual identity, the attendant forces of homophobia, and their mid-twentieth-century flo-rescence in America. More broadly, in illumining the culturally and histor-ically specific composition of past realities and selves, these artists' story shines a light on the composed status of our own. Ultimately their story reveals the revolutionary possibility that these present realities and selves could take forms other than those we now know, or have yet imagined.

A striking motif in the story of the gay modernists is that homosexual identity here engendered much more than any simple fact of sexual object choice. As understood from within and without, these artists' sexual iden-tities were interwoven with group as well as individual, professional and personal, national and music-stylistic affiliations and identities. In this regard the gay modernists' story adduces rich evidence for the proposition, recently articulated by Halperin, that sexuality, "in the last analysis, is . . . an apparatus for constituting human subjects" and homosexuality thus "introduces a novel element into social organization, into the social articulation of human difference, into the social production of desire, and ultimately into the social construction of the self."[1]

A conclusion inferable from all this is that the history of homosexuality is potentially nothing less than a history of human subjectivity, that is, of "the social construction of the self." This is a provocative notion, and a notion readily gleaned from the history of the gay modernists presented here. For, looking out today over the historical landscape of American modernism, we are apt to perceive there an array of subjectivity styles—of personas, the constructedness and arbitrariness of which appear obvious in the clarity of hindsight. A listing of characters on this site might include the queer bohemian artist, the straight male macho modernist (with subtypes: futurist, surrealist, expressionist), and the lesbian novelist (also subsuming multiple subtypes), as well as the gay male tonal composer, and the straight male atonal or serial composer.

Men were composers, women were not; composers were lone geniuses, who were outsiders, as were queers; and so on, according to societal dictates and norms for subjectivity. Atonal and dissonant music was perceived as bold and forward-looking, hence masculine, hence straight; tonal and consonant music as gentle and backward-looking, hence feminine, hence gay. Of course, the relevant attributes and their clusterings can be elaborated more fully and complexly, as indeed they have been in the foregoing pages. The associated character profiles vary—from straight serialists to gay tonalists and others—but all share a common significance: They comprise some of the shapes and styles of subjectivity belonging to a particular cultural moment.

This is not to suggest, however, that the gay Americana composers or their achievements in crafting a national identity were merely the inevitable and foreseeable products of their society's structures of subjectivation. Indeed, if we return now to one of the questions raised at the beginning of the book—Why did the twentieth century witness so many prominent (and other) gay composers?—then, on the basis of the evidence we have seen, we must suspect a more multilayered answer. Composing oneself as a gay musician, as a tonal modernist, as a Francophile, as an American: All of these, to be sure, were contingent on the paths accessible to one as a gendered, national, classed, racialized, and sexualized subject. But the particular ways in which the members of the Copland-Thomson circle navigated the paths they trod, the individual and, importantly, the collective identifications and strategies they forged in relation to their circumstances—these too were crucial determinants in their story, and hence in the story of American cultural identity, past, present, and ongoing. Like all of us, these gay artists both produced and were produced by the subjectivities of their cultural-historical locus. But remarkably, their productions here have resonated audibly and influentially in the national and international public sphere.

Thus, the gay modernists' story suggests how histories of homosexuality might constitute histories of subjectivation, and it reveals particular subjects' creative responses to the social and cultural structures of their time and place. It also shows how having a musical identity, "being musical," could function in the mid–twentieth century in many of the ways we now associate with sexual identity, informing and even transforming one's position vis-à-vis gender, sexuality, nationality, and social class. It suggests that music, like sex, offered experiences of desubjectivation, which seemingly held strong allure for persons subject to the stigma and overdeterminations of queer identity, in an era preoccupied with defining and regulating homo- and heterosexual subjects. And it shows how music-stylistic and national-cultural identifications operated as potent codes for gender and sexual identity (and vice versa) on the homophobic American cultural scene of the 1920s through the 1960s and 1970s.

Of course, homophobia was a central element in all this, functioning both destructively and productively. If, for example, homophobia was significant in the postwar decline of Americana tonality, it was surely also significant in its earlier rise. Perhaps most pivotally, homophobia impelled gay composers to form social and professional networks—the productive effects of which we have examined at some length. Homophobia was also crucial or, more precisely, constitutive in the musical devotions and careers of the many queer persons who flocked to music in the twentieth century, including the gay Americana composers of the Copland-Thomson circle. Their culture's homophobia instilled in these queer musicians a sense of profound and fundamental difference. For queer children, adolescents, and adults, classical music was often a solitary outlet—a medium affording nonverbal emotional release, and an "abstract" channel for sublimation and expression of forbidden desires. Queer subjects' perceived sociosexual difference, moreover, facilitated ready identification with images of bohemianism, solitary genius, and artistic "priesthood." For whereas queerness was a target of pathologizing and scorn, classical music was sublime and transcendent, and as such largely beyond reproach—and so, similarly, those deemed to possess talent in this rarefied art, who were thereby rendered exceptional and transcendent, if not vindicated. As Rorem observes of his own compositional impetus, "Much of it came from 'I'll Show Them,' those ignorant admired bullies who whipped me in grade school."[2]

A great deal has changed since the gay tonalists' prime. But still in countless ways and by various means we continue to invent, imagine, and re-create ourselves as individuals, as collective and national entities, and, increasingly, as a global body. Thus is one engaged, no less than in Thomson and Copland's day, in composing oneself—in that modern enterprise, eager, reluctant, and ongoing, by which the present and future are orchestrated in concert with the past.

Notes

INTRODUCTION

1. Jacqueline Clarys, Douglas Cox, and Tedd Griepentrog, liner notes for the United States Army Field Band, *The Legacy of Aaron Copland*, 9, ii (unnumbered in actual document); Jacqueline Clarys, Douglas Cox, and Tedd Griepentrog, liner notes for the United States Army Field Band Soldiers' Chorus, *The Legacy of Aaron Copland*, ii (unnumbered in actual document).

2. Clarys et al., liner notes for the United States Army Field Band, *The Legacy of Aaron Copland*, 2. The essay "The Legacy of Aaron Copland" comprises pages 2–9 in both sets of liner notes, those issued by the Field Band and by the Soldiers' Chorus.

3. Clarys et al., liner notes for the United States Army Field Band Soldiers' Chorus, *The Legacy of Aaron Copland*, 19, 22, 2, 21, and 16.

4. Howard Pollack, *Aaron Copland: The Life and Work of an Uncommon Man* (New York: Henry Holt, 1999).

5. See Jennifer L. DeLapp, "Copland in the Fifties: Music and Ideology in the McCarthy Era" (Ph.D. diss., University of Michigan, 1997), 134–51.

6. Aaron Copland, "At the River," from *Old American Songs II* (1952). Copland started work on the *Old American Songs* in 1950, with a commission from Benjamin Britten and Peter Pears. Britten was Britain's premier modernist composer and pianist in a performing duo with the tenor Pears, his life partner; both thought the song repertory would benefit by having more contributions from their American associate: Pollack, *Aaron Copland*, 74. A justly famous recording of "At the River" is the 1985 session by mezzo-soprano Marilyn Horne with the English Chamber Orchestra, Carl Davis conducting. It is included, along with several other works discussed in this book, on the 1996 double-disk compilation *Fanfare for the Common Man, Appalachian Spring, El salón México, Dance Symphony, Rodeo—Dances, Lincoln Portrait, Old American Songs, Music for Movies* (London Records 448-261).

7. This is not to deny the distinctly American aspects of the *Adagio*'s per-

formance history, which include particularly its radio broadcast in 1945 following the death of Franklin Delano Roosevelt, and its use as the musical theme for Oliver Stone's Vietnam war movie *Platoon* (1986).

8. In a long list that is nevertheless (and avowedly) far from exhaustive, Pollack cites testimony to the status, from national and international, critical and popular perspectives, of Copland's music as "a national American sound" (in the words of the Americana tonalist William Schuman, ca. 1981) and "an aural image of what America . . . sounds like" (according to Samuel Lipman, ca. 1976): see *Aaron Copland*, 526–31.

9. Lee is quoted in Pollack, *Aaron Copland*, 528.

10. I noted the persistence of this blackout on the facts of Copland's sexual-social life and identity in my essay "Classical Music and Opera," *The St. James Press Gay and Lesbian Almanac,* ed. Neil Schlager (Detroit: St. James Press, 1998), 425.

11. I have previously deployed this scenario to illustrate the prevalence of prominent gay composer-musicians in twentieth-century U.S. concert music, and the long-standing avoidance of any acknowledgment of their shared queer identity status: see ibid., 421.

12. Here I invoke Eve Kosofsky Sedgwick's refiguring of the formerly legalistic term *homosexual panic* to mark the modern double bind attending male homosocial bonds, which are simultaneously stigmatized and mandated for men who would claim the full entitlements of patriarchal masculine privilege: see *Between Men: English Literature and Male Homosocial Desire* (New York: Columbia University Press, 1985), 88–89, and elsewhere; and *Epistemology of the Closet* (Berkeley: University of California Press, 1990), 184–88 esp.

13. Prairie cowboys and pioneer newlyweds were the central figures in *Billy the Kid* (1938) and *Appalachian Spring* (1944), respectively, both ballets to Copland scores. My statement here should not be taken to suggest that Copland's contributions to the musical emblematics of Americanism lay only in pastoral or western topics, for he also created the sound of modern urban ethnic America heard, for example, in *Music for the Theater* (1925), *Quiet City* (1940), and *Music for a Great City* (1964). We might note several distinctions, however, between the Coplandian urban industrial idiom and that of American vastness and nature: First, this city sound now tends to be heard as dated, as specifically evoking modernist twentieth-century streetscapes ca. 1920–1965, whereas "America" representation in the pastoral trope evidently retains currency, albeit nostalgically, in a postindustrial and postmodern American present. Second, the urban idiom might also present itself as less original, audibly indebted as it is to a certain musical trope of the Parisian as developed by French composers and, notably, by George Gershwin (most famously in *Rhapsody in Blue* [1924] and *An American in Paris* [1928]). And last, the association of urbanism with Brooklynite, homosexual, leftist, and Jewish identities is of course conventional, and thus less useful for my purposes of underscoring the apparent counterconventional paradox of Copland's artistic and professional prominence, as against his personal identity positioning. Howard Pollack dis-

cusses both Copland and Gershwin in relation to pastoral and urban industrial idioms in "Copland and Gershwin" (paper presented at the annual meeting of the American Musicological Society, Toronto, November 2000).

14. According to Ethan Mordden, *West Side Story* is, with *Gypsy*, the first example of a Broadway musical that presented itself as high art, "Broadway's equivalent of Richard Wagner's *Gesamtkunstwerk*." Interestingly, Mordden also reads implications of a gay romance in the story between Riff and Tony, and their mirroring thus of Romeo and Mercutio in Shakespeare's *Romeo and Juliet*, of which *West Side Story* is a modern retelling: see *Coming Up Roses: The Broadway Musical in the 1950s* (New York: Oxford University Press, 1998), 8, 240, 242.

15. My assessment of the homophobia of this era, ca. 1934–54, is supported by the assessment of George Chauncey, Nancy F. Cott, John D'Emilio, Estelle B. Freedman, and six other prominent historians who summarized the history of homosexuality in American society and law for a January 2003 amicus brief to the U.S. Supreme Court. According to Chauncey et al., "[w]idespread discrimination against a class of people on the basis of their homosexual status developed only in the twentieth century . . . and peaked from the 1930s to the 1960s" under the leadership of "the medical profession, government officials, and the mass media." See "Brief of Professors of History George Chauncey, Nancy F. Cott . . . as *Amici Curiae* in Support of Petitioners" (January 2003): 2 (available at www.lambdalegal.org/binary-data/LAMBDA_PDF/pdf/183.pdf). The historians wrote in support of John Geddes Lawrence and Tyron Garner's successful case against the State of Texas, which had charged them with sodomy.

16. Michael Warner, "Introduction," in *Fear of a Queer Planet: Queer Politics and Social Theory*, ed. Michael Warner (Minneapolis: University of Minnesota Press, 1993), xxi.

17. And the reason for this is not, as some critics of queer musicology have argued in recent years, that music history has never focused on personal relationships or effects of sexuality. Nancy Yunhwa Rao's fine essay on the personal and professional relationship between the modernist composer Ruth Crawford and her once-teacher and eventual spouse Charles Seeger, for example, did not shatter any musicological paradigms by virtue of its topic (see "Partnership in Modern Music: Charles Seeger and Ruth Crawford, 1929–1931," *American Music* 15, no. 3 [1997]: 352–80). Indeed, it is but one recent instance from an extensive, long-established corpus of musicological discourse that thematizes heterosexuality in accounting for musical activities and developments.

18. Philip Brett and Elizabeth Wood, "The ORIGINAL Version of the *New Grove* Article [s.v. 'Gay and Lesbian Music']," *GLSG Newsletter: For the Gay and Lesbian Study Group of the American Musicological Society* 11, no. 1 (2001): 3–4; also available online at http://www.rem.ufpr.br.

19. Eric A. Gordon, *Mark the Music: The Life and Work of Marc Blitzstein* (New York: St. Martin's Press, 1989), 19; Gordon describes Smallens as "[a]lmost twice Marc's age" in 1924. Further details of Thomson's dealings with Smallens, Bowles, and the *Herald Tribune* are given in Anthony Tom-

masini's magnificent biography: see *Virgil Thomson: Composer on the Aisle* (New York: W. W. Norton, 1997), 317–18, 227–28, and elsewhere. Bowles's biographer Gena Dagel Caponi emphasizes the "invaluable" importance of his *Herald Tribune* job to Bowles's writing and composing crafts and careers: *Paul Bowles: Romantic Savage* (Carbondale: Southern Illinois University Press, 1994), 93–94.

20. Michael Warner, *The Trouble with Normal: Sex, Politics, and the Ethics of Queer Life* (Cambridge, Mass.: Harvard University Press, 1999), 116.

21. Goffman's notion is more precise in that it theorizes the homophobia or "ambivalence" experienced by homosexual subjects in its own right, as a mechanism peculiar to these subjects' positioning in relation to their stigmatized identity—by contrast to the (later) notion of a single structure, homophobia, that might manifest either internally (among homosexuals) or externally (among heterosexuals). Goffman writes:

> Whether closely allied with his own kind or not, the stigmatized individual may exhibit identity ambivalence when he obtains a close sight of his own kind behaving in a stereotyped way. . . . The sight may repel him, since after all he supports the norms of the wider society, but his social and psychological identification with these offenders holds him to what repels him, transforming repulsion into shame, and then transforming ashamedness itself into something of which he is ashamed.

Erving Goffman, *Stigma: Notes on the Management of Spoiled Identity* (New York: Touchstone, 1986), 107–8 (first published, Englewood Cliffs, N.J.: Prentice-Hall, 1963). The term *homophobia* was coined by George H. Weinberg, *Society and the Healthy Homosexual* (New York: St. Martin's Press, 1972).

22. Robert D. Dean, *Imperial Brotherhood: Gender and the Making of Cold War Foreign Policy* (Amherst: University of Massachusetts Press, 2000), 164. On homosexual conspiracy theories in modern European politics see two studies by George L. Mosse: *Nationalism and Sexuality: Middle Class Morality and Sexual Norms in Modern Europe* (Madison: University of Wisconsin Press, 1988), 138; and *The Image of Man: The Creation of Modern Masculinity* (New York: Oxford University Press, 1996), 68–70.

23. George Chauncey, *Gay New York: Gender, Urban Culture, and the Makings of the Gay Male World, 1890–1940* (New York: Basic Books, 1994), 276. We might examine in this light Bernstein's rebuff from Copland when the former urged his friend, former mentor, and perhaps once-lover to come out: "I think I'll leave that to you, boy." See Humphrey Burton, *Leonard Bernstein* (Boston: Faber and Faber, 1994), 473. Likewise Thomson's distancing from his friend and once-pupil Rorem when the latter's tell-all *Paris Diary* was published in 1966. The younger men both were acting in ways that transgressed the gay honor code by which Copland and Thomson had lived their lives. On

Copland and Bernstein's apparent sexual liaison (ca. the late 1930s) see the anecdote in Meryle Secrest, *Leonard Bernstein: A Life* (New York: Alfred A. Knopf, 1994), 96.

24. For more than three decades following the repeal of Prohibition, the State Liquor Authority, the police, the military, and the courts in New York imposed "disorderly conduct" prohibitions on bar patrons deemed homosexual. This "amounted to a virtual ban on the public assembly of gay men and women" (347): see Chauncey, *Gay New York*, 337–47. For an excellent and lucid summary of Foucault's analysis, presented over the course of several works, of state powers of control and punishment and their internalization, see David M. Halperin, *Saint Foucault: Towards a Gay Hagiography* (New York: Oxford University Press, 1995), 15–21 esp.

25. Sherrie Tucker, "When Subjects Don't Come Out," in *Queer Episodes in Music and Modern Identity*, ed. Sophie Fuller and Lloyd Whitesell (Urbana: University of Illinois Press, 2002), 293–310.

26. See ibid., 305. The musicians in question were the informants for Tucker's fascinating study in *Swing Shift: "All-Girl" Bands of the 1940s* (Durham: Duke University Press, 2000).

27. See, for example, Karen Brodkin, *How Jews Became White Folks and What That Says about Race in America* (New Brunswick, N.J.: Rutgers University Press, 1998), 138–39 esp.

28. Kara Anne Gardner argues, in fact, that the success criterion embraced by the "ultramodern" Americanist composers, including Charles Ives, Henry Cowell, Carl Ruggles, and Edgard Varèse, was precisely that of the independent, self-made man—a man so independent that he wrote only for himself, with no regard for audiences: "The American Composer Becomes a Self-Made Man: Modernist Misogyny and Its Consequences," paper presented at the annual meeting of the Society for American Music, Lexington, Ky., March 2002.

29. The notion of compulsory heterosexuality originates in Adrienne Rich, "Compulsory Heterosexuality and Lesbian Existence" (1980), in *Blood, Bread, and Poetry: Selected Prose, 1979–1985*, 23–75 (New York: W. W. Norton, 1986). "Priest of music" serves as titular image in William R. Trotter's 1995 biography of the gay conductor, pianist, and composer Dimitri Mitropoulos, *Priest of Music: The Life of Dimitri Mitropoulos* (Portland: Amadeus Press, 1995).

30. Pollack, *Aaron Copland*, 237.

31. Theodor W. Adorno, "On the Fetish-Character in Music and the Regression of Listening" (1938), reprinted in *The Essential Frankfurt School Reader*, ed. Andrew Arato and Eike Gebhardt (New York: Urizen Books, 1978), 270.

32. Philip Brett, "Musicality, Essentialism, and the Closet," in *Queering the Pitch: The New Gay and Lesbian Musicology*, ed. Philip Brett, Elizabeth Wood, and Gary C. Thomas (New York: Routledge, 1994), 12, 22, 17, 18, 21–22. Alan Sinfield also discusses how bohemia "as a social category" provides the grounds for both avant-garde art and "sexually dissident" (i.e., homosexual, bisexual,

gender-queer) practices in this period: see *Out on Stage: Lesbian and Gay Theatre in the Twentieth Century* (New Haven: Yale University Press, 1999), 49–50.

33. For a cogent critique of the patriarchal and homophobic ideology of radical individualism in musical composition see Lloyd Whitesell, "Men with a Past: Music and the 'Anxiety of Influence,'" *19th Century Music* 18, no. 2 (1994): 152–67.

34. See Pollack, *Aaron Copland*, 234, 53, on Copland's readerly engagements with Gide. See Alan Sheridan, *André Gide: A Life in the Present* (London: Hamish Hamilton, 1998), 376–78, on the particular focus of Gide's apologia in *Corydon*.

35. Nadia Boulanger (1887–1979) was a Parisian pedagogue, conductor, and organist, and the most influential composition teacher of the twentieth century through her long work at the Conservatoire Américain at Fontainebleau (est. 1921).

36. This account of Thomson's first encounter with Stein's work is given by the composer in "Diana Trilling: An Interview with Virgil Thomson," in Virgil Thomson, *A Virgil Thomson Reader* (Boston: Houghton Mifflin, 1981), 545–46 (first published in *Partisan Review* 47, no. 4 [1980]). Here Thomson also recalls the date of his first visit to the Stein-Toklas household, with the composer George Antheil, as occurring in January 1926.

37. In his 1966 memoir Thomson writes of Satie's music that "built into it is an attitude of reserve which by avoiding all success-rhetoric has permitted the creation of a musical reality as real as an apple or a child. . . . [I]ts way of speaking, as if nobody were there, was the kind of communication that I liked": *Virgil Thomson by Virgil Thomson* (New York: Alfred A. Knopf, 1966), 64. The Frenchman Satie was an "eccentric, celibate recluse who preferred homosocial artistic circles and published a passionate statement about his friendship with Debussy yet who vehemently disapproved of open homosexuals such as Cocteau. . . . [A]t some level, his detached and paradoxical [anti-art] authorial stance represented a response to the new injunctions surrounding privacy and sexuality": Sophie Fuller and Lloyd Whitesell, "Introduction: Secret Passages," in Fuller and Whitesell, eds., *Queer Episodes in Music and Modern Identity*, 15. Jane Palatini Bowers discusses Stein's rejection and parody of masterful discourse, specifically in her second opera with Thomson, *The Mother of Us All:* see *"They Watch Me as They Watch This": Gertrude Stein's Metadrama* (Philadelphia: University of Pennsylvania Press, 1991), 114–15.

38. Thomson quote is from John Rockwell, "A Conversation with Virgil Thomson," in Thomson, *A Virgil Thomson Reader*, 527; the piece features Thomson's own 1977 statements on his artistic debt to Stein. For an account of Thomson's debts to both Stein and Satie incorporating some later (1982) input from Thomson, see Peter Dickinson, "Stein Satie Cummings Thomson Berners Cage: Toward a Context for the Music of Virgil Thomson," *Musical Quarterly* 72, no. 3 (1986), 409 esp.

39. Rorem quote is from Ned Rorem, *Knowing When to Stop: A Memoir*

(New York: Simon and Schuster, 1994), 396. David Diamond, interview with the author, November 13, 2001.

40. In this regard I draw particularly on the work of Carol J. Oja in *Making Music Modern: New York in the 1920s* (New York: Oxford University Press, 2000), including "Women Patrons and Activists," 201–27.

41. As has been noted by several historians of homosexuality, most famously Foucault, the homosexual was born—that is, as a full-blown human type—in the scientific discourse of medicine, psychology, and sexology around 1870. "Homosexuality appeared as one of the forms of sexuality when it was transposed from the practice of sodomy onto a kind of interior androgyny, a hermaphrodism of the soul. The sodomite had been a temporary aberration, the homosexual was now a species": Michel Foucault, *The History of Sexuality,* vol. I: *An Introduction,* trans. Robert Hurley (New York: Pantheon Books, 1978), 43. See also Jeffrey Weeks, *Coming Out: Homosexual Politics in Britain from the Nineteenth Century to the Present* (London: Quartet Books, 1977). Lillian Faderman argues that lesbians internalized nineteenth-century sexologists' notions of congenital inversion or homosexuality, perhaps because these granted their relationships and life patterns more "seriousness," or because women's social position and history vis-à-vis medicine made it difficult to contravene the authority of masculinist medicoscientific discourses: see "The Morbidification of Love between Women by Nineteenth Century Sexologists," *Journal of Homosexuality* 4, no. 1 (1978): 73–90 (reprinted as "The Contributions of the Sexologists," in *Surpassing the Love of Men: Romantic Friendship and Love between Women from the Renaissance to the Present* [New York: William Morrow, 1981], 239–53).

In *Gay New York* Chauncey argues that the hetero/homo sexual binarism is effectively an even more recent creation in the United States, homosexual behavior having become consolidated as "the primary basis for [men's] labeling and self-identification . . . as 'queer' only around the middle of the twentieth century." Up to that time, particularly in working-class culture, sexual abnormality, or queerness, was ascribed only to homosexually active men who appeared as gender-abnormative—that is, effeminate—and thus Chauncey criticizes the misrepresentations instigated by those histories of sexuality that conflate elite discourses with social reality overall (13, 26).

42. On Thomson's orientation to his own sexuality see Tommasini, "I Didn't Want to Be Queer," in *Virgil Thomson,* 64–73. On Copland's tendencies in this regard see Pollack, "Personal Affairs," in *Aaron Copland,* 234–56; see 524 on the apparent conventionality of Copland's gender identification.

43. On Thomson's effeteness and camp see Rorem, "Virgil," in *Knowing When to Stop,* 217–19 esp. Again, expression of the antihomosexual and antifeminine biases in question was not limited to heterosexuals: Bernstein in the forties reportedly pursued effete men and, concurrently, reserved his fiercest derision for them. In 1945 he told Tennessee Williams, referring to a certain pair of "queens" they had met, that "when the revolution came they would be stood up against a wall and shot": Secrest, *Leonard Bernstein,* 148.

44. In prewar New York both "pansy" and "fairy" designated effeminate homosexual men: see Chauncey, *Gay New York*, 14–17.

45. See Neil William Lerner, "The Classical Documentary Score in American Films of Persuasion: Contexts and Case Studies, 1936–1945" (Ph.D. diss., Duke University, 1997), 60, 92, 108–9, 115, and elsewhere.

46. See David Metzer, "'Spurned Love': Eroticism and Abstraction in the Early Works of Aaron Copland," *Journal of Musicology* 15, no. 4 (1997): 417–43. For a sophisticated reading of musical encodings of gay desire that likewise posits orientalist means see Philip Brett, "Eros and Orientalism in Britten's Operas," in Brett et al., eds., *Queering the Pitch*, 235–56. Copland's encoding of homosexual desire in his songs of the early to mid-1920s relies, in Metzer's reading, on emblems of cognate otherness invoking musical orientalism and African-Americanisms. Concerning Copland's late-thirties move toward greater accessibility following the late-twenties establishment of his abstract style, Metzer sees here no retreat from abstraction but only its further cultivation in the populist ballets *Billy the Kid*, *Rodeo*, and *Appalachian Spring*, with their "hallmark leanness, precision, and rhythmic elasticity": "'Spurned Love,'" 440–41.

47. The gendered, sexual, and racial semiotics of repetition might constitute a fascinating subject for further inquiry in connection with such modernist musical and literary idioms as Thomson's and Stein's. Repetition is a device that is both taken as emblematic of African American discursive and aesthetic style, and stigmatized in connection with sexual excess and perversion. Thus repetition, musical and verbal alike, can raise simultaneously the racialized specters of embodiment and sexuality, and implicate the (pathologized) repetition attributed to onanism, homosexuality, and other, frequently undifferentiated, perversions newly scrutinized and regulated within the modernist era.

48. Humphrey Carpenter notes that Stein's influence on Hemingway came initially through Sherwood Anderson, who befriended Hemingway in Chicago in early 1921 and gave the unknown aspirant advice on achieving literary success. Anderson's style in *Winesburg, Ohio* and other works was Stein-influenced, and he shared with Hemingway his view that literary modernism, "especially Gertrude Stein—was not just high art, but really did hold opportunities for fame and commercial success." Hemingway's writing efforts from this point show the influence of Stein via Anderson, though, as Carpenter notes, Hemingway's deployment of Steinian "insistence," or word repetition, immediately differed from that of the source model: Stein repeats irrelevant or insignificant words to artificial effect, whereas Hemingway recasts the device to naturalistic ends, evoking the real-speech situation in which "people repeat the same word rather than search for a synonym." Steinian influence is evident in Hemingway's "incantatory manner" and "carefully contrived syntax . . . 'unpacking' the sentence's meaning piece by piece rather than compressing its ideas or fitting them together." After Hemingway and his wife Hadley moved to Paris and met Gertrude Stein in 1922 her influence on him was direct,

through the friendship and mentoring relationship that developed. "Gertrude Stein and me are just like brothers and we see a lot of her," Hemingway wrote to Anderson soon after meeting Stein. See Carpenter, *Geniuses Together: American Writers in Paris in the 1920s* (London: Unwin Hyman, 1987), 58–68.

49. Sedgwick, *Epistemology of the Closet*, 73–74. Also suggestive here is Sedgwick's notion of the "glass closet," and elsewhere, D. A. Miller's statement that "the social function of secrecy . . . is not to conceal knowledge, so much as to conceal knowledge of the knowledge": "Secret Subjects, Open Secrets," in *The Novel and the Police* (Berkeley: University of California Press, 1988), 206. The paired characterizations of Thomson are quoted from Glenn Watkins, *Soundings: Music in the Twentieth Century* (New York: Schirmer, 1988), 451, but they are essentially similar to phrasings found in many other writings. See, for example, Rorem, who recalls being shocked by his first encounters with Thomson's music, which he heard as "sappy and charmless yet pretentious in its false naïveté," and which he describes (in conspicuously gendered terms) as markedly differing from the contemporary music of leading composers, "men with guts, sensuality, rhapsody, violence": *Knowing When to Stop*, 198. Pollack similarly cites Thomson's musical "wit and mock naïveté" as (here, indicatively othered) sources of "refreshing contrast at concerts of modern music": *Aaron Copland*, 171.

50. Marcel Schneider in *Combat*, review of 1952 Paris revival of *Four Saints in Three Acts*; quoted in Thomson, *Virgil Thomson by Virgil Thomson*, 409.

51. Chauncey, *Gay New York*, 274–75.

52. See, for example, Tommasini, "I Didn't Want to Be Queer," also 356 and elsewhere in *Virgil Thomson*. See also Rorem, who remarks of Thomson, "Campy and gossipy and aggressively effeminate as he was at home, so he was circumspect in the world": *Knowing When to Stop*, 219.

53. Queer world and community making in various spheres of twentieth-century American life has previously been chronicled by John D'Emilio, *Sexual Politics, Sexual Communities: The Making of a Homosexual Minority in the United States, 1940–1970* (Chicago: University of Chicago Press, 1983); Allan Bérubé, *Coming Out under Fire: The History of Gay Men and Women in World War Two* (New York: Free Press, 1990); Lillian Faderman, *Odd Girls and Twilight Lovers: A History of Lesbian Life in Twentieth-Century America* (New York: Columbia University Press, 1991); Elizabeth Lapovsky Kennedy and Madeline D. Davis, *Boots of Leather, Slippers of Gold: The History of a Lesbian Community* (New York: Routledge, 1993); Esther Newton, *Cherry Grove, Fire Island: Sixty Years in America's First Gay and Lesbian Town* (Boston: Beacon Press, 1993); Martin B. Duberman, *Stonewall* (New York: Dutton, 1993); Chauncey, *Gay New York*; Gayle S. Rubin, "The Valley of the Kings: Leathermen in San Francisco, 1960–1990" (Ph.D. diss., University of Michigan, 1994); and Marc Stein, *City of Sisterly and Brotherly Loves: Lesbian and Gay Philadelphia, 1945–1972* (Chicago: University of Chicago Press, 2000). The

notion of queer world making (i.e., the creation of queer counterpublics) originates in Lauren Berlant and Michael Warner, "Sex in Public (Intimacy)," *Critical Inquiry* 24, no. 2 (1998): 547–66.

CHAPTER 1

John Todhunter, *The Black Cat* (1893); quoted in Neil Bartlett, *Who Was That Man? A Present for Mr Oscar Wilde* (London: Serpent's Tail, 1988), 121. Gertrude Stein, *Four Saints in Three Acts: An Opera to Be Sung* (New York: Random House, 1934), 45–46.

1. As witness the recent revivals of the work by, for example, the Houston Grand Opera (1996) and the Mark Morris Dance Group (2000), the PBS broadcast of Steven Watson's documentary on the 1934 premiere (March 1999), and the growing body of scholarly treatments of *Four Saints*. This literature includes Watson's cultural history of the opera and its original production, *Prepare for Saints: Gertrude Stein, Virgil Thomson, and the Mainstreaming of American Modernism* (New York: Random House, 1998), and numerous essays in literary, musical, theatrical, and gender-sexuality studies: see the sources cited throughout this chapter. The on- and offstage spectacle of *Four Saints'* Hartford premiere is delineated by Watson, "Opening Night," in *Prepare for Saints*, 265–80.

2. Lucius Beebe in the *New York Herald Tribune* (February 9, 1934); quoted in Tommasini, *Virgil Thomson*, 258.

3. Watson, *Prepare for Saints*, 276. "Scenario" can have multiple meanings in this context, but what Grosser contributed to the opera should be understood as its plot—which was not at all delineated by Stein's text.

4. Claudia Roth Pierpont, "The Mother of Confusion: Gertrude Stein," in *Passionate Minds: Women Rewriting the World* (New York: Alfred A. Knopf, 2000), 34; emphasis mine. Pierpont further locates the suspected significance of Stein's writings "somewhere between the studies of Freud and the logic of the Red Queen." The music critic John Rockwell similarly flags Thomson's musical setting as more meaningful than meets the eye—or ear: "[A] remarkable depth of emotion lurks beneath the lulling tunefulness and folkish abstraction of [Thomson's] two Gertrude Stein operas": "Introduction," ix.

5. This effect surely owed a debt to *Four Saints'* particular uses of an African American cast. As Barbara Webb notes, onstage blackness still functioned here as it had in minstrelsy, to facilitate for white audiences an imagined and desired "regression." It allowed them, in watching *Four Saints*, "to become 'ignorant' themselves and vicariously experience a comforting, simple faith in an increasingly faithless time colored by the Depression, scientific advances, and persistent memories of the horrors of World War I": "The Centrality of Race to the Modernist Aesthetics of Gertrude Stein's *Four Saints in Three Acts*," *Modernism/Modernity* 7, no. 3 (2000): 453–54, 456.

6. In 1982 liner notes to a new recording of the opera (from a revival hon-

oring his eighty-fifth birthday), Thomson identified "Steinese" as the author's "own language." See Virgil Thomson, "About 'Four Saints'": liner notes for *Four Saints in Three Acts* (Elektra Nonesuch 9 79035). Thomson reported these audience effects (produced by his private, one-man performances) in a letter of July 17, 1927, to Briggs Buchanan: Tim Page and Vanessa Weeks Page, eds., *Selected Letters of Virgil Thomson* (New York: Summit Books, 1988), 81–82.

7. Maurice Grosser, "Scenario," in Virgil Thomson, *Four Saints in Three Acts* (New York: G. Schirmer, 1948), iii. This edition comprises a complete vocal score with piano reduction of the orchestral score.

8. Olin Downes in the *New York Times* (February 25, 1934); quoted in Tommasini, *Virgil Thomson*, 261. I would locate Thomson's stereotypic staging of African Americans as people of simple faith not primarily onstage in the drama, which concerns the purportedly sophisticated (if ritualistic) Roman Catholic faith, but offstage in his decision to cast the opera with African Americans and his explanations of this decision in terms of "Negroes'" alleged naturalness and unselfconsciousness in conveying both religious themes and Steinian "nonsense" language.

9. Carl Van Vechten, "Introduction: A Few Notes about 'Four Saints in Three Acts,'" in Stein, *Four Saints in Three Acts*, 9.

10. Watson, *Prepare for Saints*, 276.

11. *The New Yorker* Paris correspondent Janet Flanner (a.k.a. Genêt) famously bestowed this byline: see *Paris Was Yesterday: 1925–1939* (New York: Viking, 1972), xx–xxi. In his critical discussion of *Four Saints* John Cage deploys a happy-marriage metaphor that is taken up in some subsequent sources: Kathleen Hoover and John Cage, *Virgil Thomson: His Life and Music* (New York: Thomas Yoseloff, 1959), 157.

12. Stein's *Four Saints* serves as the exemplar of "abstract libretto" in Patrick J. Smith's history of the genre, *The Tenth Muse: A Historical Study of the Opera Libretto* (New York: Alfred A. Knopf, 1970), 282.

13. Sidonie Smith, "'Stein' Is an 'Alice' Is a 'Gertrude Stein,'" in *Subjectivity, Identity, and the Body: Women's Autobiographical Practices in the Twentieth Century* (Bloomington: Indiana University Press, 1993), 74.

14. Gertrude Stein, *The Geographical History of America; Or, The Relation of Human Nature to the Human Mind*, reprint ed. (Baltimore: Johns Hopkins University Press, [1936] 1995), 139.

15. Ibid., 175.

16. For a lucid discussion of Stein's artistic theories and philosophies in this regard see Bonnie Marranca, "Presence of Mind," in *Ecologies of Theater: Essays at the Century Turning* (Baltimore: Johns Hopkins University Press, 1996), 3–24.

17. Daniel Albright, "An Opera with No Acts: Four Saints in Three Acts," *Southern Review* 33, no. 3 (1997): 584, 574. On Stein's "cubism," see also Thomson, *Virgil Thomson by Virgil Thomson*, 172–73.

18. Quoted in Sidonie Smith, "'Stein' Is an 'Alice' Is a 'Gertrude Stein,'" 72. Lisa Ruddick identifies this passage as originating in notebook DB, p. 12,

C.21, following the pagination in Leon Katz's transcription of the notebooks: see Ruddick, *Reading Gertrude Stein: Body, Text, Gnosis* (Ithaca: Cornell University Press, 1990), 65. See also Leon Katz, "The First Making of *The Making of Americans*" (Ph.D. diss., Columbia University, 1963).

19. Otto Weininger, *Sex and Character* (1906), 189; quoted in Linda Simon, *The Biography of Alice B. Toklas* (Garden City, N.Y.: Doubleday, 1977), 58–59.

20. Weininger, *Sex and Character*, 66; quoted ibid., 59. In the 1920s Stein would begin "to cut the cord she and Western culture had tied between masculinity and towering creativity," according to Catharine R. Stimpson, "The Somagrams of Gertrude Stein" (1985), in *The Lesbian and Gay Studies Reader*, ed. Michèle Aina Barale, Henry Abelove, and David M. Halperin (New York: Routledge, 1993), 646.

21. M. A. K. Halliday, "Anti-Languages," *American Anthropologist* 78, no. 3 (1976): 570–84; quoted in Stimpson, "The Somagrams of Gertrude Stein," 648.

22. Stimpson, "The Somagrams of Gertrude Stein," 649.

23. Dean, *Imperial Brotherhood*, deploys the term *lavender scare* in his analysis of the U.S. government's Cold War policies and inquisitions and their gender and sexual vectors. For discussion of homosexuality's implication in "fears of a conspiratorial 'state within a state,'" see 164.

24. This deciphering work is advanced in Richard Bridgman, *Gertrude Stein in Pieces* (New York: Oxford University Press, 1970); Simon, *The Biography of Alice B. Toklas*; Catharine R. Stimpson, "The Mind, The Body, and Gertrude Stein," *Critical Inquiry* 3, no. 3 (1977): 489–506; Elizabeth Fifer, "Is Flesh Advisable? The Interior Theater of Gertrude Stein," *Signs: Journal of Women in Culture and Society* 4, no. 3 (1979): 472–83; and other writings. It is carried further in later work including Ruddick, *Reading Gertrude Stein*. Blazing a trail for such scholarship was Donald Sutherland, *Gertrude Stein: A Biography of Her Work* (New Haven: Yale University Press, 1951).

25. Van Vechten, "Introduction," 10; his quotation of Stein is from *The Autobiography of Alice B. Toklas* (New York: Harcourt, Brace and Company, 1933), 259.

26. Emily Crandall suggests the interpretation of Van Vechten's closing sentence as envisaging a more ideal *Four Saints* audience in some less homophobic future world. Her perspicacious reading appears in "'When this you see remember me': Queerness/Musicality/Collaboration in *Four Saints in Three Acts*," unpublished manuscript written for a winter 2002 seminar in the University of Michigan: Queer World Making in American Musical Modernism, 1934–54.

27. Copland, for example, having sailed to France in 1921 for a year of study, later noted, "I thought a lot more about Brooklyn when I was in Paris than I ever did in Brooklyn," and "It's curious that one can sometimes see America more clearly from across the ocean than when living right inside it": quoted in Pollack, *Aaron Copland*, 55. Watson notes some statements to the same effect from Stein, and that "Thomson often quipped that he went to Paris

in order to write about Kansas City": *Prepare for Saints*, 55–56. For queer Americans like Stein, Thomson, and Flanner (quoted above in her designation of Paris as "capital of hedonism"), as for African Americans like Josephine Baker, Paris was a paradise affording freedom from the social and legal sanctions America imposed on bearers of certain minoritized identities. French law, unlike its English and American counterparts, was based on a separation of church and state, having been purged during the Revolution of such theologically based norms as the distinction between natural and unnatural sexual relations and "strictures against blasphemy, heresy, sacrilege, witchcraft, and incest." Twentieth-century Paris, particularly between the wars, had an international reputation, well known among queer persons, "as a tolerant, wide-open city." I quote here from Michael D. Sibalis, "Homophobia, Vichy France, and the 'Crime of Homosexuality': The Origins of the Ordinance of 6 August 1942," *GLQ: A Journal of Lesbian and Gay Studies* 8, no. 3 (2002): 302, 306.

Thomson retrospectively characterized the music scene of 1920s Paris as one that appealed precisely by its relatively arcane, subcultural flavor, as contrasted with the dominant music scenes of Vienna, Berlin, and other Austro-German centers: *Virgil Thomson by Virgil Thomson*, 118–20. Rorem characterizes France as having "never been an especially musical nation": *Knowing When to Stop*, 392; see also 413.

28. Tommasini, *Virgil Thomson*, 261.

29. One might protest that these terms—decadent, Parisian, perhaps foppish—can impute Old World aristocracy and class privilege, particularly when used by a leftist critic, which Downes was. And they can indeed, but never apart from their homophobic imputations: From the 1895 Wilde trials through the Cold War lavender scare, the aristocratic, artistic-bohemian, and sexually perverse are fused concepts in the American cultural imaginary, and they (and their attributions) operate metonymically in relation to one another. And as Sinfield notes, bohemia "as a social category" provides the grounds for both avant-garde art and "sexually dissident" practices in this period (urban bohemias having formed in the nineteenth and early twentieth centuries in London, New York, and Paris): *Out on Stage*, 49–50.

30. The former phrase appears twice in Thomson, "About 'Four Saints.'" Grosser refers to "Saint Ignatius" and "his men" in "Scenario," v.

31. In March 1927 Stein wrote to Thomson of the elements she was beginning to confect in her libretto: "Four saints in three acts. And others. . . . All four and then additions. We must invent them": Thomson, *Virgil Thomson by Virgil Thomson*, 91 (Watson's citation of this letter dates it at March 26, 1927: *Prepare for Saints*, 45). The lines from the Prologue appear in Thomson's score at rehearsal no. 9 + 8 bars: Thomson, *Four Saints in Three Acts*, 10.

32. Grosser, "Scenario," iii.

33. "Particular friendship" (or "special friendship") is the term by which same-sex pairings have long been labeled and proscribed in Catholic monastic life.

34. Thomson, *Virgil Thomson by Virgil Thomson*, 179. Sara Blair analyzes

the site of Stein and Toklas's "tranquil life," 27 rue de Fleurus, as a new "social form," a site of both avant-garde production and bourgeois domesticity that can usefully challenge reigning theoretical notions of literary modernism in relation to modern domesticity: "Home Truths: Gertrude Stein, 27 Rue de Fleurus, and the Place of the Avant-Garde," *American Literary History* 12, no. 3 (2000): 417–37.

35. Thomson connects Saint Ignatius with Stein's Paris-based literary rival James Joyce: *Virgil Thomson by Virgil Thomson*, 91. But Thomson's biographer Tommasini notes the parallel temperaments of Saint Chavez and Grosser, Ignatius and Thomson: "Like Saint Chavez, the character Maurice [Grosser] dreamed up to act as confidant to the imperious Saint Ignatius in *Four Saints*, Maurice had infinite tolerance for Virgil's fits and sputterings": *Virgil Thomson*, 5.

36. Stein, *The Autobiography of Alice B. Toklas*, 141–42. Simon, *The Biography of Alice B. Toklas*, 327, cites Bridgman, *Gertrude Stein in Pieces*, 177 ff., and Leon Katz, "The First Making of *The Making of Americans*," 277, as reading Saint Therese as a "tribute" to Toklas.

37. Noted in Meg Albrinck, " 'How can a sister see Saint Theresa suitably': Difficulties in Staging Gertrude Stein's *Four Saints in Three Acts*," *Women's Studies* 25 (1995): 10.

38. Stein, *Four Saints in Three Acts*, 36. This compares with depictions of Alice in various works, for example, "I can be as stupid as I like because my wife is always right" ("Reread Another. A Play. To be played indoors or out. I wish to be a school."; 1921), and, in Alice's voice, "I love to be right. It is so necessary" ("This One Is Serious," 1915); quoted in Simon, *The Biography of Alice B. Toklas*, 345, 349 (see 328 and 348 for further relevant examples).

39. Stein, *Four Saints in Three Acts*, 35. Thomson's remarks appear in "A Very Difficult Author," *New York Review of Books* (April 8, 1971): 4. In addition to the four lines Thomson cites I include here the line "To be belied" for its resemblance and possible relation to "Lifting Belly" (1915–17), which is, "[o]f all Gertrude's erotic pieces, . . . the most graphic recording of Lesbian love" and essentially "a long, raucous celebration of sex" (Simon, *The Biography of Alice B. Toklas*, 332). If we accept Thomson's reading of this passage, then Saint Teresa/Therese may at this point be back in a more Gertrude-like form, for it is evidently Stein who proclaims in "Susie Asado" that (by Thomson's interpretation) such effluvium "is my ice cream." He writes: "a word that occurs in an earlier Spanish period . . . seems to mean high sexual delight or, still more precisely, the sexual effluvia. The word is Susie, as in Susie Asado (*asado* being the Spanish word for 'baked'), which shortly becomes 'Toasted Susie is my ice cream' " (4).

40. The conception of music in terms of "abstraction" owes much to these notions and those of Eduard Hanslick, whose 1854 treatise *On the Musically Beautiful* argued "that the beauty of a piece of music is specifically musical, i.e. is inherent in the tonal relationships without reference to an extraneous, extramusical context": *On the Musically Beautiful*, trans. Geoffrey Payzant (Indi-

anapolis: Hackett, 1986), xxiii. For a recent account of Hanslick's enduring influence on musical aesthetics and analysis see Fred Everett Maus, "Hanslick's Animism," *Journal of Musicology* 10, no. 3 (1992): 273–92.

41. Walter Pater, *The Renaissance: Studies in Art and Poetry* (New York: Modern Library, [1873] n.d.), 111. Relevant to the present discussion (and also to the Wilde epigraph at the beginning of the next chapter) are Wayne Koestenbaum's ruminations on Oscar Wilde's and his mentor Pater's figurative use of music, during "an era of coalescing homosexual identity, . . . to symbolize a homosexuality they could not state clearly in words": *The Queen's Throat: Opera, Homosexuality, and the Mystery of Desire* (New York: Poseidon Press, 1993), 190.

42. See, for example, Ruddick, *Reading Gertrude Stein;* Stimpson, "The Somagrams of Gertrude Stein," 642–52; Smith, " 'Stein' Is an 'Alice' Is a 'Gertrude Stein' "; and Ellen E. Berry, *Curved Thought and Textual Wandering: Gertrude Stein's Postmodernism* (Ann Arbor: University of Michigan Press, 1992).

43. Michael North reads in the abstract idioms of Stein, Eliot, Pound, and certain others a concrete scenario of racial masquerade, and reveals modernist literary texts of putative semantic illegibility and syntactic singularity as veiled imitations of African American vernacular: see North, *The Dialect of Modernism: Race, Language, and Twentieth-Century Culture* (New York: Oxford University Press, 1994). Various other studies have located primary investments of modernist and nineteenth-century literature and culture in figurations of the African American. See Sieglinde Lemke, *Primitivist Modernism: Black Culture and the Origins of Transatlantic Modernism* (New York: Oxford University Press, 1998); Kenneth W. Warren, *Black and White Strangers: Race and American Literary Realism* (Chicago: University of Chicago Press, 1993); Shelley Fisher Fishkin, *Was Huck Black? Mark Twain and African-American Voices* (New York: Oxford University Press, 1993); Toni Morrison, *Playing in the Dark: Whiteness and the Literary Imagination* (New York: Vintage Books, 1992); and Leslie A. Fiedler, *Love and Death in the American Novel,* rev. ed. (New York: Stein and Day, 1966). For discussions of the structure and use of literary and artistic abstraction more generally see North, "Modernism's African Mask: The Stein-Picasso Collaboration," in *The Dialect of Modernism,* 59–76; Marjorie Perloff, *The Poetics of Indeterminacy: From Rimbaud to Cage* (1981; reprint, Evanston: Northwestern University Press, 1983), 67–108 esp.; Randa Dubnick, *The Structure of Obscurity: Gertrude Stein, Language, and Cubism* (Urbana: University of Illinois Press, 1984); and Wendy Steiner, *Exact Resemblance: The Literary Portraiture of Gertrude Stein* (New Haven: Yale University Press, 1978).

44. Robert M. Crunden, *Body and Soul: The Making of American Modernism* (New York: Basic Books, 2000), ix.

45. Raymond Williams, *The Politics of Modernism: Against the New Conformists* (New York: Verso, 1996), 58. For an examination of primitivist perspectives in relation to Van Vechten and to Thomson's casting of *Four Saints*

see Watson, "Modernism Goes Uptown," in *Prepare for Saints*, 197–208. Gail Bederman historicizes the cultural context within which conceptions of U.S. national self-identity were constructed in post-Reconstruction, pre–World War I America through recourse to racialized, and racist, notions of the primitive: Bederman, *Manliness and Civilization: A Cultural History of Gender and Race in the United States, 1880–1917* (Chicago: University of Chicago Press, 1995).

46. T. S. Eliot, "Review of *Tarr*," *The Egoist* (September 1918): 106; quoted in North, *The Dialect of Modernism*, 80. See chapter 2 in the present volume for elaboration of the cultural meanings of "civilized" and "primitive" in American discourse circa 1880–1917. White constructions of the modern in the 1930s–40s deployed blackness along the lines suggested by Sherrie Tucker's remarks on swing: "The Swing Era is, in a certain sense, the highly commodified continuation of the Jazz Age, in which young white musicians and listeners produced a subculture from African American culture, 'modernizing' themselves through the consumption of black music, language, and style and white fantasies of exotic otherness": *Swing Shift*, 245.

While Thomson's casting of African Americans was stereotypical (as mentioned above) and opportunistic in its deliberate provocativeness, it was at the same time, as Watson notes, a genuine milestone: the first casting of African Americans in a work not specifically about African American life; the first time those cast members had been paid for rehearsals; and the first time an all-black cast had performed an opera for white audiences (*Prepare for Saints*, 6). For revealing analyses of the ambivalence whereby African Americans have been simultaneously objects of both repulsion and desire within the frame of white cultural production, see Eric Lott, *Love and Theft: Blackface Minstrelsy and the American Working Class* (New York: Oxford University Press, 1993), and Michael Paul Rogin, *Blackface, White Noise: Jewish Immigrants in the Hollywood Melting Pot* (Berkeley: University of California Press, 1996).

47. The classic essay on Harlem's queer community in this period is that of the late Eric Garber: "A Spectacle in Color: The Lesbian and Gay Subculture of Jazz Age Harlem," in *Hidden from History: Reclaiming the Gay and Lesbian Past*, ed. Martin Bauml Duberman, Martha Vicinus, and George Chauncey, Jr. (New York: New American Library, 1989), 318–31. Discussions of *Four Saints* that remark on the queer emblematics of the opera's Harlem cast include those of Tommasini and Webb cited above, and Lisa Barg, "Black Voices/White Sounds: Race and Representation in Virgil Thomson's *Four Saints in Three Acts*," *American Music* 18, no. 2 (2000): 121–61. Watson, *Prepare for Saints*, discusses the nocturnal Harlem pleasure excursions of Thomson, Van Vechten, and *Four Saints*' original choreographer (the visiting Briton) Frederick Ashton, as well as Henry-Russell Hitchcock, Lincoln Kirstein, and others of Thomson's friends among the "largely homosexual constellation of Harvard-trained art professionals who would define modernist taste in America" (7): see "Modernism Goes Uptown," 197–208, also 136. Grosser's practices in this regard receive mention in Tommasini, *Virgil Thomson*, 433, and Philip Johnson's in Charles Kaiser, *The Gay Metropolis, 1940–1996* (Boston: Houghton Mifflin, 1997), 41.

48. This reading of Melanctha's blackness is something of a critical commonplace. See, for example, Sarah Schulman's invocation of it to define, by comparison, Carson McCullers's use of Jewish and physically disabled or deformed characters to represent queerness: "McCullers: Canon Fodder?" (review of Carlos L. Dews, *Illumination and Night Glare: The Unfinished Autobiography of Carson McCullers*), *The Nation* (June 26, 2000), 40; see also Ruddick, *Reading Gertrude Stein*, 32–33. Also germane is the anthropologist Karen Brodkin's demonstration that, beginning with the immigration waves of 1880–1924, Jews in U.S. society were regarded as nonwhite, and that "despite being relatively successful in material terms, many American Jews tend to think of themselves as distinctly liberal politically, as invested in social justice and in identification with the underdog, and, sometimes, as not white": *How Jews Became White Folks*, 27–28, 3.

49. The quoted phrase is from Victor Fell Yellin, "The Operas of Virgil Thomson," in Virgil Thomson, *American Music since 1910* (New York: Holt, Rinehart and Winston, 1970), 91. Yellin's phrase articulates an assessment of Thomson's declamatory art that has long been virtually universal. For discussions of Thomson's music see also Victor Fell Yellin, "Sullivan and Thomson, Gilbert and Stein," *Journal of Musicology* 11, no. 4 (1993): 478–98; Dickinson, "Stein Satie Cummings Thomson Berners Cage"; and Lerner, "The Classical Documentary Score in American Films of Persuasion," and "Copland's Music of Wide Open Spaces: Surveying the Pastoral Trope in Hollywood," *Musical Quarterly* 85, no. 3 (2001): 477–515.

50. Susan McClary analyzes "chromatic excess" as a signifier of Carmen's illicit, "dissonant" sex-gender subjectivity: see *Feminine Endings: Music, Gender, and Sexuality* (Minneapolis: University of Minnesota Press, 1991), 57.

51. Gayle S. Rubin, "Thinking Sex: Notes for a Radical Theory of the Politics of Sexuality" (1984), in Barale et al., eds., *The Lesbian and Gay Studies Reader*, 11–13.

52. Quoted passages are from Cage's discussion of *Capital Capitals* in Hoover and Cage, *Virgil Thomson*, 146.

53. The quoted phrase reproduces Grosser's description in "Scenario," iv.

54. On this point I disagree with Tommasini, who remarks on the same musical features as I do here but ascribes to them different meanings: "In opposition to the implied bickering in the text, Thomson provided quiet lyricism, turning it into a gentle exchange between the Commère and Compère . . . supported by a sturdy, sustained, and unchanging harmony." He reads the music here as "calming, content, somewhat sad," and posits that it thus suggested to Grosser "an avowal of affection between the opera's gracious hosts": *Virgil Thomson*, 208.

55. Lerner discusses Thomson's use of such melodic "open spaces" as characterize this triadic tune to represent "thematic and visual" open spaces in his 1936 score for the government documentary *The Plow That Broke the Plains*. And he compares Copland's (far more famous) deployment of the same method in subsequent opera and film scores: see "Copland's Music of Wide Open Spaces," 485–86.

56. *Tonic* harmony defines the "home base" of a given key in the Western major-minor tonal system. In any key the tonic *degree* (i.e., scale step) names the governing scale and is the basis ("root") of the tonic (I) harmony: Thus in C major the I harmony is a C-major triad, C–E–G. The IV and V harmonies are built on the fourth and fifth scale degrees, respectively—thus, in the key of C major, IV is an F-major triad, F–A–C, and V, a G-major triad, G–B–D.

57. Lerner lists "a fondness for fourths and fifths both harmonically and melodically" as also among the defining elements of Copland's "pastoral mode": "Copland's Music of Wide Open Spaces," 483.

58. *Les noces* is typically regarded as the culmination of Stravinsky's first, "Russian" style period, but it also bears close relations to the primitivism of *The Rite*. As Watkins notes, *Les noces'* singular effect was "exotic-primitive more than Russian": *Soundings*, 230.

59. Copland's remarks on *Four Saints* are reported in Thomson, *Virgil Thomson by Virgil Thomson*, 243; see also Tommasini, *Virgil Thomson*, 290.

60. Lerner, "Copland's Music of Wide Open Spaces," 486; see also "The Classical Documentary Score in American Films of Persuasion," 189, 272, and elsewhere.

61. Ned Rorem, *A Ned Rorem Reader*, foreword by J. D. McClatchy (New Haven: Yale University Press, 2001), 244. Rorem, Thomson's former assistant and student, attests similarly in *Knowing When to Stop*, 229, 231, 233, 244, 281, 322. Pollack acknowledges Thomson's importance as an influence on Copland, particularly in *Billy the Kid*, some of whose "more daringly rough-hewn moments . . . seem to leap from the pages of any number of Thomson scores." Pollack counters, however, that Copland absorbed "a wide variety of sources," including Stravinsky, and cautions that the "whole matter . . . awaits careful scrutiny": *Aaron Copland*, 174; on Thomson's influence see also 307, 552–53. To Pollack's comments I would respond, first, that the Stravinskian element is well known and long remarked, particularly in relation to Copland's early work under the influence of Boulanger, and in his continued composition in a so-called serious or severe style. It is in this connection that Copland was bound, as Thomson put it, to a "correct façade of dissonance," his abandonment of which was (a) the most essential ingredient in his breakthrough to a populist idiom, and (b) facilitated precisely by his adoption of Thomsonian simplicities. Moreover, the argument herein (and in Lerner) is not simply that Thomson's music importantly informed Copland's music, but that it importantly informed and indeed provided the crucial components for, specifically, the Coplandian idiom that is best known and most distinctly associated with the American topos—an idiom in which Stravinskian influences are not especially relevant. Second and finally, the careful scrutiny that Pollack rightly calls for is now available in the work of Neil Lerner (see previous note). Lerner's conclusions underscore the influence of Thomson's film scores on not only Copland's film music but his Americana music generally—and thus support my position here.

62. Tommasini, *Virgil Thomson*, 563. Copland was by this time still alive but in an advanced stage of senility.

63. Thomson, *American Music since 1910*, 53–55. The Copland quote comes from a July 17, 1942, postcard asking Thomson to send some scores for purposes of two lectures he was preparing. Following his request for Satie's *Socrate* and Thomson's *Four Saints*, Copland added, "I heard The River yesterday over the air. Its *[sic]* awful nice music—and a lesson in how to treat Americana": Yale MSS 29, series III, box 33, folder 1. Tommasini reports that Copland was also significantly influenced by Thomson's *Symphony on a Hymn Tune* (1928), and he discusses Copland's self-professed modeling on Thomson's 1937 ballet *Filling Station* in his own breakthrough *Billy the Kid* the next year: *Virgil Thomson*, 156, 290–91.

64. Rockwell, "Introduction," x.

65. Corinne E. Blackmer, "The Ecstasies of Saint Teresa: The Saint as Queer Diva from Crashaw to *Four Saints in Three Acts*," in *En Travesti: Women, Gender, Subversion, Opera*, ed. Corinne E. Blackmer and Patricia J. Smith (New York: Columbia University Press, 1995), 309. The full citation for Teresa's *Life* is Teresa of Ávila, *The Life of Saint Teresa of Ávila by Herself*, trans. J. M. Cohen (Harmondsworth: Penguin, 1957).

66. Thomson confirms that Stein did so "probably during her pre–World War I stay in Avila"—thus, when she visited that city with Toklas in 1912: "A Very Difficult Author," 5.

67. Ernest Hemingway identifies Firbank ("and, later, Scott Fitzgerald") as the only writer Stein spoke well of "in the three or four years we were friends" (i.e., ca. 1922–26), beyond those who had somehow advanced her career: *A Moveable Feast* (New York: Charles Scribner's Sons, 1964), 27. His mention of Firbank here may be an effort to flag Stein's "perversion" and to discredit her tastes. Blackmer, "The Ecstasies of Saint Teresa," 312, designates Firbank as sapphically identified, citing on this point Brigid Brophy, *Prancing Novelist: A Defense of Fiction in the Form of a Critical Biography in Praise of Ronald Firbank* (New York: Harper and Row, 1973). The English Firbank was also known to the literary Sitwell sibs of London, at least one of whom, Edith, was among Stein's associates.

68. Blackmer, "The Ecstasies of Saint Teresa," 309. John Boswell, *Same-Sex Unions in Premodern Europe* (New York: Villard, 1994), 111; quoted in Blackmer, "The Ecstasies of Saint Teresa," 310. Homosexuality's complex, contradictory positionings within Catholicism are explored in Mark D. Jordan, *The Silence of Sodom: Homosexuality in Modern Catholicism* (Chicago: University of Chicago Press, 2000).

69. Blackmer, "The Ecstasies of Saint Teresa," 340 n. 3.

70. Ibid., 329.

71. Albrinck's argument appears in "'How can a sister see Saint Therese suitably,'" 4. Catharine R. Stimpson explores the "Gertrice/Altrude" concept at length in "Gertrice/Altrude: Stein, Toklas, and the Paradox of the Happy Marriage," in *Mothering the Mind: Twelve Studies of Writers and Their Silent Partners*, ed. Ruth Perry and Martine Watson Brownley (New York: Holmes and Meier, 1984), 122–39.

72. Stein, *Four Saints in Three Acts*, 25.

73. Tommasini, *Virgil Thomson*, 168.

74. Bridgman, *Gertrude Stein in Pieces*, 187; quoted in Bowers, "*They Watch Me as They Watch This*," 50.

75. Bowers, "*They Watch Me as They Watch This*," 50, 61.

76. Virgil Thomson, "About 'Four Saints.'"

77. Stein was particularly engaged with affectionate and erotic themes in her writings of 1913–31, her "period of greatest dependence on Alice": Simon, *The Biography of Alice B. Toklas*, 315. For textual instances see Simon's appendix, "An Annotated Gertrude Stein," 315–54, offered as a supplement to Bridgman's (1970) "dissection of Gertrude Stein into pieces" (315)—that is, his decoding of discrete elements of Stein's language across the range and span of her oeuvre.

78. Watson, *Prepare for Saints*, 47.

79. Van Vechten, "Introduction," 10. His quotation of Stein is from *The Autobiography of Alice B. Toklas*, 259, where Stein's reason for destroying associational emotion is given thus: since "beauty, music, decoration, the result of emotion should never be the cause."

80. Martin Puchner, "Gertrude Stein: *Four Saints in Three Acts*—A Closet Drama to Be Performed," in *Stage Fright: Modernism, Anti-Theatricality, and Drama* (Baltimore: Johns Hopkins University Press, 2002), 111, 114.

81. Thomson himself translates *commère* and *compère* as "end men" in *Virgil Thomson by Virgil Thomson*, 107. For further minstrelsy comparisons see Webb, "The Centrality of Race to the Modernist Aesthetics of Gertrude Stein's *Four Saints in Three Acts*"; and Barg, "Black Voices/White Sounds."

82. Grosser, "Scenario," iii–iv.

83. Ibid., iii.

84. Ibid., iv.

85. Albrinck, "'How can a sister see Saint Therese suitably,'" 11.

86. Thomson, *Virgil Thomson by Virgil Thomson*, 107.

87. Puchner, "Gertrude Stein," 112.

88. In fact, one might read Commère and Compère as stand-ins for Stein and Thomson, as Blackmer does (further reading these roles humorously in "stage-managing" terms) in "The Ecstasies of Saint Teresa," 329. I concur with this reading but would further specify that Commère and Compère represent Stein and Thomson exclusively in their work as creators of *Four Saints*, in which regard their collaboration renders them partners in a creative "marriage." Such a reading finds support in Thomson's later use of more explicitly developed narrational characters in *The Mother of Us All* (1947), now called Gertrude S and Virgil T. As for Commère and Compère's depiction of romantic melodrama: Surely a reading of their characters as Stein and Thomson stand-ins can only serve—now, as at the time of their debut—to undermine further any credible or serious appearance of heterosexuality in the opera. Hence Blackmer sees them as "enact[ing] a queer love duet" (336).

89. In this instance Cage is discussing not *Four Saints in Three Acts* but its

"warm-up" work *Capital Capitals:* Hoover and Cage, *Virgil Thomson,* 146. Cage's contribution to the 1959 Hoover-Cage biography was completed in summer 1957: Tommasini, *Virgil Thomson,* 445. More recently, Oja has explicitly located in this "tenderness" passage a clue to *Capital Capitals'* encoding of "a string of homosexual allusions within its churchliness": *Making Music Modern,* 257.

90. Thomson's 1966 memoir *Virgil Thomson by Virgil Thomson* omitted any hint of his own or his male associates' homosexuality and offered tales of its author's putative heterosexual intrigues. But Tommasini's 1997 biography treats Thomson's queerness frankly and integratively, and suggests that the composer granted him implicit permission thus to "tell the whole story" after his death: *Virgil Thomson,* xii. This claim finds corroboration in Susan McClary's statement that Thomson had invited her to be his official biographer "because he knew [she] would not shy away from [gay] issues": Susan McClary, Philip Brett, and Elizabeth Wood, "Letters: McClary and the *New York Times,*" GLSG Newsletter: For the Gay and Lesbian Study Group of the American Musicological Society 2, no. 1 (1992): 14.

91. Thomson, "About 'Four Saints.'"

92. Thomson in a letter to Stein, September 1927; quoted in Watson, *Prepare for Saints,* 48.

93. Bowers, *"They Watch Me as They Watch This,"* 4.

94. Gertrude Stein, "Plays" (1935), in *Lectures in America* (Boston: Beacon Press, 1985): 93, 104–5; quoted in Bowers, *"They Watch Me as They Watch This,"* 77.

95. The quoted phrase is from Puchner, "Gertrude Stein," 114.

96. Blackmer, "The Ecstasies of Saint Teresa," 328. Blackmer echoes here a phrase of D. A. Miller (first quoted earlier in her essay): "incitements to narrative," from *Narrative and Its Discontents: Problems of Closure in the Traditional Novel* (Princeton: Princeton University Press, 1981), ix. Miller's phrase in turn tropes on a (by now) well-known phrase of Foucault's, "The Incitement to Discourse." Referring to the modern "proliferation of discourses concerned with sex" (18), this phrase serves as title and aegis for the first chapter in *The History of Sexuality,* vol. I.

97. Stein's earliest work, *Q.E.D.* (1903), treated her early, painful relationship with May Bookstaver in straightforward language and a style resembling that of Henry James. On account of its clear treatment of its lesbian subject matter, Stein would not allow the story to be published during her lifetime. In 1950 it was published under the title *Things as They Are,* taken from a line at the end of the book. See below for Stein's 1939 remarks on this work and the issues it raised for her, as reported by a friend, the writer Samuel Steward.

98. The taboos attending such matters are evidenced in an incident of a half-century later. In December 1983 Thomson was a guest of the Reagan White House, as a recipient of a Kennedy Center lifetime arts achievement award. In his speech on Thomson's behalf, *Four Saints'* original director John

Houseman mentioned that Thomson, though not himself religious, had composed deeply felt religious music. The mention was edited out of the subsequently televised coverage of the awards event: Tommasini, *Virgil Thomson*, 532.

99. Blackmer, "The Ecstasies of Saint Teresa," is the most notable exception in this regard. Its rich and nuanced argument illuminates queerness in the history of Teresian hagiography, in *Four Saints'* Teresian and Catholic engagements, and in what the author identifies as the opera's "dynamic musical-theatrical mode of socially organizing and dramatically performing erotic pleasure and intimacy" amid a free circulation and exchange of power (331).

100. Thomson in an interview with Tommasini, May 12, 1988; quoted in Tommasini, *Virgil Thomson*, 69. According to Sedgwick, the turn to abstraction in male high modernist literature was motivated by the contemporaneous post-Wildean crisis around homo/heterosexual definition: "male modernism serves a purpose of universalizing, naturalizing, and thus substantively voiding—depriving of content—elements of a specifically and historically male homosexual rhetoric." Sedgwick argues that the male body in particular was thus "voided," hence keeping at bay any possible hints of homosexuality: see "Abstraction/Figuration," 163–67, in *Epistemology of the Closet*.

101. This last fact alone could justify Stein's admonishment (reported in the same passage), "But you don't get the point at all": Hemingway, *A Moveable Feast*, 15.

102. Quoted passages are ascribed to Stein in Samuel M. Steward, *Dear Sammy: Letters from Gertrude Stein and Alice B. Toklas* (Boston: Houghton Mifflin, 1977), 56–57. "Melanctha" is one of the stories in Stein's *Three Lives* (New York: Random House, 1936). Ruddick discusses the story and Stein's stylistic evolution in relation to Henry James and, more centrally, to Stein's former teacher (and Henry's brother) William James: *Reading Gertrude Stein*, 33–41.

103. Ellis Hanson, *Decadence and Catholicism* (Cambridge, Mass.: Harvard University Press, 1997), 17.

104. Thomson, *Virgil Thomson by Virgil Thomson*, 174.

105. Stein, *The Autobiography of Alice B. Toklas*, 21.

106. Paul Bowles in a letter to Daniel Burns (n.d. [1931]); quoted in Caponi, *Paul Bowles*, 48–49.

107. For an insightful critique of the receptive and critical tradition of "not-seeing" (here traced back to the baroque era), and of its dire depoliticizing effects in the sphere of contemporary visual art, see Dave Hickey, *The Invisible Dragon: Four Essays on Beauty* (Los Angeles: Art Issues Press, 1993).

108. Thomson, "A Very Difficult Author," 4. *A Long Gay Book*, from 1909–12, was another of Stein's titles. The Brett quotation is from "Musicality, Essentialism, and the Closet," 21, where Brett is discussing a decision of the Kent and Sussex (England) Education Committees, ca. 1989, to cancel a performance of Benjamin Britten's *Death in Venice*.

109. Watson, *Prepare for Saints,* 74; emphasis mine. Quotations of Thomson are from Watson's interviews with the composer in the late 1980s.

110. Thomson's Wildean phrase is given (with different orthographics) in Tommasini, *Virgil Thomson,* 561.

111. Hemingway, *A Moveable Feast,* 92. Hemingway finished this manuscript in 1960. My phraseology here is indebted to D. A. Miller, *Place for Us: Essay on the Broadway Musical* (Cambridge, Mass.: Harvard University Press, 1998), 22. The dating of the completion of mass culture's appropriation of camp is subject to debate, and some observers might place it earlier than I do here. My point of reference in citing the late 1980s is the ascendance of "retro"-oriented (so-called) "camp" in such loci as David Letterman's late-night TV show and the Nickelodeon channel's Nick at Nite, and, following these, the early-nineties lounge music and cocktail-and-cigar style trends. Camp in this mainstreamed version is undoubtedly a simplified and reduced conceit, marked principally by the juxtaposition of high and low styles and of naturalism with artifice, but generally lacking other rich dimensions present in camp's queer-subcultural usage, including masculine-feminine, tragedy-artifice, and abject-transcendent dynamics. Moe Meyer emphasizes that this "heterosexual/Pop colonization" of camp began in the sixties, and he denies the label *camp* to those colonizing instances that have voided it of its queerness: "Reclaiming the Discourse of Camp," in *The Politics and Poetics of Camp,* ed. Moe Meyer (New York: Routledge, 1994), 9.

112. Susan Sontag, "Notes on 'Camp,'" in *Against Interpretation* (New York: Dell, 1966), 277–93 (reprinted from *Partisan Review* [fall 1964]: 515–30). Esther Newton, *Mother Camp: Female Impersonators in America* (Englewood Cliffs, N.J.: Prentice-Hall, 1972), xx. Newton discusses Sontag's intervention and cites the response of one of her midsixties drag-queen informants to Sontag's having nearly "edited homosexuals out of camp": *Mother Camp,* 106. Meyer puts a finer point on this reading of Sontag as sanitizing corrupter of camp, writing that she "killed off the binding referent of camp—the homosexual," after which camp "became confused and conflated with rhetorical and performative strategies such as irony, satire, burlesque, and travesty": "Reclaiming the Discourse of Camp," 7.

113. Newton, *Mother Camp,* 106.

114. Meyer, "Reclaiming the Discourse of Camp," 10. For further recent theorizing of camp see David Bergman, ed., *Camp Grounds: Style and Homosexuality* (Amherst: University of Massachusetts Press, 1993).

115. On Thomson's relationship with Murray, including hints of a sexual involvement, see Tommasini, *Virgil Thomson,* 30–38, 42–43, 68.

116. I recall some of my own youthful experiences in fused musical-homosexual realms of the final quarter of the twentieth century in "Why Gay Shame? Why Now?" in *Gay Shame,* ed. David M. Halperin and Valerie Traub, forthcoming. The phrase "discreet homosexual" comes from Alan Sinfield, *Out on Stage,* 16–17. "The closet" has been the term most often used to refer to dis-

creet homosexuality since this model first came under critical scrutiny, especially from younger, liberation-minded "gays," in the 1960s (24).

117. Tommasini, *Virgil Thomson*, 68. The book is cataloged among the
items in Thomson's possession at the time of his death: Yale MSS 29A, box 238.

118. Sinfield, *Out on Stage*, 114–15, 32–34. Sinfield explores the reverberations of the Wilde trials at greater length in *The Wilde Century* (London: Cassell, 1994).

119. Quotation is from Hanson, *Decadence and Catholicism*, 237.

120. Thomson in a letter of May 6, 1943; quoted in Page and Page, *Selected
Letters of Virgil Thomson*, 186.

121. Carpenter, *Geniuses Together*, 30.

122. Quotes are from Hemingway, *A Moveable Feast*, 15–16.

123. Hoover and Cage, *Virgil Thomson*, 62.

124. This list is drawn from Hanson, *Decadence and Catholicism*, 366 and
299, which here considers together queer and nonqueer converts both to
Catholicism and to "a distinctly High Church Anglicanism" (366), and further
lists the modernist literati E. F. Benson, Graham Greene, C. S. Lewis, and T. S.
Eliot.

125. Quotations are from ibid., 7, 26.

126. In *Decadence and Catholicism* Hanson delineates both the Neo-
Catholic literary movement and the 1880s' popular countermovement of sci-
entifically allied anticlericalism. The latter excoriated "Wagnerism," Huysmans, and the symbolist poets, especially Baudelaire and Verlaine, and sought
to reinterpret mysticism in psychologizing terms of hysteria (116–18). The
queer resonances of fin-de-siècle aestheticized or "decadent" Catholicism are
apparent in Hanson's description of *À Rebours* (literally: "In Reverse," often
translated as "Against Nature"), which was published in 1884 and reissued in
1903. Hanson calls it a "highly ornamented, oneiric, satirical novel about a
dandy who, in a neurotic fit of ennui, retreats into a monastic yet sumptuous
solitude." Featuring characters who "wander along an always already transgressed boundary line between conversion and mysticism on the one hand and
hysteria and perversion on the other," the book "exasperated [Huysmans's]
Catholic critics precisely because he insisted upon the paradox of decadent
Catholicism, what he called the 'medieval' coexistence of the perverse and the
divine, brutality and grace, hysteria and mysticism, in Verlaine no less than in
himself" (109, 111).

See also Richard D. E. Burton, "Homosexuality, Catholicism and Modernism," in *Francis Poulenc* (Bath: Absolute Press, 2002), 43–60. Burton examines Catholicism and Catholiphilia specifically in connection with the modernist
composer Poulenc and limns certain distinctions between the French and
English versions of the phenomena. As Burton notes, "[t]here is no French
equivalent of the Oscar Wilde trial" (9), and relatedly Ross Chambers suggests
that homosexuality was perceived less as a "threat to the social fabric" in France
than in Britain and America, though it represented in all three cultures a shameful embarrassment. Chambers remarks that the French response to this shame

had more to do with "surreptitiousness (*'raser les murs'*)" and, vis-à-vis Catholicism, with "the morbid and masochistic theology . . . of the Ultramontane . . . [and] Maritain-Claudel persuasion," whereas "in Anglo-America it's about camp" and "the fascination with liturgy that responds . . . to camp sensibility": personal correspondence with the author, February 9, 2003. One might trace further eruptions of this Catholiphilic impulse in certain recent queer artistic contexts as well, for example, Derek Jarman's films; Andrew Holleran's gay novel *Dancer from the Dance* (New York: William Morrow, 1978), whose central metaphor renders the discothèque as gay church and gay revelers its supplicants; and the Pet Shop Boys' 1994 concert video *Discovery: Live in Rio* (EMI Records [UK] MVN 491451–3), in the Jarman-video-infused disco medley "I Will Survive/It's a Sin," with its spectacular fusion of queer, camp, and Catholic rituals and sensuality.

127. Crunden, *Body and Soul*, ix–x.

128. Sedgwick's phrase is from *Epistemology of the Closet*, 160. Ronald Firbank, *Valmouth*, in *Five Novels by Ronald Firbank* (New York: New Directions, 1961), 149–239. Quotation is from Blackmer, "The Ecstasies of Saint Teresa," 312. William Lane Clark further illuminates Firbank's clustering and surrogation of binarisms in his construction of (roughly autobiographical) characters of transgressive personality: see Clark, "Degenerate Personality: Deviant Sexuality and Race in Ronald Firbank's Novels," in Bergman, ed., *Camp Grounds*, 134–55.

129. Carpenter, *Geniuses Together*, 116. Thomson's years at Harvard were 1919–21 and (following a year's study with Boulanger in Paris) 1922–23. For further discussion of homosexuality at Harvard in this (and other) periods see Douglass Shand-Tucci, *The Crimson Letter: Harvard, Homosexuality and the Shaping of American Culture* (New York: St. Martin's Press, 2003).

130. Hanson, *Decadence and Catholicism*, 45, identifies this term in relation to the Church.

131. Clark, "Degenerate Personality," 153.

132. See Chauncey, *Gay New York*, 17–19, for a discussion (focusing on the evolution of the usage *gay*) illustrating the importance of discursive multiple meanings for creating queer space and allowing queer communication and expression in the early twentieth century.

133. Yale Collections: MSS 29, series I.H, box 12, folder 5: Psalm 130, *De Profundis*, set for SATB chorus (sketches marked "July, 1920 / Cambridge"; 1951 published version marked "Cambridge, Mass., 1920"). Tommasini, *Virgil Thomson*, 90, discusses another work, "Vernal Equinox," also dated July 1920. Whether the ink dried on one before the other I do not know, but the date shared by both works is the earliest in Thomson's oeuvre.

134. Quoted passage is from Hanson, *Decadence and Catholicism*, 237.

135. Thomson, "About 'Four Saints.'"

136. Tommasini accompanies the tenor Paul Kirby in a performance of the "Commentaire" on *Virgil Thomson: Mostly about Love* (Northeastern Classical Arts NR 250-CD, track 6).

137. My translation of the French text as given in the original score in Thomson's hand, which bears attribution to Sade and the inscription "Paris 8 Octobre de 1928." Yale Collections: MSS 29, series I.I, box 14, folder 4. In his memoir Thomson makes reference to this song as having been written "for a young literary group in Lille, about to publish a magazine called *Les Cahiers Sade*": *Virgil Thomson by Virgil Thomson*, 124.

138. I refer here to a letter from Mencken (Yale MSS 29, series III, box 66, folder 22) that is dated October 23, 1924, and thus precedes the 1925 dating of Thomson's manuscript (in the Virgil Thomson Collection, Columbia University Rare Book and Manuscript Library). Apparently because of these dating questions, Oja identifies "My Jesus, I Love Thee" with some uncertainty, as either the essay that Mencken rejected in 1924 or an essay written in response to that rejection. She discusses the piece in *Making Music Modern*, 261–63. Tommasini's is, to my knowledge, the first published discussion of this essay: *Virgil Thomson*, 298–99. He identifies "My Jesus" unequivocally as the essay submitted to Mencken in 1924 and rejected by him in October of that year. Given that Tommasini was a personal friend of Thomson's in the composer's final decade, and that his biography was written in consultation with its subject, it is possible that Thomson himself confirmed this information about the 1925 essay and its provenance. But here I conjecture, for Tommasini does not explain the source of his certainty on these points. My own discussion assumes that the 1925 Paris manuscript represents some version of the essay rejected by Mencken's letter, which refers tellingly to "investigations of the hymns" focusing on the texts rather than the music and ultimately failing to make a clear point: "I can't rid myself of the feeling that you actually say nothing here."

139. Thomson, "My Jesus, I Love Thee," 5.

140. D. A. Miller, "Secret Subjects, Open Secrets," 206.

141. For further illumination of this tradition see Richard Rambuss's examination of "sacred eroticism" in devotional lyric of the Renaissance and elsewhere: *Closet Devotions* (Durham: Duke University Press, 1998).

142. D. A. Miller, "Anal *Rope*," in *Inside/Out: Lesbian Theories, Gay Theories*, ed. Diana Fuss (New York: Routledge, 1991), 124.

143. Thomson's profession of nonfaith is given in *Virgil Thomson by Virgil Thomson*, 356; Simon, *The Biography of Alice B. Toklas*, 308–9.

144. Ibid., 293.

CHAPTER 2

The passage from Thomson opens his first chapter, "Our Island Home, or What It Feels Like to Be a Musician," and thus his book overall, in *The State of Music* (New York: William Morrow, 1939), 3. Thomson's chapter title highlights the potential double meaning in his book title, invoking "state" both in the sense of "condition" and as a physical locale, a site of residence for its devotees. Charles E. Ives, *Memos*, ed. John Kirkpatrick (New York: W. W. Norton, 1972), 130–31. Oscar Wilde, *The Picture of Dorian Gray* (1891), in *The Complete Works of*

Oscar Wilde (New York: Harper and Row, 1989), 30, where the narration pertains to Wilde's archetypal fin-de-siècle homosexual dandy, Dorian Gray.

1. Article in the form of a letter (dated April 18, 1940) to editor Minna Lederman, published in *Modern Music*. The complete text appears, with minor deviations from the above wording, in Page and Page, *Letters of Virgil Thomson*, 136–42. My quotations here are from the (evidently tweaked) excerpts given in Thomson, *Virgil Thomson by Virgil Thomson*, 314. Thomson lived in Paris from 1921 to 1923, while a student of Boulanger, and again, by his telling, from 1925 to 1940 (though in fact he returned to the United States in the final days of 1932 to oversee the production of *Four Saints'* premiere, moving back to Paris in June 1938). In June 1940 he finally left Paris, after the Nazis began bombarding the city. With regard to Mozart's sonatas Thomson was apparently testing a hypothesis that they were camp (which term then, unlike now, invariably carried homosexual connotations). In the spring of 1940 he wrote to Grosser with a conclusion: "They are not camp, as I had thought": Tommasini, *Virgil Thomson*, 316.

2. Simon, *The Biography of Alice B. Toklas*, 308–9.

3. Perhaps relatedly, the rock musician Don Henley (of 1970s Eagles fame) has noted a similar tendency in pop and rock musicians. Apropos of his recent activist work on behalf of artists in the recording industry Henley cites "a sort of cantankerous independence, an anti-club mentality coupled with a cultivated naiveté about all things political" as typifying the "bohemian" position of most pop artists: "Don Henley Speaks Out," *Rolling Stone* 891 (March 14, 2002): 28, 31. In the realm of American classical music Thomson may have had a hand in shaping the political disengagement that characterized many twentieth-century composers and other musicians—with notable exceptions, including Blitzstein, Copland, Roy Harris, and Bernstein. By at least his own assessment, he was indeed influential in this regard. Recounting in his memoir the 1939 publication of *The State of Music*, Thomson notes that his book, despite its modest sales,

> was not ineffective. Composers took to heart its exhortation that
> they give up political politics and take up musical. And not for
> killing one another off but for assuming power, for directing musical
> matters instead of being directed. I had given them two instruments
> for doing that, a composer's alliance for collecting fees and a com-
> posers' cooperative for publishing their works . . . both presided
> over by Aaron Copland.

The State of Music, by Thomson's 1966 account, "became instantly a handbook for that operation [of self-governance] which has not yet been replaced. It still circulates, indeed, among the knowing ones": *Virgil Thomson by Virgil Thomson*, 300.

4. Henry Kingsbury's ethnographic study of later-twentieth-century East Coast conservatory culture importantly illumines the construction of (the cul-

tural notion of) talent and its functions in the classical music world: see *Music, Talent, and Performance: A Conservatory Cultural System* (Philadelphia: Temple University Press, 1988).

5. Christopher Isherwood, *Christopher and His Kind: 1929–1939* (New York: Farrar, Straus and Giroux, 1976), 36. Isherwood was a longtime friend of Paul Bowles's, dating from 1931, when Bowles accompanied Copland to Berlin and there met Isherwood with the poet Stephen Spender. He also became one of Bowles's principal influences as a writer, according to the latter's biographer, who identifies this British colleague as the source of Bowles's method of "objectively freezing reality as a thing outside himself, separate from his being—a place where others existed and had lives": Caponi, *Paul Bowles*, 46. Isherwood was also a friend of Thomson's, beginning in the early sixties: see Tommasini, *Virgil Thomson*, 469, also 473, 482.

6. Philip Brett blazed the trail for serious analysis of the vernacular usage of "musical" identified here and of the cultural associations between musicality and homosexuality. His percipient and influential work in this regard includes "Are You Musical? Is It Queer to Be Queer?" *Musical Times* 135, no. 1816 (1994): 370–76; and esp. "Musicality, Essentialism, and the Closet." The subject is revisited in Brett and Wood, "The ORIGINAL Version of the *New Grove* Article," 3–5.

7. Such queer persons include not only sexual queers but gender queers and what one might call straight–social misfit queers. Wayne Koestenbaum evocatively limns the latter, and several other queer characters familiar to the twentieth-century American classical music world, in "Queering the Pitch: A Posy of Definitions and Impersonations," in Brett et al., eds., *Queering the Pitch*, 1–5. The Anglo-American association of music and femininity has been traced as far back as the Renaissance in Linda Phyllis Austern, "'Alluring the Auditorie to Effeminacie': Music and the Idea of the Feminine in Early Modern England," *Music and Letters* 74, no. 3 (1993): 343–54.

8. *Essentialist* and *social-constructionist* are terms with considerable history in critical discourse and polemics, particularly in the essentialism-constructionism debates of the late 1980s. In the present context the terms may be understood as corresponding roughly with the "nature" and "nurture" poles, respectively, of the classic "nature/nurture" etiological duality. Or, to borrow from Steven Epstein, an essentialist sense of identity "is the type we mean when we speak of identity as describing who someone *really* is," whereas a constructionist sense of identity involves "the internalization . . . [of] socially constructed labels or roles": "Gay Politics, Ethnic Identity: The Limits of Social Constructionism" (1987), reprinted in *Social Perspectives in Lesbian and Gay Studies: A Reader*, ed. Peter M. Nardi and Beth E. Schneider (New York: Routledge, 1998), 144; emphasis in original.

9. On nineteenth- and twentieth-century lesbian diva worship see Elizabeth Wood, "Sapphonics," in Brett et al., eds., *Queering the Pitch*, 27–66; and Blackmer and Smith, *En Travesti*. On the late-nineteenth-century cult of Wagnerism and its homosexual affiliations see Hanson, *Decadence and Catholi-*

cism. On the opera queen and "her" culture see (among other writings) Wayne Koestenbaum, *The Queen's Throat;* and Mitchell Morris, "Reading as an Opera Queen," in *Musicology and Difference: Gender and Sexuality in Music Scholarship,* ed. Ruth A. Solie (Berkeley: University of California Press, 1993), 184–200.

10. Koestenbaum, "Queering the Pitch," 5.

11. Chauncey, *Gay New York,* 13, 26–27. Chauncey has also argued against the notion that the medical model was the sole determinant in conceptualizations of lesbian sexuality around this time: see "From Sexual Inversion to Homosexuality: Medicine and the Changing Conceptualization of Female Deviance," *Salmagundi* 58–59 (1982–83): 114–46.

12. Foucault, *The History of Sexuality,* vol. I, 43. Foucault's continuation in this passage includes these much-quoted phrases: "Homosexuality appeared as one of the forms of sexuality when it was transposed from the practice of sodomy onto a kind of interior androgyny, a hermaphrodism of the soul. The sodomite had been a temporary aberration; the homosexual was now a species" (43). David M. Halperin has recently offered a lucid corrective to the conventional (mis-) reading of this passage as drawing a distinction between premodern and modern conceptual paradigms hinging on sexual acts and sexual identities, respectively: see "Forgetting Foucault," in *How to Do the History of Homosexuality,* 24–47 (Chicago: University of Chicago Press, 2002).

13. Chauncey, *Gay New York,* 27.

14. Chauncey discusses these factors, excepting that of African Americans; ibid., 111–27. For a book-length analysis of all these "threats" and their cultural effects see Bederman, *Manliness and Civilization.*

15. Chauncey, *Gay New York,* 126–27.

16. Diamond was born in Rochester, New York (home of the Eastman School). The family's impoverished economic situation is further suggested by the fact that they lost their home in 1927 and temporarily moved to Cleveland to live with relatives: Victoria J. Kimberling, *David Diamond, A Bio-Bibliography* (Metuchen, N.J.: Scarecrow Press, 1987), 3.

17. Rorem quote is from *Knowing When to Stop,* 104. Blitzstein's murder is recounted in Gordon, *Mark the Music,* 526–27. The proletariat sympathies of Blitzstein, Copland, and Bernstein might fruitfully be considered in relation to their upper-middle-class Jewish backgrounds. See Brodkin for examination of a perceived tendency on the part of many U.S. Jews, "despite being relatively successful in material terms, . . . to think of themselves as distinctly liberal politically, as invested in social justice and in identification with the underdog": *How Jews Became White Folks,* 3. See also Michael Alexander's claim that "[a]s Jews moved up, they identified down" and his analysis of the "origins, influences, and consequences of this exceptional Jewish liberalism," in *Jazz Age Jews* (Princeton: Princeton University Press, 2001), 1.

18. Rorem, *Knowing When to Stop,* 308.

19. Rorem ascribes this pattern to Diamond as he knew him around 1944: ibid., 261.

20. Tommasini recounts Thomson's episode in *Virgil Thomson*, 353–61. For a thorough account of Cowell's trial and imprisonment see Michael Hicks, *Henry Cowell, Bohemian* (Urbana: University of Illinois Press, 2002).

21. Rorem refers to Diamond's pit orchestra work for *On the Town* ca. 1944, garnered "thanks to Lenny Bernstein" (*Knowing When to Stop*, 262). Again "thanks to Lenny," Diamond was playing for *Candide* in 1956 when he was subpoenaed by the Red-, Jew-, and lavender-baiting House Committee on Un-American Activities: see chapter 4 in this volume. Diamond's celebrity intimates included friends and lovers: He had a love affair with Reeves McCullers in the early forties, in the interim between the latter's two marriages to the queer writer Carson McCullers (Schulman, "McCullers," 41); and he was the once-housemate of the Hollywood icon Lana Turner and counterpoint tutor of the bandleader Artie Shaw after Shaw had become Turner's husband (Rorem, *Knowing When to Stop*, 263).

22. Chauncey, *Gay New York*, 126.

23. This last point is queried in the title of Brett's article "Are You Musical? Is It Queer to Be Queer?"

24. Quoted phrase is from Judith Tick, "Charles Ives and Gender Ideology," in Solie, ed., *Musicology and Difference*, 83. A historicizing and culturally contextualizing perspective on Ives, as opposed to one regarding his utterances as merely personal or idiosyncratic, is given especially in Tick's essay, which concludes that the "project" of Ives's vituperations "was the emasculation of the [old, restrictive, European] cultural patriarchy"; in Lawrence Kramer, "Cultural Politics and Musical Form: The Case of Charles Ives," in *Classical Music and Postmodern Knowledge* (Berkeley: University of California Press, 1995), 174–200; and in Catherine Parsons Smith, "'A Distinguishing Virility': Feminism and Modernism in American Art Music," in *Cecilia Reclaimed: Feminist Perspectives on Gender and Music*, ed. Susan C. Cook and Judy S. Tsou (Urbana: University of Illinois Press, 1994), 94–96. While each of these studies examines the phobia and venom in Ives's utterances (musical or verbal), none addresses these as they were expressed in his actions, as in his renunciation of Henry Cowell, a close friend and important promoter of Ives's music, when Cowell was imprisoned on sodomy charges. Stuart Feder's posthumous psychoanalysis of Ives examines the composer's misogynist and homophobic utterances, but places them in a less historicizing and more individualizing light. Feder cites certain of Ives's "excitable" statements on music as evidence of his marked alternations of mood and retrospectively diagnoses him with cyclothymia, a "mood disorder": *Charles Ives: "My Father's Song"* (New Haven: Yale University Press, 1992), 183, 219.

25. Oja, *Making Music Modern*, 296.

26. Mary Herron DuPree, "The Failure of American Music: The Critical View from the 1920s," *Journal of Musicology* 2, no. 3 (1983): 305–15. For further discussion of the literature on gender and music, 1890–1930, see Tick, "Charles Ives and Gender Ideology," 90–96 esp. See Lawrence W. Levine, *Highbrow/Lowbrow: The Emergence of Cultural Hierarchy in America* (Cam-

bridge, Mass.: Harvard University Press, 1988), on the native inferiority complex and the significant growth and elitist turn of concert music in nineteenth-century America.

27. DuPree, "The Failure of American Music," 313.

28. This date according to Ives himself: see *Memos*, 74, 123.

29. See Siobhan B. Somerville, *Queering the Color Line: Race and the Invention of Homosexuality in American Culture* (Durham: Duke University Press, 2000), 29.

30. Rorem, *Knowing When to Stop*, 161, 173.

31. Paul Rosenfeld, "Musical Chronicle: Introit," *The Dial* 69 (November 1920), 550; quoted in DuPree, "The Failure of American Music," 314. See Oja, *Making Music Modern*, 297–310 esp., on Rosenfeld's importance as "one of the defining figures in American modernism" (15).

32. The indistinct figure of the "sex pervert" would emerge most conspicuously in U.S. sex-crime panics beginning in the 1930s. The warnings of medical and law-enforcement officials that parents protect their young daughters from homosexual men illustrate the operation of a multiplicitous and undifferentiated notion of sexual pervert in which any type of pervert was at once, or potentially, every type of pervert. Also operative here are assumptions of a generalized sexual lability on the part of the pervert, whereby a man who would "give in" to "unnatural" impulses toward another man was capable of equal "lack of control" with regard to children, including (and by this refracted logic, including especially) female children. See George Chauncey, "The Postwar Sex Crime Panic," in *True Stories from the American Past*, ed. William Graebner (New York: McGraw-Hill, 1993), 160–78; also Estelle B. Freedman, "'Uncontrolled Desires': The Response to the Sexual Psychopath, 1920–1960," in *Passion and Power: Sexuality in History*, ed. Christina Simmons and Kathy Peiss (Philadelphia: Temple University Press, 1989), 199–225. Foucault identifies the medicojuridical discourses of normalization by which, starting in the late eighteenth century, manifold types of nonconjugal, nonprocreative sexual behavior (by the late nineteenth century including homosexuality, zoophilia, onanism, etc.) were at once specified and consolidated under the aegis of unnatural, incomplete sexual practices, in a simultaneous *"specification of individuals"* and *"incorporation of perversions"*: see *The History of Sexuality*, vol. I, 42–43, 37–48 esp.; emphasis in original.

33. Sedgwick, *Epistemology of the Closet*, 44–48 esp., exposes this definitional incoherence and its consequences. See also Halperin, "How to Do the History of Male Homosexuality," in *How to Do the History of Homosexuality*, 104–37, for elaboration of genealogical categories of male gender and sexual deviance.

34. DuPree, "The Failure of American Music," 315, notes that American music's "failure" ceased by the late twenties to be an issue, the outcry quelled not by a reversal of the situation but by the appearance of some significant works by mostly younger composers just coming of age artistically—composers of Thomson and Copland's generation.

35. Kramer, "Cultural Politics and Musical Form," 175, 184. Kirkpatrick dates Ives's composition of the Second Quartet to 1911–13 and further specifies that the second movement dates from 1907: Ives, *Memos*, 266.

36. Ives, *Memos*, 74.

37. Quotations are from Kramer, "Cultural Politics and Musical Form," 184, 181. For his theorization of nineteenth-century American identity formation and its problematics (176–77, 179) Kramer draws on Philip Fisher, "Democratic Social Space: Whitman, Melville, and the Promise of American Transparency," *Representations* 24 (1988): 61–62, 75–79.

38. On the latter two points Kramer ("Cultural Politics and Musical Form," 180) cites Michael Rogin's reading in " 'The Sword Became a Flashing Vision': D. W. Griffith's *The Birth of a Nation*," *Representations* 9 (1985): 163, 174.

39. Kramer, "Cultural Politics and Musical Form," 185, 189.

40. On this vision and its ascendance see especially "Theodore Roosevelt: Manhood, Nation, and 'Civilization,' " 170–215, in Bederman, *Manliness and Civilization*.

41. Ibid., 5.

42. This according to the same mechanism by which, in western stories, "white heroes achieve manhood by becoming 'like' Indian warriors," while remaining white and superior to the Indians: ibid., 173, citing Richard Slotkin in *Regeneration through Violence: The Mythology of the American Frontier, 1600–1860* (Middletown, Conn.: Wesleyan University Press, 1973); and in *The Fatal Environment: The Myth of the Frontier in the Age of Industrialization, 1800–1890* (New York: Atheneum, 1985).

43. Bederman, *Manliness and Civilization*, 84–88, 185–87.

44. These masculine incapacities of drinking and reproduction are described in the classic reference text on neurasthenia, George M. Beard's *American Nervousness: Its Causes and Consequences* (New York: G. P. Putnam's Sons, 1881), 153–54; cited in Bederman, *Manliness and Civilization*, 88 (see also 85). The quotation of Bederman is from *Manliness and Civilization*, 84. An important recent study of the neurasthenia phenomenon is Tom Lutz, *American Nervousness, 1903: An Anecdotal History* (Ithaca: Cornell University Press, 1991).

45. Bederman, *Manliness and Civilization*, 15.

46. Somerville, *Queering the Color Line*, 16.

47. Ibid., 31.

48. See ibid., 26–29.

49. Bederman, *Manliness and Civilization*, 17–19, discusses the term *masculinity* and its meaning in this period. See 22–24 on middle-class white men's appropriation, from ca. 1870, of "primitive masculinity" as complement to the "civilized manliness" they already claimed exclusively.

50. Ives quotes are from *Memos*, 133, 134.

51. Gardner discusses artists' perceived physical weakness within this cultural moment in "The American Composer Becomes a Self-Made Man," 2. See also Brett's assertion that the "nervousness" identified by Havelock Ellis as a characteristic of both the musician and the male homosexual "is, after all, the

chief *female* condition of late Victorianism." Brett cites this instance as symptomatic of the condition of twentieth-century male musicians: "Much of what men in music feared during the twentieth century was that they were broadly perceived as less than men, that is, as homosexuals." Philip Brett, "Musicology and Sexuality: The Example of Edward J. Dent," in Fuller and Whitesell, eds., *Queer Episodes in Music and Modern Identity*, 180.

52. This in his health crises of 1906 and 1918, by Sherwood's hypothesis: Gayle Sherwood, "Charles Ives and 'Our National Malady,'" *Journal of the American Musicological Society* 54, no. 3 (2002): 555–84. I find Sherwood's overall argument persuasive, though I do not share her opinion on the historical meaning of the diagnosis: She contends that neurasthenia would have been for Ives, at least in "pre-Freudian" America, a mark of class distinction bearing no gender stigma. Sherwood takes a firm stand on this latter point, on which she repeatedly invokes the contention that no less virile a man than Theodore Roosevelt had likewise been diagnosed as neurasthenic (see ibid., 560, 566 n. 47; and in the same issue, Sherwood's "Ives and Neurasthenia: A Response to Stuart Feder," 643). But male neurasthenia was described in emasculating and effeminizing terms already in Beard's *American Nervousness* (1881). And according to Bederman's periodization of styles of American manhood, physical emasculation would have been stigmatized following the turn of the century and Roosevelt's championing of "the strenuous life." Bederman also casts credible doubt on the claim (which originates in Lutz, *American Nervousness, 1903*, 63) that Roosevelt ever received a neurasthenia diagnosis: *Manliness and Civilization*, 87–88, 275 n. 20.

53. Brett, "Musicality, Essentialism, and the Closet," 11–12.

54. In Adams's 1759 diary he contrasts "a Life of Effeminacy, Indolence and obscurity" with one of "Industry, Temperance, and Honour" and instructs himself, "return to your Study, and bend your whole soul to the Institutes of the Law. . . . Let no trifling Diversion or amuzement or Company decoy you from your Books . . . no Girl, no Gun, no Cards, no flutes, no Violins, no Dress, no Tobacco, no Laziness." L. H. Butterfield, Wendell D. Garrett, and Marjorie E. Sprague, eds., *Adams Family Correspondence* (Cambridge, Mass.: Harvard University Press, 1963–), vol. II, 96–97, vol. III, 333; quoted in Philip J. Greven, *The Protestant Temperament: Patterns of Child-Rearing, Religious Experience, and the Self in Early America* (New York: Alfred A. Knopf, 1977), 246.

55. Ives, *Memos*, 30.

56. Smith, "'A Distinguishing Virility,'" 98.

57. Ibid., 93–94.

58. Ibid., 95–99.

59. Sandra M. Gilbert and Susan Gubar, *No Man's Land: The Place of the Woman Writer in the Twentieth Century*, vol. 1, *The War of the Words* (New Haven: Yale University Press, 1988).

60. Smith, "'A Distinguishing Virility,'" 98.

61. Ibid., 95.

62. Tick, "Charles Ives and Gender Ideology," 98–99. I would note that this historicizing account is no less feminist for its relegation of women to the periphery of Ives's Oedipal exercise. On the contrary, it aligns exactly with Gayle S. Rubin's feminist analysis of the place of women within patriarchal culture—that is, as objects of exchange in relations between men: see Rubin, "The Traffic in Women: Notes on the 'Political Economy' of Sex," in Rayna R. Reiter, ed., *Toward an Anthropology of Women* (New York: Monthly Review Press, 1975), 157–210.

63. See Tick's literature survey for some further examples, mostly from the 1920s: "Charles Ives and Gender Ideology," 93–96.

64. Sir Thomas Beecham, "Women Ruin Music: A Pessimist's View of Women Musicians—Heirs to a Dying Art," *Vogue* (July 15, 1942): 52. Brett and Wood trace the popular notion that music is rife with homosexuals to the discourses of sexology, and particularly turn-of-the-century writings by Edward Carpenter and Havelock Ellis: see "The ORIGINAL Version of the *New Grove* Article," 3.

65. Brett also flags the "intertwin[ing] of homophobia and misogyny" in music and its illustration in Ives's rhetoric: see "Musicality, Essentialism, and the Closet," 22.

66. Sedgwick, *Epistemology of the Closet*, 44–48; on what is condensed under the homosexual aegis, see 8–9.

67. In this passage I draw upon ibid., 8–9, 44–48; and Halperin, *How to Do the History of Homosexuality*, 109–36. Halperin elaborates the idea that homosexual definition condensed in complex and incoherent ways a plurality of prior categories from both official and folk sources, entailing not only qualities of sexual orientation but of erotic preference and gender style, and various peculiarities of personal style—speech, dress, and manner.

68. The gender invert, a persona invented before the homosexual, was defined as a woman's soul trapped in a man's body, or vice versa, and was *not* presumed necessarily to exhibit same-sex desire or sexual behaviors.

69. "Tangents," *One* (February 1965), 17. These comments respond to Anna Frankenheimer, "A Much-Needed Upbraiding of Long-hair Music," *Fact* 1 (November–December 1964), 12.

70. Oja, *Making Music Modern*, 238.

71. Smith, "'A Distinguishing Virility,'" 100.

72. On hypermasculinity in Ives, see above; on Schoenbergian atonality and midcentury serialism, see chapter 4. The same tendencies surface in surrealism, which in its hypermasculinity shuns music altogether; see note 94 below.

73. Smith, "'A Distinguishing Virility,'" 94; quotation is from Tick, "Charles Ives and Gender Ideology," 95.

74. Thomson quoted in Rorem, *Knowing When to Stop*, 383.

75. Crunden, *Body and Soul*, iv.

76. Another apparent instance of this usage surfaces in K. Robert Schwarz's landmark 1994 *New York Times* article on gay composers. Referring to the members of the Copland-Thomson circle, Schwarz states that "the gay com-

posers were writing the tonal, lyrical, more conservative music America wanted to hear." He then quotes Susan McClary as saying: "There was almost a kind of self-selection in American music. . . . The straight boys claimed the high moral ground of modernism and fled to the universities, and the queers literally took center stage in concert halls and opera houses and ballet, all of which are musics that people are more likely to respond to." Again, the language seems to position gay composers' tonal music as antithetical to compositional modernism, rather than as a species of it. Schwarz, "Composers' Closets Open for All to See," *New York Times* (June 19, 1994), sec. 2: 1, 24.

77. Terry Teachout, "The New Tonalists," *Commentary* 104, no. 6 (1997): 55, 54. Thomson attributes a similarly imperialist, even Darwinian, drive to Schoenberg and his followers, writing in 1950 that "many atonalists believe . . . this style must either kill off all others or wholly die": Virgil Thomson, *Music Right and Left* (New York: Henry Holt, 1951), ix.

78. Leon Botstein, s.v. "modernism," *New Grove Dictionary of Music and Musicians*, 2nd ed., ed. Stanley Sadie and John Tyrell (New York: Grove's Dictionaries, 2001).

79. See Oja, *Making Music Modern*.

80. Oja also places Fine among the ultramoderns "as we conceive of them today": ibid., 194. As a child prodigy in both piano and composition Vivian Fine became a student of Crawford in Chicago, was later encouraged in her dissonant experimentalism by Cowell, came under Copland's mentorship upon moving to New York in 1931, and shifted to tonal writing while a student of Roger Sessions (ca. 1934–41): Judith Cody, *Vivian Fine: A Bio-Bibliography* (Westport, Conn.: Greenwood Press, 2002), 4–16. The recent literature on Crawford, Fine, and these other modernist women composers includes Judith Tick, *Ruth Crawford Seeger: A Composer's Search for American Music* (New York: Oxford University Press, 1997); Rao, "Partnership in Modern Music"; Ellie M. Hisama, *Gendering Musical Modernism: The Music of Ruth Crawford Seeger, Marion Bauer, and Miriam Gideon* (Cambridge: Cambridge University Press, 2001); and Oja, "A Forgotten Vanguard: The Legacy of Marion Bauer, Frederick Jacobi, Emerson Whithorne, and Louis Gruenberg," in *Making Music Modern*, 155–76.

81. The relevant diary passage (in which the descriptor "withering" originates), dated August 31, 1927, is cited in Gardner, "The American Composer Becomes a Self-Made Man," 1.

82. Richard Franko Goldman, "Aaron Copland," *Musical Quarterly* 47, no. 1 (1961): 1–3.

83. Pollack credits the Young Composers group hosted and advised by Copland in 1932–33 with popularizing Copland's title as "Dean of American Music": *Aaron Copland*, 186.

84. The quoted characterization of Ives and Ruggles is a translation of the title of one of Cowell's several 1930 articles on the subject in the German music journal *Melos*, "Die beiden wirklichen Amerikaner: Ives und Ruggles." Other quotations are from Pollack, *Aaron Copland*, 519, 656 nn. 5–6. For further dis-

cussion of racial and national identity in Copland's career see Pollack, "Identity Issues," ibid., 518–31.

85. Scott Bravmann sounds a sustained note of caution on this historiographic front in *Queer Fictions of the Past: History, Culture, and Difference* (New York: Cambridge University Press, 1997).

86. Thomson's letter, dated February 5, 1947, is reprinted (without the reader's letter that inspired it) in *Selected Letters of Virgil Thomson*, ed. Page and Page, 209.

87. See Pollack, *Aaron Copland*, 236.

88. Ibid., 53, 234.

89. Halperin, *How to Do the History of Homosexuality*, 109. In presenting this and the other three discursive categories—of "effeminacy," "friendship or male love," and "passivity or inversion"—Halperin demonstrates that they all persist within the modern conception of homosexuality, even to the present day, and indeed that "what 'homosexuality' signifies today is an effect of [a] cumulative process of historical overlay and accretion" of these traditions (109).

90. Ibid., 113–17.

91. Ibid., 115–16. Other theorists might emend Halperin's relatively radical assessment of the "lopsided" distribution of desire and pleasure in pederastic partnering, to allow, for example, that those of the younger partner are perhaps lesser and probably of a different nature than those of the older partner.

92. See Pollack, *Aaron Copland*, 3–4, on Copland's looks and physical self-perception.

93. Rorem's phrase is from *Knowing When to Stop*, 207.

94. "Diana Trilling," 548. See chapter 1 in this volume for Thomson's remarks elsewhere concerning meaning amid the "obscure thing" in *Tender Buttons*. I find intriguing contextualization for Thomson's account of his "little controversy" with Breton in Rorem's remarks on surrealism as a "male chauvinist" movement characterized by both homo- and musicophobia. Rorem writes that "surrealism . . . was a literary (sometimes by extension a painterly) movement that excluded the art of music as sissified and irrelevant." He notes, "I did not know [the artist Kurt] Seligmann well, . . . perhaps because, like all surrealists in principle, he was heterosexual—homosexuality, like music, being taboo (Charles-Henri [Ford] had been granted, he claims, 'special dispensation' by Breton, while [Federico García] Lorca and [Salvador] Dali [sic] were simply banished)": Rorem, *Knowing When to Stop*, 556, 216, 256.

95. Brett, "Musicality, Essentialism, and the Closet," 13.

96. Sándor Márai, *Embers*, trans. Carol Brown Janeway (New York: Alfred A. Knopf, 2001), 198; the novel was originally published as *A gyertyák csonkig égnek* in Budapest in 1942.

97. Koestenbaum, *The Queen's Throat*, 189–90.

98. Texted music, of course, invites more "pinning down" of concrete meanings than does "pure" instrumental music, the ideally abstract musical medium.

99. Koestenbaum, *The Queen's Throat*, 11, 16.

100. For evidence of the author's self-awareness about the pre-Stonewall locus of his queer nostalgia see ibid., 84 and elsewhere.

101. See ibid., 47.

102. Ibid., 20.

103. Brett discusses this "social contract" in relation to music and bohemia in "Musicality, Essentialism, and the Closet," 16–18. On music's regulation of patriarchal order see 12–16 (concerning such regulation within the domain of music itself) and 16–23 (concerning such regulation within culture at large).

104. Ibid., 17, quoting Allan Bloom, *The Closing of the American Mind* (New York: Simon and Schuster, 1988), 235.

105. Brett, "Musicality, Essentialism, and the Closet," 17.

106. Ibid., 22.

107. Suzanne G. Cusick, "On a Lesbian Relationship with Music: A Serious Effort Not to Think Straight," in Brett et al., eds., *Queering the Pitch*, 67–83.

108. See Leo Bersani, *Homos* (Cambridge, Mass.: Harvard University Press, 1995), 75–76.

109. Warner, "Introduction," xiii.

110. Thomson traveled overland to Lisbon and from there embarked in mid-August on a ship bound for New York (and carrying also Man Ray and Salvador Dalí): see *Virgil Thomson by Virgil Thomson*, 307, 315–20.

111. Rorem, *Knowing When to Stop*, 217.

112. Donald Webster Cory [pseud.], *The Homosexual in America: A Subjective Approach* (New York: Greenberg, 1951; reprint ed., New York: Arno Press, 1975), 154.

113. Interestingly, Rorem's *petite phrase* is directed here to fending off those who would draw connections between music and homosexuality: *The Later Diaries, 1961–1972* (New York: Da Capo Press, 2000), reprint of *The Final Diary, 1961–1972* (New York: Holt, Rinehart, and Winston, 1974), 433.

114. This recent tally of Rorem's song output comes from Ned Rorem, *Lies: A Diary* (Washington, D.C.: Counterpoint, 2000), 304.

115. See chapters 3 and 4 for discussion of postwar "complexity music" and its relations to U.S. gay composers.

116. Koestenbaum, *The Queen's Throat*, 131.

117. Tommasini, *Virgil Thomson*, 427.

118. Thomson quote is from Page and Page, *Selected Letters of Virgil Thomson*, 262. For accounts of the *Lincoln Portrait* cancellation and Thomson's response see DeLapp, "Copland in the Fifties," 123–34; and Tommasini, *Virgil Thomson*, 425–27.

119. Tommasini, *Virgil Thomson*, 427.

120. As Brett notes and as this instance can illustrate, the "discretionary model of homosexuality" also "brought with it distinct advantages as well as drawbacks": Philip Brett, "Britten, Copland, and Transatlantic Queer Musical Connexions," paper presented at the annual meeting of the American Historical Association and its Committee on Lesbian and Gay History, San Francisco, January 2002, 13.

121. Rorem, *Knowing When to Stop*, 219.

122. Lederman was editor of *Modern Music:* see Tommasini, *Virgil Thomson*, 356.

123. Tommasini, *Virgil Thomson*, 475.

124. Ibid., 464, 149, 537–38.

125. An early (and homophobic) articulation of the now conventional sex-transposition reading of Proust's *À la recherche* is Justin O'Brien, "Albertine the Ambiguous: Notes on Proust's Transposition of the Sexes," *PMLA* 64, no. 5 (1949): 933–52. The notion has been further scrutinized and developed in more recent criticism including J. E. Rivers, *Proust and the Art of Love: The Aesthetics of Sexuality in the Life, Times, and Art of Marcel Proust* (New York: Columbia University Press, 1980); and Elisabeth Ladenson, *Proust's Lesbianism* (Ithaca: Cornell University Press, 1999). The quoted phrase is from Blackmer, "The Ecstasies of Saint Teresa," 340 n. 3.

126. Thomson, *Virgil Thomson by Virgil Thomson*, 89, 179, 95, and elsewhere. For examples of Thomson's statements and innuendoes here see his discussion of Stein in "A Portrait of Gertrude Stein," in *Virgil Thomson by Virgil Thomson*, 169–80 (179 esp.); and the same essay published under the same title in the *New York Review of Books* (1966) and reprinted in *A Virgil Thomson Reader*, 69–78 (77 esp.). See also Thomson, "A Very Difficult Author."

127. Tommasini, *Virgil Thomson*, 227.

128. As Warner notes in his discussion of Goffman's classic formulations on "spoiled identity," racial and sexual identities alike are subject to the inflection of stigmatization: "The shame of a true pervert—[not ordinary shame but] stigma— . . . is a social identity that befalls one like fate. Like the related stigmas of racial identity or disabilities, it may have nothing to do with acts one has committed. It attaches not to doing, but to being; not to conduct, but to status": *The Trouble with Normal*, 28.

129. Warner regards this awareness of shame's absurdity as a striking feature of queer culture: ibid., 33–34.

130. Brett, "Musicality, Essentialism, and the Closet," 17.

131. See Trotter's biography of Mitropoulos, *Priest of Music*.

132. Cory, "Till Death Do Us Part," in *The Homosexual in America*, 201.

133. Quoted phrases are from Warner, *The Trouble with Normal*, 99–100.

134. Cusick, "On a Lesbian Relationship with Music," 80.

135. Another locus in which a gender-obsessed modernist (part-time) musician expresses deep distrust and disregard toward words is Charles Ives's 1919 short story "George's Adventure and the Majority." Ives's protagonist expounds upon "his pet theme: . . . The Futility of Words as Such": "Words are the one invention of man that has done more to cause war and retard civilization than the discovery of gunpowder" (see Ives, *Memos*, 208).

136. Chauncey, *Gay New York*, 273. Further relevant sources on the construction of identities include Jeffrey Weeks, "Questions of Identity," in *The Cultural Construction of Sexuality*, ed. Pat Caplan (New York: Tavistock, 1987), 31–51; Stuart Hall, "Ethnicity: Identity and Difference," *Radical Amer-*

ica 23, no. 4 (1989), 9–20; and Werner Sollors, ed., *The Invention of Ethnicity* (New York: Oxford University Press, 1989).

137. See Chauncey, *Gay New York*, 107–10, 220–23, and elsewhere.

138. Newton, *Mother Camp*, 21. Newton notes the exceptional status of such "highly sophisticated urban occupational groups" as the art, theater, and fashion worlds, "whose occupations form subcultures of their own" and as such contrast with most other "job-based and professional groups," which are either explicitly or implicitly heterosexual (28–29).

139. Rubin, "Thinking Sex," 21, 23.

INTERMEZZO

1. Rorem, *Knowing When to Stop*, 148–49, 221–23. The young Rorem was introduced to the music of Satie in 1944 by one of Virgil Thomson's self-accompanied performances, in his small "composer's voice," of *Socrate* (ibid., 211)—just as Stein and Toklas in 1926 had received their introduction to Satie's work. John Cage was likewise initiated, and like Rorem he thereafter deemed *Socrate* his favorite piece of music, though according to Rorem he "gleaned from it what I never heard. Where for me Satie's quips were plaintive, to John they were campy." Cage under Satie's influence pursued a direction completely different from Rorem's, "tak[ing] Satie literally where he was being merely whimsical," and thus "rent[ing] a hall plus a relay of pianists" to carry out—for twenty-five hours—Satie's instructions in *Vexations*, a three-minute work for piano that is to be repeated 840 times (see ibid., 232). At other points Paul Bowles and (ca. 1943) Lou Harrison too joined the ranks of those who were "recruited" to *Socrate* by Thomson: see Tommasini, *Virgil Thomson*, 368, 372.

2. Quoted passages are from *Rorem, Knowing When to Stop*, 222. In a 1970 diary entry Rorem identifies Bowles's aria as "Te de Llevar." Rorem here further remarks (with flippant camp anachronism) that the same gesture of a descending minor third occurs in Messiaen, Mahler, Mompou's Catalonian songs, Franck, and the Copland *Organ Symphony*, but that all such uses strike him "as coming from Messiaen or Bowles": *The Later Diaries, 1961–72*, 346.

3. Rorem, *Knowing When to Stop*, 223. Similarly, according to Pollack, Copland "became a faithful reader of Bowles's books and was struck by how strangely dark his fiction was compared to his music, whose freshness and charm he had long admired": *Aaron Copland*, 185.

4. This is the chronology given by Bowles's biographer Caponi in *Paul Bowles*, 41–42. Pollack, *Aaron Copland*, 182, however, places Bowles's (born December 30, 1910) and Copland's first meeting in 1930.

5. Caponi, *Paul Bowles*, 46.

6. Ibid., 41–44; see also Pollack, *Aaron Copland*, 182–83.

7. Tommasini, *Virgil Thomson*, 291.

8. In 1947 Bowles emigrated to Tangier from New York, with his wife Jane Auer Bowles (married February 1938): Pollack, *Aaron Copland*, 185; Rorem, *Knowing When to Stop*, 346.

9. Caponi, *Paul Bowles*, 48.

10. Ibid., 57. The song's complete text is given in the liner notes to *Paul Sperry Sings Romantic American Songs* (Albany Records TROY043).

11. Pollack, *Aaron Copland*, 183. Pollack cites one piece of evidence "point[ing] to physical intimacy," but it seems merely to suggest the possibility: That is, a 1933 letter from Bowles to Thomson referring to Copland's new relationship with Victor Kraft, in the passage, "Aaron of course has a new pet so there is no snuggling there" (604 n. 16). Decades later, in 1969, Copland described Bowles to Phillip Ramey as "a cold fish," and still later when Ramey pressed Copland for details on Bowles, he said only, "Oh, he was a bad boy" (185).

12. Pollack, *Aaron Copland*, 183. Pollack's footnote (604 n. 16) attributes this quote to Thomson, *Virgil Thomson by Virgil Thomson*, 206, but this is erroneous: Thomson's memoirs throughout are fiercely closeted vis-à-vis his own sexuality and that of all his gay male—though not his lesbian—friends and associates: The page cited, in fact, makes vague but ostentatious mention of a Parisian girl he alleges to have been "Paul's dainty and devoted sweetheart" of 1931.

13. Tommasini, *Virgil Thomson*, 293.

14. Ibid., 353; emphasis mine.

15. Regina Weinrich and Catherine Warnow, producers, *Paul Bowles: The Complete Outsider* (New York: First Run/Icarus Films, 1993). In remarking on the absence of any particular indication of bisexuality in Bowles I am implicitly but deliberately rejecting those quasi-clinical perspectives that would label an individual as bisexual on no other basis than the empirical evidence of his or her having been involved erotically with members of each sex—in disregard of sociocultural context and of the subject's self-identification.

16. Tangier was an independent city within the International Zone (governed by eight countries plus Tangier itself) from 1923 until 1956, when it became part of Morocco.

17. Joan Peyser writes that Copland used this phrase among friends with reference not to Bowles but to Bernstein: *Bernstein: A Biography* (New York: William Morrow, 1987), 52. Perhaps amending this account, Secrest reports (citing Bernstein's sister Shirley as source) that Copland called Bernstein "B.H.," for "bluff homosexual": *Leonard Bernstein*, 180.

18. See Somerville, *Queering the Color Line*, for a discussion of the co-construction of "Negro" and homosexual identities in early-twentieth-century America, in which the terms of miscegenation explicit in the former are revealed as implicit in the latter.

19. Kaiser, *The Gay Metropolis*, 89. Rorem declares that "all homosexual conductors of the period (except Mitropoulos) . . . married," and elaborates: "male orchestra conductors . . . were and remain married worldwide, though most of them fool around: being absolute monarchs, anything is permitted them, provided they are protected with a wedding ring": *Knowing When to Stop*, 570, 346–47. I have discussed the complexities and misrepresentations

attending Bernstein's life and persona in "Bernstein's *Mass* Appeal: Eclecticism, Omnivorism, Dirty Laundry, Musical Knowledge," paper presented at the annual meeting of the Society for American Music, Cleveland, March 2004.

20. Pollack, *Aaron Copland,* 171. One such letter is that of November 26, 1931, in which Thomson (in Paris) explains to Copland (in New York) his own reservations concerning Boulanger as potential teacher for young Bowles, and asks Copland to write Bowles as soon as possible with guidance: Page and Page, *Selected Letters of Virgil Thomson,* 100–101; see also 103–4.

21. Caponi, *Paul Bowles,* 54–55; see also Pollack, *Aaron Copland,* 184.

22. Thomson, *Virgil Thomson by Virgil Thomson,* 206–7.

23. Pollack, *Aaron Copland,* 182–83; Tommasini, *Virgil Thomson,* 293.

24. Rorem, *Knowing When to Stop,* 149. The Bowles composition goes unidentified, but Rorem recalls that it might have been a documentary film score. In any case it could not have influenced Copland's *Music for the Theater* of 1925; whatever influence Bowles might have had on Copland could not have preceded their first communications in early 1930.

25. Ibid., 223.

26. Ibid., 192.

27. See ibid., 178–79.

28. Ibid., 242. He continues, "For the moment the overall optimism, plus the specific acceptance—unimaginable today—of High Art, was the electric tone in that madly healthy air."

29. This phrase according to ibid., 253.

30. Paul Bowles, *Without Stopping* (New York: G. P. Putnam, 1972), 98.

31. Caponi, *Paul Bowles,* 48.

32. Rorem, *Knowing When to Stop,* 253–54. The piano duo Double Edge released a fine recording of Bowles's *Night Waltz* on their 1992 disk *U.S. CHOICE* (CRI CD 637).

33. Under the heading "Incidental Theater Music" Caponi lists thirty-three works, twenty of which were composed between 1936 and 1948: *Paul Bowles,* 249.

34. Rorem, *Knowing When to Stop,* 355, 576.

35. Ibid., 222, 491, 148, 194, 218.

36. Ibid., 148.

37. Rorem continues: For "didn't 'they' [famous people] all know about each other?": ibid., 431. One boyfriend meeting reported here by Rorem involved his having met "Paul's teenaged Spanish boyfriend" on a visit to Tangier in 1950 (492).

38. Rorem might have known more about Bowles's erotic persona if on their second meeting (in Manhattan, 1943), when Bowles invited Rorem to spend the night at his apartment in the Chelsea Hotel, Rorem had not pretended to pass out drunk. A famed beauty as well as a heavy drinker in his youth, Rorem claims also to have used this tactic to elude the seductions of Samuel Barber (ca. 1947). Tennessee Williams accused Rorem of having performed the same act with him, whereas Rorem reports having dodged Virgil

Thomson (ca. 1944) by less contrived means. According to Rorem he did not forgo "Lenny" Bernstein, however, when they first met in 1943. See ibid., 193, 308, 383, 212–13, 177.

39. Interestingly, according to Pollack Copland nurtured a "special liking" for *L'Immoraliste*—as he did, of course, for Bowles: see Pollack, *Aaron Copland*, 54.

40. Bersani, *Homos*, 119–20.

41. Rorem, *Knowing When to Stop*, 124–25.

42. Bersani, *Homos*, 122; emphasis in original, 123.

43. Rorem, *Knowing When to Stop*, 455.

44. Quoted in Stephen Davis, "Mercury at 80," *Boston Globe Magazine* (March 4, 1990): 14–20, 24–25; reprinted in Gena Dagel Caponi, *Conversations with Paul Bowles* (Jackson: University Press of Mississippi, 1993), 228.

45. The charm perceived in Bowles's music is variously attested and discussed in Owsley Brown III's independent film *Night Waltz: The Music of Paul Bowles* (2001).

46. For this account of musical modernism see esp. Robert P. Morgan, "Secret Languages: The Roots of Musical Modernism," *Critical Inquiry* 10, no. 3 (1984): 442–61.

47. Metzer, "'Spurned Love,'" 431–40. Metzer sees this turn beginning in such "transitional" works as *Poet's Song* (1927), *Vocalise* (1928), and *Symphonic Ode* (1929), and culminating in the *Piano Variations* (1930). One finds here a "silencing of the human voice" insofar as these works also punctuate the decade of Copland's most extensive song composition (418). As the phrase "scorched-earth campaign" may suggest, Metzer (418) goes so far as to read in the abstraction of the later works a revisionist renunciation of the earlier works' homoerotics and racial borrowings. I concur with the author's characterization of a "back[ing] away" (418) from such associations, and I assume a refiguring of the musical rhetoric in the new works, but I see no evidence of any aggressive revisionism toward the earlier ones.

48. James Baldwin, "This Morning, This Evening, So Soon" (1960), in *Early Novels and Stories*, ed. Toni Morrison (New York: Library of America, 1998), 878.

49. Personal correspondence with the author, February 17, 2003.

50. Rorem, *Knowing When to Stop*, 223. In addition to Rorem's admissions of the general influence of Bowles's composition on his own music, he cites Bowles's song "David" specifically as a disguised model (its piano part having been cut and pasted into "a background fabric") for the piano accompaniment in his own 1946 song "On a Singing Girl" (258–59).

CHAPTER 3

The English barrister is quoted in H. Montgomery Hyde, ed., *The Trials of Oscar Wilde* (London: William Hodge, 1948), 375; quoted in Cory, *The Homosexual in America*, 89. Cory, *The Homosexual in America*, 107. Rorem, *Know-*

ing When to Stop, 402. We might remark that the pseudonym Don(ald) Cory itself embeds a markedly French and queer reference (notably inverted) to Gide's *Corydon*. Also illustrative is Henry Gerber's choice of pseudonym for his 1932 defense of homosexuals, responding to a condemnatory article in *The Modern Thinker:* See Parisex [pseud.], "In Defense of Homosexuality," *The Modern Thinker* (June 1932); reprinted in Martin Duberman, *About Time: Exploring the Gay Past* (New York: Gay Presses of New York, 1986), 119; and cited in Chauncey, *Gay New York*, 282.

1. This letter is cited in multiple sources including the Barber biographies by Nathan Broder and Barbara B. Heyman, whose quotations differ in certain orthographic details. I follow Heyman's version here, and likewise her argument that Barber was nine (not eight) years old when he wrote the letter. Heyman's persistence, however, even at the late date of 1992, in thoroughly closeting Barber's sexuality and his lifelong partnership with fellow composer Gian Carlo Menotti inevitably casts a shadow on her book's credibility. A further discrepant detail concerning this boyhood incident is that Heyman's version has Barber leaving the finished letter on his own desk, whereas in Broder's 1954 account he leaves it "on his mother's dressing table." See Heyman, *Samuel Barber: The Composer and His Music* (New York: Oxford University Press, 1992), 7; and Broder, *Samuel Barber* (New York: Schirmer, 1954), 9.

2. Brett, "Musicality, Essentialism, and the Closet," 11–12, 18.

3. Cusick, "On a Lesbian Relationship with Music," 70–71. I use the hyphenated construction *music-lover* to mark a fervency and erotics beyond those typically denoted by the (unhyphenated) phrase, as when this latter is more blandly applied to symphony subscribers.

4. Ibid., 70–71, 78–79. Lest my abridgment of it suggest otherwise, I will attest that Cusick's culminating query is no mere rhetorical flourish but a formulation that resonates powerfully with her fellow musicians. In fact, her first presentation of this paper, to an audience of queer and straight musicians and music scholars in 1991, inspired one of the most sympathetic and cathartic audience responses to an academic paper I have ever witnessed, and a subsequent spate of similarly interior, embodied musical inquiry by other musical thinkers.

5. Ibid., 80, 73. It would be a difficult task to prove that music-loving, or lesbian sex, in fact allows such an escape from identity and its "consolidated power." Whether or not verifiable, the claim is undoubtedly consequential within Cusick's extended comparison of music-loving and lesbian sex. And it can be suggestive for purposes of understanding the kinds of appeal that concert (and perhaps other) music might have offered to twentieth-century queer (and undoubtedly other) subjects, particularly those who constructed lives and identities in intimate affiliation with music.

6. T. S. Eliot, *Four Quartets* (New York: Harcourt, Brace, 1943), 27.

7. Cusick, "On a Lesbian Relationship with Music," 77. *Musical identity* rings paradoxical insofar as the music(al) term, pace Cusick, nullifies the identity term (within the phrase's conventional sense of musically defined subjec-

tivity) and polysemous insofar as the phrase takes on also the logical-mathematical sense of "identity"—hence, denoting a oneness with music. Also relevant here is Fred Everett Maus's analysis of a central function of music-critical discourse, that of counteracting music's threat of emasculating by penetrating the (perilously passive, receptive) listening subject—I would say, in other words, of counteracting music's identity-dissolving effects; see Maus, "Masculine Discourse in Music Theory," *Perspectives of New Music* 31, no. 2 (1993): 264–93.

My paraphrase echoes Bersani's question "Who are you when you masturbate?" which is (in its ensuing elaboration) likewise concerned with interior processes of identification and thence with identity. Such concerns in Bersani are enabled by his rendering (needlessly foreclosed, in my view) of autoeroticism as essentially alloerotic in a fantasmatic realm: He avows, "I find unimaginable a successful session . . . without fantasy," which fantasy is conceived (as his subsequent discussion reveals) in terms involving an other.

8. On Foucault's identification of the modern history and techniques of subjectivation and his pursuit of desubjectivation via pleasure, see Halperin, *Saint Foucault*, 90–112 esp.

9. Warner, *The Trouble with Normal*, 166, 195.

10. Bersani, *Homos*, 103, 122–29.

11. Leo Bersani, "Is the Rectum a Grave?" in *AIDS: Cultural Analysis, Cultural Activism*, ed. Douglas Crimp (Cambridge, Mass.: MIT Press, 1988), 217, 222. See also Bersani, *Homos*, 98–99 esp.

12. Bersani, "Is the Rectum a Grave?" 218, 217, 222.

13. Rorem recounts the Bowles anecdote in *Knowing When to Stop*, 193.

14. Ibid., 345–46. In a 1966 diary entry Rorem updates and emends this account:

> Generalities given to Kinsey eighteen years ago (but times have changed) *re* homoerotics in the male sex. Composers in the '40s: 75 percent (and conveniently, three of the Top Four). Composers today: no more than 50 percent—the musical style doesn't lend itself. Of the leading youngish composers singly representing America, France, Italy, and Germany (I don't know about Scandinavia or the Orient), only one: the German. . . . Pianists, then as now, about 50 percent. Organists: 90 percent (not because of attraction to the word but their sissified Protestant background—though in France it's otherwise). Harpsichord: 95 percent. Violinists: no more than 10 percent (the solid Jewish family). Soloists, though, of course are more neurotic than the orchestra players for whom music is a living wage and who are 99 percent heterosexual. . . . Harpists: fewer than you'd think. . . . Abstract expressionists of yesterday: almost none. Pop artists of today: almost all (a question of humor; they don't drink much either).

Ned Rorem, *The Later Diaries*, 195–96. For more on "the German" to whom

Rorem apparently refers see Hans Werner Henze, *Bohemian Fifths: An Auto-biography*, trans. Stewart Spencer (London: Faber and Faber, 1998).

15. See Rorem, *Knowing When to Stop*, 140 (on Rorem's attraction to Jews), 143–44 and 349 (on his alcoholism), and elsewhere.

16. See Michel Foucault, *The History of Sexuality*, vol. I; and Vernon A. Rosario, *The Erotic Imagination: French Histories of Perversity* (New York: Oxford University Press, 1997).

17. Sedgwick, *Epistemology of the Closet*, 8–9. The "varied and acute implications and consequences" (9) of the privileging of and obsession with homo/heterosexual definition in Anglo-American modernity and modernism are explored throughout *Epistemology of the Closet*.

18. Most adults of the period were heterosexually married. This included many if not most homosexuals, among whom the concept "marriage of convenience" was well known. Of the composers in the present circle, Bernstein, Blitzstein, and Bowles were married to women, and even Thomson (in the terms of the period, a notorious *pansy*, albeit one perennially uncomfortable with his homosexuality) and Rorem (though an unabashed and exclusive gay bottom, and unusually accepting of his homosexuality) entertained the possibility of marrying. See Watson, *Prepare for Saints*, 195–96, on the prevalence of "queer marriages" (as Thomson called them) in high bohemian circles, and for mention of Thomson's proposal to enter into such a union with Theodate (sister of the gay architect Philip) Johnson. For fuller treatment of this proposal—including Thomson's surprise appearance, naked, in Johnson's bed—see Tommasini, *Virgil Thomson*, 315–16.

19. For further discussion of Partch's work and life, including his sexuality, see Philip Blackburn, ed., *Enclosure Three: Harry Partch* (St. Paul: American Composers Forum, 1997); and Bob Gilmore, *Harry Partch: A Biography* (New Haven: Yale University Press, 1998). Relevant writings on Cage include Caroline A. Jones, "Finishing School: John Cage and the Abstract Expressionist Ego," *Critical Inquiry* 19, no. 3 (1993): 628–65; Thomas S. Hines, "Then Not Yet 'Cage': The Los Angeles Years, 1912–1938," in *John Cage: Composer in America*, ed. Marjorie Perloff and Charles Junkerman (Chicago: University of Chicago Press, 1994), 65–99; and Jonathan D. Katz, "John Cage's Queer Silence or How to Avoid Making Matters Worse," *GLQ: A Journal of Lesbian and Gay Studies* 5, no. 2 (1999): 231–52. On Harrison see Leta E. Miller, *Lou Harrison: Composing a World* (New York: Oxford University Press, 1998).

20. Harrison "disdained" Copland's art, according to Rorem, *Knowing When to Stop*, 228; and Cage ca. 1941 was "rebuffed" by Copland, according to Thomson, *Virgil Thomson by Virgil Thomson*, 353.

21. Rorem, *Knowing When to Stop*, 229.

22. Ibid., 207. For analysis of gay discursive codes, including camp, see William L. Leap, *Word's Out: Gay Men's English* (Minneapolis: University of Minnesota Press, 1996). By his own account, Rorem was never a member of Copland's or Thomson's "entourage," but "dipped [his] toe in both streams": Rorem, "Aaron Copland," in *A Ned Rorem Reader*, 233.

Pollack also finds exaggeration in Rorem's account of the separateness of Copland's and Thomson's "factions" and discusses multiple instances of their significant association: *Aaron Copland,* 173. One such association, documented by several writers, was Thomson's and (especially) Copland's affiliation, beginning in the 1920s, with the League of Composers and its magazine, *Modern Music.* In this connection the two composers were indeed embroiled in a rivalry, between competing composers' organizations (see chapter 4), but here were members of the same "team."

23. References to such gay-conspiracy theories are, not surprisingly, vastly fewer in the daylight of published prose than in the disavowable discourse of speech acts—which persist on these themes even today. This scenario illustrates the means by which the closet (as a space of furtiveness and secrecy) is constructed around and against queer subjects, by a homophobic cultural system—a point that bears repeating, in view of the ubiquity of figures depicting the closet as a space either chosen or abandoned by a supremely agentic queer subject. Among the few conspiracy mentions in print, see Secrest, *Leonard Bernstein,* 256–57, for some uncritically cited examples; and Michael Tippett, *Those Twentieth-Century Blues: An Autobiography* (London: Hutchinson, 1991), 214, for critical mention of Britain's 1940s scuttlebutt, which invariably focused on Britten and his partner, the renowned tenor Peter Pears, and often on the composer Tippett as well. See chapter 4 in this book for gay-conspiracy theories in the correspondence of the straight-identified modernist Edgard Varèse.

Surely more characteristic is the studiously vague—and thus more broadly insinuative—sort of (non-) mention perfected in discourses of the Cold War era. For instance, Brett flags a coyly closeted remark on "bachelor composers" in the conversation books of Igor Stravinsky with (his amanuensis) Robert Craft (see "Musicality, Essentialism, and the Closet," 19, 25 n. 27). In a critical discussion of Menotti's *Last Savage* Stravinsky is quoted as saying, "The predatory female idea might have possibilities, though—I am thinking of Mr. Robbins's ballet about her to the music of my String Concerto—especially to talented bachelor composers such as Britten, Henze, Tchaikovsky, and Menotti." The word *bachelor* in any literal sense is gratuitous here; its use purely as a code word is affirmed by the fact that every artist at which (the nonbachelor) Stravinsky reportedly points his curiously asynchronous finger—all four composers and one choreographer—is a gay man: Stravinsky and Craft, *Themes and Episodes* (New York: Alfred A. Knopf, 1967), 100–101.

Other conspiracy rumors circulated in this era, implicating other identity groups: Virgil Thomson was among those who speculated on Copland's involvement in a syndicate of Jewish composers. He referred to the League of Composers as "the League of Jewish Composers" (Oja, *Making Music Modern,* 218) and proposed to Minna Lederman an article for *Modern Music* on "the thirteen Jews who ran music in New York" (Tommasini, *Virgil Thomson,* 301). Elsewhere, the African American composer William Grant Still ca. 1949 publicly implicated Copland, Bernstein, and Blitzstein in an alleged racist and communist conspiracy to impede the careers of conservative composers, including himself: see Catherine Parsons Smith, *William Grant Still: A Study in Contradictions* (Berkeley: University of California Press, 2000), 195–96.

The 1940s were the prime moment for these composers as a group, not to say each of them individually; certainly Rorem's career apex came later.

24. K. Robert Schwarz, "Composers' Closets Open for All to See," *New York Times* (June 19, 1994), sec. 2: 1, 24.

25. Stories of homosexual purges in the Eastman School during Howard Hanson's tenure as director (1924–64) surfaced among queer, and some straight, musicians for decades. An account, attributed to Diamond, alleging homosexual purges by Hanson in the 1930s appears in Schwarz's landmark *New York Times* feature (ibid.). And Rorem refers to conversation among his music-student cohort ca. 1947, all of whom (save Rorem) had "recently immigrated to Manhattan" from the Eastman School and disparaged Hanson as having "fostered homosexual purges": *Knowing When to Stop*, 335–36. In an interview with the present author (November 13, 2001), Diamond named three Eastman faculty members who were dismissed and one student who was asked to leave under these circumstances, all males. But Diamond emphasized that he considered Arthur Larson (Eastman Registrar, 1929–61) the "spy" and guilty party in these purgings, and that Schwarz's 1994 *Times* article misrepresented his own account of the matter, particularly by its demonization of Hanson.

26. Ives, *Memos*, 135. See also (among innumerable other examples) Rorem's story of Rosario Scalero—composition teacher of Barber and Menotti in the late 1920s and early 1930s, and briefly Rorem (in 1943), at the Curtis Institute—and his response when Thomson's name arose: "Silly man—he wears bracelets" served effectively to dismiss both the artist and his oeuvre (*Knowing When to Stop*, 178). In the event, Scalero was deriding one of his queer students to another: Thomson in 1923 had briefly, warily, studied composition with Scalero, then newly emigrated, at the Mannes College of Music (Tommasini, *Virgil Thomson*, 111).

27. My assessment of Chopin's popular reputation finds confirmation in Cory, *The Homosexual in America*. Writing from a homosexually identified subject position, Cory invokes Chopin in a critique of some heterosexual critics' rejection (or ghettoization) of the work of homosexual artists: "Just as the homosexuals do not reject the music of Chopin, although it is imbued with the tragic romance of his love for women; or the literary influences of a Dickens or a Joyce, so is it equally absurd for the 'normal man' to reject an art, a philosophy, a music, a political thought, because it came from the creative mind of a homosexual" (165).

28. Tick's argument is exactly this—that misogynist and homophobic utterances in Ives's discourse figured resistance toward the established European art-musical tradition: "Charles Ives and Gender Ideology." For a revealing study of the gender- and genre-coded language of nineteenth-century music

criticism concerning Chopin and other keyboard composers, see Jeffrey Kallberg, "The Harmony of the Tea Table: Gender and Ideology in the Piano Nocturne," *Representations* 39 (1992): 102–33.

29. This anecdote was related in a letter from the composer and critic Robert Parris to the *New York Times* in response to Schwarz, "Composers' Closets Open for All to See": see "Gay Composers: Exception To the Rule?" *New York Times* (July 10, 1994), sec. 2: 2. There is no dating here of Thomson and Weber's first meeting, but references to Weber in Thomson's memoir date their acquaintance at least as far back as 1946, when Weber is mentioned as having made, as copyist, "a handsome new orchestral score" of *Four Saints in Three Acts:* Thomson, *Virgil Thomson by Virgil Thompson,* 387. Joseph R. Dalton recounts the anecdote from this (Parris's) letter to the *Times* and adds the observation that Weber was the only gay composer among serialists of his generation, which included George Perle, Milton Babbitt, and Elliott Carter: Dalton, liner notes for *Gay American Composers,* vol. 2, CRI CD 750, 10–11.

30. Dalton, liner notes, 10.

31. Sedgwick introduces the notion of "nonce taxonomy" under her "Axiom 1" in *Epistemology of the Closet,* 22–23. Concerning the proposition posed by her first and "most obvious" axiom—that is, "People are different from each other"—she writes,

> [P]robably everybody who survives at all has reasonably rich, unsystematic resources of nonce taxonomy for mapping out the possibilities, dangers, and stimulations of their human social landscape. It is probably people with the experience of oppression or subordination who have most *need* to know it; and I take the precious, devalued arts of gossip, immemorially associated in European thought with servants, with effeminate and gay men, with all women, to have to do . . . with the refinement of necessary skills for making, testing, and using unrationalized and provisional hypotheses about what *kinds of people* there are to be found in one's world.

I share Sedgwick's sense that gay men have been among those strongly impelled to formulate nonce taxonomies. And I would note that Rorem and Thomson's formulations demonstrate unusual clarity and eloquence about the identity mechanisms that operated in U.S. musical modernism. But I would also emphasize that the homophobic movements of nongay composers evince that these identity structures operated throughout the music world and shaped—albeit differentially—the experiences and work of all musicians, queer and nonqueer.

32. Thomson's quip implies that heterosexuals can be twelve-tone composers and clearly specifies that homosexuals can never be twelve-tone composers, but omits any mention of whether heterosexuals can be non–twelve tone composers (read here: tonalists). One intended function of my qualifying "to whatever extent" is that of placeholder for this unspecified meaning.

33. See, for instance, Roger Sessions's galling of Thomson by his humorless and aesthetically tone-deaf review of the latter's *Sonate d'Eglise* for a 1926 issue of *Modern Music:* Tommasini, *Virgil Thomson*, 192. Johnson, referring to an episode of late 1932, is quoted in Watson, *Prepare for Saints*, 137.

34. Rorem, *Knowing When to Stop*, 195.

35. Kramer, "Cultural Politics and Musical Form," 183. The phrase "a good dissonance like a man" is attributed to Ives, and it appears most famously as the title of Ted Timreck's film about Ives and his music: see Theodor William Timreck, producer and director, "A Good Dissonance Like a Man" (Framingham, Mass.: Home Vision, 1976). According to the Ives scholar James B. Sinclair, Timreck may have encountered the phrase in oral history archives of interviews with Ives (personal correspondence with the author, October 16, 2002).

36. Parris, "Gay Composers"; emphasis mine.

37. Alfred Towne, "The New Taste in Humor," *American Mercury* 333 (1951): 27.

38. Andrew Elfenbein, *Romantic Genius: The Prehistory of a Homosexual Role* (New York: Columbia University Press, 1999), reveals shared key attributions sustaining and interlinking the eighteenth-century creative genius and the nineteenth-century homosexual.

39. I first noted these shared motifs in my essay "Classical Music and Opera," 425.

40. Oja, *Making Music Modern*, 225, 125–26; Varèse's remark is attributed to a 1939 lecture (426 n. 24).

41. Chauncey, *Gay New York*, 276.

42. Lawrence D. Mass, "An Interview with Ned Rorem," in Brett et al., eds., *Queering the Pitch*, 85–112. Mass comments on such generational and sensibility clashes, involving Rorem and several other gay critics and artists, in "Musical Closets: A Personal and Selective Documentary History of Outing and Coming Out in the Music World," in *Taking Liberties: Gay Men's Essays on Politics, Culture, and Sex*, ed. Michael Bronski (New York: Richard Kasak, 1996), 387–440.

43. Halperin, *Saint Foucault*, 59.

44. Bernard-Henri Lévy, "Non au sexe roi" (interview with Michel Foucault), *Le Nouvel Observateur* (March 12, 1977): 95, 98; quoted ibid., 58–59 (Halperin's translation, based on that of David J. Parent).

45. It is within nineteenth-century Romanticism that the artist is lifted up to an exalted plane. For elucidation of the means by which talent and musicality are constructed (while also naturalized and essentialized) in late-twentieth-century conservatory culture see Henry Kingsbury, *Music, Talent, and Performance: A Conservatory Cultural System* (Philadelphia: Temple University Press, 1988).

46. Gordon, *Mark the Music*, 17.

47. A recent essay argues that intimations of Tchaikovsky's homosexuality appeared in print, in English, as early as 1899, but that certain critics began to characterize the sensitive and Romantic qualities of his music in feminizing

and pathologizing terms mostly after the language of psychosexual pathology became common in the 1910s: Malcolm Hamrick Brown, "Tchaikovsky and His Music in Anglo-American Criticism, 1890s–1950s," in Fuller and Whitesell, eds., *Queer Episodes in Music and Modern Identity*, 138, 145.

48. Not only inborn but immutable according to then-current views, including those of the gay composers in question. A female confidante to whom Blitzstein revealed his homosexuality "imagined a hormonal root to it, citing the work of Krafft-Ebing and Havelock Ellis, and thus forgave it as an unchangeable element in his psychology" (Gordon, *Mark the Music*, 19). Copland's similar "belief that homosexuality was a natural and inherited phenomenon" was reportedly influenced by his reading of Gide and of Ellis (Pollack, *Aaron Copland*, 234–35).

For Rorem at least—and perhaps more broadly, in connection with a further, Protestant/Catholic binarism attaching to my axis of hetero/homo, German/French, etc.—an emphasis on one's immutable nature, *la nature bête*, either inborn or fixed early in childhood, appears as definitively French and Catholic. Such an emphasis indeed resonates with the richly connotative and often-repeated French dictum "*Je suis comme je suis*" (with a Gallic shrug: "I am as I am"). And the pathways along which Rorem might link this attitude to Catholicism—which, like Frenchness, he fetishizes (Catholicism appeared to the young Quaker as "an exciting, strange, even wicked condition")—are hinted at in his statement "The Catholic priest is right: we're all pretty much 'made' by age seven" (*Knowing When to Stop*, 25, 585). Rorem's Catholiphilia, like Stein and Thomson's Catholic fascinations in *Four Saints*, may suggest a persistence of the markedly queer Neo-Catholic impulse that surfaced in late-nineteenth-century French literature.

49. Brett acknowledges potential dangers in projects of the present sort, "[p]roducing knowledge about homosexual artists of the past," dangers including "a tendency to essentialize homosexuality as a condition of creativity, . . . which at its most grotesque reflects [a subcultural] elitism": "Britten's Dream," in Solie, ed., *Musicology and Difference*, 260. More generally such a tendency may reflect the mutually imbricated meanings, pace Elfenbein in *Romantic Genius*, of homosexuality and creativity. In any event, I would hope that my formulation of a constructed homosexual-outsider-artist correlation will be distinguished from any essentializing homosexual-artist correlation.

50. Dalton, liner notes for *Gay American Composers*, vol. 2, 7.

51. See Gary C. Thomas, "'Was George Frideric Handel Gay?' On Closet Questions and Cultural Politics," in Brett et al., eds., *Queering the Pitch*, 155–204. For the record, I find Thomas's argument sound and cogent, and subsequent work, especially Ellen T. Harris, *Handel as Orpheus: Voice and Desire in the Chamber Cantatas* (Cambridge, Mass.: Harvard University Press, 2001), further bears it out. We might also compare Rorem's insinuations concerning Beethoven. Writing of his own three-time rejection by the military draft board as one who, according to his psychiatrist, "had not yet developed mature sexual impulses," Rorem counterpoints the theme of his (purportedly incorrigibly

French) failure to place Beethoven "at the core of the cosmos": "When I did mature I had not learned to appreciate Beethoven more intensely, though I did learn that Beethoven himself never developed mature sexual impulses": *Knowing When to Stop,* 173.

52. Chauncey discusses constructions of gay folklore and its dissemination in writings of queer authors of the 1910s through 1930s: "Few gay men [or lesbians, I would add] heard their teachers discuss the possible significance of homosexuality in Plato, Whitman, or Shakespeare, but they could find it mentioned in almost every gay novel published in the early 1930s." *Gay New York* cites Richard Meeker's *Better Angel* and (the female writer) Blair Niles's *Strange Brother* as novels demonstrating "both the [1930s] currency of such ideas [of an eminent gay historical tradition] among gay intellectuals and their allies and their determination to disseminate them among gay readers" (284–85).

53. Letter dated April 9, 1935, from Sigmund Freud in Vienna, addressed (in English) "Dear Mrs. ———" (name crossed out), in the collections of The Kinsey Institute for Research in Sex, Gender, and Reproduction, Inc. Used by permission.

54. In fact, Rorem identifies his above-cited musicosexual taxonomy as having been first imparted in 1948 to Dr. Kinsey, following a formal interview granted for Kinsey's research toward a new book: "he was planning a book on the sexuality of artists, which was why he was in New York visiting Juilliard and other sacred conclaves," Rorem notes parenthetically. Rorem reports that his parents were interviewed for the same project by Kinsey's assistant Dr. (Wardell B.) Pomeroy, and that he corresponded with Kinsey after this meeting until Kinsey's 1956 death (*Knowing When to Stop,* 345–46). This claim is confirmed by a file in the Kinsey Institute at Indiana University containing correspondence between Rorem, then a young and aspiring composer, and the world-renowned sex researcher, dated from February 13, 1949 (Kinsey's acknowledgment of the Rorems' contribution to his study) to February 21, 1955.

The study mentioned was never brought to fruition, and I have not been able to determine whether it was to have focused on the sexuality of artists, as Rorem reports, or sexuality as represented and expressed in the arts—or perhaps some combination of the two. In his written recollections, *Dr. Kinsey and the Institute for Sex Research* (New York: Harper and Row, 1972), Pomeroy seems to suggest the second possibility: In a chapter entitled "Kinsey and the Arts," he reports that Kinsey wrote to Tennessee Williams in early 1950, "we are making an extensive study of the erotic element in the arts . . . painting, music, writing, the stage, etc." (191), and notes that this study invoked the word *erotic* "in the broadest sense of an evocation of emotion more or less related to sexual interest in the subject matter." Pomeroy attests that "[h]undreds of artists gave [Kinsey] their histories, and scores of them spent considerable time discussing their work with him"—in the same way, presumably, as young Rorem did. But this testimony was directed, by Pomeroy's account, toward "helping [Kinsey] judge the erotic content of [their own and] other artists' work" (198–99).

Elsewhere, however, Pomeroy suggests that the study was concerned with artists' sexuality: "we took the history of nearly everyone in the three separate companies playing [Williams's] *A Streetcar Named Desire* and were able to demonstrate, at least to our own satisfaction, that Stanley, or Blanche, or Mitch, as portrayed by one actor emerged differently when played by another because of differences in the actors' sexual backgrounds" (191). The connection with artists' sex lives arises again in Pomeroy's recollection that Kinsey, upon meeting the novelist Glenway Wescott—another homosexual artist, like Rorem and Williams—in early summer 1949, had asked "if he would help develop a theory of literature as a key to the sex life of artists, exploring the interrelationships [Kinsey] had already begun to develop through taking histories of the various *Streetcar* casts" (194–95). In a 1972 interview transcript Wescott, who became a friend to Kinsey and a contributor to his research, recalls that "Kinsey wanted to make a special category of the research—the usual questionnaire plus a set of questions directed to visual artists—and I think he ended up with about 500 of these histories." Such questions, however, may have been directed more to art and its sexual representations than to artists and their sexual particularities—or so we might infer from Wescott's testimony: "[Kinsey] consulted me about modern contemporary literature as a source of information about human sexual behavior," Glenway Wescott, Oral History Interview by James H. Jones (June 27, 1972): 22, 24; in The Kinsey Institute for Research in Sex, Gender, and Reproduction, Inc. Used by permission.

55. Dalton, liner notes for *Gay American Composers*, vol. 2, 7.

56. Cowell had homosexual involvements but, like many of his contemporaries straight and gay (including Bernstein, Blitzstein, and Bowles), lived for years in a heterosexual marriage, marrying soon after his release from imprisonment on sodomy charges. Any of the standard classifications, homo-, hetero-, or bisexual, might be controversial with reference to Cowell. My use of the label *gay* here is not intended to beg or to settle the question of which one best applies; rather, it follows Harrison's classification for the purpose of (re-) constructing a lineage into which gay composers might have self-consciously placed themselves.

57. A pair of remarks from Rorem, *Knowing When to Stop*, serves illustratively here. Recalling the goings-on in his sphere in 1948, he notes that "lesbianism had a certain naughty cachet in those days, while male inversion was simply a stigma" (347; but see also 461, 463, and 482), and: "The grand [European] tour was the goal of American graduates then. . . . For us the reflection of Paris's postwar aura from the twenties was forceful enough to impel an equally forceful mystique in the fifties" (349).

58. Holleran, *Dancer from the Dance*, 19.

59. Rorem cites Boulanger as the source for Copland's *dépouillement* (*Knowing When to Stop*, 282). According to Pollack, Copland's French found use in the bedroom as well. One of Copland's more significant loves, John Kennedy, recalls for Pollack "how, in bed, Copland might read Goncourt or Gide in the original French, translating into English out loud" (*Aaron Copland*, 236).

60. Tommasini, *Virgil Thomson,* 127, 91. Thomson's essay appeared in *Vanity Fair* (April 1925): 46. According to Stein, writing later in *The Autobiography of Alice B. Toklas,* Thomson's idol Satie had himself made a point of separating French music from the Germanic on a singular occasion around 1915:

> Only once in the half dozen times that Erik Satie was at the house did he talk about music. He said that it had always been his opinion and he was glad that it was being recognized that modern french music owed nothing to modern Germany. That after Debussy had led the way french musicians had either followed him or found their own french way. (208–9)

For an excellent recent analysis of Ravel's complex persona and carefully guarded privacy in relation to modern regimes of sexual identity see Lloyd Whitesell, "Ravel's Way," in Fuller and Whitesell, eds., *Queer Episodes in Music and Modern Identity,* 49–78.

61. Rorem, *Knowing When to Stop,* 221. Cf. also 219–20: "Virgil, who . . . had the wittiest English language repartee of anyone around . . . spoke always in French-style generalities, which are anathema to literal-minded American children." Rorem similarly explains Thomson's personal manner: "I was prepared for the swishy voice . . . but not for the patronizing friendliness and icy impatience, a mixture I later found to be native to uppercrust French females" (197). Thomson's explication of "instrumentation" is conceived in binary terms of two rival traditions, German and French (or, sometimes: Franco-Russian), and defined by further binarisms including emotional power/clarity, tonal weight/brilliance, timbral composites/timbral separation: *The State of Music,* 98–100. According to his pupil Rorem, Thomson considered orchestration the only teachable craft related to the composer's art, instruction in composition itself being nonexistent, "an esthetic study best left to analytical Germans": *Knowing When to Stop,* 220.

62. Report published in *Modern Music,* excerpted in Thomson, *Virgil Thomson by Virgil Thomson,* 294. By age eighty Thomson had not relented in his struggle against German culture, telling John Rockwell, "You always have to fight the Germans. Everybody has to fight the Germans": Rockwell, "A Conversation with Virgil Thomson," in Thomson, *A Virgil Thomson Reader,* 528.

63. Kimberling, *David Diamond,* 3.

64. Rorem, *Knowing When to Stop,* 392.

65. Their reverence for Boulanger was by no means simple or unproblematic. On various occasions "Mademoiselle" was lionized in print by Copland, Diamond, Rorem, and Bernstein. On other occasions she was patronized or even vilified by Copland, Diamond, Rorem, and Thomson, who thus gave voice to the prevailing misogyny of their times.

66. William Westbrook Burton, *Conversations about Bernstein* (New York: Oxford University Press, 1995), 16; Burton, *Leonard Bernstein,* 149.

67. Rorem writes of Boulanger giving "critical and unpaid perusal" and commentary on his latest compositional "outpourings" in visits he made

around 1950. During such visits Boulanger also expressed her concern, ardently yet diplomatically, about Rorem's then notorious alcoholic excesses. Rorem writes of Boulanger,

> she didn't want me to become her pupil: I was already twenty-five, she pointed out, not seventeen, and my character was formed, *tant bien que mal*—my *nature bête*, which her prodding could only sterilize.
>
> But we loved one another. She arranged for me to receive the annual Lili Boulanger award [in 1950] . . . performed my works in public . . . invited me as a peer to her table.

Rorem, *Knowing When to Stop*, 500, 198–99, 398.

68. Aaron Copland, *Our New Music: Leading Composers in Europe and America* (New York: McGraw-Hill, 1941), 219.

69. These passages are quoted from government documents in Dean, *Imperial Brotherhood*, 107; emphasis mine.

70. Bowles biographer Caponi chronicles this instance and notes Bowles's enthusiasm around this time for the "French moderns" Honegger, Milhaud, and Poulenc, as well as Hindemith and Stravinsky: *Paul Bowles*, 41–42.

71. Copland clearly reveals his pro-French and anti-German biases in *Our New Music*, where he laments, for example, the reduced vitality of Berg's music because of its ties "to the German past," which render it (and here Copland negates Wagner's *Zukunftmusik* formulation) "music without a future" (56). His pupil and friend Arthur Berger reports that Copland's "leaning towards French style . . . was strongly present [even] before he went abroad, while he was under the tutelage of a musician so inclined towards mid-European sources as Rubin Goldmark": Berger, *Aaron Copland* (New York: Oxford University Press, 1953), 42. From 1917 to 1921 Copland studied with Goldmark, who revered German Romantic music "as best representing 'universal' ideals": Pollack, *Aaron Copland*, 34–35.

72. Blitzstein, review of Paul Hindemith, *Hin und Zurück*, in *Modern Music* (May-June 1928); quoted in Gordon, *Mark the Music*, 33.

73. Gordon, *Mark the Music*, 30; emphasis in original. Along similar aesthetic lines, and like Thomson, Copland, and other members of the gay tonalists' circle, Blitzstein also harbored an antipathy for German late-Romantic music: see ibid., 250.

74. Thomson, *Virgil Thomson by Virgil Thomson*, 118. Tommasini discusses the prevalence of an antagonistic thematics of Germanic music in Thomson's memoirs, his music reviews, and his conversation: *Virgil Thomson*, 181–84.

75. Halperin, *Saint Foucault*, 37–38; emphasis mine.

76. Ibid., 38.

77. Rorem, *Knowing When to Stop*, 207.

78. Blitzstein, lecture at Brandeis University, April 2, 1962; quoted in Gordon, *Mark the Music*, 28.

79. This is also, of course, an attack on Stravinsky's stylistic, qua historical,

affiliations. In relation to the Wagner/Brahms dichotomy that preceded this one, Watkins notes that Stravinsky was both anti-Wagner and (if quietly) anti-Brahms: "the post-Beethoven Germans . . . who could provide a continuing thread" were "discounted" by Stravinsky (who engaged neoclassically with earlier music, including that of Italian Baroque composers). Schoenberg, on the other hand, "endorsed [the post-Beethoven Germans] for this very reason" of continuity. Thus Watkins sees "a chronological as well as a cultural bias, both of which contributed to the Stravinsky-Schoenberg dichotomy at an early date": *Soundings*, 327.

80. Gordon, *Mark the Music*, 26.

81. Watkins reads *Three Satires* as evidence that Schoenberg by this point conceives of his position as "diametrically opposed" to that of Stravinsky. The work's foreword "sounds a warning and promotes the idea that history is in the making": *Soundings*, 328.

82. Smith, "'A Distinguishing Virility,'" 100.

83. The homosocial and homosexual tightness of these gay modernists' sphere is especially evident from recent queer-explicit biographies, including Pollack, *Aaron Copland*, and Tommasini, *Virgil Thomson*, and from Rorem's diaries and memoirs. One introspective passage from Rorem is particularly illustrative:

> When JH [life partner James Holmes] asked me last night if I'd ever had a close male friend who was straight (recalling Copland and Harold Clurman), I realized that the question had never occurred to me. No, I guess not. Though in the old [student] days, when we all saw each other socially every day, many of my male friends were straight—Eugene [Istomin], Seymour [Barab], the husbands of girlfriends.
> Are you too young to understand?

With this last question, addressed directly to the reader, Rorem effectively underlines the historically specific origins of his social proclivities and sphere, suggesting that they belong to a vanished past (and indeed all this serves to introduce a large extract from his then-forty-eight-year-old 1946 diary, which follows shortly): *Knowing When to Stop*, 324.

84. Blitzstein and Hellman were personally and professionally associated from 1946 until Blitzstein's death in 1964. Most notable of their several collaborations was *Regina* (1949), an operatic version of Hellman's play *The Little Foxes*. See Gordon, *Mark the Music*, 287–88 and 294–317 esp.

85. Smith argues, of course, that this reaction destroyed the pre–World War I gains of romantic Americanism, within which "many middle-class white women [had] emerged as composers." She also cites DuPree's previous demonstration, in "The Failure of American Music," "that the critical vogue of the 1920s that asserted the failure of romantic Americanism is in fact antifeminist." See "'A Distinguishing Virility,'" 90, 94.

86. Copland registered his objections to Romanticism's persistence and

prevalence over many years and in various forums, including his books *What to Listen for in Music* (1939) and *Music and Imagination* (1952). His position in this regard is discussed in DeLapp, "Copland in the Fifties," 18–22.

87. Brett, "Musicality, Essentialism, and the Closet," 13–14. In fact the foundations of modern systematic and abstract theories of music were laid by a Frenchman, Jean-Philippe Rameau, in his *Traite de l'harmonie* (*Treatise on Harmony*) of 1722. But the Austro-Germans soon took over and developed this vein of discourse (sometimes, as in the case of Heinrich Schenker, with express disavowal of Rameau's influence), such that for nineteenth- and twentieth-century purposes it became a markedly Germanic tradition.

Another important characteristic of the gay composers examined here that is demonstrably anti-Romantic—and equally contravenes high modernism—is their pursuit of the popular marketplace as a venue for their work. Copland, Thomson, Blitzstein, and Bernstein, especially (in their performance and critical, as well as compositional, activities), enacted a high-profile refusal of the dichotomies that served to regulate artistic legitimacy and authority: artistic purity versus commercial engagement, secluded garret versus popular sphere, elite versus demotic discourses. Bernstein's position here (and his career generally) was obviously and self-avowedly influenced by his mentors from the previous generation, especially Copland and Dimitri Mitropolous. Copland's and Thomson's positions were influenced by their admiration of certain French models: Satie, particularly, in Thomson's case, and in general a French anti-authority, anti-masterpiece, anti-art mentality that was conspicuous already in Debussy.

88. Thomson's letter to Copland (March 20, 1939) is reprinted in Page and Page, *Selected Letters of Virgil Thomson*, 127. Thomson's own 1939 book, *The State of Music*, debunks, in tandem, analytic listening and the "Platonic authority" by which the unquestioned masterworks are sanctioned and sanctified (125–26). Thomson's argument thus shares ground with Brett's 1994 (poststructuralist- and feminist-informed) exegesis, which likewise cites Plato and music-analytic ordering en route to remarkably similar conclusions about the mechanisms of knowledge and power in the Germanic musical tradition.

89. I read such indications in two passages: "Your book . . . contains a lot of stuff that I don't believe and that I am not at all convinced you believe"; and "I'm not trying to write your book for you. I'm just complaining that you didn't write it for yourself." See Tommasini, *Virgil Thomson*, 340, for extracts from a *Herald Tribune* column (May 17, 1942) of three years later in which Thomson criticized the ideology of the absolute in Arturo Toscanini's work as a conductor. Anticipating by about four decades similar criticisms of musical canonicity by New Historicist and poststructuralist musicology, Thomson declared Toscanini "essentially a reactionary" whose interpretation "is very little dependent on literary culture and historical knowledge. It is disembodied music and disembodied theater [that] opens few vistas to the understanding of men and epochs." Thomson's critique was, in short, directed against that voiding of cultural and historical specificity through which musical works are pre-

sented as "absolute"—representing values and meanings that are (putatively) eternal and transcendent.

90. Chauncey, *Gay New* York, 2–3.

CHAPTER 4

Cory, *The Homosexual in America*, 6, 7.

1. Rorem, *Knowing When to Stop*, 242.

2. J. D. McClatchy, Foreword, in Rorem, *A Ned Rorem Reader*, xv.

3. Diamond, in an interview with the author, November 13, 2001, reported that he has said this directly to Rorem at times when the latter has announced intentions to write about him. Whether or not related to such exchanges, Rorem's *Reader* (released in October 2001) contains portraits of Virgil Thomson, Marc Blitzstein, Franco Zeffirelli, and others, but none of Diamond.

4. Quoted by McClatchy, Foreword, xii.

5. I was unable to elicit elaboration from Rorem in correspondence and phone conversation with him in October 2001. On the postwar queer situation see esp. D'Emilio, *Sexual Politics, Sexual Communities*. For an especially cogent assessment of the significance of Kinsey's reports here, particularly the first one (1948), on males, see the 1975 author's foreword to the reprint edition of Cory, *The Homosexual in America*, 6–7. For a contemporaneous application of Kinsey's findings to antihomophobic sociological inquiry see the chapter (published in 1951) "Is Our Number Legion?", 76–91.

6. One such indication-indictment comes from an item attributed to Inez Robb in the *Toledo Times:* "Who can remember the good, old days . . . when the Broadway success formula was 'boy meets girl'? . . . The formula, after the war, was quickly revised to . . . 'boy meets boy'": quoted in "Tangents," *One* (March 1966); reproduced in Michael Sherry, "The 'Homintern' in the Arts: Gay Men in America's Cultural Empire, 1945–70" (unpublished manuscript, 2000), cover page.

Rorem hints at such a shift in another passage from *Knowing When to Stop,* 346: "Among composers, who until the war had been mainly Gentile and defiantly effete (Thomson, Griffes) or defiantly virile (Ives, Sessions) the ratio was fifty-fifty. The ratio remained fifty-fifty." This passage derives from the longer one, cited previously, in which Rorem holds forth on the homo/hetero (and other) correlates of classical musicians of various stripes: harpists, string players, brass players, etc.

7. One part of Rorem's claim that I do not include in my own proposition is the purported "goyische" element. It is not entirely clear to me how Rorem might see this aspect manifested in late-wartime American arts. Beyond the Bowles and Williams example cited here, he does mention elsewhere Williams, Gore Vidal, and Truman Capote as representatives in a "boiling fertility of all the creative arts in the United States between 1945 and 1950," one that was "if not in music at least in literature . . . suddenly Gentile, nonheterosexual,

non–*Partisan Review,* nonpolitical": ibid., 385. My own researches, which are admittedly attuned primarily to sexual identity valences, have not suggested any evidence of a particular "goyische" turn in this moment.

8. Ibid., 185.

9. Rorem, *A Ned Rorem Reader,* 231.

10. Thomson, *Virgil Thomson by Virgil Thomson,* 419. The picture painted by Rorem and Thomson here is contested in Joseph N. Straus, "The Myth of Serial 'Tyranny,'" *Musical Quarterly* 83, no. 3 (1999): 301–43. Straus argues against claims for the privileged position of U.S. serialist composers and their music in the Cold War years. He undertakes an ambitious project of gathering and analyzing statistical data on composition prizes, faculty appointments, and other indices in correlation with U.S. composers identified as serial and nonserial in the fifties and sixties. By this process he purports to rebut a myth of U.S. Cold War–era serial ascendance that remains, as he acknowledges, well entrenched among serialists and nonserialists alike. But Straus's extensive statistics do not explain why the central players in this historical moment, on both sides of the tonal/serial fence, still hold to a putatively mythical view on it: His collection of facts fails to illuminate the truth in this matter, which requires a reckoning with the largely unquantifiable realms of cachet, consecration, and numinosity. As Thomson aptly observes in another context, certain "authors and composers" may "enjoy a prestige that is not expressed in their income level": Virgil Thomson, "'La Môme' Piaf," *New York Herald Tribune* (November 9, 1947), reprinted in *Music Right and Left* (New York: Henry Holt, 1951), 51.

11. In describing serialism as music that "would seep over and damage the globe like a liquid tumor" in the decades following World War II, Rorem not only concurs with the assessment of his once-mentor Thomson concerning the postwar U.S. music scene, but echoes language that Thomson had used much earlier with reference to the Germanic music that had prevailed *before* the rise of tonal Americana. In 1934, in the wake of his triumph with *Four Saints,* Thomson in a public lecture proclaimed a "new deal in music" entailing "a revolt against the complicated hyperbole of the exaggerated romantic period which is a *tumor on the body of music.*" Thomson quoted in the *Kansas City Times* (May 1934); quoted in Tommasini, *Virgil Thomson,* 263; emphasis mine.

12. Undoubtedly a crucial factor in the postwar American art music scene was the enormous influx into U.S. university music departments of war emigrés ca. 1930–45, musicians and scholars from Germany, Austria, and Eastern Europe. The topic is taken up in a recent collection: Reinhold Brinkmann and Christoph Wolff, eds., *Driven into Paradise: The Musical Migration from Nazi Germany to the United States* (Berkeley: University of California Press, 1999).

13. Oja, *Making Music Modern,* 186, 221–27.

14. As Rorem further notes, the two groups would merge in 1954: *Knowing When to Stop,* 229.

15. Burton offers this report as proof of his homophobia-tinged statement

that Aaron Copland "never flaunted his homosexuality in the way certain of his friends did": Burton, *Leonard Bernstein*, 43.

16. Oja, "Creating a God: The Reception of Edgard Varèse," in *Making Music Modern*, 25–44.

17. Quotations of Varèse are from his letter to Ruggles (November 14?, 1944): Yale MSS 26, box I.5, folder 115. It is unlikely that "healthy and white" here marks an express racial reference. Rather, "white" appears to invoke the figurative usage denoting "pure" or "wholesome"—itself surely entangled in racial constructions—in contrast to the putative perversions described in the subsequent passage. Varèse's usage in this instance apparently aligns with that of the Women's Christian Temperance Union in their labeling of "The White Life," the social-purity lifestyle they endorsed ca. 1885 (see Kramer, "Cultural Politics and Musical Form," 180). Composers of color were not a powerful presence on the New York modernist scene: Beyond the African American tonalist William Grant Still, who attracted some very high critical notice in the 1920s, they were nonexistent among its principal actors.

18. Secrest, *Leonard Bernstein*, uncritically states the following: "The composer Benjamin Lees claimed it was a disadvantage not to be a homosexual in the music world and that careers of many heterosexuals had suffered from a form of discrimination. He claimed to know many a well-known composer who had deliberately changed his sexual orientation in order to improve his career prospects" (256).

19. See Lerner, "Copland's Music of Wide Open Spaces," 477, for further contextualization and commentary on this milestone in Copland's, and Hollywood's, career.

20. Lazare Saminsky, *Living Music of the Americas* (New York: Howell, Soskin and Crown, 1949), 123–27; quoted in Pollack, *Aaron Copland*, 520. In Saminsky's rendering Copland is a minor talent and "a devious personality with a feline *savoir faire*": Here, as elsewhere, the coding of anti-Semitic and homophobic slurs depends on established figures of misogyny.

21. The purges at Eastman had begun by the early thirties, according to Diamond's account. As we have seen, a queer taint has been imputed to American art music since at least Ives's time: The queer composers Charles Tomlinson Griffes and Henry Cowell and the 1910s–20s gender panic in U.S. music are among the relevant figures and movements on this early-century scene.

22. "The Homosexual in America," *Time* (January 21, 1966), 40–41.

23. The quoted phrase is from Gene Marine, "Who's Afraid of Little Annie Fanny?" *Ramparts* (February 1967): 26–30; quoted in Sherry, "The 'Homintern' in the Arts," 13. The perception of increased gay presence in the arts is expressed variously in contemporaneous commentaries, for example, by Howard Taubman: "It is time to speak openly and candidly of the increasing incidence and influence of homosexuality on New York's stage—and, indeed, in the other arts as well": "Not What It Seems: Homosexual Motif Gets Heterosexual Guise," *New York Times* (November 5, 1961): X-1.

24. Pollack, *Aaron Copland*, 202; see also 554, 608 n. 73, and 609.

25. The "chance revelation" was that of Under Secretary of State John Peurifoy, who testified to members of the Senate Appropriations Committee on February 28, 1950, that "most of ninety-one employees dismissed for moral turpitude were homosexuals." Republicans then seized on these remarks in an effort to discredit Truman and his handling of national security: D'Emilio, *Sexual Politics, Sexual Communities*, 41.

26. Louise S. Robbins, "The Library of Congress and Federal Loyalty Programs, 1947–1956: No 'Communists or Cocksuckers,'" *Library Quarterly* 64, no. 4 (1994): 365–85.

27. 81st Congress U.S. Senate, 2nd Session, Document No. 241, "Employment of Homosexuals and Other Sex Perverts in Government (report to the Committee on Expenditures in the Executive Departments)" (1950), in *Government versus Homosexuals*, ed. Leslie Parr (New York: Arno Press, 1975).

28. William N. Eskridge, Jr., "Privacy Jurisprudence and the Apartheid of the Closet, 1946–1961," *Florida State University Law Review* 24, no. 4 (1997): 709–10. "Fifth column" refers to a group comprising peripheral communist supporters prepared to jump into the fray upon the start of a revolution.

29. The headline is from *Physical Culture* (April 1953), 12–13; reproduced in Sherry, "The 'Homintern' in the Arts," cover page.

30. Print items cited in Sherry, "The 'Homintern' in the Arts," 27 nn. 1, 9, 10, and 12, include William Barrett, "New Innocents Abroad," *Partisan Review* (March 1950): 272–91; Alfred Towne, "Homosexuality in American Culture: The New Taste in Literature," *American Mercury* (August 1951): 3–9, and "The New Taste in Humor"; Philip Roth, "The Play That Dare Not Speak Its Name," *New York Review of Books* (February 25, 1965): 4; Wilfred Sheed, "The Heterosexual Backlash," *Commentary* (May 21, 1965): 289–90; "The Homosexual in America." See also Howard Taubman, "Not What It Seems," and "Modern Primer: Helpful Hints to Tell Appearances vs. Truth," *New York Times* (April 28, 1963): 125; and Stanley Kauffmann, "Homosexual Drama and Its Disguises," *New York Times* (January 23, 1966): 93, and "On the Acceptability of the Homosexual," *New York Times* (February 6, 1966): X-1. In the CBS documentary Wallace reported on "talk of a homosexual mafia in the arts": see Kaiser, *The Gay Metropolis*, 165.

31. Sherry, "The 'Homintern' in the Arts," 18.

32. John D'Emilio, "The Homosexual Menace: The Politics of Sexuality in Cold War America," in *Making Trouble: Essays on Gay History, Politics, and the University* (New York: Routledge, 1992), 64, 68.

33. Copland was a fellow traveler according to the account given in Aaron Copland and Vivian Perlis, *Copland: 1900 through 1942* (Boston: Faber and Faber, 1984), 218. For details of Copland's involvements in front groups see DeLapp, "Copland in the Fifties," 71–82 esp.

34. In 1950 Blitzstein and Bernstein, along with both Copland and the music critic Olin Downes, were listed in a widely known source, *Red Channels: The Report of Communist Influence in Radio and Television* (New York: Amer-

ican Business Consultants, 1950), on pages 16–17, 20–23, and 45–47, respectively: DeLapp, "Copland in the Fifties," 155 n. 155. See 117–18 for further details on *Red Channels* and its use in blacklisting; see also Gordon, *Mark the Music*, 347–48. Testimony to the House Committee on Un-American Activities (HUAC) had already linked Blitzstein, Bernstein, and Copland as agents in a "Red Offensive" allegedly deployed via a group known as People's Songs, Inc. The allegations arose in the July 1947 testimony before a HUAC committee of Walter S. Steele, chairman of a group called the American Coalition of Patriotic, Civic, and Fraternal Societies. Transcripts of Steele's testimony include five pages' discussion of People's Songs, Inc., which Steele describes as a leader among "present-day movements specializing in various fields of so-called 'culture' but which have become part and parcel, in fact, of the Red propaganda and agitational machine in the United States." He lists Bernstein, Blitzstein, and Copland among those involved in its operations: DeLapp, "Copland in the Fifties," 156–57. Steele quotation is from House Committee on Un-American Activities, *Testimony of Walter S. Steele Regarding Communist Activity in the United States*, 80th Cong., 1st sess., July 21, 1947, 99; cited in DeLapp, "Copland in the Fifties," 156.

The three composers' names would again surface in HUAC investigations and public hearings of 1955–56, along with that of dancer-choreographer Jerome Robbins (DeLapp, "Copland in the Fifties," 155 n. 158). Robbins had a minor role in the 1938 premiere of Copland's *Billy the Kid* and achieved fame as a choreographer collaborating with Bernstein on *Fancy Free* (1944) and *Facsimile* (1946), as he would again on *West Side Story* (1957). He privately cooperated with HUAC and thus in 1951 had his name officially cleared of any suspicion. Such name clearing typically entailed "naming names" among one's associates. Whatever the details of Robbins's process, his subsequent relationship with at least one associate, Blitzstein, reportedly cooled, according to Gordon, *Mark the Music*, 343. Rorem's 1993 memoir reveals that Robbins spent the three weeks preceding his 1951 McCarthy hearings on holiday in France with Rorem and his patron, the Vicomtesse Marie-Laure de Noailles (*Knowing When to Stop*, 576–79).

In connection with Robbins's deal-cutting with HUAC to clear his name, at least one historian has speculated that he may have been one of the "reliable informants" on Copland deployed by the FBI throughout the fifties (DeLapp, "Copland in the Fifties," 161). Beginning in that decade, the rumor circulated that Robbins had "turned informer to keep the Committee's investigators from publicizing evidence that he was a homosexual": Victor S. Navasky, *Naming Names* (New York: Viking Press, 1980), 75; cited in DeLapp, "Copland in the Fifties," 120. The rumor, regardless of its veracity, can illustrate some of the double-binding effects of queer identity under the refractions of the contemporary paranoia: For example, Robbins's homosexuality served as an axis along which gays and straights alike found ripe grounds for contempt. Tracing these effects further, we might examine Robbins's alleged actions in terms of a preemptive strike against other homosexuals by an informant bent on guarding his own homosexual secrets—but to give that matter its due, according to some commentators, we would have to bring Roy Cohn, J. Edgar Hoover, and Joseph McCarthy into the discussion. For several of the principal figures in the post-war anticommunist and antihomosexual hysteria may have formed their suspicions about "secret infiltrators" based on knowledge of their own deeply buried sexual secrets.

Some recent writings on McCarthy, Cohn, and Hoover have explored such questions: David M. Oshinsky, *A Conspiracy So Immense: The World of Joe McCarthy* (New York: Free Press, 1983), 310–11, 328–29, discusses the reactionary Senator McCarthy in connection with his longtime bachelorhood, and rumors alleging his homosexuality; Nicholas Von Hoffman, *Citizen Cohn* (New York: Doubleday, 1988), reveals that McCarthy's chief counsel Roy Cohn was a closeted homosexual; and Anthony Summers, *Official and Confidential: The Secret Life of J. Edgar Hoover* (New York: G. P. Putnam's Sons, 1993), discusses the cross-dressing and possible homosexuality of FBI Director Hoover, identifying Clyde Tolson as Hoover's longtime companion and the only person with whom he had emotional intimacy. Cohn's homosexuality has been confirmed since his death from AIDS in the 1980s. But Summers's evidence regarding Hoover is refuted in Athan G. Theoharis, *J. Edgar Hoover, Sex, and Crime* (Chicago: Ivan R. Dee, 1995).

35. Rorem, *Knowing When to Stop,* 578.

36. The city was at this time independent but would become part of Morocco in 1956.

37. Kimberling, *David Diamond,* 29. Kimberling also cites a 1965 *New York Times* feature in which Diamond is quoted as saying, "I left for Europe in 1951 when all that McCarthy business was going on. . . . Extremism . . . [of] any kind is dangerous. . . . But [especially] if it gets recognition, and the mass simply moves with it" (30). Diamond went to Italy in 1951 and stayed for most of the decade.

38. David Diamond, interview with the author, November 13, 2001. Diamond reports having been questioned about his own homosexuality and about the sex lives of other composers and writers, and being brazenly candid about the former and professing ignorance about the latter (he also recounts that Blitzstein too was called up and questioned at the federal buildings in downtown Manhattan). Diamond recalls having been adjourned in short order and attributes this to the complete candor of his sexual self-descriptions—by which he may mean to suggest that there was no need for more drawn-out grilling. I, however, would not ignore the possible links between Diamond's relatively quick and painless treatment here and committee members' reportedly charmed reception of his revelations concerning his childhood sexual self-awareness and predilection for older men—older men, one might imagine, not unlike the congressmen themselves, who reportedly responded with smiling, laughter, and intrigued follow-up questions. The scene appears as potentially prurient, not to mention flirtatious, and I would suggest that this could have contributed to the brevity and ease of Diamond's interrogation.

39. Diamond, interview with the author, November 13, 2001.

40. See Aaron Copland and Vivian Perlis, *Copland since 1943* (New York: St. Martin's Press, 1989).

41. Letter from Thomson to Ernst Bacon (February 24, 1953) reproduced in Page and Page, *Selected Letters of Virgil Thomson*, 266. See also the letters to a reader (January 29, 1953) and to Charles Denby (February 3, 1953): ibid., 262.

42. Tommasini, *Virgil Thomson*, 464, 149, 537.

43. Lott, *Love and Theft*, 6; referring to Homi K. Bhabha, "The Other Question: The Stereotype and Colonial Discourse," *Screen* 24, no. 6 (1983): 18.

44. Rorem writes of Thomson: "When in 1954 he retired from the paper, the performance frequency of his music plummeted to the surprise of no one but himself" (*Knowing When to Stop*, 208).

45. Quoted phrases are from Watkins, *Soundings*, 454.

46. Thomson's use of the phrase "complexity boys" is noted in Tommasini, *Virgil Thomson*, 506, among other places. According to Diamond, in Thomson's usage it referred to "Milton Babbitt and any of them who became interested in Pierre Boulez and his twelve-note theory": interview with the author, November 13, 2001.

47. One might observe the workings of tonal-versus-serial lines of affiliation, as related to gay-versus-straight compositional "sensibility," in Rorem's recent remarks on the classical music world in mid-twentieth-century France. Rorem's recollections of his late-1990s appearance with Elliot Carter (and others) on a French radio panel depict diametrical differences between the two composers' constructions of musical history: "But when [Carter] said that after 1951 the musical world really started in France, I had to interrupt to say, 'Oh, but that's about when it *stopped.*'" Rorem offers no explicit accounting for the conversity of his and Carter's perspectives here, but some context is provided by 1951's well-known status as a watershed, the year of Schoenberg's death and Boulez's Oedipally triumphant essay "Schoenberg est mort," which punctuated the start of both Boulez's and Carter's flourishing as composers in a *serial* language that expanded the implications of Schoenberg's method within further realms—of not just pitch, but (for example) rhythm, timbre, and form. Rorem, on the 1990s radio panel, did offer elaboration on his own perspective, revealing an orientation to gay, often campy, auteurs and oeuvres that he expressly imagines Carter not to share: "True, Poulenc still had *The Dialogues of the Carmelites* in him (I could see Elliot flinch), and true, Cocteau still had a play or two left in him, and Gide would die the following year, but the *great* France—and I'm right, of course—was over." Rorem, "The Art of the Diary" (1999 conversation with J. D. McClatchy), in *A Ned Rorem Reader*, 19; emphasis in the original.

48. Babbitt, "Who Cares if You Listen?" *High Fidelity* 8, no. 2 (1958): 38–40. This title was given by the magazine's editors without consulting the author. My use of the word *men* in this paragraph is deliberate: The domain being described was indicatively male.

49. Arnold Schoenberg, "New Music, Outmoded Music, Style and Idea"

(1946), in *Style and Idea: Selected Writings of Arnold Schoenberg,* rev. ed., ed. Leonard Stein, trans. Leo Black (New York: St. Martin's Press, [1950] 1975), 124. On Ruggles's elitism see Claire R. Reis, *Composers, Conductors, and Critics* (New York: Oxford University Press, 1955), 7; quoted in Tommasini, *Virgil Thomson,* 186.

50. Martin Brody argues that Babbitt's position also derives from different motives as compared with Schoenberg's. Babbitt's exclusivity should be understood specifically in relation to "the anti-Stalinist/mass cult anxieties he and his contemporaries experienced in the 1930s and 1940s" (179), anxieties in which mass culture was figured as an instrument of totalitarian oppression. In this light Babbitt's elitism represents an actively "critical perspective within the cultural mainstream," as contrasted with Schoenberg's "ascetic retreat" (in Adorno's view, at least) into the margins of modernist alienation (180). See Brody, "'Music for the Masses': Milton Babbitt's Cold War Music Theory," *Musical Quarterly* 77, no. 2 (1993): 161–92.

51. Both quotes are from Blitzstein, the first from a letter of March 19, 1927, to William E. Walter at the Curtis Institute, and the second from mid-1930s notes for an article on Schoenberg: Gordon, *Mark the Music,* 27.

52. Thomson, *Virgil Thomson by Virgil Thomson,* 248.

53. Botstein discusses the postwar influence of Adorno's views of Webern and especially Schoenberg as the exclusive avatars of historically, politically, and ethically valid music in the twentieth century. Under Adorno's theoretical lens, "[t]he conflict between an audience and the rejection of inherited conventions of musical expression became virtues and signs of authenticity." The extent to which Adorno's theories shaped the U.S. music-cultural landscape is discussed in Botstein, s.v. "modernism."

54. The quoted phrase is from Brett, who notes that the "complexity boys," however successful in the Cold War era, were ultimately "diverted from broader success through the lure of intellectual superiority aided and abetted by the University and Foundation, those twentieth-century American equivalents to the outmoded courts of Europe": "Britten, Copland, and Transatlantic Queer Musical Connexions," 13.

55. Gordon provides a contemporaneous definition: "in the postwar era of the late 1940s, art seemed more and more to be dominated by alienating, dehumanized, escapist forms—or *formalism,* the term the committed left used to disparage such an outlook": *Mark the Music,* 320.

56. See DeLapp, "Copland in the Fifties," 99. The seemingly irreproachable thematics of the *Lincoln Portrait* was also rendered suspect and cited in Copland's FBI files as an instance of a smoke screen tactics ascribed to the American Communist Party of the 1930s (179).

57. Teachout, "The New Tonalists," 55, 54.

58. I refer here to dialogues involving Schoenberg, Copland, and Thomson, as chronicled by DeLapp, "Copland in the Fifties," 100–104. It was Thomson, in his weekly newspaper column, who directly linked serial music and Soviet prohibitions: *New York Herald Tribune* (January 29, 1950); reprinted in Thomson,

Music Right and Left, 181. But Copland had made implicit reference to such linkage in a letter published in Thomson's column four months earlier (September 25, 1949): "since when is [failure to embrace the twelve-tone system] a crime? . . . In America it is still possible (I hope) to share a platform with [Soviet 'anti-formalist' Dmitri Shostakovich] without being judged guilty by association." The letter was a response to Schoenberg's sudden and unexpected attack on Copland, as reported in Thomson's column of September 11, 1949. In a radio broadcast Schoenberg had named Stalin and Copland in the same breath, as would-be agents of artistic degeneration and restriction on artistic freedom, including particularly Schoenberg's own. Copland's and Thomson's remarks in response were directed to decoupling Copland from the notion of artistic censorship and surely were not intended to privilege twelve-tone serialism in relation to artistic liberty. Perhaps most significant here is the fact that the tenor of Copland's self-defense suggests he already perceived the possible, if not actual, operation of such privileging in the burgeoning Cold War environment.

59. This is not to suggest that the meanings and associations attaching to particular musical styles and idioms were, or are, fixed or universal. In fact, my example illustrates just the contrary. A further illustration of the variability of such associations can be found in Edmund Wilson's 1963 comments on serialism:

> [T]he serial system has, in any case, by this time become something of a cult. I'm told that in the schools of music, the Schoenberg technique is now so much the thing that the students have to withstand a strong pressure, and even to risk something like ostracism, if they don't want to become twelve-toners. A friend of mine who has seen a good deal of these students tells me that it is almost like the pressure of a homosexual group—though he didn't mean to imply that there was any connection between homosexuality and serial music. Except, of course, that they're both *culs de sac.* It strikes me that—in America, at least—the composers are the most ingrown group of any in the major arts. Their audience is so limited, and it is almost as if, finding themselves doomed to this, they take pride in defying the neglect of them by making it more limited still. They feel safer in the Kafka-esque burrow of the dark and hidden twelve-tone row.

Edmund Wilson, *The Bit between My Teeth: A Literary Chronicle of 1950–1965* (New York: Farrar, Straus and Giroux, 1965), 594.

60. Serge Guilbaut, *How New York Stole the Idea of Modern Art: Abstract Expressionism, Freedom, and the Cold War* (Chicago: University of Chicago Press, 1983).

61. Hickey, *The Invisible Dragon,* 55.

62. Copland's *Lincoln Portrait* is well known as a patriotic tribute and is still performed frequently. And it bears a Thomsonian connection that is by now scarcely known—specifically, to Thomson's portraiture practice, which followed

that of Stein. Copland's *Lincoln Portrait* shows little resemblance to the sound and word portraits of Thomson and Stein: Both of the latter employed techniques of automatic writing, and Thomson always composed his only from live sittings. But it was nevertheless because of Thomson's portraits (which included both Copland and Stein as subjects) that Copland wrote his: "In 1942, [the conductor] André Kostalanetz, having heard about the Portraits, proposed to Thomson that he and a few other composers write portraits to be premièred during [various] Kostalanetz guest engagements. . . . Aaron Copland, Jerome Kern, and Thomson accepted the project." Hoover and Cage, *Virgil Thomson*, 193.

63. *New York Times* (January 16, 1953); cited in DeLapp, "Copland in the Fifties," 123. See 123–34 on the cancellation of Copland's *Lincoln Portrait* by the 1953 inaugural concert committee and its repercussions. According to Botstein, "the close link between fascism and totalitarianism and a reactionary musical aesthetic [e.g., of Strauss, Pfitzner, Orff, and Egk in Nazi Germany], as well as the intense ideological campaign against it [under both Nazism and Stalinism], lent [high] Modernism a unique prestige and visibility in the 1930s that continued well into the postwar era." Hence this account suggests that the "moral-political privilege" I ascribe to "complexity music" in the postwar United States arises earlier, in the 1930s. But Botstein's focus in this regard is exclusively on Europe and Russia. He notes, for example, "the irony in the attack by Hitler and Stalin was that by the late 1920s the continuing failure of Modernism to gain a wide audience had led to defections (in terms of compositional practice) within the Modernist camp by composers on the political left, notably Hanns Eisler and Kurt Weill." The most obvious parallel in the American compositional realm, unremarked here, is with Copland and Blitzstein, whose leftist politics were likewise motivating factors in their embrace of populist idioms beginning in the twenties and thirties.

At this point I am aware of no evidence for any meaningful moral-political privileging of modernist complexity music emergent on the U.S. scene until the postwar period. And Botstein's narrative, in its continuation, is compatible with the story I tell above (including its dates): "In part as a result of the political significance and ethical overtones of [post-Webernian] Modernism, its moment of relative dominance among composers occurred in the late 1940s, the 50s and the 60s, the decades most influenced by the shock of the Holocaust and Hiroshima." Botstein, s.v. "modernism." Botstein's language of "relative dominance" and my account in this chapter contradict Straus's contention in "The Myth of Serial 'Tyranny'" that modernist complexity composers in fact never enjoyed dominance in the American twentieth-century music world.

64. Recalled in a 1967 interview: see Edward T. Cone, "Conversation with Aaron Copland," in *Perspectives on American Composers*, ed. Benjamin Boretz and Edward T. Cone (New York: W. W. Norton, 1971), 141.

65. DeLapp, "Copland in the Fifties," 222; DeLapp's exegesis appears in her dissertation as chapter 4, "Copland's *Piano Quartet:* The Construction and Deconstruction of a Musical Dichotomy," 182–222.

66. Ibid., 95.

67. See Guilbaut, *How New York Stole the Idea of Modern Art,* 138–47, for a discussion of the "doctrine" and contemporaneous political and artistic responses to it.

68. DeLapp, "Copland in the Fifties," 177–78. Copland's first operatic foray, *The Second Hurricane* (1936), was a play-opera for high school students. Daniel E. Mathers reads the troubled reception history of *The Tender Land* in connection with its inscription of the queer outlooks and interests of Copland and his librettist and lover Erik Johns, including an encoding of gay-male subjectivity in the opera's female protagonist Laurie: see "Expanding Horizons: Sexuality and the Re-zoning of *The Tender Land,*" in *Copland Connotations: Studies and Interviews,* ed. Peter Dickinson (Woodbridge: Boydell Press, 2002), 118–35.

69. Richard Taruskin, "'Nationalism': Colonialism in Disguise?" *New York Times* (August 22, 1993), sec. 2: 24. DeLapp, "Copland in the Fifties," for example, 180–81.

70. Rorem, *Knowing When to Stop,* 284.

71. Lerner, "Copland's Music of Wide Open Spaces," 479.

72. Ibid., 508 n. 12. On the basis of her interviews with a number of Hollywood composers Claudia Gorbman locates a Coplandian revival in film and TV music in the bicentennial year. Her ethnographic findings are reported in "A Part of Our World: Music for Network News," paper presented at the annual meeting of the American Musicological Society, Oakland, November 1990, cited and summarized in Lerner, "Copland's Music of Wide Open Spaces," 508 n. 12.

73. Classical music had constituted a master narrative in America since the mid–nineteenth century but had lost this status by about the mid-1980s—one index of which is Allan Bloom's jeremiad in his chapter "Music," in *The Closing of the American Mind* (1987), 68–81: As Bloom notes (with evident disapproval), "Classical music is now a special taste, like Greek language or pre-Colombian archeology, not a common culture of reciprocal communication and psychological shorthand" or the sole "regularly recognizable class distinction between educated and uneducated in America" (69). Indeed, whereas formerly classical music for many intents and purposes *was* music, the insuperable cultural and intellectual credentials once encapsulated in the smug understatement of a phrase like "good music" by the mid- to late eighties no longer attached to this music in America (arguably such notions survive here mostly with regard to jazz, albeit even then only in small, connoisseurial circles). Mark Slobin's framework for understanding Western classical music as one style and practice among many responds to these postmodern actualities: see "Micromusics of the West: A Comparative Approach," *Ethnomusicology* 36, no. 1 (1992): 1–87.

74. For definition and analysis of the open secret see Miller, "Secret Subjects, Open Secrets," 206–7.

75. On legal repressions in this cultural context see Eskridge, "Privacy Jurisprudence and the Apartheid of the Closet, 1946–1961," 708–9. The effects

of the 1930–68 Motion Picture Production (a.k.a. Hays) Code and its prohibitions on representing queer persons and lives is illuminated at length in Vito Russo, *The Celluloid Closet: Homosexuality in the Movies* (San Francisco: Harper and Row, [1981] 1987). On the "pansy craze" in New York see Chauncey, "'Pansies on Parade': Prohibition and the Spectacle of the Pansy," in *Gay New York*, 301–29. The post–World War I sex-crime panic demonized homosexuals as uncontrolled sex perverts intent on molesting children (particularly via the image, oddly enough, of homosexual men preying on little girls): see Chauncey, "The Postwar Sex Crime Panic"; also Freedman, "'Uncontrolled Desires.'"

76. One relevant factor not created by the war but intensified by it (in connection with the increase in homosexual visibility discussed above) was the proscription against the appearance or representation of homosexuals and homosexuality in America, not only in movies as enforced by the Hays Code, but in real life as enforced by police, courts, and increasingly virulent homophobia in society and the media.

77. Robbins, "The Library of Congress and Federal Loyalty Programs, 1947–1956," lends support to this notion of postwar remanning of the workforce, of replacing the homosexuals who, having been rejected 4-F for military service, had assumed certain civilian positions in the absence of the "real men" during World War II.

78. Rorem may have hinted at this inimicality when he remarked in 1966 that the proportion of homosexuals among composers in the 1940s had comprised "75 percent (and conveniently, three of the Top Four)," whereas they then comprised "no more than 50 percent"—because "the [midsixties' complex] musical style doesn't lend itself": *The Later Diaries, 1961–72*, 195–96.

79. Teachout, "The New Tonalists," 55.

80. Sherry, "The 'Homintern' in the Arts," 25.

81. Taras quote is from Nancy Reynolds, *Repertory in Review: 40 Years of the New York City Ballet* (New York: Dial Press, 1977), 231; Wuorinen is quoted in Teachout, "The New Tonalists," 54. Taras was the choreographer for *Shadow'd Ground*, a ballet on Copland's *Dance Panels* (1962) that premiered at Lincoln Center. His assessment pertains to Copland's standing in the New York arts world ca. 1965, but as Michael Sherry points out, matters may have been otherwise in the provinces and in smaller cities across the country (correspondence with the author, June 18, 2003).

82. For example, see Rorem's remark, "I *am* a little bit anti-queer" (*Knowing When to Stop*, 556), and Bernstein's collusions with homophobia as discussed in Hubbs, "Bernstein's *Mass* Appeal."

83. Quotes are from Tommasini, *Virgil Thomson*, 340, and Thomson, *Virgil Thomson by Virgil Thomson*, 330.

84. Quoting John Shepherd, who compares "'classical' music" with *écriture classique*, noting that the former "has *appeared* to many to approach the condition of music itself": Shepherd, "Music and Male Hegemony," in *Music and Society*, ed. Richard Leppert and Susan McClary (New York: Cambridge University Press, 1987), 162. For Barthes's discussion of *écriture classique* and the

means of its cultural authority see Roland Barthes, *Writing Degree Zero* (1953), trans. Annette Lavers and Colin Smith (New York: Hill and Wang, 1977).

85. Rorem, *Knowing When to Stop*, 229.

CODA

1. Halperin, *How to Do the History of Homosexuality*, 88, 134. Halperin credits these ideas to his reading of Foucault in *The History of Sexuality*, vol. I.

2. Rorem, *The Later Diaries 1961–72*, 8.

Works Cited

Adorno, Theodor W. "On the Fetish-Character in Music and the Regression of Listening" (1938). In *The Essential Frankfurt School Reader,* edited by Andrew Arato and Eike Gebhardt, 270–99. New York: Urizen Books, 1978.

Albright, Daniel. "An Opera with No Acts: *Four Saints in Three Acts.*" *Southern Review* 33, no. 3 (1997): 574–604.

Albrinck, Meg. "'How can a sister see Saint Theresa suitably': Difficulties in Staging Gertrude Stein's *Four Saints in Three Acts.*" *Women's Studies* 25 (1995): 1–22.

Alexander, Michael. *Jazz Age Jews.* Princeton: Princeton University Press, 2001.

Austern, Linda Phyllis. "'Alluring the Auditorie to Effeminacie': Music and the Idea of the Feminine in Early Modern England." *Music and Letters* 74, no. 3 (1993): 343–54.

Babbitt, Milton. "Who Cares if You Listen?" *High Fidelity* 8, no. 2 (1958): 38–40.

Baldwin, James. "This Morning, This Evening, So Soon" (1960). In *Early Novels and Stories,* edited by Toni Morrison, 865–907. New York: Library of America, 1998.

Barale, Michèle Aina, Henry Abelove, and David M. Halperin, eds. *The Lesbian and Gay Studies Reader.* New York: Routledge, 1993.

Barg, Lisa. "Black Voices/White Sounds: Race and Representation in Virgil Thomson's *Four Saints in Three Acts.*" *American Music* 18, no. 2 (2000): 121–61.

Barthes, Roland. *Writing Degree Zero* (1953). Translated by Annette Lavers and Colin Smith. New York: Hill and Wang, 1977.

Bartlett, Neil. *Who Was That Man? A Present for Mr Oscar Wilde.* London: Serpent's Tail, 1988.

Bederman, Gail. *Manliness and Civilization: A Cultural History of Gender and Race in the United States, 1880–1917.* Chicago: University of Chicago Press, 1995.

Beecham, Sir Thomas. "Women Ruin Music: A Pessimist's View of Women Musicians—Heirs to a Dying Art." *Vogue*, July 15, 1942, 52, 77.

Berger, Arthur. *Aaron Copland*. New York: Oxford University Press, 1953.

Bergman, David, ed. *Camp Grounds: Style and Homosexuality*. Amherst: University of Massachusetts Press, 1993.

Berlant, Lauren, and Michael Warner. "Sex in Public (Intimacy)." *Critical Inquiry* 24, no. 2 (1998): 547–66.

Berry, Ellen E. *Curved Thought and Textual Wandering: Gertrude Stein's Postmodernism*. Ann Arbor: University of Michigan Press, 1992.

Bersani, Leo. *Homos*. Cambridge, Mass.: Harvard University Press, 1995.

———. "Is the Rectum a Grave?" In *AIDS: Cultural Analysis/Cultural Activism*, edited by Douglas Crimp, 197–222. Cambridge, Mass.: MIT Press, 1988.

Bérubé, Allan. *Coming Out under Fire: The History of Gay Men and Women in World War Two*. New York: Free Press, 1990.

Blackburn, Philip, ed. *Enclosure Three: Harry Partch*. Saint Paul: American Composers Forum, 1997.

Blackmer, Corinne E. "The Ecstasies of Saint Teresa: The Saint as Queer Diva from Crashaw to *Four Saints in Three Acts*." In Blackmer and Smith, eds. *En Travesti: Women, Gender, Subversion, Opera*, 306–47.

Blackmer, Corinne E., and Patricia J. Smith, eds. *En Travesti: Women, Gender, Subversion, Opera*. New York: Columbia University Press, 1995.

Blair, Sara. "Home Truths: Gertrude Stein, 27 Rue de Fleurus, and the Place of the Avant-Garde." *American Literary History* 12, no. 3 (2000): 417–37.

Bloom, Allan. *The Closing of the American Mind*. New York: Simon and Schuster, 1987.

Boretz, Benjamin, and Edward T. Cone, eds. *Perspectives on American Composers*. New York: W. W. Norton, 1971.

Botstein, Leon. S.v. "modernism." In *New Grove Dictionary of Music and Musicians*, edited by Stanley Sadie and John Tyrell. 2nd ed. New York: Grove's Dictionaries, 2001.

Bowers, Jane Palatini. *"They Watch Me as They Watch This": Gertrude Stein's Metadrama*. Philadelphia: University of Pennsylvania Press, 1991.

Bowles, Paul. *Without Stopping*. New York: G. P. Putnam, 1972.

Bravmann, Scott. *Queer Fictions of the Past: History, Culture, and Difference*. New York: Cambridge University Press, 1997.

Brett, Philip. "Are You Musical? Is It Queer to Be Queer?" *Musical Times* 135, no. 1816 (1994): 370–76.

———. "Britten, Copland, and Transatlantic Queer Musical Connexions." Paper presented at the annual meeting of the American Historical Association and its Committee on Lesbian and Gay History, San Francisco, January 2002.

———. "Britten's Dream." In Solie, ed. *Musicology and Difference*, 259–80.

———. "Eros and Orientalism in Britten's Operas." In Brett et al., eds., *Queering the Pitch*, 235–56.

———. "Musicality, Essentialism, and the Closet." In Brett et al., eds., *Queering the Pitch*, 9–26.

———. "Musicology and Sexuality: The Example of Edward J. Dent." In Fuller and Whitesell, eds., *Queer Episodes in Music and Modern Identity*, 176–88.

Brett, Philip, and Elizabeth Wood. "The ORIGINAL Version of the *New Grove* Article [s.v. Gay and Lesbian Music]." *GLSG Newsletter: For the Gay and Lesbian Study Group of the American Musicological Society* 11, no. 1 (2001): 1–20.

Brett, Philip, Elizabeth Wood, and Gary C. Thomas, eds. *Queering the Pitch: The New Gay and Lesbian Musicology*. New York: Routledge, 1994.

Bridgman, Richard. *Gertrude Stein in Pieces*. New York: Oxford University Press, 1970.

Brinkmann, Reinhold, and Christoph Wolff, eds. *Driven into Paradise: The Musical Migration from Nazi Germany to the United States*. Berkeley: University of California Press, 1999.

Broder, Nathan. *Samuel Barber*. New York: G. Schirmer, 1954.

Brodkin, Karen. *How Jews Became White Folks and What That Says about Race in America*. New Brunswick, N.J.: Rutgers University Press, 1998.

Brody, Martin. " 'Music for the Masses': Milton Babbitt's Cold War Music Theory." *Musical Quarterly* 77, no. 2 (1993): 161–92.

Brophy, Brigid. *Prancing Novelist: A Defense of Fiction in the Form of a Critical Biography in Praise of Ronald Firbank*. New York: Harper and Row, 1973.

Brown, Malcolm Hamrick. "Tchaikovsky and His Music in Anglo-American Criticism, 1890s–1950s." In Fuller and Whitesell, eds., *Queer Episodes in Music and Modern Identity*, 134–49.

Brown, Owsley, III, director. *Night Waltz: The Music of Paul Bowles*. 2001. Film.

Burton, Humphrey. *Leonard Bernstein*. Boston: Faber and Faber, 1994.

Burton, Richard D. E. "Homosexuality, Catholicism and Modernism." In *Francis Poulenc*, 43–60. Bath: Absolute Press, 2002.

Burton, William Westbrook, ed. *Conversations about Bernstein*. New York: Oxford University Press, 1995.

Caponi, Gena Dagel. *Conversations with Paul Bowles*. Jackson: University Press of Mississippi, 1993.

———. *Paul Bowles: Romantic Savage*. Carbondale: Southern Illinois University Press, 1994.

Carpenter, Edward. *The Intermediate Sex: A Study of Some Transitional Types of Men and Women*. London: George Allen and Unwin, 1908.

Carpenter, Humphrey. *Geniuses Together: American Writers in Paris in the 1920s*. London: Unwin Hyman, 1987.

Chauncey, George. "From Sexual Inversion to Homosexuality: Medicine and the Changing Conceptualization of Female Deviance." *Salmagundi* 58–59 (1982–83): 114–46.

———. *Gay New York: Gender, Urban Culture, and the Makings of the Gay Male World, 1890–1940*. New York: Basic Books, 1994.

————. "The Postwar Sex Crime Panic." In *True Stories from the American Past*, edited by William Graebner, 160–78. New York: McGraw-Hill, 1993.

Chauncey, George, et al. "Brief of Professors of History George Chauncey, Nancy F. Cott, John D'Emilio, Estelle B. Freedman, Thomas C. Holt, John Howard, Lynn Hunt, Mark D. Jordan, Elizabeth Lapovsky Kennedy, and Linda P. Kerber as *Amici Curiae* in Support of Petitioners." Brief filed in the U.S. Supreme Court in *John Geddes Lawrence and Tyron Garner v. State of Texas* (January 2003).

Clark, William Lane. "Degenerate Personality: Deviant Sexuality and Race in Ronald Firbank's Novels." In Bergman, ed., *Camp Grounds*, 134–55.

Clarys, Jacqueline, Douglas Cox, and Tedd Griepentrog. Liner notes for the United States Army Field Band, *The Legacy of Aaron Copland.*

————. Liner notes for the United States Army Field Band Soldiers' Chorus, *The Legacy of Aaron Copland.*

Cody, Judith. *Vivian Fine: A Bio-Bibliography.* Westport, Conn.: Greenwood Press, 2002.

Cone, Edward T. "Conversation with Aaron Copland." In Boretz and Cone, eds., *Perspectives on American Composers*, 131–46.

Copland, Aaron. *Our New Music: Leading Composers in Europe and America.* New York: McGraw-Hill, 1941.

Copland, Aaron, and Vivian Perlis. *Copland: 1900 through 1942.* Boston: Faber and Faber, 1984.

————. *Copland since 1943.* New York: St. Martin's Press, 1989.

Cory, Donald Webster [pseud.]. *The Homosexual in America: A Subjective Approach.* New York: Greenberg, 1951. Reprint. New York: Arno Press, 1975.

Crandall, Emily. "'When this you see remember me': Queerness/Musicality/Collaboration in *Four Saints in Three Acts.*" Unpublished manuscript, 2002.

Crunden, Robert M. *Body and Soul: The Making of American Modernism.* New York: Basic Books, 2000.

Cusick, Suzanne G. "On a Lesbian Relationship with Music: A Serious Effort Not to Think Straight." In Brett et al., eds., *Queering the Pitch*, 67–83.

Dalton, Joseph R. Liner notes for *Gay American Composers*, vol. 2. CRI CD 750.

Dean, Robert D. *Imperial Brotherhood: Gender and the Making of Cold War Foreign Policy.* Amherst: University of Massachusetts Press, 2000.

DeLapp, Jennifer L. "Copland in the Fifties: Music and Ideology in the McCarthy Era." Ph.D. diss., University of Michigan, 1997.

D'Emilio, John. "The Homosexual Menace: The Politics of Sexuality in Cold War America." In *Making Trouble: Essays on Gay History, Politics, and the University*, 57–73. New York: Routledge, 1992.

————. *Sexual Politics, Sexual Communities: The Making of a Homosexual Minority in the United States, 1940–1970.* Chicago: University of Chicago Press, 1983.

Dickinson, Peter. "Stein Satie Cummings Thomson Berners Cage: Toward a Context for the Music of Virgil Thomson." *Musical Quarterly* 72, no. 3 (1986): 394–409.

Duberman, Martin B. *Stonewall.* New York: Dutton, 1993.

Duberman, Martin Bauml, Martha Vicinus, and George Chauncey, Jr., eds. *Hidden from History: Reclaiming the Gay and Lesbian Past.* New York: New American Library, 1989.

Dubnick, Randa. *The Structure of Obscurity: Gertrude Stein, Language, and Cubism.* Urbana: University of Illinois Press, 1984.

DuPree, Mary Herron. "The Failure of American Music: The Critical View from the 1920s." *Journal of Musicology* 2, no. 3 (1983): 305–15.

Elfenbein, Andrew. *Romantic Genius: The Prehistory of a Homosexual Role.* New York: Columbia University Press, 1999.

Eliot, T. S. *Four Quartets.* New York: Harcourt, Brace, 1943.

Ellis, Havelock. *Sexual Inversion.* 3rd ed. New York: Random House, 1910.

Epstein, Steven. "Gay Politics, Ethnic Identity: The Limits of Social Constructionism" (1987). In *Social Perspectives in Lesbian and Gay Studies: A Reader,* edited by Peter M. Nardi and Beth E. Schneider, 134–59. New York: Routledge, 1998.

Eskridge, William N., Jr. "Privacy Jurisprudence and the Apartheid of the Closet, 1946–1961." *Florida State University Law Review* 24, no. 4 (1997): 703–838.

Faderman, Lillian. "The Morbidification of Love between Women by Nineteenth Century Sexologists." *Journal of Homosexuality* 4, no. 1 (1978): 73–90. Reprint. "The Contributions of the Sexologists." In *Surpassing the Love of Men: Romantic Friendship and Love between Women from the Renaissance to the Present,* 239–53. New York: William Morrow, 1981.

———. *Odd Girls and Twilight Lovers: A History of Lesbian Life in Twentieth-Century America.* New York: Columbia University Press, 1991.

Feder, Stuart. *Charles Ives: "My Father's Song."* New Haven: Yale University Press, 1992.

Fiedler, Leslie A. *Love and Death in the American Novel.* Rev. ed. New York: Stein and Day, 1966.

Fifer, Elizabeth. "Is Flesh Advisable? The Interior Theater of Gertrude Stein." *Signs: Journal of Women in Culture and Society* 4, no. 3 (1979): 472–83.

Firbank, Ronald. *Five Novels by Ronald Firbank.* New York: New Directions, 1961.

Fishkin, Shelley Fisher. *Was Huck Black? Mark Twain and African-American Voices.* New York: Oxford University Press, 1993.

Flanner, Janet [a.k.a. Genêt]. *Paris Was Yesterday: 1925–1939.* New York: Viking, 1972.

Foucault, Michel. *The History of Sexuality.* Volume I: *An Introduction.* Translated by Robert Hurley. New York: Pantheon Books, 1978.

Frankenheimer, Anna. "A Much-Needed Upbraiding of Long-hair Music." *Fact* (November–December 1964): 12.

Freedman, Estelle B. " 'Uncontrolled Desires': The Response to the Sexual Psychopath, 1920–1960" (1987). In *Passion and Power: Sexuality in History,* edited by Christina Simmons and Kathy Peiss, 199–225. Philadelphia: Temple University Press, 1989.

Fuller, Sophie, and Lloyd Whitesell. "Introduction: Secret Passages." In Fuller and Whitesell, eds., *Queer Episodes in Music and Modern Identity,* 1–21.

———, eds. *Queer Episodes in Music and Modern Identity.* Urbana: University of Illinois Press, 2002.

Garber, Eric. "A Spectacle in Color: The Lesbian and Gay Subculture of Jazz Age Harlem." In Duberman et al., eds., *Hidden from History,* 318–31.

Gardner, Kara Anne. "The American Composer Becomes a Self-Made Man: Modernist Misogyny and Its Consequences." Paper presented at the annual meeting of the Society for American Music, Lexington, Ky., March 2002.

Gilbert, Sandra M., and Susan Gubar. *No Man's Land: The Place of the Woman Writer in the Twentieth Century.* Volume 1: *The War of the Words.* New Haven: Yale University Press, 1988.

Gilmore, Bob. *Harry Partch: A Biography.* New Haven: Yale University Press, 1998.

Goffman, Erving. *Stigma: Notes on the Management of Spoiled Identity.* Englewood Cliffs, N.J.: Prentice-Hall, 1963. Reprint. New York: Touchstone, 1986.

Goldman, Richard Franko. "Aaron Copland." *Musical Quarterly* 47, no. 4 (1961): 1–3.

Gordon, Eric A. *Mark the Music: The Life and Work of Marc Blitzstein.* New York: St. Martin's Press, 1989.

Greven, Philip J. *The Protestant Temperament: Patterns of Child-Rearing, Religious Experience, and the Self in Early America.* New York: Alfred A. Knopf, 1977.

Grosser, Maurice. "Scenario." In Thomson, *Four Saints in Three Acts,* iii–v.

Guilbaut, Serge. *How New York Stole the Idea of Modern Art: Abstract Expressionism, Freedom, and the Cold War.* Chicago: University of Chicago Press, 1983.

Hall, Radclyffe. *The Well of Loneliness* (1928). New York: Anchor, 1990.

Hall, Stuart. "Ethnicity: Identity and Difference." *Radical America* 23, no. 4 (1989): 9–20.

Halperin, David M. *How to Do the History of Homosexuality.* Chicago: University of Chicago Press, 2002.

———. *Saint Foucault: Towards a Gay Hagiography.* New York: Oxford University Press, 1995.

Hanslick, Eduard. *On the Musically Beautiful* (1854). Translated by Geoffrey Payzant. Indianapolis: Hackett, 1986.

Hanson, Ellis. *Decadence and Catholicism.* Cambridge, Mass.: Harvard University Press, 1997.

Harris, Ellen T. *Handel as Orpheus: Voice and Desire in the Chamber Cantatas.* Cambridge, Mass.: Harvard University Press, 2001.

Hemingway, Ernest. *A Moveable Feast.* New York: Charles Scribner's Sons, 1964.

Henley, Don. "Don Henley Speaks Out." *Rolling Stone* 891 (March 14, 2002): 28, 31.

Henze, Hans Werner. *Bohemian Fifths: An Autobiography.* Translated by Stewart Spencer. London: Faber and Faber, 1998.

Heyman, Barbara B. *Samuel Barber: The Composer and His Music.* New York: Oxford University Press, 1992.

Hickey, Dave. *The Invisible Dragon: Four Essays on Beauty.* Los Angeles: Art Issues Press, 1993.

Hicks, Michael. *Henry Cowell, Bohemian.* Urbana: University of Illinois Press, 2002.

Hines, Thomas S. "Then Not Yet 'Cage': The Los Angeles Years, 1912–1938." In *John Cage: Composer in America,* edited by Marjorie Perloff and Charles Junkerman, 65–99. Chicago: University of Chicago Press, 1994.

Hisama, Ellie M. *Gendering Musical Modernism: The Music of Ruth Crawford Seeger, Marion Bauer, and Miriam Gideon.* Cambridge: Cambridge University Press, 2001.

Holleran, Andrew. *Dancer from the Dance.* New York: William Morrow, 1978.

"The Homosexual in America." *Time,* January 21, 1966, 40–41.

Hoover, Kathleen, and John Cage. *Virgil Thomson: His Life and Music.* New York: Thomas Yoseloff, 1959.

Hubbs, Nadine. "Bernstein's *Mass* Appeal: Eclecticism, Omnivorism, Dirty Laundry, Musical Knowledge." Paper presented at the annual meeting of the Society for American Music, Cleveland, March 2004.

———. "Classical Music and Opera." In *The St. James Press Gay and Lesbian Almanac,* edited by Neil Schlager, 420–29, 432–34. Detroit: St. James Press, 1998.

———. "A French Connection: Modernist Codes in the Musical Closet." *GLQ: A Journal of Lesbian and Gay Studies* 6, no. 3 (2000): 389–412.

———. "Why Gay Shame? Why Now?" In *Gay Shame,* edited by David M. Halperin and Valerie Traub. Forthcoming.

Isherwood, Christopher. *Christopher and His Kind: 1929–1939.* New York: Farrar, Straus and Giroux, 1976.

Ives, Charles E. *Memos,* edited by John Kirkpatrick. New York: W. W. Norton, 1972.

Jones, Caroline A. "Finishing School: John Cage and the Abstract Expressionist Ego." *Critical Inquiry* 19, no. 3 (1993): 628–65.

Jordan, Mark D. *The Silence of Sodom: Homosexuality in Modern Catholicism.* Chicago: University of Chicago Press, 2000.

Kaiser, Charles. *The Gay Metropolis, 1940–1996.* Boston: Houghton Mifflin, 1997.

Kallberg, Jeffrey. "The Harmony of the Tea Table: Gender and Ideology in the Piano Nocturne." *Representations* 39 (1992): 102–33.

Katz, Jonathan D. "John Cage's Queer Silence or How to Avoid Making Matters Worse." *GLQ: A Journal of Lesbian and Gay Studies* 5, no. 2 (1999): 231–52.

Katz, Leon. "The First Making of *The Making of Americans*." Ph.D. diss., Columbia University, 1963.

Kennedy, Elizabeth Lapovsky, and Madeline D. Davis. *Boots of Leather, Slippers of Gold: The History of a Lesbian Community*. New York: Routledge, 1993.

Kimberling, Victoria J. *David Diamond, A Bio-Bibliography*. Metuchen, N.J.: Scarecrow Press, 1987.

Kingsbury, Henry. *Music, Talent, and Performance: A Conservatory Cultural System*. Philadelphia: Temple University Press, 1988.

Kinsey, Alfred, et al. *Sexual Behavior in the Human Female*. Philadelphia: W. B. Saunders, 1953.

———. *Sexual Behavior in the Human Male*. Philadelphia: W. B. Saunders, 1948.

Koestenbaum, Wayne. *The Queen's Throat: Opera, Homosexuality, and the Mystery of Desire*. New York: Poseidon Press, 1993.

———. "Queering the Pitch: A Posy of Definitions and Impersonations." In Brett et al., eds., *Queering the Pitch*, 1–5.

Kramer, Lawrence. "Cultural Politics and Musical Form: The Case of Charles Ives." In *Classical Music and Postmodern Knowledge*, 174–200. Berkeley: University of California Press, 1995.

Ladenson, Elisabeth. *Proust's Lesbianism*. Ithaca: Cornell University Press, 1999.

Leap, William L. *Word's Out: Gay Men's English*. Minneapolis: University of Minnesota Press, 1996.

Lears, T. J. Jackson. *No Place of Grace: Antimodernism and the Transformation of American Culture, 1880–1920*. New York: Pantheon Books, 1981.

Lemke, Sieglinde. *Primitivist Modernism: Black Culture and the Origins of Transatlantic Modernism*. New York: Oxford University Press, 1998.

Lerner, Neil William. "The Classical Documentary Score in American Films of Persuasion: Contexts and Case Studies, 1936–1945." Ph.D. diss., Duke University, 1997.

———. "Copland's Music of Wide Open Spaces: Surveying the Pastoral Trope in Hollywood." *Musical Quarterly* 85, no. 3 (2001): 477–515.

Levine, Lawrence W. *Highbrow/Lowbrow: The Emergence of Cultural Hierarchy in America*. Cambridge, Mass.: Harvard University Press, 1988.

Lott, Eric. *Love and Theft: Blackface Minstrelsy and the American Working Class*. New York: Oxford University Press, 1993.

Lutz, Tom. *American Nervousness, 1903: An Anecdotal History*. Ithaca: Cornell University Press, 1991.

Márai, Sándor. *Embers [A gyertyák csonkig égnek]* (1942). Translated by Carol Brown Janeway. New York: Alfred A. Knopf, 2001.

Marranca, Bonnie. "Presence of Mind." In *Ecologies of Theater: Essays at the Century Turning*, 3–24. Baltimore: Johns Hopkins University Press, 1996.

Mass, Lawrence D. "An Interview with Ned Rorem." In Brett et al., eds., *Queering the Pitch*, 85–112.

———. "Musical Closets: A Personal and Selective Documentary History of Outing and Coming Out in the Music World." In *Taking Liberties: Gay Men's Essays on Politics, Culture, and Sex*, edited by Michael Bronski, 387–440. New York: Richard Kasak, 1996.

Mathers, Daniel E. "Expanding Horizons: Sexuality and the Re-zoning of *The Tender Land*." In *Copland Connotations: Studies and Interviews*, edited by Peter Dickinson, 118–35. Woodbridge: Boydell Press, 2002.

Maus, Fred Everett. "Hanslick's Animism." *Journal of Musicology* 10, no. 3 (1992): 273–92.

———. "Masculine Discourse in Music Theory." *Perspectives of New Music* 31, no. 2 (1993): 264–93.

McClary, Susan. *Feminine Endings: Music, Gender, and Sexuality*. Minneapolis: University of Minnesota Press, 1991.

———. "Terminal Prestige: The Case of Avant-Garde Music Composition." *Cultural Critique* 12 (1989): 57–81.

McClary, Susan, Philip Brett, and Elizabeth Wood. "Letters: McClary and the *New York Times*." *GLSG Newsletter: For the Gay and Lesbian Study Group of the American Musicological Society* 2, no. 1 (1992): 14–16.

Metzer, David. "Reclaiming Walt: Marc Blitzstein's Whitman Settings." *Journal of the American Musicological Society* 48, no. 2 (1995): 240–71.

———. "'Spurned Love': Eroticism and Abstraction in the Early Works of Aaron Copland." *Journal of Musicology* 15, no. 4 (1997): 417–43.

Meyer, Moe. "Reclaiming the Discourse of Camp." In *The Politics and Poetics of Camp*, edited by Moe Mayer, 1–22. New York: Routledge, 1994.

Miller, D. A. "Anal *Rope*." In *Inside/Out: Lesbian Theories, Gay Theories*, edited by Diana Fuss, 119–41. New York: Routledge, 1991.

———. *Narrative and Its Discontents: Problems of Closure in the Traditional Novel*. Princeton: Princeton University Press, 1981.

———. *Place for Us: Essay on the Broadway Musical*. Cambridge, Mass.: Harvard University Press, 1998.

———. "Secret Subjects, Open Subjects." In *The Novel and the Police*, 192–220. Berkeley: University of California Press, 1988.

Miller, Leta E. *Lou Harrison: Composing a World*. New York: Oxford University Press, 1998.

Mordden, Ethan. *Coming Up Roses: The Broadway Musical in the 1950s*. New York: Oxford University Press, 1998.

Morgan, Robert P. "Secret Languages: The Roots of Musical Modernism." *Critical Inquiry* 10, no. 3 (1984): 442–61.

Morris, Mitchell. "Reading as an Opera Queen." In Solie, ed., *Musicology and Difference*, 184–200.

Morrison, Toni. *Playing in the Dark: Whiteness and the Literary Imagination*. New York: Vintage Books, 1992.

Mosse, George L. *The Image of Man: The Creation of Modern Masculinity*. New York: Oxford University Press, 1996.

———. *Nationalism and Sexuality: Middle Class Morality and Sexual Norms in Modern Europe.* Madison: University of Wisconsin Press, 1988.

Newton, Esther. *Cherry Grove, Fire Island: Sixty Years in America's First Gay and Lesbian Town.* Boston: Beacon Press, 1993.

———. *Mother Camp: Female Impersonators in America.* Englewood Cliffs, N.J.: Prentice-Hall, 1972.

North, Michael. *The Dialect of Modernism: Race, Language, and Twentieth-Century Culture.* New York: Oxford University Press, 1994.

O'Brien, Justin. "Albertine the Ambiguous: Notes on Proust's Transposition of the Sexes." *PMLA* 64, no. 5 (1949): 933–52.

Oja, Carol J. *Making Music Modern: New York in the 1920s.* New York: Oxford University Press, 2000.

Oshinsky, David M. *A Conspiracy So Immense: The World of Joe McCarthy.* New York: Free Press, 1983.

Page, Tim, and Vanessa Weeks Page, eds. *Selected Letters of Virgil Thomson.* New York: Summit Books, 1988.

Parr, Leslie, ed. *Government versus Homosexuals.* New York: Arno Press, 1975.

Pater, Walter. *The Renaissance: Studies in Art and Poetry* (1873). New York: Modern Library, n.d. (ca. 1960).

Perloff, Marjorie. *The Poetics of Indeterminacy: From Rimbaud to Cage* (1981). Reprint. Evanston: Northwestern University Press, 1983.

Pet Shop Boys. *Discovery: Live in Rio.* EMI Records (UK) MVN 491451–3 (1995). Videocassette.

Peyser, Joan. *Bernstein: A Biography.* New York: William Morrow, 1987.

Pierpont, Claudia Roth. "The Mother of Confusion: Gertrude Stein." In *Passionate Minds: Women Rewriting the World,* 33–49. New York: Alfred A. Knopf, 2000.

Pollack, Howard. *Aaron Copland: The Life and Work of an Uncommon Man.* New York: Henry Holt, 1999.

———. "Copland and Gershwin." Paper presented at the annual meeting of the American Musicological Society, Toronto, November 2000.

———. "The Dean of Gay American Composers." *American Music* 18, no. 1 (2000): 39–49.

Pomeroy, Wardell B. *Dr. Kinsey and the Institute for Sex Research.* New York: Harper and Row, 1972.

Puchner, Martin. "Gertrude Stein: *Four Saints in Three Acts*—A Closet Drama to Be Performed." In *Stage Fright: Modernism, Anti-Theatricality, and Drama.* Baltimore: Johns Hopkins University Press, 2002.

Rambuss, Richard. *Closet Devotions.* Durham: Duke University Press, 1998.

Rao, Nancy Yunhwa. "Partnership in Modern Music: Charles Seeger and Ruth Crawford, 1929–1931." *American Music* 15, no. 3 (1997): 352–80.

Red Channels: The Report of Communist Influence in Radio and Television. New York: American Business Consultants, 1950.

Reynolds, Nancy. *Repertory in Review: 40 Years of the New York City Ballet.* New York: Dial Press, 1977.

Rich, Adrienne. "Compulsory Heterosexuality and Lesbian Existence" (1980). In *Blood, Bread, and Poetry: Selected Prose, 1979–1985,* 23–75. New York: W. W. Norton, 1986.

Rivers, J. E. *Proust and the Art of Love: The Aesthetics of Sexuality in the Life, Times, and Art of Marcel Proust.* New York: Columbia University Press, 1980.

Robbins, Louise S. "The Library of Congress and Federal Loyalty Programs, 1947–1956: No 'Communists or Cocksuckers.'" *Library Quarterly* 64, no. 4 (1994): 365–85.

Rockwell, John. "A Conversation with Virgil Thomson." In Thomson, *A Virgil Thomson Reader,* 525–41.

Rogin, Michael. *Blackface, White Noise: Jewish Immigrants in the Hollywood Melting Pot.* Berkeley: University of California Press, 1996.

Rorem, Ned. *Knowing When to Stop: A Memoir.* New York: Simon and Schuster, 1994.

———. *The Later Diaries, 1961–72.* New York: Da Capo Press, 2000. Reprint of *The Final Diary, 1961–1972.* New York: Holt, Rinehart, and Winston, 1974.

———. *Lies: A Diary.* Washington, D.C.: Counterpoint, 2000.

———. *A Ned Rorem Reader.* Foreword by J. D. McClatchy. New Haven: Yale University Press, 2001.

———. *The Paris Diary of Ned Rorem.* New York: George Braziller, 1966.

Rosario, Vernon A. *The Erotic Imagination: French Histories of Perversity.* New York: Oxford University Press, 1997.

Rotundo, E. Anthony. *American Manhood: Transformations in Masculinity from the Revolution to the Modern Era.* New York: Basic Books, 1993.

Rubin, Gayle S. "Thinking Sex: Notes for a Radical Theory of the Politics of Sexuality" (1984). In Barale et al., eds., *The Lesbian and Gay Studies Reader,* 3–44.

———. "The Traffic in Women: Notes on the 'Political Economy' of Sex." In *Toward an Anthropology of Women,* edited by Rayna R. Reiter, 157–210. New York: Monthly Review Press, 1975.

———. "The Valley of the Kings: Leathermen in San Francisco, 1960–1990." Ph.D. diss., University of Michigan, 1994.

Ruddick, Lisa. *Reading Gertrude Stein: Body, Text, Gnosis.* Ithaca: Cornell University Press, 1990.

Russo, Vito. *The Celluloid Closet: Homosexuality in the Movies* (1981). Rev. ed. San Francisco: Harper and Row, 1987.

Schoenberg, Arnold. "New Music, Outmoded Music, Style and Idea" (1946). In *Style and Idea: Selected Writings of Arnold Schoenberg* (1950), edited by Leonard Stein, 113–24. New York: St. Martin's Press, 1975.

Schulman, Sarah. "McCullers: Canon Fodder?" Review of Carlos L. Dews,

Illumination and Night Glare: The Unfinished Autobiography of Carson McCullers. The Nation, June 26, 2000, 39–41.

Secrest, Meryle. *Leonard Bernstein: A Life.* New York: Alfred A. Knopf, 1994.

Sedgwick, Eve Kosofsky. *Between Men: English Literature and Male Homosocial Desire.* New York: Columbia University Press, 1985.

———. *Epistemology of the Closet.* Berkeley: University of California Press, 1990.

Shand-Tucci, Douglass. *The Crimson Letter: Harvard, Homosexuality and the Shaping of American Culture.* New York: St. Martin's Press, 2003.

Shepherd, John. "Music and Male Hegemony." In *Music and Society,* edited by Richard Leppert and Susan McClary, 151–72. New York: Cambridge University Press, 1987.

Sheridan, Alan. *André Gide: A Life in the Present.* London: Hamish Hamilton, 1998.

Sherry, Michael. "The 'Homintern' in the Arts: Gay Men in America's Cultural Empire, 1945–70." Unpublished extracts from *The "Homintern" in the Arts: Gay Men in America's Cold War Cultural Empire.* Forthcoming.

Sherwood, Gayle. "Charles Ives and 'Our National Malady.'" *Journal of the American Musicological Society* 54, no. 3 (2002): 555–84.

———. "Ives and Neurasthenia: A Response to Stuart Feder." *Journal of the American Musicological Society* 54, no. 3 (2002): 641–43.

Sibalis, Michael D. "Homophobia, Vichy France, and the 'Crime of Homosexuality': The Origins of the Ordinance of 6 August 1942." *GLQ: A Journal of Lesbian and Gay Studies* 8, no. 3 (2002): 301–18.

Simon, Linda. *The Biography of Alice B. Toklas.* Garden City, N.Y.: Doubleday, 1977.

Sinfield, Alan. *Out on Stage: Lesbian and Gay Theatre in the Twentieth Century.* New Haven: Yale University Press, 1999.

———. *The Wilde Century.* London: Cassell, 1994.

Slobin, Mark. "Micromusics of the West: A Comparative Approach." *Ethnomusicology* 36, no. 1 (1992): 1–87.

Smith, Catherine Parsons. "'A Distinguishing Virility': Feminism and Modernism in American Art Music." In *Cecilia Reclaimed: Feminist Perspectives on Gender and Music,* edited by Susan C. Cook and Judy S. Tsou, 90–106. Urbana: University of Illinois Press, 1994.

———. *William Grant Still: A Study in Contradictions.* Berkeley: University of California Press, 2000.

Smith, Patrick J. *The Tenth Muse: A Historical Study of the Opera Libretto.* New York: Alfred A. Knopf, 1970.

Smith, Sidonie. "'Stein' Is an 'Alice' Is a 'Gertrude Stein.'" In *Subjectivity, Identity, and the Body: Women's Autobiographical Practices in the Twentieth Century,* 64–82. Bloomington: Indiana University Press, 1993.

Solie, Ruth A., ed. *Musicology and Difference: Gender and Sexuality in Music Scholarship.* Berkeley: University of California Press, 1993.

Sollors, Werner, ed. *The Invention of Ethnicity.* New York: Oxford University Press, 1989.

Somerville, Siobhan B. *Queering the Color Line: Race and the Invention of Homosexuality in American Culture.* Durham: Duke University Press, 2000.

Sontag, Susan. "Notes on 'Camp.'" *Partisan Review* (fall 1964): 515–30. Reprint. In *Against Interpretation,* 277–93. New York: Dell, 1966.

Stein, Gertrude. *The Autobiography of Alice B. Toklas.* New York: Harcourt, Brace and Company, 1933.

———. *Four Saints in Three Acts; An Opera to Be Sung.* New York: Random House, 1934.

———. *The Geographical History of America; Or, The Relation of Human Nature to the Human Mind* (1936). Reprint. Baltimore: Johns Hopkins University Press, 1995.

———. *Three Lives.* New York: Random House, 1936.

Stein, Marc. *City of Sisterly and Brotherly Loves: Lesbian and Gay Philadelphia, 1945–1972.* Chicago: University of Chicago Press, 2000.

Steiner, Wendy. *Exact Resemblance: The Literary Portraiture of Gertrude Stein.* New Haven: Yale University Press, 1978.

Steward, Samuel M. *Dear Sammy: Letters from Gertrude Stein and Alice B. Toklas.* Boston: Houghton Mifflin, 1977.

Stimpson, Catharine R. "Gertrice/Altrude: Stein, Toklas, and the Paradox of the Happy Marriage." In *Mothering the Mind: Twelve Studies of Writers and Their Silent Partners,* edited by Ruth Perry and Martine Watson Brownley, 122–39. New York: Holmes and Meier, 1984.

———. "The Mind, The Body, and Gertrude Stein." *Critical Inquiry* 3, no. 3 (1977): 489–506.

———. "The Somagrams of Gertrude Stein" (1985). In Barale et al., eds., *The Lesbian and Gay Studies Reader,* 642–52.

Straus, Joseph N. "The Myth of Serial 'Tyranny.'" *Musical Quarterly* 83, no. 3 (1999): 301–43.

Stravinsky, Igor, and Robert Craft. *Themes and Episodes.* New York: Alfred A. Knopf, 1967.

Summers, Anthony. *Official and Confidential: The Secret Life of J. Edgar Hoover.* New York: G. P. Putnam's Sons, 1993.

Sutherland, Donald. *Gertrude Stein: A Biography of Her Work.* New Haven: Yale University Press, 1951.

"Tangents." *One,* Feb. 1965, 14–17.

Teachout, Terry. "The New Tonalists." *Commentary* 104, no. 6 (1997): 53–57.

Teresa of Ávila. *The Life of Saint Teresa of Ávila by Herself.* Translated by J. M. Cohen. Harmondsworth: Penguin, 1957.

Theoharis, Athan G. *J. Edgar Hoover, Sex, and Crime.* Chicago: Ivan R. Dee, 1995.

Thomas, Gary C. "'Was George Frideric Handel Gay?' On Closet Questions and Cultural Politics." In Brett et al., eds., *Queering the Pitch,* 155–204.

Thomson, Virgil. *American Music since 1910.* New York: Holt, Rinehart and Winston, 1970.

———. *Everbest Ever: Correspondence with Bay Area Friends.* Gathered and edited by Charles Shere with Margery Tede. Berkeley: Fallen Leaf Press, 1996.

———. *Four Saints in Three Acts* (complete vocal score). New York: G. Schirmer, 1948.

———. "How Modern Music Gets That Way: Some Notes on Schoenberg, Stravinsky, and Satie as Representative Moderns." *Vanity Fair,* April 1925, 46.

———. *Music Right and Left.* New York: Henry Holt, 1951.

———. "My Jesus, I Love Thee" (1925). Virgil Thomson Collection: Music Criticism. Columbia University Rare Book and Manuscript Library, New York.

———. *The State of Music.* New York: William Morrow, 1939.

———. "A Very Difficult Author." *New York Review of Books,* April 8, 1971, 3–5, 8.

———. *Virgil Thomson by Virgil Thomson.* New York: Alfred A. Knopf, 1966.

———. *A Virgil Thomson Reader.* Boston: Houghton Mifflin, 1981.

Tick, Judith. "Charles Ives and Gender Ideology." In Solie, ed., *Musicology and Difference,* 83–106.

———. *Ruth Crawford Seeger: A Composer's Search for American Music.* New York: Oxford University Press, 1997.

Timreck, Theodor William, producer and director. *A Good Dissonance Is like a Man.* Framingham, Mass.: Home Vision, 1976. Video.

Tippett, Michael. *Those Twentieth-Century Blues: An Autobiography.* London: Hutchinson, 1991.

Tommasini, Anthony. *Virgil Thomson: Composer on the Aisle.* New York: W. W. Norton, 1997.

Towne, Alfred. "The New Taste in Humor." *American Mercury* 333 (1951): 22–27.

Trilling, Diana. "An Interview with Virgil Thomson." *Partisan Review* 47, no. 4 (1980). Reprinted in Thomson, *A Virgil Thomson Reader,* 545–46.

Trotter, William R. *Priest of Music: The Life of Dimitri Mitropoulos.* Portland: Amadeus Press, 1995.

Tucker, Sherrie. *Swing Shift: "All-Girl" Bands of the 1940s.* Durham: Duke University Press, 2000.

———. "When Subjects Don't Come Out." In Fuller and Whitesell, eds., *Queer Episodes in Music and Modern Identity,* 293–310.

Van Vechten, Carl. "Introduction: A Few Notes about 'Four Saints in Three Acts.'" In Stein, *Four Saints in Three Acts,* 5–10.

Von Hoffman, Nicholas. *Citizen Cohn.* New York: Doubleday, 1988.

Warner, Michael. "Introduction." In *Fear of a Queer Planet: Queer Politics and Social Theory,* edited by Michael Warner, vii–xxxi. Minneapolis: University of Minnesota Press, 1993.

—————. *The Trouble with Normal: Sex, Politics, and the Ethics of Queer Life.* Cambridge, Mass.: Harvard University Press, 1999.

Warren, Kenneth W. *Black and White Strangers: Race and American Literary Realism.* Chicago: University of Chicago Press, 1993.

Watkins, Glenn. *Soundings: Music in the Twentieth Century.* New York: Schirmer, 1988.

Watson, Steven. *Prepare for Saints: Gertrude Stein, Virgil Thomson, and the Mainstreaming of American Modernism.* New York: Random House, 1998.

Webb, Barbara. "The Centrality of Race to the Modernist Aesthetics of Gertrude Stein's *Four Saints in Three Acts.*" *Modernism/Modernity* 7, no. 3 (2000): 447–69.

Weeks, Jeffrey. *Coming Out: Homosexual Politics in Britain from the Nineteenth Century to the Present.* London: Quartet Books, 1977.

—————. "Questions of Identity." In *The Cultural Construction of Sexuality,* edited by Pat Caplan, 31–51. New York: Tavistock, 1987.

Weinberg, George H. *Society and the Healthy Homosexual.* New York: St. Martin's Press, 1972.

Weinrich, Regina, and Catherine Warnow, producers. *Paul Bowles: The Complete Outsider.* New York: First Run/Icarus Films, 1993.

Wescott, Glenway. Oral History Interview by James H. Jones (June 27, 1972). The Kinsey Institute for Research in Sex, Gender, and Reproduction, Inc., Bloomington, Ind.

Whitesell, Lloyd. "Men with a Past: Music and the 'Anxiety of Influence.'" *19th Century Music* 18, no. 2 (1994): 152–67.

—————. "Ravel's Way." In Fuller and Whitesell, eds., *Queer Episodes in Music and Modern Identity,* 49–78.

Wilde, Oscar. *The Complete Works of Oscar Wilde.* New York: Harper and Row, 1989.

Williams, Raymond. *The Politics of Modernism: Against the New Conformists.* New York: Verso, 1996.

Wilson, Edmund. *The Bit between My Teeth: A Literary Chronicle of 1950–1965.* New York: Farrar, Straus and Giroux, 1965.

Wood, Elizabeth. "Sapphonics." In Brett et al., *Queering the Pitch,* 27–66.

Yellin, Victor Fell. "The Operas of Virgil Thomson." In Thomson, *American Music since 1910,* 91–109.

—————. "Sullivan and Thomson, Gilbert and Stein." *Journal of Musicology* 11, no. 4 (1993): 478–98.

Discography

Listed are selected recordings of compositions discussed in this book, which are available commercially as of press time.

Bowles, Paul. "Letter to Freddy," and songs by various artists, including Virgil Thomson. William Sharp, vocals; Steven Blier, piano. *William Sharp, Baritone.* New World Records 80369 (1 compact disc). P 1992.

———. "Letter to Freddy," and songs by various artists, including Virgil Thomson. Paul Sperry, vocals; Irma Vallecillo, piano. *Paul Sperry Sings Romantic American Songs.* Albany Records TROY043 (1 compact disc). P 1995.

———. *Night Waltz.* Performed by the piano duo Double Edge. *U.S. Choice.* CRI CD 637 (1 compact disc). P 1993.

Copland, Aaron. *Fanfare for the Common Man; Appalachian Spring; Lincoln Portrait;* "At the River," from *Old American Songs; Dance Symphony;* "Hoe-Down," from *Rodeo.* Various artists. *Fanfare for the Common Man, Appalachian Spring, El salón México, Dance Symphony, Rodeo—Dances, Lincoln Portrait, Old American Songs, Music for Movies.* London Records 448-261 (2 compact discs). P 1996.

Thomson, Virgil. "Commentaire sur Saint Jérome" and other songs. Nancy Armstrong, vocals; Anthony Tommasini, piano. *Virgil Thomson: Mostly about Love.* Northeastern Classical Arts NR 250-CD (1 compact disc). P 1994.

———. *Four Saints in Three Acts.* Orchestra of Our Time; Joel Thome, conductor. *Four Saints in Three Acts.* Elektra Nonesuch 9 79035 (2 compact discs). P 1982.

Index

Cory, Donald Webster, 95–96, 99–100, 117, 152, 166, 220–21n, 225n27, 235n5
Covarrubias, Miguel, 20
Coward, Noël, 104
Cowell, Henry, 13, 67, 69, 84–85, 125, 129, 138–39, 144, 170, 183n28, 208nn20,24, 213nn80,84, 230n56, 237n21
Craft, Robert, 224n23
Crandall, Emily, 190n26
Crashaw, Richard, 44, 60
Crawford, Ruth, 84–85, 181n17, 213n80
creativity, notions of, 9, 31, 80, 94, 137–39, 143, 169, 190n20, 198n88, 225n27, 228n49. *See also* genius, notion of
Crunden, Robert M., 31, 83
cubism, 24, 49, 89, 189n17
Curtis Institute of Music, 110, 125, 142, 225n26
Cusick, Suzanne G., 93, 100, 119–23, 136, 221nn4,5,7

Dada, 24, 83
Dalí, Salvador, 214n94, 215n110
Dalton, Joseph R., 226n29
Dancer from the Dance (Holleran), 140, 202n126
Davis, Madeline D., 187n53
Dean, Robert D., 7, 143, 190n23
Debussy, Claude, 38, 104, 140–41, 184n37, 231n60, 234n87
DeLapp, Jennifer L., 165–66
D'Emilio, John, 153, 157–59, 181n15, 187n53
Denby, Charles, 241n41
deniability, of homosexual knowledge, 62, 170
desubjectivation (sexual and musical), 101, 113, 119–22, 176, 222n8. *See also* subjectivity
Diaghilev, Sergei, 143
Diamond, David, 4, 8, 12, 67, 69, 70, 71, 84, 125, 141–42, 152, 155, 160,

207n16, 208n21, 225n25, 231n65, 235n3, 237n21, 240nn37,38, 241n46
Dickens, Charles, 225n27
Dickinson, Peter, 184n38, 225n27
dissonance. *See* atonality and dissonance
Donne, John, 60
Downes, Olin, 20–21, 27–28, 168, 191n29, 238n34
draft board evaluation: of Bowles, 122; of Rorem, 72–73, 228n51
Duberman, Martin Bauml, 53, 194n47
Dubnick, Randa, 193n43
DuPree, Mary Herron, 72, 79, 209n34, 233n85

Eastman School of Music, 69, 127, 156, 207n16, 225n25, 237n21. *See also* purges, of homosexuals
écriture classique, 172, 246n84
Egk, Werner, 244n63
Eisenhower, Dwight D., 97, 154, 160, 165
Eisler, Hanns, 244n63
electronic music, 156, 162, 169
Elfenbein, Andrew, 227n38, 228n49
Eliot, T. S., 31–32, 122–23, 193n43, 202n124; "The Dry Salvages," 120
Ellis, Havelock, 76, 139, 210n51, 212n64, 228n48
England. *See* Great Britain and Britons
Epstein, Steven, 206n8
Eskridge, William N., 245n75
eugenics, 76
experimentalism, compositional, 83–84, 125, 129, 170, 213n80
expressionism, 84, 165, 176, 222n14

Faderman, Lillian, 185n41, 187n53
fascism, 64
Feder, Stuart, 208n24
Fehl, Fred, *88*
femininity and effeminacy, 9, 13, 56, 64, 65–67, 71–74, 78–83, 90, 118, 123, 127–28, 133, 136, 140–41,

femininity and effeminacy (*cont.*)
147–50, 171, 176, 185n43, 201n111,
206n7, 211n52, 222n7, 227n47. *See
also* women
feminism, 68, 75, 79, 212n62, 233n85,
234n88
Fiedler Leslie A., 193n43
Fifer, Elizabeth, 190n24
fifth column, 158, 238n28
Fine, Irving, 123
Fine, Vivian, 85, 213n80
Firbank, Ronald, 44, 58, 197n67,
203n128
Fishkin, Shelley Fisher, 193n43
Fizdale, Robert, 111
Flaherty, Robert, 161
Flanagan, William, 67, 125
Flanner, Janet, 153, 189n11, 190n27
Ford, Charles-Henri, 214n94
formalism, aesthetic, 89, 164–65, 169,
171, 242nn55,58
Forte, Allen, 162
Foucault, Michel, 8, 13, 68, 117, 120,
121, 135, 145, 155–56, 183n24,
185n41, 199n96, 207n12, 209n32,
222n8, 247n1
France, 15, 64, 95, 117, 141–42,
190n27, 202n126, 222n14, 238n34,
241n47. *See also* Paris
Franck, César, 217n2
Freedman, Estelle B., 209n32
Frenchness and Francophilism, 117,
128–29, 132, 155–56, 176, 180n13,
202n126, 220–21n, 228nn48,51,
230nn57,59, 231nn60,61,
232nn70,71, 234n87, 241n47
French Revolution, 190n27
Freud, Sigmund, 121, 124, 138–39,
188n4, 211n52, 229n53
Friedhofer, Hugo, 167
Fuller, Donald, 125
Fuller, Sophie, 12, 184n37
futurism, 176

Garber, Eric, 194n47
García Lorca, Federico, 214n94
Garden, Mary, 140

Gardner, Kara Anne, 183n28, 210n51
genealogy and history, queer: as constructed by queer artists, 10–13,
43–49, 57, 59–60, 138–39, 229n52.
See also kinship; lineages
genius, notion of, 9, 10, 24–25, 132,
137, 176, 227n38
gentiles (also *goyim*), 110, 123–24,
152–53, 155, 176, 227n38, 235nn6,7
Gerber, Henry, 220–21n
Germanness (incl. Austro-German),
39, 49, 83, 84, 107, 125, 132,
140–41, 144–50, 154, 156, 165,
190n27, 213n84, 222n14, 228n48,
231nn60,62, 232nn71,73,74,79,
234nn87,88, 236n11
Germany, 147, 163, 222n14, 231n60,
236n12, 244n63
Gershwin, George, 180–81n13
Gide, André, 11, 13, 184n34, 228n48,
230n59, 241n47; *Corydon*, 11, 87,
184n34, 220–21n; *L'Immoraliste*,
112–13, 121
Gideon, Miriam, 85
Gilbert, Sandra M., 79
Gilmore, Bob, 223n19
Goffman, Erving, 7, 182n21,
216n128
Gold, Arthur, 111
Goldbeck, Eva, 105
Goldman, Richard Franko, 85
Goldmark, Rubin, 232n71
Gorbman, Claudia, 167, 245n72
Gordon, Eric A., 181n19, 207n17,
242n55
government, U.S., 14, 42, 143, 158–59,
168–69, 181n15, 190n23, 195n55;
House Committee on Un-American
Activities, 160, 208n21, 238n34;
Library of Congress, 1, 158; Office
of War Information, 160; purges of
homosexuals in, 158, 169; Senate, 2,
158; Works Progress Administra-
tion, 14, 111
Graham, Martha, 41–42, 149
Great Britain and Britons, 32, 43, 44,
50, 56, 76, 80, 93, 130, 138, 140, 143,

Plessy v. Ferguson, 76
Pollack, Howard, 2, 3, 85, 87, 109, 157,
    180nn8,13, 184n34, 187n49,
    196n61, 213n83, 217n3, 218n11,
    220n39, 223n22, 230n59, 233n83
Pollock, Jackson, 137, 165
Pomeroy, Wardell B., 229n54
Poulenc, Francis, 141, 144, 202n126,
    232n70, 241n47
Pound, Ezra, 31, 193n43
primitivism: artistic, 31–32, 41,
    193n45, 196n58, 210n49; cultural,
    72, 75, 77, 193n45, 194n46, 210n49
Princeton University, 162
projective displacement, of Otherness
    or sexual interest, 31–33, 60–62,
    98–99, 161, 194n48. *See also* Alber-
    tine strategy; closet codes
Prokofiev, Sergey, 33
Protestantism, 31, 33, 47, 58, 61, 74,
    78, 85, 222n14, 228n48; Anglican-
    ism, 22, 33, 202n124; Calvinism,
    118; Southern Baptism, 47, 55, 61.
    See also Quakerism
Proust, Marcel, 98, 113, 216n125
Puccini, Giacomo, 22, 33
Puchner, Martin, 46
Pulitzer Prize, 130, 152, 157, 161
purges, of homosexuals: in Eastman
    School of Music, 127, 156, 168, 169,
    225n25, 237n21; in U.S. govern-
    ment, 158, 169

Quakerism, 228n48

Rainey, Ma: "Prove It on Me Blues,"
    98
Rambuss, Richard, 204n141
Rameau, Jean-Philippe, 234n87
Rand, Ayn, 164
Rao, Nancy Yunhwa, 181n17, 213n80
Ravel, Maurice, 140, 141, 145, 231n60
Ray, Man, 215n110
Red baiting and Red Scare, 9, 157, 159,
    164, 165. *See also* anticommunism;
    Red Channels
Red Channels, 159, 238n34

Reis, Claire, 12, 241n49
religion, vis-à-vis art, 20, 27, 28, 34,
    44, 48, 54–63, 65, 189n8, 199n98
repetition, artistic use and meanings
    of, 15, 34, 53, 115, 186nn47,48
Reynolds, Nancy, 246n81
Rich, Adrienne, 183n29
Rivers, J. E., 216n125
Robb, Inez, 235n6
Robbins, Jerome, 4, 100, 111, 224n23,
    238n34
Robbins, Louise S., 238n26, 246n77
Rochester (New York), 207n16
Rockwell, John, 43, 188n4, 231n62
Rogin, Michael, 194n46
Rome, 63
Roosevelt, Franklin Delano, 179n7
Roosevelt, Theodore, 77, 211n52
romantic Americanism, 79, 83, 149,
    233n85
Romanticism, 12, 49, 83, 89, 103,
    125, 136, 137, 144, 148, 149, 151,
    227nn45,47, 232nn71,73, 233n86,
    234n87, 236n11; neoromanticism,
    173
Rorem, Ned, 4, 12, 13–15, 42, 67,
    69, 72, 85, 89, 95–96, 97, 103–4,
    108, 109–12, 114–16, 117, 126,
    128–30, 134, 141, 142–43, 142,
    146, 152–55, 156, 159, 166,
    172, 177, 187nn49,52, 191n27,
    196n61, 207n19, 208n21, 214n94,
    215nn113,114, 217nn1,2, 218n19,
    219nn24,37, 223n22, 224n23,
    225nn25,26, 227n42, 229n54,
    230nn57,59, 231nn65,67, 233n83,
    235nn3,5,6,7, 236nn10,11,14,
    238n34, 241n44, 246n78; as camp
    commentator, 13, 126, 217n2,
    241n47; French and anti-German
    affiliations of, 141, 144–45, 149,
    153–54, 228n48; gender and sexual
    identity of, 136, 223n18, 228n51,
    246n82; musicosexual taxonomy of,
    122–25, 128–29, 222n14, 226n31,
    235n6; sexual and romantic life of,
    69, 124, 219n38, 223n18; as tonal

Shiletto, Violet, 44
Shostakovich, Dmitri, 242n58
Sibalis, Michael D., 190n27
Siloti, Alexander, 136
Simon, Linda, 190n24, 192n36,
    198n77
Sinclair, James B., 227n35
Sinfield, Alan, 56, 183n32, 191n29,
    201n116, 202n118
Sitwell, Edith, 197n67
skepticism, as conditioned by homo-
    sexual experience, 94–99, 169
Slobin, Mark, 245n73
Slotkin, Richard, 210n42
Smallens, Alexander, 6, 181n19
Smit, Leo, 123
Smith, Billie, 32
Smith, Catherine Parsons, 79–84,
    148–49, 208n24, 224n25, 233n85
Smith, Colin, 247
Smith, Patrick J., 189n12
Smith, Sidonie, 23, 193n42
Socrates, 12
Sollors, Werner, 216–17n136
Somerville, Siobhan B., 76–77, 218n18
Sondheim, Stephen, 5, 100
Sontag, Susan, 55, 201n112
Southern Baptism, 47, 55, 61
Soviet Union. *See* Union of Soviet
    Socialist Republics
Spencer, Stewart, 222–23n14
Stalin, Joseph, 158, 242n58, 244n63
Stanton, Elizabeth Cady, 13
Steele, Walter S., 238n34
Stein, Gertrude, 5, 11, 22, 137, 138,
    148, 192n38, 196n61, 197nn66,67,
    198n77, 216n126, 217n1; abstrac-
    tion and modernism in work of,
    15, 20–21, 23–33, 43–54, 89–90,
    115, 184n37, 186n47, 188nn4,6,
    189nn8,12,16,17, 191n34, 193n43,
    198n79; "anti-language" of, 25–26,
    48, 59; influence on Bowles, 53, 104,
    105, 110; and clothes, 57; gender
    and sexual identity of, 5, 11, 24–25,
    27, 98, 190nn20,27; influence on
    Hemingway, 15, 51, 186n48,

200n101; literary portraits by, 12,
    243n62; influence on Thomson,
    11–12, 16, 184nn36,38, 243n62.
    Works: *The Autobiography of Alice
    B. Toklas*, 44–45, 52–53, 231n60;
    Four Saints in Three Acts, 6, 11–12,
    13, 19–63, 35, 37–38, 39, 115,
    188n3, 191n31, 192n35, 198n88,
    228n48; *The Geographical History
    of America; Or, The Relation of
    Human Nature to the Human
    Mind*, 23; "Letter to Freddy," 105,
    106; "Lifting Belly," 192n39; *A
    Long Gay Book*, 54, 200n108; *The
    Making of Americans*, 52, 59;
    "Melanctha," 33, 52, 200n102; *The
    Mother of Us All*, 12, 184n37,
    198n88; *Q.E.D. (Things as They
    Are)*, 52, 199n97; "Susie Asado,"
    192n39; *Tender Buttons*, 11, 54,
    89
Stein, Marc, 187n53
Steiner, Wendy, 193n43
Stettheimer, Florine, 28, 30, 54
Steward, Samuel M., 51–52, 199n97
Stewart, John, *167*
Still, William Grant, 224–25n23,
    237n17
Stimpson, Catharine R., 25–26,
    190nn20,24, 197n71
St. John, Christopher, 44
Stone, Oliver, 179n7
Stonewall riots, 7, 25, 47, 92–93, 94,
    102, 133–34, 215n100
Strange Brother (Blair), 138, 229n52
Straus, Joseph N., 236n10
Strauss, Johann, 244n63
Stravinsky, Igor, 33, 38, 41, 84, 103,
    123–24, 126, 131, 143, 145–48, 169,
    196nn58,61, 224n23, 232nn70,79,
    233n81
subjectivity, 4, 13, 23–25, 27, 31, 44,
    47, 58–60, 76, 87, 90–92, 95,
    100–101, 113–14, 120–22, 135,
    175–77, 195n50, 222n8, 224n23,
    225n27, 245n68. *See also* desubjec-
    tivation

Wilde, Oscar (*cont.*)
  56–57, 59, 92; *Picture of Dorian
  Gray,* 56, 204–5n; trials of, 31,
  50, 56–57, 69, 117, 191n29,
  202nn118,126
Williams, Raymond, 31
Williams, Tennessee, 110, *112,*
  185n43, 219n38, 229n54, 235n7
Wilson, Edmund, 243n59
Wolff, Christoph, 236n12
women, 8, 12–13, 31, 57, 60, 68, 72,
  74–76, 78, 79–80, 91, 98, 123, 133,
  148–49, 150, 185n41, 212n62,
  223n18, 226n31; as composers, 12,
  79–80, 84–85, 148, 176, 213n80,
  233n85; as patrons, 12–13, 156.
  See also femininity and effemi-

nacy; feminism; misogyny and sex-
  ism
Wood, Elizabeth, 5, 206n9, 212n64
Workers' Music League, 159, 212n64
Works Progress Administration
  (WPA), 14, 111
World War I, 43, 56, 59, 79, 188n5,
  193n45, 197n66, 233n85, 245n75
World War II, 7, 8, 72–73, 83, 96, 122,
  133, 153, 154, 155, 161, 163, 164,
  168, 169, 236n11, 246n77
Wuorinen, Charles, 84, 170

Yellin, Victor Fell, 195n49

Zatkin, Nathan, 21
Zeffirelli, Franco, 235n3